GANDHI

GANDHI

Geoffrey Ashe

STEIN AND DAY / *Publishers* / New York

Contents

v

Illustrations

Preface

As the diplomat Chester Bowles once observed, everybody on earth has been affected by Gandhi. Because of him the British Empire ceased to exist as such, and when his own people threw Europe off, the rest of Asia and Africa followed. His special teachings and techniques have inspired other struggles for human deliverance, in quarters where armed revolt would have been out of the question. America's Civil Rights campaign was foretold by him, and led by his avowed admirers and imitators. There and elsewhere, the spectacular wave of 'protest' movements has not always displayed the same discipleship, yet without his broadening of horizons it might never have begun to roll. Hazy as the Mahatma's image may have become, his triumphant paradox of power through non-violence continues to haunt imaginations.

All the issues he wrestled with—war and the atomic bomb, racism, exploitation, excess population—are still most painfully with us. So is another problem, the place of the religious personality in the modern world, which he explored himself before most people realized that it existed. As his contributions remain unique, the case for an effort to rediscover and reassess is a highly practical one. But more is involved than a series of generalities. Gandhi's labours, hopes and forebodings for India are still fearfully relevant to India. And to follow his life through is to see that this is British history also, and that Britain's transformation cannot be fully understood without him. Every Cabinet had to reckon with Gandhi. In a sense, even, he was a British politician himself, and among the greatest. His mind took shape when he was a student in London. Throughout almost all his public career he was a citizen of the Empire. Throughout half of it he was a loyal citizen, fighting within its framework for what he believed to be its ideals.

In attempting a new study of him, I am concerned with his personality as well as his influence. The other colossi of his time—Churchill, Roosevelt, Stalin, Hitler—are all well known to us. Gandhi, who is more of a living presence than any of them, and more deserving to be known than at least two, is far more elusive. Yet when a contemporary of Lenin and Freud was a divine saviour even to intelligent westerners, and the centre of a mystique that altered millions of lives; when we find that twenty years after his murder he remains an object of popular cult verging on godhead— then it is worth asking what kind of man he was, and what, if anything, he still has to say to us.

Nor is it any aspersion on past biographers to suggest that certain restraints and preoccupations have hindered a satisfying answer. In books written close to Gandhi's death, he tended to be obscured by political details which were interesting then but have now faded. A reluctance to be frank about the case against him, and about what must be called (for want of a better term) his private life, made him more like a paragon of simple virtue than he actually was, and less vivid and provocative. It has become common knowledge that one important memoir was partly suppressed. I had some difficulty locating what may be the only copy in England. Yet he was frank enough himself. Today, with the unfolding of such projects as the monumental *Collected Works* published by the Indian Government, it is possible to improve on previous books; though the last word is far from being said.

I have not discovered any completely new material. But I have drawn on writings and researches which are hardly known outside India, and perhaps not given their proper weight even there. My chief object is to interpret, to trace the growth and workings of the Mahatma's mind in its intensely active context. He is helpful— supplying, for instance, a full account of his reading during his formative years. I have gone through those books myself in as nearly as possible the same order, and achieved, I think, one or two fresh insights. Also we must face the fact that at the close of his life, despite apparent success, he said he was a failure. I have tried rather carefully to define what he was aiming at, and how far his aspirations possess permanent value. Again the effort has been fruitful.

Personal acknowledgements are no easy matter where so many have been kind. My special thanks are due to Vinoba Bhave, who is Gandhi's successor so far as anyone is; to Jayaprakash Narayan, the Socialist leader; to Chhaganlal Joshi and Shantikumar Morarji; to Frank Moraes, Nehru's biographer; to S. K. Dé of the Gandhi Memorial Trust and Bhushan Rao of the *Times of India;* to Didi Contractor and Marilyn Silverstone. Particularly the last. Of course, in spite of the immensity of my debt, none of them can be held directly responsible for what I say. Beyond these I can only make an all-embracing salute to a medley of generous Indians who are not in the history books. Memory lingers on the splendid figure of Udmi Ram, who lives in Lado Sarai near Delhi. He and I have no language in common. But to me he was enough in himself to dispel half the nonsense talked by the sillier sort of Mahatma-worshippers.

I am grateful to the following proprietors of copyright works for kindly granting me permission to reprint extracts: the Navajivan Trust for the works of Mahatma Gandhi; Prime Minister Mrs Indira Nehru Gandhi and Asia Publishing House for *A Bunch of Old Letters* by Jawaharlal Nehru; and Harper & Row, Inc., and Jonathan Cape Ltd., for *The Life of Mahatma Gandhi* by Louis Fischer.

Indian names sometimes present difficulties, and I do not claim to have solved every one. When referring to Gandhi's wife I have called her 'Kasturbai', as he does himself in his *Autobiography*. In her later years the suffix *bai* was replaced by the more matronly *ba*. Some books therefore call her 'Kasturba'. However, I have followed Louis Fischer's practice in the Gandhi biography best known to English-speaking readers, and said 'Kasturbai' throughout, with a note at the appropriate point in the text but no actual change.

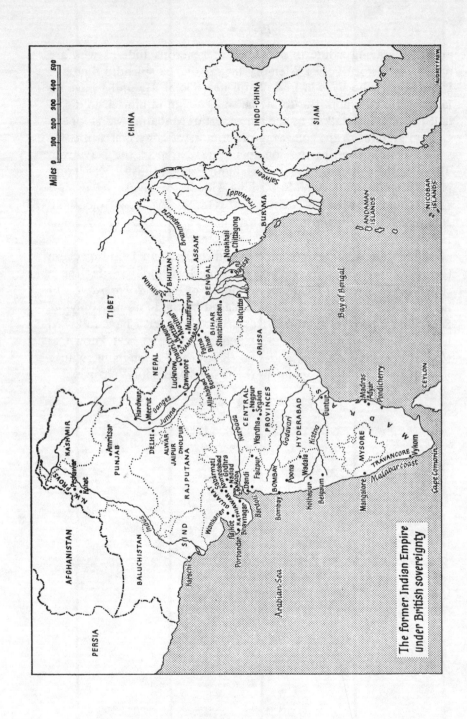

The former Indian Empire under British sovereignty

Four Estimates

Generations to come, it may be, will scarce believe that such a one as this ever in flesh and blood walked upon this earth.

Albert Einstein

He stopped at the thresholds of the huts of the thousands of the dispossessed, dressed like one of their own. He spoke to them in their own language; here was living truth at last, and not quotations from books. . . . In direct contact with truth, the crushed forces of the soul rise again; when love came to the door of India that door was opened wide. . . . At Gandhi's call India blossomed forth to new greatness, just as once before in earlier times, when Buddha proclaimed the truth of fellow-feeling and compassion among all living creatures.

Rabindranath Tagore

It is alarming and also nauseating to see Mr. Gandhi, a seditious Middle Temple lawyer, now posing as a fakir of a type well known in the East, striding half-naked up the steps of the Viceregal Palace, while he is still organizing and conducting a defiant campaign of civil disobedience, to parley on equal terms with the representative of the King-Emperor.

Winston Churchill

. . . The ascetic defender of property in the name of the most religious and idealist principles of humility and love of poverty; the invincible metaphysical-theological casuist who could justify anything and everything in an astounding tangle of explanations and arguments which in a man of common clay might have been called dishonest quibbling, but in the great ones of the earth like Mac-Donald or Gandhi is recognized as a higher plane of spiritual reasoning; the prophet who by his personal saintliness and selflessness could unlock the door to the hearts of the masses where the moderate bourgeois could not hope for a hearing—and the best guarantee of the shipwreck of any mass movement which had the blessing of his association.

                                                        R. Palme Dutt

1

Son to the Prime Minister

1

He was born in Porbandar on 2 October 1869.

Porbandar is a western coastal city of India, in what is today the state of Gujarat. It slopes gently to the Arabian Sea, and is the terminus of a railway line running inland. But its once-important harbour has decayed rather than flourished. The most famous local industry is the quarrying of Porbandar stone, a creamy-white free-stone formed by the deposit of windblown sand. Old Porbandar was largely made of the stuff, and was therefore called 'the White Town'. Builders in grander cities, including Bombay, have used it by choice. It is easily worked, yet after it has been exposed to the weather, the blocks coalesce and you have a rock-like wall that can be smashed but not dismantled.

In 1869 Porbandar had its harbour and white stone, some prosperous trading houses, but no railway. By Indian standards it was short of trees and greenery. Its eye-catching features were the city wall and a number of temples. At dawn and sunset (the rapid businesslike dawn and sunset of Gujarat) its pinnacles caught the light and looked gracious. On the whole, however, it was not a place to awaken a love of beauty or a sense of the past. An active mind, planted there, would be likely to seek fulfilment in human society.

Its hinterland was the Kathiawar peninsula. Lying off the main routes, Kathiawar had been, over the centuries, a land of refuge. It harboured a variety of communities and an assortment of sects. Hindus, Muslims, Jains, Parsees, Christians, mingled or declined to mingle. But the people of Gujarat, whether inside or outside the peninsula, generally preferred action to speculation. Early in the Christian era they had supplied many recruits to the wave of adventurers who carried Hindu culture through south-east Asia. In the nineteenth century the Gujarati merchant or craftsman was apt to be unusually hard-working; the Gujarati peasant had staved off the worst oppressions of landlordism.

Geography and language had once made this area fairly cohesive. But when Gandhi was born, no single Gujarati political unit existed. Even the sharply defined peninsula was fragmented almost beyond belief. In Porbandar stood the palace of a Rana or prince, who was entitled to an eleven-gun salute, and possessed, beyond his gardens and city, a Porbandar principality to be ruler of. But this was no more than a coastal strip covering much the same acreage as Hertfordshire, with a population of about seventy thousand. All Kathiawar was jigsawed into similar states, most of them even smaller. The exact number depended on what the enumerator was prepared to count as a state. However, one reckoning gave 193.

These political midgets were not under direct British rule. They all had Indian sovereigns like the Rana of Porbandar, who were controlled through agents. The Empire-builders had long since grasped that a purely colonial government could not be imposed on the entire sub-continent. Therefore they allowed native states to exist under their protection, here and elsewhere in India, 'without political power but as royal instruments'—to quote Canning. The puppet princes softened the lines of foreign imperialism with a shadow of nationality. Despotic toward their subjects, they collaborated most humbly with the British, and set up obstacles to any spread of unrest.

Kathiawar's extreme subdivision was bad for the economy. Yet it brought its compensations. The wealthier princes had their would-be-imposing establishments to maintain, and made their small cities into capitals . . . of a sort. British law courts and colleges gave the region a spectral unity through shared institutions. The arrangement was stable and peaceful, if utterly artificial. Among the states that amounted to something, besides Porbandar itself, were Rajkot and Wankaner, over a hundred miles inland. The three ruling dynasties had friendly connections, and a traffic in court personnel went on between the cities. Each prince employed a Diwan or prime minister. These were appointed, not elected, and might owe their status in practice to private obligations and family ties rather than merit. But at least one family combined influence with ability. It kept the princely favour in all three states for several decades, with only temporary breaks. Premiership became almost hereditary in it.

This was the Gandhi family.

Although they held office and were Hindus, the Gandhis did not belong to either of the superior castes. The four divisions of Hindu society were the Brahmins (priests and scholars), the Kshatriyas (nobles and war-leaders), the Vaisyas (farmers and merchants), and the Sudras (workers). These, however, had split long before into many sub-castes, not all of which even pretended to an occupational basis. The Gandhis were Vaisyas and belonged to the Modh Bania sub-caste, theoretically a sort of bourgeoisie. 'Bania' means a businessman. 'Gandhi'—a quite common name in parts of India— means a grocer. In the ancestral background, and not far off, real grocers were present. But despite the caste label a certain Uttamchand or Ota Gandhi became prime minister of Porbandar.

Ota showed abnormal integrity and was forced into exile. The fifth of his six sons was named Karamchand or Kaba. Kaba too became premier of Porbandar, and, after more than twenty years' service, held the same office in Rajkot and Wankaner successively. When he went to Rajkot, a brother took over the job in Porbandar. At Rajkot Kaba lived up to the family standard of moral courage. He defended the prince, his chief, against an overbearing British political agent, and was briefly under detention.

In his official capacity he was above bribery and intrigue. Outside it, he was not a person of austere moral rectitude. At one stage he owned a house in each of the three states, but he never saved much, and drifted downhill. The Wankaner premiership proved unrewarding. Some of his money went on charity and some on plain spending. He justified this by saying it would be bad for his children to inherit a fortune. Quick-tempered and rather highly sexed, Kaba married a fourth wife in what for an Indian was middle age—past forty. He had no formal education. But he profited by his ministerial hat-trick to gain an acute grasp of practical affairs and the management of human beings. His knowledge left its impression on his household.

In October 1869 he was living in Porbandar. There, on the second day of the month, his fourth and last wife Putlibai produced her fourth and last child. It was a boy, the future Mahatma. After consulting an astrologer they gave him the names Mohandas Karamchand.

The Gandhis' house was a three-storey building round a court-yard. Acquired in 1777, it was home for five generations of the family, and bore the scars of cannon-balls fired at it by a lady Regent during the differences which led to the exile of Ota. It stood on the outskirts of the town. Most of the rooms were small and stuffy. The birth occurred in a corner of one of them on the ground floor, about nineteen feet by thirteen: not as cramped as some, but gloomy and airless. The house, though altered, is still there, a relic of old Porbandar in a city which has grown past it. Visitors today see a memorial and a museum. The site of the birth under a barred window is marked with a good-luck swastika.

2

Mohandas Karamchand—Mohan as they called him—spent his childhood in a home that was neither illiterate nor notably cultured. There were a few books about. However, they were mostly religious texts which a Hindu family might possess as English families used to possess Bibles. Without being rich, Mohan's people had an air of comfort and distinction. His father's visible status symbol was a gold necklace. Of his two older brothers, the senior, Laxmidas, was to become a lawyer in Rajkot and later a treasury official in Porbandar. The second, Karsandas, who was only a couple of years older than Mohan, became a sub-inspector of police. The other child was a girl, Raliatbehn.

One problem exercised Kaba: which of his sons should be groomed for the family premiership? The choice, eventually, was to fall on Mohandas. It is not clear how early the shaping of his brothers' interests began to single him out for this role. Later he had no remembrance of being a candidate till the end of his school-days. But long before that, his father had only to be present to make political eminence a reality to him, a thing he could see as belonging to his own world.

If his father stood for politics, his mother Putlibai stood for religion; and she meant more to him. The Gandhis were Vaishnavites, worshipping Vishnu as Supreme God. Putlibai supplied most of the devotion. She gave it her own bias. Her parents belonged to a sect which infused Islamic ideas into Hinduism, and had strict attitudes to sex, alcohol and tobacco. Putlibai kept up the connection, taking her youngest son to visit their temple. At home, she stayed for most of the time in the room where she had given birth to him. She prayed daily and was precise about fasts.

Yet her piety was sane and cheerful, not a display of sanctimonious gloom. She was a welcome guest at the princes' courts, a sparkling conversationalist. Her children adored her. She could turn even rigidity into a game. Once, in cloudy weather, she vowed not to eat till she saw the sun. The children watched for the sun to appear and rushed in to tell her when it did. By the time she got outside to look, it had vanished again. 'It doesn't matter,' she said. 'God doesn't want me to eat today.' In her moral guidance she at least tried to be positive rather than prohibitive. She taught Mohan the importance of telling the truth and sticking to his undertakings. A nurse, Rambha, reinforced her. Mohan was deeply attached to Rambha too. As the baby of the family he was somewhat fussed over.

He first went to school in Rajkot, when Kaba became prime minister there and the Gandhis moved. For years the little boy did nothing remarkable. He stumbled over the multiplication table. He played tennis and cricket, spun tops, blew up balloons, and failed to master a mouth-organ. His favourite exercise was walking, his favourite hobby was gardening. He was quick with his hands. His ears stuck out. Investigators looking for the man in the child have noted that he was self-willed but not violent. He never hit other boys; not even when they hit him. So far, so good. But what he did in one such case, most regrettably, was to tell his father. That is not the only piece of sneaking ascribed to him. There is another story about some mischievous thieving by a gang, when Mohan turned Queen's Evidence.

He grew out of that kind of thing. Children do. Yet sneaking—telling the full truth when telling is mean or treacherous—is often their first encounter with an authentic problem: how far is it right to be virtuous at other people's expense? This was one of the issues which Gandhi's thought and conduct were to raise repeatedly. It is no accident that even the childhood stories all have the same slightly distressing effect. However trivially, they pose moral queries with no plain answer. Yet even Gandhi's tale-bearing is a foretaste of the peculiar interest his career was to acquire. While his life can be read as a saint's life, it is a saint's life in modern idiom, appropriate to an age when saints are apt to look priggish and inhuman.

Whatever one's final judgement as to his success in overcoming that obstacle, he was confronting it from the outset. He formed his character out of unclear situations, often by refusing to admit that they were unclear.

Toward the age of twelve he passed on to the Alfred High School. He was a mediocre student, shy and slow to mix. Every day he walked to school and ran home, trying to be exactly punctual, neither early nor late. This was a task he set himself. The quality of mind which his previous exploits had foreshadowed was beginning to show. One day the inspector, an Englishman, visited the classroom. As a spelling test he dictated five English words. The teacher, looking over the boys' shoulders, saw that Mohandas had mis-spelt 'kettle'. He gave him a prod, drawing his attention to his neighbour's slate. Mohandas failed to take the hint. It did not occur to him to cheat, even at the teacher's prompting. His own error spoilt the class's record. The teacher was annoyed and spoke to him afterwards, but without result.

Young Gandhi was a George Washington with a difference. He not only practised unbending honesty, he let the side down by doing so.

Doubtless he was more in the right this time, and anyhow he may not have cared much. School and school work failed to inspire him with zeal or loyalty. For a while he took an interest in plays. He read one on the legend of Shravana. Travelling minstrels showed him a picture illustrating the play, and sang a lament which occurred in it. He picked up the tune and did his best with it on a concertina. But the moral pleased him most. He admired the hero's touching devotion to his parents.

Then he saw a complete live performance of another play, about King Harischandra. It captured him. He went to it several times, re-enacted scenes himself, 'identified' with Harischandra, and wished he could go through the same trials. It is worth noting what these trials were. Harischandra is an Indian Job. The plot turns on his perfect truthfulness. An ascetic, Viswamitra, undertakes for a bet to make him lie, traps him into a promise involving the loss of his wealth and kingdom, and then offers to put everything right again if Harischandra will concur in a pretence that the promise was not made. The King refuses to pretend. He gives up his kingdom to Viswamitra, and wanders off with his wife and son. His wife is sold as a slave, his son dies, and he himself becomes an

Untouchable's servant, forced to handle the corpses in a public burning-ghat. Further horrors ensue, but he still will not utter even a token fib, the merest verbal equivocation. Finally Viswamitra admits defeat and the gods restore the King and Queen to their former state.

That is the legend which enraptured Mohandas. A westerner may have qualms about Harischandra. You may be steadfast in a conviction, and accept loss and suffering for it. But how far can you force the consequences on others—above all, those who depend on you? Apparently, however, the boy Gandhi was not even aware of a crux. He simply wished that everyone could be as truthful as Harischandra. The ideal of Absolute Truth, and Absolute Duty corresponding to it, had come to him with the charm, the excitement, the mad logic of a fairy-tale. He embraced the ideal in earnest.

One observes with some relief that his passion for fanatical uprightness did not make him always fanatically upright. Nor (in spite of that other drama about the filial Shravana) did his respect for his elders prevent stirrings of revolt. With a young relative as his accomplice, he began collecting his uncle's cigarette-ends and smoking them. He smoked surreptitiously, knowing his parents would object. The conspirators went further. They pilfered a servant's wretched pocket-money to buy complete cigarettes. They rolled unpleasant herbal ones of their own. Their sense of guilt drove them to rationalize by inveighing against the power of adults. Disgusted with restriction, they made a suicide pact to poison themselves in a temple, but didn't. Mohandas recoiled from the entire silly business and gave up smoking. As a man he never resumed the habit. On the railway he used to head for a non-smoking compartment. Tobacco-laden air choked him.

Here as in more important cases, he acted in a way which a western mind could misconstrue. There was no question of surrendering to a narrow religious ethic, his mother's or anybody else's. He did not forswear a harmless pleasure because of its alleged sinfulness. His temper of mind was experimental. Cigarettes incurred his disapproval as unhealthy. Today he would seem to have had the last laugh.

3

Petty theft and illicit fags, love-hate relations with pedagogues and parents, games and lessons and good resolutions . . . it is almost the world of a pre-1914 English school story. But now the gap between England and India suddenly yawns. At thirteen, with his text-books on the table and his furtive cigarette-stubs hardly disposed of, Mohandas was married.

Hindu child marriage was then normal. He accepted it with no foreboding of the hate which he was soon to feel for it. His parents had already betrothed him to two little unknown girls. Both had died, so this was the third attempt. His senior brother Laxmidas was already married; Karsandas and Mohandas were now to go to their weddings together, with a cousin who was not much older. The reason was quite frankly that a triple ceremony would be cheaper than three single ones.

To say so is to make the parents sound meaner than they were. An orthodox Hindu wedding could in fact be ruinously expensive (it can still). Mohandas's bride was Kasturbai, a child his own age, the daughter of a Porbandar merchant. For months beforehand the preparations were going on—dressmaking, banquet arrangements, plans for the obligatory music. Mohandas and his brother were given only a general idea of what the grown-ups were doing. When all was ready they were taken from Rajkot to Porbandar, five days' journey by cart, and smeared all over with turmeric paste. Meanwhile their father Kaba, deep in official business, had had difficulty in getting leave of absence. By the time he could be released, it was so late that the prince had to order special stage-coaches to bring him to Porbandar in three days. On the last day his coach capsized. He was badly hurt and arrived covered in bandages, but insisted that the show must go on. With subdued gaiety the marriage was performed. The battered Prime Minister sat stoically in his place, doing all that was required of him.

His family did not yet realize the gravity of his injuries, and even if they had, Mohandas was in no state to take it in. Placed at the centre of attention, finely dressed, with that intriguing permanent playmate beside him—how could he not respond to the moment? They sat on a dais, he and his bride, while the holy fire burned; they walked together reciting vows of fidelity, seven steps, neither more nor less; they dropped symbolic food into each other's mouths.

It was all highly exciting. But when left together in their bedroom, Mohandas and Kasturbai were engulfed in confusion. Both had been instructed, yet most of what mattered seemed to have been left out. Still, they managed. Looking back ruefully in middle age, Gandhi thought the ease of sexual adjustment could only be explained by reincarnation. Couples are carried through by subconscious memories of past lives. Whatever the value of this very Indian theory, it fitted the facts as they were for him at thirteen, a just sufficiently adolescent Indian boy. Certainly there was never to be any question as to his sexual competence. He was Kaba's son.

They settled down in the family home at Rajkot. Mohandas read pamphlets giving advice on happy marriage, and applied the bits that appealed to him. Full of ideals, he expected Kasturbai to be as faithful to him as he was to her. No doubt she was. But his perfectionism, at this point, took the form of infantile jealousy. He resented her going anywhere without him, even to the temple or on visits to friends. She was indignant, and their life jerked along through a series of tiffs and sulks.

His notion of his rights was combined with an oppressive hothouse devotion. At last he had an occupation he could throw himself into, and he did. Kasturbai was small and quiet and self-possessed. She found him trying. He not only made love to her with importunate energy, he also wanted to educate her. At night, if he was not keeping her awake one way, he was doing it the other way. She could not read or write, and though she finally learned to follow Gujarati script and painfully compose sentences in it, he felt that the two pursuits had not mixed and that the education had failed.

The marriage was made bearable by the Hindu practice of not leaving a child-couple together continuously. Kasturbai would spend a few months with her husband and the next few months with her father and mother. The separations were distressing, but helpful.

A teenage husband was not expected to go to work immediately in support of his teenage wife. Mohandas returned tamely to school in Rajkot. But he had lost a year, and the prospect of family responsibilities preyed on his mind. He tried harder and won some prizes— a creditable result, because he achieved it largely against the grain. The fact that the subjects were taught in English (by Imperial edict)

slowed him down and made it hard for him to discuss them with
his elders at home. In any case his tendency was to be cold toward
a subject till something made him enjoy it, or at least value it. With
that experimental outlook which was now fast developing, he had
to be shown. To shine at school, however, you must persevere
whether you are shown or not, and usually you are not. In Victorian
India the showing was even rarer.

Sometimes it did happen. After a sluggish start in geometry,
Gandhi suddenly 'saw' it with a pure intellectual delight at the
thirteenth proposition of Euclid, which states that if a straight line
is drawn from any point to intersect another straight line, the angles
formed on that side add up to two right angles. He relished such
lucid and precise insights ever afterwards. With Sanskrit, on the
other hand, full acceptance came only in adulthood, as did his
enthusiasm for languages in general. Several subjects misfired altogether. He neglected his handwriting till it was too late to do anything but be sorry.

His struggle against his own mental road-blocks extended his
perfectionism to school. He became over-sensitive and could not relax. His best loved exercise was still solitary walking. Games and
gym, which he was to think highly of later, had no charms for him
now. Furthermore he had a real reason for wanting to be excused:
Kaba, who had never quite got over his injuries, was now failing
in health, and help was needed at home with nursing. Gandhi
genuinely liked caring for his father. Once he missed a gym period
through doing so, and suffered one of the blackest hours of his
schooldays when the headmaster disbelieved his explanation and
accused him of lying. But he had few amusements, and at fifteen
he was badly unsettled. He remained timid. Also he had not shaken
off a fear of the dark and ghosts, and kept a nightlight in his
room.

Then a series of unlooked-for experiences jolted him violently.
Kasturbai's husband showed signs of growing up. He became the
friend—the humble hero-worshipping friend—of Sheikh Mehtab,
a Muslim youth. Mehtab not only overshadowed him but
challenged the Gandhis' manner of life. He was a powerful, no-
nonsense fellow, and belonged to the party of progress, in so far as
Rajkot had such a thing. For Hindus the modish way of being progressive was to eat meat. Vegetarianism, which their religion taught
as virtuous and even obligatory, was denounced as a source of weak-

ness and the main cause of Indian abasement. The boys at school recited a verse by Narmad, a Gujarati poet:

> Behold the mighty Englishman,
> He rules the Indian small,
> Because being a meat-eater
> He is five cubits tall.

Some of the teachers, it was whispered, had secretly turned carnivorous out of patriotism.

Sheikh Mehtab boasted that his own athletic prowess was due to meat. Mohandas was torn between loyalty to his parents and the allurements of Mehtab and ideological fashion. His tempter won. They went to a lonely spot by a river, and there he ate strips of goat's flesh with bread. It gave him nightmares. Still, over the next year he got through half a dozen of these doctrinaire meals. He could stand the meat, but the deception of his mother was too much for him. While still believing in meat-eating as a patriotic duty, he decided to suspend its practice till his parents were dead.

Mehtab drew him into other adventures in enlightenment, including a visit to a brothel. Again he had no conscious objection to the act in itself, but again he revolted, and fled in panic. About the same time he stole a bit of gold from his brother's armlet—allegedly to settle a debt owed by the brother himself, but in any case without his knowledge. This was going too far; the moral tide turned. Mohandas took a written confession to his sick father, who read it, wept for an instant, and tore it up. The beatitude of forgiveness gave him his first inkling of Ahimsa, so feebly translated as Non-Violence. Mehtab temporarily drifted away from him and became rather malicious.

In 1885 a traumatic disaster made his moral bias irrevocable. Kaba was sinking. Kasturbai was pregnant. Mohandas one night sat massaging his father, his mind elsewhere, in a quarter where it habitually hovered. When an uncle offered to relieve him he shot off to his bedroom and launched himself at Kasturbai, though she was asleep, and at a late stage of pregnancy when intercourse was unwise. A servant interrupted him: Kaba was dying. Before he could reach the sickroom Kaba was dead, deserted by the son who should have been with him.

Gandhi had to live with that moment for the rest of his days. It made him shudder at the latent mischief in the sexual nature of man. Kaba, damaged by the wounds due to the wedding, had now died like this because of his son's passions. Kasturbai's child, when born, lived only a few days. For that tragedy too Gandhi blamed himself.

They continued marital relations for many years, with recovered ardour on his part at least, and produced children who survived. But his mistrust of self-indulgence was never to leave him. It led him to a renunciation, some quarrels, and a bizarre scandal. Not to the puritanism which regards sex as unmentionable; that notion was as foreign to Gandhi as to the author of the *Kama Sutra.* But at sixteen an impulse had been given. Some of the effort that had gone into study began to go into self-training and searching. He lacked direction. Early teaching had given him few certainties as to what was right. It was a conviction that he had gone wrong which now impelled him on a religious quest.

At the outset he faced Hinduism itself. So far he knew little beyond externals. He had learnt a few prayers, he had absorbed habits and sentiments, he respected his devout mother. But there was nothing definite in this, and the air of restriction put him off. The showy temples displeased him and he steered clear of them, again deceiving his parents. Also, when an Untouchable scavenger called to clean the lavatories, he never understood why it was sinful to come in contact with him.

His best impressions of Hinduism thus far were derived from something that had happened during Kaba's illness. A friend named Ladha Maharaj had come a number of times to read to the patient. He read the epic *Ramayana,* commenting as he went along. The original is in Sanskrit, which the Gandhis could not have followed, but the reader used a vernacular version by Tulsidas. This poet venerated Rama as an incarnation of the Supreme God Vishnu, and his verses extol the saying of Rama's name as an act of devotion. (Ladha Maharaj was alleged to have cured himself of leprosy by that method.) The plot of the epic turns on a rash vow by Rama's father, which leads to the hero's banishment, and which he insists must be kept: 'Truth is the foundation of all merit and virtue.' Rama's integrity, like Harischandra's, is taken very far and causes much misery. As before, Gandhi responded. Even when he knew many other sacred writings, he still thought Tulsidas's *Ramayana* the greatest book in all devotional literature.

But the readings had not made him content with his own religion.

He took soundings in several others. The family's connections brought visits from Muslims, Parsees, and Jains. Especially Jains—prosperous, industrious pacifists on the fringe of Hinduism, the Quakers of India. They rejected caste and carried a doctrine of non-violence to such extremes that if taken literally, it would have made life impossible. After Kaba died Putlibai needed somebody to consult on family problems, and turned for help to a Jain monk, Becharji Swami. Her son, whose whole future was to be changed by Becharji's advice, fortunately approved. He also found good in most of the other callers. But one religion, which never entered the house, defeated his broad-mindedness. Christianity was too much for it. The missionaries insulted the people and gods of India. Their proselytes became sham Europeans with an alien garb, an alien diet. After listening to one sermon he could stand no more.

Little forays into comparative religion could not mobilize his purposiveness. He tried harder. His father's modest library included the Hindu law-book of Manu, a text roughly equivalent to the Mosaic Law in the Bible. Gandhi read this. It inclined him toward atheism. Its crucial difference from the commandments of Sinai—that the code is given in a void, without any historical setting—meant that, unlike a Jew, he had no way of relating it to his nation or ancestry, or to anything he had read of the past. He could only check it against his own knowledge and find it wanting, its mythology pointless, its logic incoherent, its rules contradicted by daily practice. The book claimed a divine origin, yet had nothing in it to make the claim credible.

The gods had withdrawn. Hinduism, despite Rama, had withered, and the other religions had no power to convert. One tenet remained with Gandhi: the conviction (as he put it) that morality is the basis of things, and that truth is the substance of all morality. Truth became his sole objective. His naïve delight in the Harischandra play, his hearings of the epic, had given him that to hang on to. Drama and poetry had had more effect on him than precept and ritual. Poetry had also supplied the single specific moral truth he was sure about, that he should return good for evil. It came from the final couplet of some lines by the Gujarati poet Shamal Bhatt, which used to run through his head:

> For a bowl of water give a goodly meal;
> For a kindly greeting bow thou down with zeal;

For a simple penny pay thou back with gold;
If thy life be rescued, life do not withhold.
Thus the words and actions of the wise regard;
Every little service tenfold they reward.
But the truly noble know all men as one,
And return with gladness good for evil done.

4

The question of his career became urgent. At school, he was
slipping back on a downward spiral of anxiety and poor performance, each making the other worse. In November 1887 he sat for
his Bombay University matriculation at Ahmedabad, and scraped
through only because the pass level was low: he got a total of $247\frac{1}{2}$
marks out of 625. A term at Samaldas College in Bhavnagar was a
fiasco. Academically he floundered. Also he suffered from nose-
bleeding and headaches, supposedly because of the heat, though one
would suspect psychosomatic reasons.

He returned to Rajkot, and to a circle of relatives and family
advisers, crowding round with ideas for his future. They were
voluble and divided. The premiership of Porbandar was in the fore-
front of the debate. It had grown clear that if any of Kaba's boys
was to succeed to this, Mohandas was the one. What training would
prepare him best? He might go in for law or for medicine. He
would have liked to be a doctor himself, but his elders crushed him.
A doctor couldn't become a prime minister. They concluded on
law, partly because this was said to have been Kaba's wish, but
chiefly because the Porbandar ruling house—being under an obligation to the Gandhis—would probably offer at least some sort of
ministerial job if a suitable Gandhi could be put up for it. Having
settled Mohandas's career, they next had to decide on the place of
his studies. Here the difficulty came. If he was to qualify properly,
there was no real choice but to send him to England, to an Inn of
Court.

The proposal lifted his heart like the opening of a prison door.
He was ready to do almost anything, not only to escape from Rajkot
but to get to England—'the land of philosophers and poets, the
very centre of civilization', in his own words. But his brother Laxmidas wondered where the money could come from, since the family
was no longer affluent, and his mother recoiled from the notion of

his going at all. Her grief at the prospect of losing him was reinforced by religious misgivings. Strict Hindus doubted the possibility of keeping oneself pure among the heathen.

Putlibai sent him to consult Kaba's surviving brother in Porbandar. Laxmidas remarked that the British Administrator there, Mr Frederick Lely, approved of the Gandhis and might provide help from the public funds. Mohandas rushed off in wild enthusiasm on the same road that had brought Kaba to grief. Kathiawar still had no railway, and he impatiently plodded seaward by bullock-cart and camel. Unluckily he found his uncle setting out for a pilgrimage, with every scruple at its height. The elderly gentleman grumbled that he didn't like the conduct of other Indians who studied in London. They went morally to pieces, they became like Englishmen. But he wouldn't object if Putlibai consented.

So the ball returned to her, and Mohandas to Rajkot. Before going he tackled Mr Lely at his residence. The Administrator was just climbing the stairs when Gandhi crossed the hall towards him, bowing with joined palms and stammering a rehearsed speech. He glanced down at the awkward youth, and said curtly that for anybody without a degree, no state aid could be considered. Gandhi went his way, and Lely went his, unaware that he had stood face to face with the ruin of the Empire.

Back in Rajkot the wavering went on. Laxmidas admitted that enough money could be found, if necessary by borrowing, or selling Kasturbai's ornaments. The religious obstacle remained. Putlibai sent for Becharji, the helpful Jain monk, who hit on a method of allaying her fears. Setting her son before him, he administered a solemn oath not to touch meat, wine or women while abroad. On the subject-matter of this oath, Mohandas now had no real convictions; but, thanks to Rama and Harischandra, he had very real convictions indeed about keeping his word. Putlibai knew that in this respect her teaching had taken root, and the vow satisfied her. He could go.

On 4 July 1888 the High School boys gave a party for Gandhi. They expected him to make a speech. Although he wrote it down in advance, his stage fright almost silenced him. A paragraph in the *Kathiawar Times* embalms one interesting sentence which he did manage to blurt out: 'I hope that some of you will follow in my footsteps and after you return from England you will work whole-heartedly for big reforms in India.'

Parting came in August. It was agony. The Gandhis had all the
Hindu horror of separation. Though Mohandas was going with his
elders' blessing, he found himself at the centre of fifty distressed
people, chattering and lamenting in strident Gujarati voices. His
wife—who had recently given birth to their first child that lived, a
boy named Harilal—begged him to change his mind. Her parents
were most resentful. At last, however, he was safely off to Bombay
with Laxmidas, in a state of undisguised relief.

He still had obstacles to surmount. Bombay citizens advised
against venturing on the rough ocean before November. Laxmidas
left him with friends, entrusting the money to a brother-in-law for
safe keeping. Gandhi dreamed of England continually. His wait in
Bombay was a long boredom broken only by arguments with his
caste organization. No Modh Bania had ever been to England, and
a committee summoned him and warned him against the impiety of
going. The occasion was intimidating, but now, when he really
cared, his nervousness fell from him. He answered firmly, mention-
ing the vow and the parental approval. The headman swore at him
without the slightest effect, and then pronounced sentence of excommunication: no Modh Bania should assist him or see him off.

Afraid that pressure might be exerted, Gandhi judged it best to
sail quickly. He heard that a lawyer acquaintance named Mazmudar was leaving aboard S.S. *Clyde,* and resolved to join him.
Already the pressure was beginning. The brother-in-law who had
the money dared not hand it over. With his new-found determination Gandhi arranged a loan, booked his second-class passage, and
bought his outfit. This included a necktie, which he disliked,
though, as with other things, he learned to appreciate it; a short
jacket which he thought immodest; and some fruit and sweets
(sweets in the substantial Indian sense) for his vegetarian voyage.

He embarked on 4 September 1888. In almost nineteen years of
education and wedlock, he had shown no outward signs of any
distinctive ideas, outstanding virtues, or special talents. He was not
a saint even incipiently, but a sceptic or even apostate, under a
religious ban. As for being a nationalist, he was cherishing adora-
tion of England as his first mature passion. The 'reforms' which he
had spoken of would not have been such as to disturb the overlords. And as for being a leader . . . well, he had trembled all over
when he rose to read a few words to his schoolfellows.

II

The Crown's Brightest Jewel

1

In the same year as Gandhi's crisis over the death of his father, an association was formed called the Indian National Congress. Here he was to rediscover the politics which Kaba had represented for him. But not yet.

Because of what Congress did afterwards, and Gandhi's part in this, it would be natural to assume that it was always a rebellious body and that Gandhi was at heart anti-British. Neither inference would be right. Similar causes produced similar effects, with the group as with the individual. Gandhi's Anglophile zeal was authentic and symptomatic, by no means a state of mind to gloss over or explain away.

It may seem odd that the heir of an ancient and splendid culture should have conceded superiority to a younger and cruder one, which Indians had little reason to love. It may seem odder that he should have joyfully gone to train himself for a job as collaborationist. Yet he was not exceptional. Many Indians thought as he did. One of the most enlightened, Rabindranath Tagore, also saw England as standing for civilization—for 'rational and moral force'. The poet therefore 'set the English on the throne of his heart'. His disenchantment, like Gandhi's, was still far off. To grasp their attitude one must re-create the Indian mood before the resurgence which they themselves so largely inspired.

Viewed with hindsight, the British regime looks brief and flimsy. A single long lifetime would span the whole epoch from the Crown's assumption of power in 1858 to its withdrawal in 1947. But in Gandhi's student days the edifice towered up unchallengeable, both over what is now India and over what is now Pakistan. His India was Kipling's. Most of its people had scarcely more awareness of

17

their inherited glories than Kipling had. The best anybody could claim was that a few had emerged, or were emerging, from demoralized nullity. The masses were not yet doing that.

India had fallen far, over many generations. The golden creative age of the Hindu world was as remote as Graeco-Roman antiquity. Its grandeur accentuated the later fall.

In the second millennium B.C., the Aryan conquests covered northern India with well-governed states, including elective as well as feudal monarchies, and even republics. Out of their long-enduring civilization came the Vedas, the Upanishads, the majestic epics, lyricism and art and science. Village communes dotted the land with strongholds of peasant democracy. The Maurya Empire of the third century B.C., under the saintly Asoka, embraced nearly all the sub-continent.

But then it became despotic and corrupt, and broke apart. Hindu culture remained vigorous, and spread through south-east Asia, but it was living mainly on capital and exploiting past success. Centuries of subtle decline at home culminated in collapse through a Hun invasion. The warrior-nobles lost control. With temporary exceptions like the Gupta kingdom, most of the nominal monarchies had already ceased to matter. India crumbled into a chaos of small units—village communes, depressed but still active; guilds and voluntary societies; craft-unions and religious orders. Over all in practice presided the Brahmins, a Mandarin officialdom, but hereditary, not strengthened as in China by outside recruitment. No national spirit drew the people together, and the Brahmins preached non-violence as mere passivity.

From about the ninth century A.D. onward, a further wave of invasions wrecked even this world. Hosts of Muslims, chiefly Afghans and Turks, poured in from the north-west. Spineless and leaderless, the Hindus succumbed and sank into self-pity. Toward the new masters they were neither frankly co-operative nor frankly defiant. They led an unhealthy double life, accepting, obeying, yet trying to despise. The trend established by the first Muslim conquests was confirmed by the later one which set up the Mogul Empire in 1525. Many Indians became converts to Islam. Even with these added, the Muslims were a minority; but an able, confident minority, superimposing a culture of its own. The Hindu millions laboured on in servile resentment. Their last solid institution, the village council, weakened under Muslim autocracy. An eighteenth-century Hindu revival in the shape of the Maratha kingdom remained unfulfilled.

Last came the British, the East India Company, Robert Clive. They restored a certain balance by subduing the Muslims without elevating the Hindus. When Gandhi was completing his schooldays they had been powerful in India for well over a hundred years. The Crown had been in charge, as the Company's successor, for nearly thirty. Victoria had been Empress for a decade. India's native greatness had receded into shadow behind the conquerors. The glorious Hindu civilization was reduced to mythology, still beloved, but without potency in the present.

The recurrent term 'Hindu' might suggest a basis of positive union for most Indians. Like 'Jew', however, it refers to a religion as well as a people, indeed to a religion rather than a people; and the shape which that religion took in the nineteenth century was neither inspiring nor unifying.

Hinduism has its sources in the Vedas, products of the heroic era of Aryan triumph. It has never been a creed. Rather, it is a huge medley of cults and legends and customs and ideas, ranging from exalted monotheism and profound mysticism to gross idolatry, and fitting in both without the slightest feeling of contradiction. It affirms almost everything and denies almost nothing. A few themes hold it together—for instance, transmigration, and the concept of a single divine Reality behind all appearances. Yet even these were arrived at only gradually through a long zigzag of debate and protest, conflict between priests and lay thinkers, and digestion of heretical notions taught by Buddhists and Jains.

The Hinduism contemporary with the Caesars was still a growing system. Then it began to petrify. The philosophers of Vedanta came after, and so did many writers and artists, but as builders on foundations already laid. Priestly enactments grew ever more oppressive. By the nineteenth century the religion was clogged with incrustations which had acquired a sordid sanctity, and to a great extent these *were* Hinduism, for adherents and infidels alike. In the words of the learned patriot Aurobindo, if an Indian of the time of the Upanishads had been placed in that setting, he would have seen his race clinging to 'forms and shells and rags of the past', and missing nine-tenths of its nobler meaning. The ingredients of the debased Hinduism which confronted the British included child marriage, as inflicted on Gandhi; suttee, the burning alive of dead

men's widows; human sacrifices to the Goddess Kali, performed by
professional assassins from whose nickname the word Thug
originated; and of course caste, the most notorious of all.

India's four main social divisions—Brahmins, Kshatriyas,
Vaisyas, Sudras—had taken shape during the Aryan conquests and
were functional, with a religious sanction. The word translated
'caste' is in this case *varna,* literally 'colour'. The first Sudras or
workers were probably dark Dravidians, whom the light-skinned
Aryans enslaved. The Vaisyas were the Aryan rank-and-file, the
Kshatriyas their nobles, the Brahmins their priests. Intermarriage,
discouraged but not prevented, reduced the contrasts of colour
without destroying the structure. It was at the upper levels that
functionalism began to fail. Brahmins and Kshatriyas struggled for
ascendancy, and the Brahmins won the battle. When it died away
they had spread out into other fields besides ritual and scholarship.
Kshatriyas had ceased to carry their former weight as an aristocracy,
and men of other castes were encroaching on their preserves. The
colours had run.

To do the Brahmins justice, they were something better than
vulgar exploiters. But they enjoyed their scripturally ordained status,
and had a vested interest in social stability. Hence they not only
upheld the caste hierarchy as sacred even though it had lost point,
but allowed subdivision within it, making it more elaborate and
more rigid. This process went on through numerous generations. For
a Gandhi or a Tagore or a British Sahib, the effective reality was
not the *varna* pattern but a patchwork of sub-castes—seven hundred
or more; nobody could count them. Some were occupational and
some were breakaway groups produced by occupational changes.
Some, however, were tribal or cultic, out of touch with the functional principle entirely.

Each sub-caste had a sort of autonomy and disciplinary powers
over its members (hence Gandhi's troubles with his own Modh
Bania brethren). But the vitality was all inward. The sub-castes
were hereditary, inbred, and exclusive. Every member of every one
was held to have been born into it as the just result of conduct in
a former existence. His *dharma* or duty was to live according to
the rules of his sub-caste, and it was wicked for him to do otherwise. To wander was to become unclean.

The system kept society broken up, and, through ritual and taboo,
imposed a stability that was near paralysis. Orthodox Hinduism

not only supplied the mystique but closed the door on change. The sacred books, which hallowed the caste scheme in its simpler ancient form, were interpreted as hallowing the degenerate muddle it had become. Religion, therefore, was much less of a force for patriotism than it might have been. The Brahmins fostered fragmentation rather than solidarity. Even the *esprit de corps* which the sub-castes possessed could be perverted to turn them against each other, a weakness that was to bedevil Indian affairs long after the idea of unity did take hold.

Two further factors increased India's misfortune. Outside all the sub-castes were the swarms of Untouchables without status of any kind. They were descended from tribes which had been absorbed economically but not socially. Untouchables had to do the nastier work, and were supposed to pollute caste Hindus, who refused to allow them in the temples. The bulk of the converts to Islam had been drawn (understandably) from this part of the populace.

Lastly, on top of all the rest, the British themselves were virtually another caste, with a kindred outlook but immensely more power . . . a super-caste, so to speak. Whatever their contempt for the Hindu scheme, it helped to hold India in subjection. Their policy was to conserve it rather than supplant it. Under that mighty surveillance the spirit of mass Hinduism could hardly help being timid, scrupulous, afraid of putting a foot wrong.

2

When the British penetrated India, they found most of its people lethargic. A flicker of capitalistic growth had petered out, and now, with the Company's ventures offering fresh opportunities, even the rich seldom took them except to the extent of becoming its agents. The Indians showed no interest in western technology. Capital remained largely British. The profits went to nourish the British economy, which then poured goods into India and depressed such industry as there was. Indian textiles wilted under Lancashire's competition. Lord William Bentinck, a Governor-General, observed in 1834 that the bones of the cotton weavers were 'bleaching the plains'. Official policy favoured this relationship. Industrial projects were discouraged. The constant aim was to keep India agricultural, a source of raw materials, and a passive market for British exports. The villages lost the crafts that had supported them, and the still appreciable remnant of their autonomy. The Government promoted the vesting of land-ownership in the native tax-collectors or zamindars, turning them into a new landlord class with an obligation to their patrons.

In spite of all, the mid-Victorian British were less brutal than most conquerors, and more constructive. The best of them sincerely wanted to build a durable order. But when considering what it should be like, they were conscious of the visible Hindu squalor, not the buried Hindu magnificence. The latter had to be delved for. Orientalists had only very imperfectly unearthed it, and without persuading more than a handful of the governing race to take any notice. To Englishmen of the conquest era, native culture had meant chiefly Thug murders and the incineration of women. While acting with fair success to stamp out such evils, they had handed on their scorn to their successors.

The Crown's servants, therefore, proposed to by-pass the Indian heritage altogether, Muslim as well as Hindu, and create a new loyal élite by education on British lines. This programme was adopted on the advice of Macaulay, whose ridicule of Indian culture buttressed their prejudices with a show of learning, and ended a phase of hesitation. Schools run by missionaries, carrying the prestige of the rulers, nurtured students who rejected their own background and flirted with Christianity. As adults many of these Indians declared for westernization. After the 1857 mutiny, the first who had grown up on Macaulay's principles were the first to attempt political thinking beyond Kaba Gandhi's level. Their oracles, however, were all European. They invoked Macaulay himself, Burke and Paine, Mill and Bright and Mazzini. British-sponsored universities gave them a paternal blessing. Calcutta's was founded in the Mutiny year. When Gandhi sailed, four more had been added. His respect for England is easy to understand. It was a common sentiment among the better-informed Hindus.

What other rallying point had they? There was, of course, the memory of the Mutiny. Though not a full-scale national rising, it had raised the national question, and left bitterness lingering on. Anglicized Indians were more out of step with the rest because of it, were more like puppets and therefore less at ease, than they would otherwise have been. The British themselves had grown more aloof and more distrustful of natives, even tame ones. With their women coming over increasingly to join them, they were increasingly a distinct society. Their tiny grants of self-rule to Indians were controlled experiments, not concessions. Their own sense of racial mastery was stronger than ever, just beginning to harden toward ossification, and the decadence portrayed by Forster and Orwell. Scope certainly existed for an answering rebirth of Indian morale. The problem, however, was to see what form this could take, if it was not to be merely imitation-British.

Collaborators could point to the benefits of foreign rule: the public works, efficient administration, and so forth. Against these could be set the poverty and hunger, the ruin of industry and humiliation of soul. Feelings could be stirred up and plots hatched, even locally dangerous plots. Gandhi's schoolfellows could talk wildly of expelling the meat-eating Englishman. But the basis for any broad, serious Indian movement was far from clear. Even in the limited field of social reform, it had been chiefly the British who took action. They had stopped suttee, for instance—in the face of furious protests from orthodox Hindus. The orthodox objected also to Indians going overseas, as Gandhi well knew, and their scruples slowed higher education and the grooming of Hindus for any sort of leadership or initiative. As for the Muslims, descendants of India's former masters, their wounded pride had pitched them into the Mutiny alongside the Hindus. But they had nothing more positive to offer.

Could there be such a thing as an Indian character, an Indian nationalism; whether in partnership with the British or in revolt against them?

The obvious comment on such a dream (and imperialists were to go on making it to the last gasp) was that it was meaningless. India had no single character and no basis for nationhood. Before the British themselves took charge, the sub-continent had never lived under one authority. Several races shared it. They spoke dozens of languages. Even by grouping these into related families, the number could not be reduced below five. As for religion, it too was multiple. The Muslims had at least their historians, their proud traditions, their sense of a bond. The far more numerous Hindus lacked those.

Yet a cloudy notion of India-as-a-whole, Bharata-Varsha, did persist. This was a relic of the Maurya days, when Asoka's subjects had glimpsed a vision of union under a single head. After he died, the failure of world-rejecting thinkers to impose a moral order on politics had left the vision in a void where it faded. But its bogus revival in the person of Queen Victoria might raise the issue of an authentic revival under leaders other than her successors.

Despite appearances, Hinduism held the key. Even though it divided people, even though it debased them, it was the religion of the majority. Most Indians possessed a common inheritance in the Sanskrit classics and the Hindu ceremonies and doctrines. Nationality could only come by the reawakening of vital and hopeful forces within that context. No appeal acting through other media could spread widely enough.

In Gandhi's boyhood the reawakening had begun. Thus far, however, it was confined to a small circle, and its manifestations were still unlikely to incite anybody against England. Its prime inspirer was the amazing genius Rammohan Roy, born as far back as 1772, who had foreseen the impact of the West before most Indians knew it existed. Roy was a Bengali Brahmin, extremely erudite, friendly with Muslims and at odds with his caste brethren. Damning most of Hinduism as corruption, pedantry and idolatry, he appealed from the dismal present to the creative past, and preached an ethical monotheism which he said was the real religion of the Vedas and Upanishads. He welcomed British rule as bringing a higher civilization, and argued that the true wisdom of India, when dug out from under the debris of centuries, would come to fruition in partnership with western science. Showing a flair for publicity, he championed various reforms such as press freedom and the end of suttee. He won the admiration of Bentham, and died (strangely enough) in Bristol.

An organization was founded under his auspices to carry on his liberal neo-Hinduism. It was named the Brahmo Samaj, and its Calcutta headquarters became a meeting-place of the intelligentsia. The Samaj was in essence an ethical society. On its platform the Tagore family—Bengali Brahmins like Rammohan Roy—rose to fame. Dwarkanath Tagore and then his son Debendranath, father of the poet, presided after the founder's death. In keeping with the ecumenical aim, the family showed friendliness toward Muslims, thereby annoying the orthodox. The Samaj also drifted into sympathy with Protestant Christianity. Influenced by missionaries, its members supported reforms which the British favoured. Their further hopes included the abolition of caste and the emancipation of women. Though the masses took no notice, they persevered.

Keshab Chandra Sen, who became head of the Samaj in 1862, hastened the trend toward western radicalism and was close to joining the Christians outright. For most of his active life he denounced Hindu ways in general and insisted that Indians must 'follow British ideas'. He did not carry his colleagues quite so far, and a substantial Indian-ness endured. European research was now opening up the past, and proving it to be richer than the Hindus themselves, who lacked historical consciousness, had realized.

In 1875, while the Brahmo Samaj was seeking equilibrium, a Gujarati lecturer named Dayananda Saraswati started a new body in Bombay, the Arya Samaj. This too took a reformist line, but on strictly Hindu principles. Dayananda, a fiery figure recalling Luther, proclaimed the reinstatement of Vedic truth in its ancient purity. He tried to ground everything on his own interpretation of scripture, and maintained, correctly, that the Vedas gave no warrant for the later abuses. Except in the Punjab, where his simple militancy provided a retort to Islam, his disciples had no more success than the Brahmo men in reaching the multitude. The achievement of both societies was rather to form a thinking public within Hinduism. During the 1880s Indians of the same type noted the rise of Theosophy in England and America. However grotesque this looked, it revealed that some westerners believed India had lessons for them. Self-respect could creep back. The foundation for a national ideology, seeking to restore what was best in the Hindu past, had been laid.

But there was still no broad movement, no real reassertion of India. The reformers were a handful of literates. Their ideas had saved them from sliding into a Christian or agnostic position and losing contact with the people entirely. They could even claim to have saved Hinduism, in the sense of giving it a renewed capacity for adaptation. But by cutting it down to a sort of Unitarianism, and denouncing its firmliest-rooted practices, they had crippled their own right hands. Their philosophy could never work through the Hindu masses. Seemingly its only chance lay in the British, and the growth of a co-nationhood under British aegis. If Imperial policies went on without interference . . . if the use of English gave Indians a common language . . . if railways and labour mobility cracked the caste barriers . . . if central government prepared the ground for a.

central parliament . . . if irrigation, improved health, better food supplies, more schools, raised a new citizenry above the level of desperation . . . then a self-ruling India with an enlightened faith might some day, somehow, be born.

And indeed the first symptoms had appeared. Indians had their own newspapers, their own novels. Surely the printed word would spread wider and wider (despite censorship) with far more to follow. It was in that spirit that the National Congress came together, as an expression of hopes aroused both by the religious reformers and by the outright westernizers.

3

Congress was launched in Bombay on 28 December 1885. It had had forerunners, minor 'Indian Associations' of various kinds, but none had amounted to very much. The main impulse for another attempt came from Allan Hume, an Englishman and retired civil servant. Hume believed in forestalling unrest by giving Indians more voice in public affairs. Aided by a Scottish businessman, Andrew Yule, he enrolled seventy-two members. Most of them were lawyers; British education had been fairly successful in producing a middle-class *noblesse de la robe*. Others were schoolmasters and journalists. Only two were Muslims. However, the Muslim proportion later rose to a fifth, not too bad a reflection of India's population. Congress was never a Hindu body as its enemies charged. Its secular character gave it breadth, but at first weakened its impact. Not being religious, it was no more a popular organization than the Brahmo Samaj or the Arya Samaj. No one had yet hit on the formula for an appeal—necessarily a religious appeal—that could stir the masses.

The infant Congress walked warily. It was pro-western in the manner of Rammohan Roy, and conducted business in English. Its members assembled annually and debated social reforms, little more. They were coaxed to venture further by encouragement from the summit. Lord Dufferin, the Viceroy, was rather taken with Congress. Hume had convened it in consultation with him. At that time Dufferin had been preoccupied with Burma, but once the Burmese were annexed and their king in prison, the viceregal mind could turn to the question of native participation in government.

Dufferin urged Congress to tackle politics, in the sense of offering loyal advice for improved administration.

The trouble was that he could not keep this programme on the suggestion-box level. Sixty years of Brahmo Samaj activities, however narrow their scope, proved to have been too much of a stimulant. Congress's English bias was not selective enough. It meant a general influx of English books and ideas . . . which included democracy. When Dufferin left in 1888 the atmosphere had cooled. The next year Congress's star speaker was the agnostic Charles Bradlaugh, an Englishman still, but an outsider to the Establishment. Resolutions began to be pressed demanding a faster intake of Indians into the Civil Service, and stronger legislative councils including elected members.

Here as in religion, paths were being marked out which Gandhi would explore in his own way. When he left home he knew little about Congress or the Brahmo Samaj. But progress, for their members, still meant gradual progress under the Empire. Contact with them would still only have confirmed his view that England was the centre of civilization, a land where an Indian should go to seek light. Even the Arya Samaj would not have taught him hostility. Apart from petty local outbreaks, battle was not yet joined. Not anywhere.

III

The Time-bomb

1

The voyage lasted nearly eight weeks. It placed Gandhi in an isolation which he was not used to. As an Indian among Indians, however shy, he had lived surrounded and even oppressed by company. But in the second-class saloon he was an Indian among Englishmen. Mazmudar, his lawyer companion, mixed freely and urged him to do likewise. His halting English always restrained him. Sometimes he dared to watch games or strum the piano. If addressed, however, he either failed to understand or took too long composing his answer, and conversation flagged.

So he spent much of the time in his cabin, or in lonely admiration of moonlight and starlight on the sea. He had other motives for keeping to himself. Though not seasick, he shrank from the meals—partly because of his clumsiness with a knife and fork (Indians pick up food with the right hand), and partly because of apprehensions over the meat content. Instead of coming to the table, he worked slowly through his tuck-box. Passengers who did talk assured him that in the cold English climate his diet would not keep him alive. One advised him to take up meat-eating while aboard. Another said he should lay in a stock of whisky. But he insisted on his promise.

The *Clyde* put in at Aden, Port Said, Brindisi, Malta and Gibraltar. He went ashore at each port and roamed the streets with observant eyes, noting details like the high price of lemonade in Port Said. The final docking was on 27 October. Misadventures began at once. On the ship he had worn a black suit, but now for some obscure reason he changed into white flannels. At his London hotel—the Victoria—he was the only person in white, and he could not get at his luggage on account of the Sabbath. He went about self-consciously, awestruck by the electric light and defeated by the lift.

As a prime minister's son and potential successor, he carried letters of introduction to several Indians of standing. They included Prince Ranjitsinhji, another native of Kathiawar; Dadabhai Naoroji, a learned Bombay Parsee engaged in teaching and political work, revered by his many admirers as India's 'Grand Old Man'; and Dr P. J. Mehta. The doctor called at the hotel wearing a top hat, which Gandhi picked up to look at, and unfortunately stroked the wrong way. Mehta was irritated and lectured him on how to behave in England. He mustn't raise his voice, he mustn't ask anybody questions at a first meeting, he mustn't say 'sir' at incorrect moments, he mustn't touch other people's things (hats, for instance), and he mustn't stay at expensive hotels like the Victoria.

Abashed, Gandhi moved out with Mazmudar into lodgings found for them by a fellow passenger. The last thing he saw at the hotel was the bill, which horrified him. Now that he was in England at last, elation faded and reaction set in. Everything was strange, alien, forbidding. Homesickness interfered with his sleep. But Dr Mehta, who inspected the lodgings and disapproved, arranged for him to board with a friend in Richmond, and there he became slightly more cheerful.

On 6 November he had enrolled at the Inner Temple. Among the four Inns of Court, Indians tended to prefer it as possessing social cachet. In a photograph taking during this phase he has an unsure and troubled look. However, Mehta's Richmond friend gave him invaluable support where he needed it. His latent talent for languages began to emerge, and with growing proficiency in English a great deal more came besides. Soon he was spending an hour each day reading newspapers—the first he ever had read— and absorbing all they could tell him. His favourites were the *Daily News, Daily Telegraph*, and *Pall Mall Gazette*. The first two were more or less liberal, the third was independent, with pronounced ideas about the civilizing mission of Britain. Gandhi studied them and looked around him and started a diary.

2

Food was his worst problem. It was also his salvation.

The Richmond Indian ate like the English. His landlady served their guest with porridge and spinach and bread and jam. But he

suspected rightly that the menu was inadequate, and urged a
change. Gandhi's vow, he said, had been made to please a mother
ignorant of English conditions. It was not binding. He returned to
the attack several times, and one day he began reading aloud from
Bentham's *Theory of Utility*. That was the last straw. The victim
admitted that he could not defend vegetarianism by logic, but nothing would induce him to break his word. Thereupon the subject
dropped. Gandhi was clinging to 'truth' after the pattern of his
mythical heroes, and it was still almost his only certainty. In the
absence of guidance he often prayed to the God he had no faith in;
chiefly because he had learnt the habit of invocation from his nurse,
who had taught him, as a child, to repeat the prayer called
'Ramanama' when scared of ghosts.

Richmond was too far out for comfort. In any case the solicitous
Mehta thought Gandhi should board with English people. Another
Indian found him a billet with a widow in West Kensington. The
old lady and her two daughters were sympathetic, but not much
more. His meals were all bits and pieces, and even the vegetables
themselves seemed tasteless without the hot condiments of his
country. Nobody had told him that there were vegetarians in Britain.
However, his landlady did recall hearing of meatless restaurants.
Having no notion how to locate them, he wandered miles through
London, and at last discovered two in rapid succession.

He chose the Central in Farringdon Street, and walked inside
with rising spirits. Before sitting down he bought a pamphlet from
a display case by the door. His meal consisted of porridge, which
he didn't enjoy, and pie, which he did. For the first time in England
he left the table satisfied, and free from anxiety over the prospects
of keeping his vow.* But the pamphlet was more welcome still, and
more momentous. It was *A Plea for Vegetarianism,* by Henry
Stephens Salt. Gandhi read it through and it struck him with the
force of a revelation.

The reason for its impact was psychological. This was the first
occurrence of what was to be a repeated theme in his life. The
growth from law student into demigod began at that unlikely session
in Farringdon Street.

* A year or so later, when Gandhi was probably still patronizing this
restaurant, Sherlock Holmes passed it (*The Red-Headed League*). It was
lunch time, but unfortunately Holmes went somewhere else to eat. If he had
gone in, what would he have deduced about the Indian student he might
have noticed at one of the tables?

Salt's pamphlet was published in 1886. In it he presents a cool, workmanlike case, without monomania. Rearing animals for their flesh is cruel, degrading, expensive, and unnecessary. Man is more akin to the fruit-eating apes than to carnivores. To give a vegetarian diet a fair trial is to be convinced: you will be healthier, and suffer less from cravings for tobacco and drink. And so forth. An attractive feature is the author's civilized breadth of outlook. He relates food reform to other human concerns. On the aesthetic side he cites a poet, Shelley, an essayist, Thoreau, and an art-critic, Ruskin. Also he fits food reform into the wider context of social reform, discussing its effect on the cost of living, and its value as an adjunct to Socialism, which he anticipates calmly and even hopefully.

This challenge to British folkways can still inspire a reader's respect. But Gandhi went beyond respect. The pamphlet straightened out his mind on the issue that was disturbing it. He had accepted a Hindu dogma without inward assent, as the only means of getting to England. Whatever his emotional leaning toward his mother, common sense and progressive feelings had pulled him the other way. The oath had split his allegiance and endangered his health. Now, however, the *Plea* gave him what the West alone could then give—a fresh statement of the doctrine in reasoned terms, with no childish appeals to incredible authorities. The author made sense of it, and used arguments specially apt to Gandhi, with his experimental temper and his love of morality in alliance with beauty. Moreover, Salt was English. Here was a member of the enlightened ruling race who was not a meat-eater—thereby refuting the schoolboys' verse. As a disciple Gandhi could resolve his conflict. He could be filial, honourable, patriotic and rational, all at once.

Vistas opened before the proselyte. He read further vegetarian books. *The Perfect Way in Diet,* by a woman doctor named Anna Kingsford, supplied a documented review of the food habits of different nations including Indians. 'Man', Dr Kingsford declared, 'is the master of the world . . . and working with God and Nature, he may reconvert it into Paradise.' The writings of T. R. Allinson, another doctor, enlarged vegetarianism into a whole programme for the Simple Life, full of health-giving baths and exercise and fresh air. Howard Williams's *The Ethics of Diet* was a biographical dictionary of vegetarians. Here, as in Salt and Anna Kingsford, Gandhi encountered Shelley, hymned through eighteen pages as an arch-prophet for the modern world.

To compare these and other books with what Gandhi said about them, when he recalled them many years later, is to get an insight into his mind. He tended to quote the titles wrongly, or give a slightly false notion of the contents. He was a functional reader, not scholarly, and retained what he could apply himself. Thus far it was the health aspect of food reform that chiefly interested him. No religious motive was asserting itself yet.

He had his diversions and distractions. The Richmond Indian continued to worry about him, and invited him to go to a play one evening. The theatrical part went off smoothly, but Gandhi made difficulties at a restaurant, and their dispute broke out again. Afraid of putting people off as a crank, he followed a path taken by numerous Indians, and tried to become English so as to crash English society. Visiting Bond Street and the Army & Navy Stores, he built up a Londoner's wardrobe: a nineteen-shilling top hat, disproportionately tall; a ten-pound evening suit, a morning coat, a double-breasted waistcoat and dark striped trousers; patent leather shoes with spats; leather gloves and a silver-mounted stick; flashy ties and striped silk shirts. He also asked Laxmidas to send him a gold watch-chain. Every morning he spent ten minutes before a mirror, brushing his unruly black hair and working on the knot of his tie. He enrolled for French lessons, elocution lessons, violin lessons, even (disastrously) dancing lessons. One more Bourgeois Gentilhomme, Hindu style, seemed to be in the making.

But after three months his practicality pulled him up. What use would these accomplishments be in India? He kept careful accounts and knew what they were costing. It wouldn't do. Cancelling his classes (the lady violin teacher 'encouraged him in the determination to make a complete change'), he reverted to strict economy, though he went on wearing the clothes and getting the good out of them. To save money he moved again. So long as he stayed with the Kensington family he shared in their social life and went out with them, which he could not do for nothing. Also he had to pay full board, whether he ate the meals or not. Accordingly he rented rooms by himself and did his own cooking. During a phase in Tavistock Street, he cut his weekly outlay to fifteen shillings.

The second half of 1889 was the most studious period in Gandhi's life. Remembering Lely's words about a degree, he decided to try London Matriculation. He was reconciled to Latin by its value for lawyers, and took French as his modern language and chemistry as

his science. In January 1890 he sat for the examination, but failed
in Latin. At the second attempt, in June, he passed.

3

Meanwhile he had entered English society by another route. His
diet could hardly remain a private habit. To be a vegetarian was to
align oneself with the vegetarians of England. To eat at their
restaurants was to come in contact with them. Soon after reading
Henry Salt's pamphlet he had met the author, and begun to edge
into the company which the author kept.

Some biographers, put off by an impression of faddishness, have
missed the point of this phase. One of them dismisses the 'aged,
crusading vegetarians' as having meant almost nothing to Gandhi.
But they were not all aged, and they were far more than vegetarians.
They introduced him to a circle in which he found himself at home
and developed; and it was not a coterie of cranks, it was up-to-date,
exciting, even fashionable. Thinking people were drawn into it as
they were afterwards drawn into the Bloomsbury set or the Left
Book Club. It is interesting to look up the publication dates of the
books Gandhi studied under their influence. Nearly all were recent,
and some were only just out. Whether on the right path or not, he
was striding ahead of his Indian contemporaries who still pored
over dead men like Burke and Macaulay.

In the group which he gradually came to know, Henry Salt himself played a prominent role. Salt, with his friends, carried on a
tradition deriving from Shelley, on whom he was an authority.
Additional inspiration came from Thoreau, from Ruskin, to a lesser
extent from Whitman. In 1889 Edward Carpenter was the school's
leader so far as it had one. His disciples preached a sweeping reno-
vation of society. Rejecting civilization as it stood, they called for
a fresh start from the fundamentals. They insisted on re-examining
the basic things, food and sex and religion, and they subjected
standard notions about all three to impartial probing. The results
varied, but showed recognizable trends.

Vegetarianism was only the most obvious. It was linked with
radical ideas of a larger kind, not a doctrine in isolation but part
of a scheme. On the sexual issue, some of the heretics declared for
free love or at any rate emancipation, as Shelley had done; some

for a new cult of celibacy and restraint; some for birth control. The common enemy was commercialized Victorian marriage. In religion, some—including Salt—favoured agnosticism, otherwise called Free-thought with a capital F; some groped behind the churches for a 'real teaching of Christ' or a cosmic truth underlying all religions; some embraced novel forms of mysticism. Here again they had a common enemy, established Christianity.

Many of those who shared this outlook agreed on certain social goals. They believed in the Simple Life, and in a highly moral Socialism or near-anarchism as its ideal setting (the exiled Kropotkin was among Salt's friends). Love was to be supreme. Non-violence, and non-violent protest by civil disobedience, were ideas already planted by Shelley and Thoreau, though civil disobedience remained almost entirely untried. They were in touch with Tolstoy, who was soliloquizing on the same lines in Russia. Tolstoy sent Salt a vegetarian tract of his own, and wrote the preface for a translation of Howard Williams's *Ethics of Diet*. Celebrities who were far from accepting the whole programme were attracted by parts of it. The Simple Life appealed to such diverse figures as Charles Bradlaugh and Cardinal Manning. Non-violent revolution and voluntary communism appeared in William Morris's *News from Nowhere*.

There was an overlap with the five-year-old Fabian Society. English progressives were extolling vegetarianism precisely when Hindu ones were attacking it. Salt himself was a Fabian, close to such founding fathers as Sydney Olivier. At an early meeting he proposed forming an affiliated Humanitarian League, to campaign for reforms of an ethical rather than economic type. This was launched with the support of Olivier, Edward Carpenter, Annie Besant (then a militant organizer of women workers), and W. H. Hudson the naturalist and novelist, to whom the Hyde Park Bird Sanctuary is a memorial. Howard Williams joined, and so did Edward Maitland, who had collaborated with Anna Kingsford of *The Perfect Way in Diet*. In 1889 the League gave a series of tea-parties at one of the vegetarian restaurants. Here Salt kept open house, so to speak. Most of the circle, including its more peripheral members, looked in at the parties. Guests included Sir George Greenwood the Shakespearean writer, Clarence Darrow the lawyer, and many of less note who came to meet the famous.

There was also an overlap with the thirteen-year-old Theosophical Society. Some of Salt's friends were agnostics like himself, willing to be classed with Freethinkers of the Bradlaugh school. But in 1889 Freethought was undergoing a crisis. Annie Besant, who had been a zealous co-worker with Bradlaugh as well as the Fabians, suddenly revolted into Theosophy. As taught by its high-priestess Madame Blavatsky, this purported to be an eternal religion containing all the others. Its motto was 'There is no religion higher than Truth'. It was largely Hindu in its motifs, and owed a debt to such rediscoverers of the East as Sir Edwin Arnold, editor of the *Daily Telegraph.* Arnold's poem *The Light of Asia* had introduced Buddha to English readers, and he had translated the *Bhagavad Gita,* the supreme literary expression of Hinduism. Many Theosophists were also vegetarians.

All these people knew each other, stimulated each other, and cited each other's books. Arnold was himself a diet-reformer. Carpenter studied the *Gita.* Anna Kingsford quoted *The Light of Asia* in her. vegetarian essay, expounded her own version of 'true Christianity', and held office in the Theosophical Society. Some of the group can be dismissed as eccentrics, but the group as a whole cannot. Its achievement would have been great if it had done no more than educate Gandhi. But it also educated George Bernard Shaw. He was in it and of it—a vegetarian, a Fabian, a heretic on religion and marriage. He acknowledged Salt as a mentor, and departed from habit sixty years later to write a preface to Salt's biography. Chesterton too matured largely in the same set, and some of his liveliest writing sprang from his love-hate relation with it.

The Humanitarian tea-parties were popular with Indians living in London. Gandhi's introduction to Salt occurred early in 1889 when he turned up at one. At that time he was preoccupied with his efforts to become a gentleman. He appeared bashfully in the doorway wearing his black coat and excessive top hat. The guests put him at his ease, and he asked if anybody could recommend a dancing teacher. Salt noted his name but did not remember him for anything in particular.

Months passed. Talking with fellow vegetarians over his meals, Gandhi learned that they had their own association. During his spell of thrift and hard work he was not inclined to join. However, he glanced at their newsletters and periodicals, and late that year he subscribed to *The Vegetarian,* their weekly paper. Its editor, Dr Josiah Oldfield, heard of him from an acquaintance and invited him to an international congress, held at Portsmouth in the first week of February 1890. For this function he stayed at Shelton's Vegetarian Hotel, Ventnor. A group photograph shows his continuing care for his appearance: he wears a white tie, stiff white cuffs, a white handkerchief in his breast pocket. His hair is neat.

At Portsmouth he encountered the London Vegetarian Society face to face, and in the late summer of 1890 he joined it. Dr Oldfield saw that he had unusual gifts (the doctor was the first person who ever did), and got him on to the committee. To Oldfield's disappointment he hardly ever uttered a word. By the time he had screwed up courage to speak, the subject had generally changed. However, he helped to design a badge for members. Also, under his colleagues' influence, he tried experiments at home. He drank cocoa instead of tea. He tested a bread-and-fruit diet, a cheese-milk-and-egg diet . . . though he decided finally that eggs counted as meat. Then, in Bayswater where he was now lodging, he founded his own local vegetarian club, inviting Oldfield to be president and Sir Edwin Arnold to be vice-president. While it did not last long, it gave him, as secretary, some lessons in organization.

4

As already remarked, when Henry Salt and his friends probed the fundamentals of life, their critique extended to other things besides food; but with less consistency in the results. Sex was harder to pin down. Here they agreed only in rejecting the norms, or alleged norms, of the society round them. Against the apostles of Shelleyan New Morality stood the neo-puritans, whose oracle was Tolstoy—sensual, unhappily married, and disgusted with that aspect of human nature. Theosophists also believed in celibacy as a means to the highest occult quest, though they added hastily that it was only for the select few who could rightly undertake such a quest. The hottest debating topic was birth control. Annie Besant had lectured on contraception, and, with Bradlaugh, had got into trouble for publishing obscene matter.

Gandhi had already had to cope with a personal problem. Other Indian students shared it. Victims like himself of child marriage, with wives at home, they were forced to spend years in England where lads of their own age were single. Most of them concealed their wives' existence from unsuspecting western maidens (who had never heard of child marriage) and circulated freely.

Intriguingly enough in view of his later career, Gandhi followed the fashion. Nor was he so backward as his character might have led one to expect. Even in his early lodging with the Kensington landlady, he took her daughters out to dinner on money sent by his family. Despite Hindu disapproval of contact with women other than your wife, he had few qualms of conscience about Kasturbai, back in India with their small son. However, he did worry over the fact that he was lying—or at least dissembling—by letting everyone assume that he was unmarried; and always there was the vow to his mother. Checked by these scruples as well as his ingrained shyness, he became inarticulate with girls, but not wholly uninteresting. Few took much notice of him; those who did were apt to tease him and try to draw him out.

At Ventnor during the 1890 conference, the daughter of his hotel proprietor took him walking. Miss Shelton was twenty-five. Gandhi walked fast and strenuously as usual. But she, in her high-heeled boots and long skirt, walked even faster, and dragged him up a steep hill. She talked all the time, pointing out scenery, and he could only murmur 'yes' and 'no'. When they went down again she negotiated the slope at a breakneck pace, and then stood at the bottom cheering as her poor Indian crawled and slithered after her.

This idyll was a diversion from a slightly graver involvement. During 1889 Gandhi had visited Brighton. An elderly widow who helped him with a French menu invited him to dine with her on Sundays at her London house. She turned out to have a girl living with her, and often left them alone together. Week by week the acquaintance ripened and Gandhi's uneasiness increased. At last he wrote the widow a laboriously composed letter confessing his marital secret. To his relief she took the news lightly and assured him that he could go on calling, which he did, throughout his stay in England.

His motive here was simply the overpowering need to be truthful. By temperament he was more like the neo-puritans than the free lovers, but his behaviour was not governed by rigid chastity, still less by prudery. In fact it was the delicate topic of contraception that occasioned the first public stand he ever made.

The president of the Vegetarian Society was a rich ironmaster, A. F. Hills by name, a puritan. His money kept the society going, and its committee was packed with his nominees. Among the non-Hills men was Dr Allinson, author of one of the books read by Gandhi, and an exponent of birth control. Hills accused Allinson of subverting morals. Arguing that the Society had ethical responsibilities extending beyond diet, he mustered his protégés behind a motion for the doctor's expulsion.

Gandhi was already much interested in birth control. His awareness of population came early. He admired Hills personally, and distrusted Allinson's methods. The issue, however, was whether the president could impose an ethical view on a dietetic body. Gandhi felt bound to challenge him. Still nervous, he came to the crucial meeting with a written statement which another member read out. That was his first battle, fought on 20 February 1891. His counter-attack was brief and timid and, in the upshot, unsuccessful. Yet he made it as a matter of pure principle, on behalf of a colleague whom he did not agree with. When Allinson was forced off the committee he contemplated resigning himself.

5

In spite of setbacks, Gandhi was becoming more sociable. During his involvement with the vegetarians he had also been attending meetings of a body called the National Indian Association. After a tongue-tied start, here as elsewhere, he was introduced to someone he already knew by repute—the poet Narayan Hemchandra, who had translated various foreign works into Gujarati. Dressed like a tramp, fiddling with his beard, Narayan explained that he knew several Indian languages but no English. Would Gandhi teach him? They began a series of lessons and grew very friendly, cooking vegetarian meals for each other, and working together on Narayan's gaseous projects. Eventually the poet sailed for America, where he rashly wore Indian costume and was arrested for indecent exposure. In the autumn of 1889, however, he brought Gandhi to his first interview with a public figure in the top rank, Cardinal Manning. The Cardinal's mediation during the dock strike had altered the face of labour relations and made him a national celebrity. Narayan, an ideological lion-hunter, insisted on meeting 'the sage'. Gandhi wrote a letter and Manning proved accessible. Their visit, though short, was pleasant.

For years this remained almost his only contact with Christianity,
at least in its older and richer forms. During a trip to Paris he
wandered round Notre Dame and had intimations of the love felt
by the folk who had built it. He was impressed by French churches
generally and the worshippers in them. But his response was ex-
ternal. His personal discovery of religion—the third fundamental
thing which his mentors were probing—came otherwise.

He met two bachelor brothers who were Theosophists. Primed
with notions about the Wisdom of India, they were reading Arnold's
translation of the *Gita*. Now here was Gandhi, a genuine Hindu in
the flesh. They asked him to expound it in the original, only to get
the disillusioning answer that he had never read it in any language.
So they introduced him to this classic of his own country. While
he gave what help he could with the Sanskrit, his knowledge was
luckily too slight to trap him in academic by-roads. He absorbed
the English text as a poetic statement, and found it enthralling. He
was to be enthralled more and more deeply as the years passed.

The *Bhagavad Gita* forms a section of the epic *Mahabharata*.
The title means 'Song of the Blessed Lord', i.e. Krishna, who is an
avatar or incarnation of the Supreme God Vishnu. Krishna acts as
charioteer for the hero Arjuna, in a war between the two branches
of a dynasty. Arjuna is the finest warrior on the 'good' side, but
many relatives whom he loves and reveres have joined the enemy.
Seeing them waiting across the battlefield he is stricken with grief,
and refuses to fight them. In the long dialogue that ensues, Krishna
persuades him to take up his arms again.

While many topics are discussed, the key concept is *dharma*—
duty, vocation, what a person is 'for'. This is bound up with the caste
theory: Arjuna is a warrior-noble and has responsibilities which
he must not evade, whatever his feelings. But the lesson is more
profound than the theory. Krishna's point is that mere emotion—
desire, revulsion, pity, even when seemingly praiseworthy should
never divert a man from the central truth of his nature. You are
what you are, you must find out what you are called to do in the
world's scheme, and you must do it without brooding over the
consequences. The frets and lusts of the individual self are liars.
Krishna tells Arjuna to conquer this petty self, and enter into the
higher Selfhood of God, the realm of Truth, through ardent devotion and disinterested action in keeping with his own calling.

Salvation through action, *karma-yoga*, was out of favour in

Gandhi's depressed India. Thanks partly to the *Gita,* he himself
was to be one of its chief revivalists. Meanwhile Krishna confirmed
him in the moral absolutism he had learned from Harischandra
and Rama. The divine charioteer taught an ethic not only of Truth
but of Truth at all costs, including the suffering of others: Arjuna's
duty is to slaughter his relatives and not worry. Also interesting
to Gandhi were passages about correct diet and control of the
passions. To Krishna's best disciples the Arnold version applies
the term Mahatma, meaning Great Soul. This was the first context
where Gandhi unquestionably came across it.

Afterwards he studied the Sanskrit in detail, and compared it
with other more exact translations, but always preferred Arnold's.
Its appeal to him seems to have rested on two merits. First, it reads
like a poem, and from boyhood onward he could always respond to
poetry and accept ideas which came to him in a literary medium.
Secondly, it is more coherent, more of a step-by-step argument,
than the text really warrants. Connections of thought which pre-
suppose a reader instructed in Hinduism are spelt out by Arnold
for a reader who is not. This feature too was suited to Gandhi's
mind.

When he read the English *Gita* he was repeating the process he
had undergone with Salt's pamphlet. He was discovering his own
heritage through a westerner, who focused it and made sense of it
as Indians themselves did not. It would be wrong to stress this point
if it concerned his reactions to Salt and Arnold alone. But the same
thing happened again and again. He partially described it himself
in a letter written some years later when he was reading Emerson:
'The essays to my mind contain the teaching of Indian wisdom in
a western *guru.* It is interesting to see our own sometimes thus
differently fashioned.' In his London phase it was more than interesting, it was decisive.

He had grown up with a yearning for clear ideas, precise truths,
experimental proofs, in a world where these were hard to come by;
in a society without price-tags, governed by bargaining, its loyalties
ambiguous and its morale confused. Nothing had been firm or explicit except religious rules which he could see no justification for.
He had lived in featureless landscapes, on food that was never crisp
or cold. England of course had its own evils and muddles, some far
worse than any Hindu equivalent. But England (and the West
generally) could at least supply the thinking of a temperate climate,

and a culture rooted in law and logic and definition. Even eccentricity, even revolt, had the same tinge. This was the kind of thinking that Gandhi desperately needed. Westerners could not westernize him, but they could teach him his own people's wisdom better than his own people. If, like Salt, they reached the same positions by different paths, the paths were clearer. If, like Arnold, they interpreted India directly, they brought light instead of darkness. And so the philosophy which he finally took back east with him was a fertile hybrid.

The theosophical brothers had not finished with him. After taking him through the *Gita* they took him through *The Light of Asia*, Arnold's poem on Gautama, the Buddha. It was not completely new to Gandhi, since he had read a passage quoted by Anna Kingsford, but now he explored it as a whole. Again he was fascinated. Parts of the story were peculiarly apt. Gautama's father arranges a marriage for him, and his wife bears a son, but then he leaves without a goodbye on a lonely quest for salvation. He can shed such fetters with a clear conscience in pursuit of a higher good. It is a notion more acceptable in India than the West. The country still abounds in *sadhus* or holy men, real and bogus, who have deserted their families. While Gandhi never did that, self-identification with Buddha was perhaps a foreshadowing of his solution to the marital problem which his own parents had handed him.

As the two poems sank in he realized that he was past his agnostic stage. Like most educated Indians he respected Bradlaugh, who was a staunch friend to India. He had given Bradlaugh's opinions a hearing, but unbelief now struck him as simply barren. Annie Besant's leap from Freethought to Theosophy set him pondering. He followed the controversy, and read her apologia *Why I became a Theosophist,* a marvel of adroit batting on a sticky wicket. The redeeming eloquence of its closing words about Truth might have been addressed to him personally. But could he enrol in the Theosophical Society? The brothers pressed him, and introduced him to Annie Besant herself and Madame Blavatsky. He got as far as an associate membership, but dropped it, feeling that he ought to know more.

They tried again. On their advice he toiled through Madame Blavatsky's new *Key to Theosophy.* Here he learned that 'there is no religion higher than Truth', and that all religions embody the same Truth; also, that Christianity is a pack of lies. He read a good deal about the Brotherhood of Man; also, a good deal about the gulf between initiates who can receive the Truth and the masses who are unfit for it. The authoress discussed reincarnation, and celibacy, and vegetarianism. She denounced organized charity and school education. She wrote of the unseen Mahatmas who instructed her by telepathy; and she inveighed touchily against critics who scoffed at them.

Theosophists often give the impression that while all religions are equal, Hinduism is more equal than others. Reading the *Key*, Gandhi extracted one valuable moral at any rate, that Hinduism was worth studying. Later he was to deride theosophical 'humbug', but later still, his happy memories of Theosophist friends invested their doctrine with a halo which it scarcely deserved. He praised it as 'Hinduism at its best'. But that was only a passing remark, indicative of the way he had again approached the East through Europe. His concern was with Hinduism, not Theosophy.

In 1890 he had other religious concerns. A Christian vegetarian gave him a Bible. With his Hindu blind spot toward history, he could make nothing of the Old Testament. But he loved the Sermon on the Mount, especially the precept 'Resist not evil', and tried to combine it with the sermons of Krishna and Buddha in a creed of self-abnegation. Christ led him to Muhammad, whom he discovered in Carlyle's volume of Heroes, thus encountering Asia through Europe yet again. He noted the Prophet's courage, and his simplicity—how he fasted, mended his own shoes, patched his own cloak. Carlyle's congenial phrases about the 'grand Truth' vouchsafed to the Prophet, 'setting his soul in flame', conjured up the vision of an apostolate. It also laid the foundation for Gandhi's sympathy with India's Muslims, in which he followed Rammohan Roy and the Tagores, and for which, like them, he suffered.

In January 1891 Bradlaugh died. Gandhi went to his funeral, together with most of the Indians in London. On the way back, an argument between an atheist and a clergyman disgusted him with the shallow bad taste of the Freethought party. That May he had his first feeling of the hand of God in his life, when he went with an Indian acquaintance to another vegetarian congress. This also was held in Portsmouth. One evening, after attending a session, the two of them played cards with their rather raffish landlady. Risqué jokes were exchanged, Gandhi joined in, and the woman made advances which he nearly responded to. A hint from the fourth player pulled him up. He recalled his vow (not Kasturbai, apparently) and hurried off to his room alone. To avoid the embarrassment of staying on in the same house, he moved to Ventnor for the rest of the conference. The incident was a shock. Being fully aware what he had wanted, and how little resistance he had made, he was left with a conviction that God had saved him.

6

Gandhi had been in London two and a half years. He had made his way into a certain portion of English society—a set. With all the rest of English society his record was a virtual blank.

For instance, even his religious inquiries had not brought him anywhere near the Church of England, to which the majority belonged. He had gone to hear one or two fashionable preachers, but knew no more of Anglican Christianity than of Catholic. Now and for years afterwards, the Christians whom he did meet were mostly 'low' and dissenting, with an Are-you-saved attitude that repelled him. Realization that orthodox Christianity could be other than this came too late. He remained a stranger to the Anglican Establishment and all that went with it.

He remained a stranger to a great deal besides. The England of his studies was the England of the Queen's Golden Jubilee, of Mr Gladstone, of Cecil Rhodes, of dawning Labour politics. It was also the England of *Three Men in a Boat* and *Charley's Aunt*. Doubtless Gandhi read about many things in the papers, but few left their mark on him. In most respects his Anglophile outlook was still nearly as much an outsider's as it had been in Rajkot. He was too poor and too gauche to mingle with the gentry. As for London's respectable Vaisyas and swarming Sudras, only a job could have involved his life with theirs, and he had no job.

Hence, the one bit of England which he was ever inside was Henry Salt's circle of radicals: a small group of earnest men and women, middle-class and upward, above average in intelligence, who had themselves partially seceded from the society round them. Gandhi received their influence almost unmixed. It was a creative accident, which could only have happened to an alien like himself. His English friends, however devoted to their quixotic causes, always had links outside the circle. Gandhi had none. He emerged from their tutelage a purer Truth-worshipper, Simple Lifer, and sceptic about capitalist civilization, than they were themselves.

By the time he sailed for home he had acquired most of the ideas he was to mould into a working philosophy. He had found them, or at least the essential hints and justifications, in books he had read or public events he had taken an interest in. Even some of the less obvious ones, which did not come into the open till much later, were already planted in his mind. His rejection of formal education was supplied ready-made by Madame Blavatsky. His policy toward labour disputes was prefigured by Manning's toward the dock strike. In some areas he would require a further push, in others he still had lessons to learn; and always there was his need to experiment. Yet even then the push, the lesson, the impulse to try, were to come from people associated with his English circle, people of whom he was already conscious.

His originality lay in what he did with his acquisitions. As an Indian he could relate his mentors' writings and sayings to the Indian world. He could use them as he used the *Plea for Vegetarianism*, to bring the best of that world into focus. When he eventually applied them among Indians they flourished as they never did anywhere else. In England (except with the unique genius Bernard Shaw) this ideology became diffused, faded, crankish. In India it struck root and blossomed—as an expression of India's own better nature. Through Gandhi the doctrines of a clique mobilized a multitude.

In 1891 he was far from showing the qualities that achieved this. But he was making progress. On 2 May he succeeded in reading a paper to the London vegetarians on 'The Foods of India'. They liked it, and he read it again at Portsmouth. Meanwhile his first published writings were appearing in their weekly. An article on 'Indian Vegetarians' ran in six instalments. This article is in acceptable English. Gandhi gives a careful account of Hindu diet, with some remarks about the Muslims and Parsees. Rebutting the charge that Hindu debility is due to lack of meat, he suggests other reasons for it. One is child marriage, which he denounces at painful length. Under the right conditions, he claims, Hindus are stalwart: his prize exhibit is the shepherd. Another point of portentous interest is a passing slap at the British salt tax.

After his serial Gandhi wrote three pieces on Hindu festivals. The most noteworthy feature of these is the detailed observation. Though he complains mildly about obscene language, the articles show sympathy toward the masses who take part in the festivities. They could not have been written by a prig or a snob.

In June *The Vegetarian* carried a long interview with him on the eve of departure. The inset portrait is of a very ordinary-looking young Indian with a tiny moustache and bow tie. He seems to have talked freely about his shameful wedding and the obstacles put in the way of his journey to England. Clearly his most intense memories of home were memories of those hordes of people hemming him in and shouting and weeping. Hence, perhaps, his idealization of the shepherd's life. Hence also, perhaps, what looks like a wish-fulfilling Freudian slip at the outset of his maiden magazine article—a statement that India has twenty-five million inhabitants. He has lost a zero. It is ironic that the first printed sentence by this zealot of Truth should have been a falsehood.

As for his studies, he had completed them. Eating his dinners had presented a certain difficulty, but he managed. He was a painstaking student and read more textbooks than most, especially in Roman law. Among English manuals his favourite was Joshua Williams's *Principles of the Law of Real Property;* partly because he found it readable, partly because conceptions of property interested him. Dipping rather late into John Mayne's *Treatise on Hindu Law and Usage,* he gathered that whereas individual property was the rule in England, corporate property was the rule in India. That could mean that India was a more hopeful field for the co-operative living dreamed of by his Utopian acquaintances.

Such questions, however, were not his present concern. He passed his examinations, was called to the Bar on 10 June, and enrolled in the High Court on the 11th. Towards the end he sought advice on his future practice from a Mr Frederick Pincutt. In Gandhi's own words, 'he was a Conservative, but his affection for Indian students was pure and unselfish'. Pincutt remarked on the curiously elementary fact that Gandhi knew very little about India. He urged him to read a lately published · *History of the Indian Mutiny* in six volumes by Sir John Kaye and Colonel Malleson.

Another event of Gandhi's last days in London was a farewell dinner-party he gave for some friends at the Holborn Restaurant, with a special vegetarian menu. As when he left school, he was expected to make a speech, and as when he left school, he bungled it. He started by telling a joke—a correct English opening, but out of character. Later, when he found his own style in speech-making, he hardly ever tried for laughs. At the Holborn Restaurant he could get no further. He thanked his guests for coming and then sat down. This persistent shyness when faced with more than one or two distressed him. Still, it saved him from wasting time in chatter, and taught him to think before he spoke. He made a virtue of his defect.

On 12 June he sailed for Bombay aboard S.S. *Oceana*. His parting remarks in the *Vegetarian* interview, which appeared the same week, ran as follows: 'During my nearly three years' stay in England I have left many things undone, and have done many things which perhaps I might better have left undone, yet I carry one great consolation with me—that I shall go back without having taken meat or wine, and that I know from personal experience that there are so many vegetarians in England.' Surely a lame conclusion. Gandhi always dismissed these student days as a mere preface, before he began life. The ingredients were assembled, but they were still inactive. The world had yet to draw him out.

At his landing in England he had carried that letter of introduction to the famous Dadabhai Naoroji. Throughout his stay he had never talked with the Grand Old Man for more than a moment, but he attended his lectures. In Naoroji he saw and heard—probably for the first time—a distinguished Indian who spoke against British Imperialism. But in June 1891 this was unfinished business; indeed, unstarted business. Another deferred matter was Mr Pincutt's advice to read Kaye and Malleson. In due course, however, he tackled their massive work. On the first page were some quotations from Francis Bacon. One said: 'To think that an handful of people can, with the greatest courage and policy in the world, embrace too large extent or dominion, it may hold for a time, but it will fail suddenly.' And another: 'If there be fuel prepared, it is hard to tell whence the spark shall come that shall set it on fire. The matter of seditions is of two kinds, much poverty and much discontentment.'

IV

Self-reliance

1

At Aden the India-bound passengers transferred to a smaller boat. The Arabian Sea was rough, and nearly everybody was sick. Gandhi, however, ate his porridge and paced the deck unruffled, meditating his dreams of reform. These were thrust into abeyance by a shock that awaited him in Bombay. Laxmidas met the boat and told him that their mother was dead. The news had been kept back so as not to disturb his studies. His grief was profound, but he was now capable of controlling it, and weathered the blow almost without a tear.

Dr Mehta, who had been so helpful in the first English days, was back at his Bombay home. The Gandhi brothers were his guests for a while. Through Mehta, Mohandas made one of the few friendships that ever deeply influenced him, with the Jain poet Raychandbhai. Raychandbhai was about twenty-five, a partner in a jewellery firm. Mohandas was much impressed by his blend of business acumen, literary talent, and spiritual wisdom. According to Hindu notions, every seeker of truth should have a *guru* or master. Gandhi never did. His individualism is one of the reasons why the description 'Hindu saint' does not really fit him. Raychandbhai, however, became a valued counsellor, as close to being his *guru* as anyone was.

But not immediately. Bombay had to be left behind, life had to be resumed. Gandhi's excommunication still stood. Laxmidas arranged a ceremonial cleansing, which appeased some of their caste brethren though not all. The ban was lifted enough to remove the inconvenience, not enough to clear the air. Nor were the returned husband's relations with his wife much improved. Back in the old surroundings at Rajkot, the old jealousy and domineering started again. Their household arrangements were uneasy, affected by his

47

changed taste in clothing and by his innovations in diet. Kasturbai had to come to terms with cocoa and English vegetarian dishes. However, their son Harilal was big enough to be interesting, and Harilal was a better subject for educational zeal. Gandhi's homecoming was the beginning of his lifelong fondness for children, and of that more significant thing, their fondness for him.

Laxmidas was doing fairly well as an attorney. He had served the ruler of Porbandar as secretary and general adviser. For a novice, he said, legal practice in Rajkot was a dubious proposition. It was agreed that Mohandas should move to Bombay, where he could gain experience in the courts.

Mohandas got as far as the move, but not the experience. He received one brief through a tout, made difficulties over greasing the tout's palm, and then became inarticulate when he had to cross-examine. The only legal work he succeeded in handling was paperwork. He applied for a part-time teaching post, but was turned down as having no degree. Expenses mounted. His sole clear benefit from attending court was the self-imposed exercise of walking there and back. After six futile months he retreated to Rajkot, where he could hope to establish himself by devilling for his generous brother.

Unfortunately a new factor had begun to work against him—the darkening of the family's political prospects. Laxmidas was charged with misusing his late position in Porbandar. The matter went to the British agent. Mohandas had met this agent briefly in London, and Laxmidas persuaded him, very much against the grain, to intercede. It was his first attempt to deal with a British official. He soon found that the man who had been sociable when on leave in England was cold and brusque when on duty in India. The Sahib resented a Hindu presuming on a casual personal acquaintance. But as with the caste council years before, Gandhi's obstinate streak suddenly emerged. He refused to be silenced even by the broadest hints, and went on talking till a servant dragged him out of the office. Still he would not give up. He sent in a note, and it took a stinging answer from the agent to induce him to leave. A veteran barrister told him he must swallow such insults; there was no other way of surviving with the British. The affair left him with a rooted aversion to wire-pulling and the exploitation of private contacts.

Even if the agent could be appeased, Gandhi saw no future in state politics. He was getting a few assignments from the ruler of Porbandar, and trying to strengthen that prince's pathetic dignity.

In this he made a little headway. But the corruption and intrigue sickened him. His father's premiership was neither attainable nor worth seeking. Again he yearned to escape. Again a path opened.

A firm of Muslim merchants, Dada Abdulla, had a flourishing business in South Africa. Needing a lawyer to help with a complex case, their Porbandar office approached Laxmidas, and offered his younger brother a year's work for a hundred guineas plus expenses. The proposition was a godsend. In April 1893 (leaving Kasturbai with a second baby, Manilal, six months old) Gandhi hopefully embarked for another new country. As the ship happened to be crowded, he was allowed to share the captain's quarters. They got on well; he had made further progress in that respect at least. When they reached Zanzibar the captain took him ashore for a jaunt, which included an unscheduled call at a brothel. Gandhi spent a paralytic few minutes with a Negro prostitute, neither drawn nor morally restrained, simply out of his element and ashamed of himself.

In May the ship docked at Durban. He was met by his employer Abdulla Sheth ('Sheth' means a substantial businessman). Abdulla was somewhat at a loss. The offer to Gandhi had been made at the firm's Indian end without proper consultation. Their lawsuit was going on in Pretoria, the capital of the Transvaal, and he could not see what there was for an assistant to do. However, his wealth did not prevent him from being a courteous host to a young nobody. They spent a week together, discussing Islam and visiting the city court. Gandhi made some Christian acquaintances there, who set him thinking again about their own creed.

And there also—casually, unspectacularly, on a serio-comic issue—he began his true career. It was a Durban magistrate who launched him. He had soon grasped that the large Indian minority in South Africa was divided into groups. On top were the Muslim merchants, sometimes called Arabs, who employed Hindu and Parsee clerks. They, and to some extent their staffs, enjoyed a condescending social acceptance among the more tolerant whites. But most Indians were labourers brought over on an indenture basis, and these were despised, not only by the whites but by their own compatriots. Labouring Indians were 'coolies', literally 'carriers'—in English terms, 'hewers of wood and drawers of water'. The white man, of course, was apt to apply the word to any Indian. But if he called a merchant a 'coolie', the merchant might object, and could sometimes even extract an apology. With most Indians it was different. Gandhi, being unclassifiable in any more polite way, could expect to be treated as one of them. The alternative word to 'coolie' was 'Sammy', derived from the 'swami' at the end of Indian names. It was still more contemptuous.

Entering court in the frock coat and Bengali turban which he habitually wore, he was better dressed than a coolie had any right to be. His shoes shone, his trousers were pressed. The magistrate asked him to take his turban off. He declined, and walked out. On reflection the issue did not strike him as vital. He told Abdulla that he was willing to wear a hat instead. The merchant replied, however, that he would be letting down some of his fellow countrymen who were trying to make a stand on this very point. Furthermore, if he wore a hat he would look like a waiter; and the Indian waiters —mostly the sons of indentured workmen who had turned Christian —were a base lot.

Gandhi wrote a letter to a newspaper. It provoked some correspondence, and he was described as an unwelcome visitor. Nevertheless he kept his turban.

The incident was a warning, hardly more. But Gandhi's lesson in race-discrimination was rammed home when the time came for him to go to Pretoria. Abdulla gave him a first-class ticket and he set off. At nine in the evening his train halted at Pietermaritzburg. A passenger entered his compartment, looked him over, and summoned two railway officials. They ordered the presumptuous coolie to move to the van. He sat tight and showed his ticket. They sneered at it, and fetched a policeman who hauled him out on to the platform. His luggage followed. The train steamed away.

Gandhi always spoke of the ensuing ordeal as the most creative passage in his whole life. It was winter, there in the southern hemisphere, and the night was dark and savagely cold. He sat in the waiting room and shivered, wondering what to do. His own discomfort was nothing; the racial pestilence that caused it was everything. At last he resolved to go on as planned, and see what remedies could be found. In the morning he wired Abdulla and the general manager of the railway. While he was waiting for their replies, several Indian traders wandered over to the station, and told him about their own similar misfortunes. Plainly these were typical of inter-coloured relations in South Africa.

Thanks to Abdulla, the railway manager sent word that Gandhi was not to be detained. Another train took him to Charlestown, near the battlefield of Majuba Hill. Now he had to cross into the Transvaal and make his way to Johannesburg by road. His employer had booked a seat in the stage-coach, but the coach agent immediately cancelled his ticket. Other passengers would object to a coolie. The 'leader' in charge of the coach waved him to a place on the outside, and then, at a halt, tried to shift him from even that, on to the footboard. Gandhi was terrified of opposing the big white man. Yet the strength came to him. He refused. The leader swore, hit him, and tried to drag him down. He clung desperately to a rail till the kindlier passengers intervened. Finally he was released, and the coach lumbered on. The leader muttered and threatened. Gandhi prayed.

At Standerton, where they stopped for the night, he met more Indians with stories of the same kind. Transferring to another coach, he reached Johannesburg safely and in fair comfort. But then he went to a hotel and was told that it was full—the reason for its 'fullness' being made obvious. An Indian merchant laughed at him. Did he seriously suppose that any hotel would have room for him? In South Africa they had to pocket these insults all the time; they did it for the sake of their livelihood. On the train to Pretoria, Gandhi would simply have to travel third class. They were in Boer territory, where no better tickets were even sold to Indians, let alone honoured.

He studied the railway regulations. They gave no ground for refusal. He declared that he would insist on a first-class ticket, or else hire a cab for the remaining thirty-seven miles. Having sent a note to the station-master explaining that he was a lawyer and expected to travel first class, he called on the surprised official in correct European dress, complete with tie. After some palaver he actually got his ticket. When the guard on the train asked him to move, the other passenger in the compartment said he could stay. The guard growled, 'If you want to travel with a coolie, what do I care?' and went off. So the Inner Temple barrister reached his destination in qualified triumph.

Gandhi had been frightened, but adamant—several times over. His Truth, his relentless Absolute, had taken control. He had had that experience which is occasionally given to mortals, and which Luther put in words: 'Here stand I; so help me God, I can no other.' It is ironic, all the same, that he should have made his stand on his right to travel in a first-class compartment, when in days to come he scrupulously kept out of them.

2

In the dim station at Pretoria he hesitated, uncertain where to go. An American Negro escorted him to a hotel. Mr Johnston, the proprietor, offered him a room, on condition that he stayed in it for his meals: 'I assure you I have no colour prejudice, *but.* . . .' Remarkably, Johnston consulted the other guests. They decided they would let this Indian into the dining-room. But Gandhi noted that their permission had had to be asked.

Next day he went to Abdulla's attorney, A. W. Baker, who found lodgings for him with a poor couple who were prepared not to be particular. Baker explained that there was not much work for Gandhi to do yet—none, in fact, as counsel. Their talk drifted to other topics. The attorney was a Protestant lay preacher. He asked the newcomer what his religion was. Gandhi replied that he was an inquirer, Hindu by birth, but not well instructed in that or any religion. Baker invited him to a prayer meeting, and he expressed gratitude.

His religious interests were reawakening. It appeared that instead of having his time filled immediately with the job, he would be able to continue his mental pilgrimage. Once more the impulsion was coming from a westerner, in this case from a devout Christian. But the atmosphere was changing. Because of the revelation of racism, the eternal questions were pressing into real life. His Absolute—Truth or God, whatever one called it—had descended from the empyrean and involved him in a brawl on a stage-coach. He had to look at it more closely, to compare all religions in the hope of distilling it out as the common factor. Plainly he should not move toward any alien faith before he understood his own. But with that proviso he could allow Mr Baker (who was kind, and genuinely without colour prejudice) to take him to prayer meetings.

Towards one o'clock next day, they went. Though neither knew it, Baker's religion was on trial, perhaps for its life. Gandhi was ready to welcome any aid in the struggle for Indian rights which he already foresaw. The gods were giving Christianity its first and last chance to be in at the birth of the Afro-Asian revolution.

Gandhi as a student in London, 1888 *(Radio Times Hulton Picture Library)*

Gandhi *(front row, right)* at the Vegetarian Congress, 1890 *(Sumati Morarjee Collection)*

Gandhi with his office staff in Johannesburg, 1907 *(Sumati Morarjee Collection)*

With Kasturbai, 1915 *(Sumati Morarjee Collection)*

Gandhi at work: *above*, at Juhu, 1924; *below*, speaking at Tata Ironworks, Jamshedpur, 1925 *(Radio Times Hulton Picture Library)*

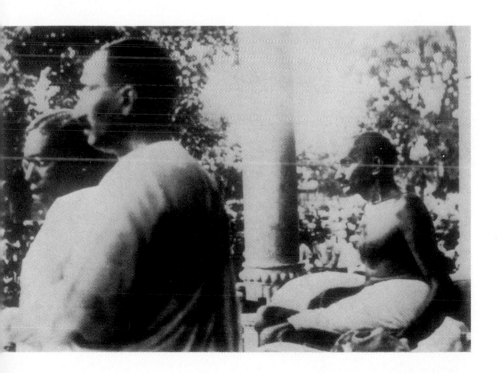

Hand-spinning, old style: *above*, Gandhi demonstrating traditional wheel in Calcutta; *below*, Kasturbai spinning *(Radio Times Hulton Picture Library)*

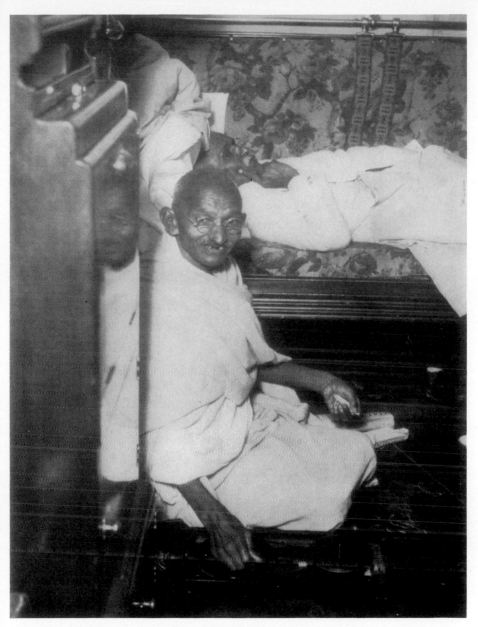

Hand-spinning, new style: Gandhi with improved wheel, on board
ship, 1931 *(Radio Times Hulton Picture Library)*

UNITED INDIA.

A cartoon by David Low, 1928 (*by arrangement with the London* Evening Standard)

A FRANKENSTEIN OF THE EAST.

GANDHI. "REMEMBER—NO VIOLENCE; JUST DISOBEDIENCE."
GENIE. "AND WHAT IF I DISOBEY *YOU?*"

(Published 12 March 1930. © PUNCH—
reproduced by permission of the Proprietors)

On the march. (*Radio Times Hulton Picture Library*)

With Sardar Patel (*center*) at Karachi Congress, 1931 (*Radio Times Picture Library*)

Gandhi with Rabindranath Tagore *(right)* and Dr Andrews *(Mansell Collection)*

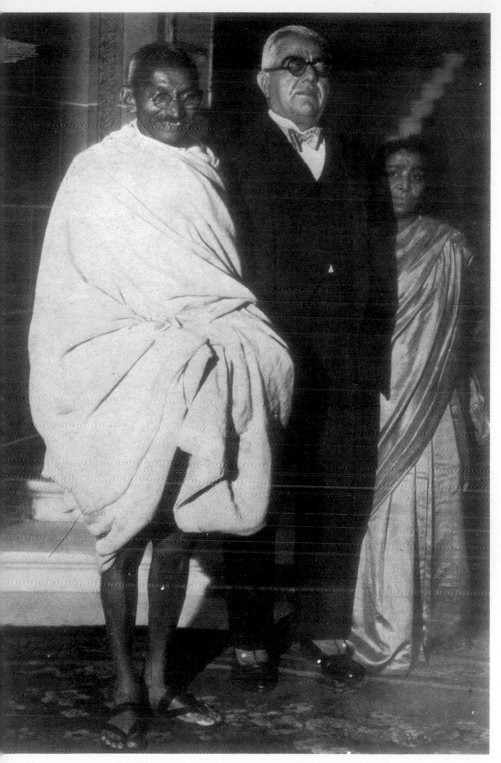

With the Aga Khan at the Ritz Hotel, London, 1931 *(Radio Times Hulton Picture Library)*

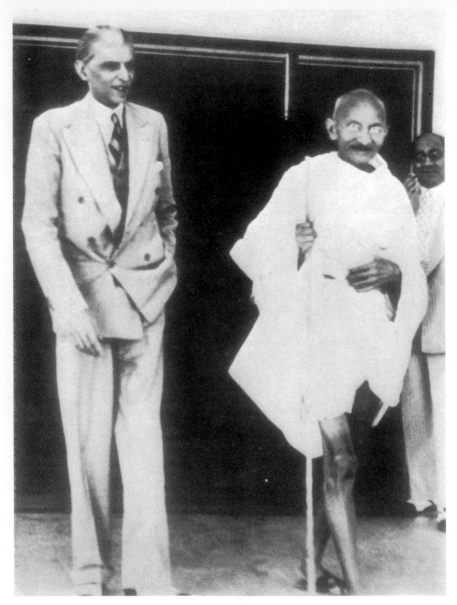

With Jinnah, 1938 *(Sumati Morarjee Collection)*

Jawaharlal Nehru in London, 1938 *(Radio Times Hulton Picture Library)*

Study of Gandhi toward the end of his life (*Mansell Collection*)

The pair arrived at the house, and Christianity, after its fashion, rose to the occasion. Gandhi was introduced to a small circle of white faces. Conspicuous members were two elderly spinsters and a youngish Quaker named Michael Coates. All knelt to pray, and Gandhi did likewise, not squatting cross-legged in the Hindu posture. Various needs were laid before the Almighty. A special petition was added for the conversion of the guest. The whole session lasted five minutes.

And that was it. The gods sat back with a sigh, and everybody went off to lunch. They had been nice to him. The spinsters, who lived together, had told him he could join them for tea any Sunday. In the ensuing weeks he often did. Coates was a frequent visitor there, and lent him books which they discussed. It was quite like his student days. But the conversion misfired. Its breakdown was one of the main reasons for his subsequent emphasis on Indian self-reliance. To turn to Europeans for help usually implied turning to missionary types, whose ideas and motives, he was forced to realize, were out of key.

Coates's failure was not for want of trying. He deluged Gandhi with books. Among them were the scriptural commentaries of Dr Parker, the well-known minister of the City Temple by Holborn Viaduct. Parker fell flat. Gandhi approved of some of the moral sentiments, but dismissed the main performance, quite justly, as question-begging. Coates tried Butler's *Analogy of Religion*. This was one of the few Anglican classics that Gandhi ever read. He respected its author's intelligence and learning. But again the attack failed. The *Analogy* was written to confute eighteenth-century atheists, and Gandhi was past atheism in that sense. Moreover, its academic tone and its appeal to history were unattractive to anyone with his moral fervour and lack of historical consciousness. Butler's case for the uniqueness of Christianity, and for Jesus as the sole divine Incarnation and Mediator, did not persuade him in the least. He could believe that a religion might reveal truths transcending reason. He could not believe that Christianity was alone in doing so.

The Quaker persisted. But although they stayed on good terms, it became evident that they were talking different languages. Gandhi wore a Vaishnava necklace given him by his mother. Coates tactlessly urged him to destroy this as superstitious, and would not see that her love or faith could mean anything. Also he introduced him to other Christians, with a curious blindness to the likely results. One of them was a Plymouth Brother. The Brother told Gandhi that he was manifestly troubled by guilt, that it was no use trying to improve oneself by moral endeavour, and that if he would just accept Christ as his personal saviour he would cease fretting and enjoy inner peace. Gandhi answered that so long as he remained the imperfect creature he was, he had no wish for such relief; he would rather fret. Privately he noted that the Plymouth Brother, true to his own doctrine, was very far indeed from trying to improve himself by moral endeavour.

Gandhi was left with a feeling that the Christians' Bible was a book to take seriously, but that these pious white South Africans had got it wrong. Surely religion and morality were indistinguishable? Yet some of what he was being told struck him as non-moral, even anti-moral. If Mr Baker's group had shown more humility, if they had approached him through his interests and not through theirs, they might have forged a momentous alliance. But they saw only an earnest young coloured lawyer whom they could ask to tea, take for walks, pray over and enlighten. Their opportunity passed.

3

It passed for ever. The earnest young lawyer had already launched his campaign. The higher certainties could wait; the Absolute could be obeyed without being anatomized.

During his first week in Pretoria he had called on Tyeb Sheth, a respected Muslim businessman, proposing to bring together the city's Indians to debate their problems. The fact that Tyeb was his employer's opponent in the lawsuit did not deter him. Nor did it deter the merchant, who promised to help. Invitations went out.

Most of the Indians who came were Muslims. But Hindus were scarce anyhow in Pretoria. Gandhi's speech was the beginning of his career as a leader, and the end of his shyness. His main theme (surely an unexpected one) was that if his hearers were to improve their status, they must shoulder their responsibilities. White people would judge all Indians by the few they observed, and react accordingly. The Indians, therefore, had a duty to think about their mode of living. They should make a point of being honest and truthful

. . . even in business. They should cultivate clean habits. They should stand together, not splitting their ranks by sectarian or regional feuds. After this homily—but only after it—he suggested forming a society to combat discrimination.

Audacity paid. The just-arrived Hindu of twenty-three carried his audience, who discussed his remarks in a friendly spirit, and offered ideas. Gandhi was quick to notice their difficulties over language; they came from different parts of India. He advised them to learn English and volunteered to teach it himself. Three pupils were enrolled, a Muslim barber and clerk, and a Hindu shopkeeper.

Having agreed to meet regularly, the Indians dispersed. Gandhi's first active move was against the abuse which had shaken him personally. In a letter to the railway company, he pointed out that its policy on tickets corresponded to nothing in its regulations. He got a reply: first- and second-class tickets would be sold to Indians who were 'properly dressed'. On such a basis, a station-master could nearly always find some ground to refuse. The ruling was another lesson in the workings of prejudice. Gandhi's efforts were not entirely wasted. That autumn an Indian who was thrown out of several second-class carriages plucked up courage to sue the railway, and won. But the exchange was only a skirmish, and more would be needed than skirmishing.

Gandhi studied the whole Indian position in South Africa. He was coached by Tyeb Sheth, and by the British agent in Pretoria, who expressed sympathy but pleaded that he was powerless because the Transvaal was not British. Gradually an account of the Indians' plight pieced itself together in Gandhi's mind, counterpointed against the weirdly irrelevant tracts issuing from Coates.

The first Indian labourers (it transpired) had been shipped to Natal from Calcutta and Madras, as far back as November 1860. The object of importing them was to ease a labour shortage in the settlers' sugar plantations, where Zulus refused to work. More and more arrived. Originally their term of indenture was three years. This was raised to five. They were provided with free board of a sort, and paid ten shillings a month. Impartial white investigators denounced the arrangement as semi-slavery. Abject illiteracy and moral collapse were widespread. Still, many who completed the term stayed on in the colony and counted as 'free'. Women joined them and families sprang up. The Asian community spread to the Transvaal in 1881, and then throughout South Africa. In the 1890s Natal had 51,000 Indians, alongside 50,000 Europeans and 400,000 Negroes. Corresponding figures in the Transvaal were 5,000 Indians, 120,000 whites, 650,000 Negroes; and in Cape Colony, 10,000 Indians, 400,000 whites, 900,000 Negroes.

It was to make money by supplying Indian needs that the Muslim traders like Abdulla had come over. The pioneer was a fellow citizen of the Gandhis in Porbandar. News of his profits lured the others over, with various employees and hangers-on, mostly from the same city and elsewhere in Gujarat. The merchants did excellent business with the Negroes as well. Gandhi, in Durban, had seen the social gulf that yawned between the two classes of Indian, however much the whites were inclined to lump them together as coolies or Sammies. The existence of 'free' ex-labourers did not bridge it— partly because they were only doubtfully free: they had to carry passes and submit to other restrictions. Nevertheless many of them were doing quite well as market gardeners. Others were in trade. What Gandhi perceived was that the Indians' thrift and hard work, their willingness to live poorly and get up early, were making them dangerous competitors. A piece of doggerel in the *Natal Mercury*, printed about this time, contrasted the white colonists' happy past with their nervous present.

> We had no squalid coolies then,
> With truthless tongues and artful ways;
> No Arab storeman's unclean den
> Disfigured West Street in those days.
> The White Man ran the kafir trade,
> And *was* the boss in days gone by;
> But now the Hindoo takes our cash,
> 'Busts up' and straightway 'does a guy'.
>   With a ha ha ha and a ho ho ho,
>   Ramsammy soon will have to go.

As the last couplet hinted, white activists had begun a counter-attack, intended not merely to keep the Asian in his place but to push him down further, and if possible, out. They had fired their opening shots in the Transvaal soon after his advent. 'These Indians', their spokesmen declared, 'have no sense of human decency. They suffer from loathsome diseases. They consider every woman as their prey.' An Indian deputation which protested to President Kruger was dismissed with quotations from the Old Testament. In 1885 the Boer government decreed that Indians could not vote or acquire citizenship. Also, they would have to live in prescribed districts for 'sanitary' reasons, and could own no property outside. Those immigrating into the country must pay a poll tax. All Indians were supposed to be under British protection as subjects of the Crown. But white opinion throughout South Africa supported the Boers, and the British High Commissioner in the Transvaal got only minor concessions.

Other acts of discrimination followed. The Boer Orange Free State deprived Indians of almost every civil right, and squeezed them all out, except for a few waiters. In Natal itself—a British colony—there were loud demands for repatriation or prohibitive taxes. With the achievement of partial self-government in 1893 the agitators grew hopeful of success. Cape Colony, which had a large English element, was less oppressive but still disposed to harass.

Gandhi's immediate concern was with the Transvaal where he was stationed. Among other indignities, Indians in Pretoria were denied the use of the sidewalk, and forbidden to be out after 9 p.m. without a permit. Luckily for him the State Attorney, Dr Krause, was a barrister of the Inner Temple. Krause provided his colleague with a letter which removed any difficulty—but the fact remained that the letter was needed. And then one day Gandhi strolled along the footpath by Kruger's house. The policeman on guard, seeing the insolent coolie, strode up without a word and kicked him into the gutter. Michael Coates happened to be riding past; he spoke to the officer in Dutch and got an apology. Gandhi did not want the apology. Once again, the fact was what mattered. As he was to remark in retrospect, 'It has always been a mystery to me how men can feel themselves honoured by the humiliation of their fellow-beings.'

For months he was learning, sometimes in this hard way, sometimes less painfully. He kept his meetings going. He gave his English lessons. He widened his range in society. Beyond that, his public actions were few. It was enough that Indians were beginning to think. In September 1893, however, he wrote to the *Natal Advertiser* to rebut an article which described them as 'parasites who live a semi-barbarous life'. This life of theirs, he retorted, was a modest and frugal one that compared well with the Europeans' luxury.

By then, a good deal of his time was taken up with Abdulla's lawsuit against Tyeb Sheth, to which he always gave due priority.

He learned two guiding principles from it. One was the prime importance of getting the facts, whatever he might be dealing with. The other arose from the way the case was concluded. He persuaded Tyeb to accept arbitration, and the arbitrator decided for Abdulla. Insistence on a lump payment of the whole amount owing would have left Tyeb bankrupt—an unthinkable disgrace for a Muslim. Gandhi, by immense efforts, persuaded his own employer to take the cash in instalments. To his delight, he ended as a mediator rather than a fighter on one side. Henceforth he always aimed at the reconciling solution rather than the crushing triumph.

In April 1894 the lawsuit was over. Despite his African concerns, he assumed there would be no more work for him, and set out to return to India. Abdulla Sheth gave him a farewell party in Durban. Its end was unforeseen. Gandhi picked up a copy of the *Natal Mercury,* and his eye fell on a paragraph under the headline 'Indian Franchise'. It referred to a bill before Natal's new Legislative Assembly which would deprive Indians of the vote. Few of the company present either knew or cared. But he refused to let the occasion relapse into mere sociability. 'This is the first nail in our coffin,' he said. The issue was specific and crucial. Indians must make a stand, must fight for their self-respect. Almost before the guests realized what was happening he had turned them into a committee, and the more articulate were pressing him to stay for another month. They agreed to subscribe to a campaign fund. With cries of 'Allah is great and merciful!' in his ears, Gandhi hurried away and roughed out a petition to the Assembly and Council.

Abdulla Sheth and a second merchant, Haji Muhammad, took the lead in forming a larger body. They were the richest and most honoured members of the Natal Indian community. The inaugural meeting took place at Abdulla's house, and Muhammad was elected as president. A call went out for volunteers. Abdulla was pessimistic about bringing in the educated young men born in Natal; alas, he said, they were mostly Christians taking their cue from the white clergy, and as such, had deserted their own people—a statement that shook Gandhi considerably. However, some of these Christians did come forward, thanks largely to the Durban court interpreter, Mr Paul, a Catholic. So also did Hindus, Parsees, and others with a wide range of occupational and regional backgrounds. The discovery of a common purpose (even if they did not quite understand it) gave them a unity never felt before.

Telegrams were dispatched to the Speaker of the Assembly and the Prime Minister of the colony, asking that the Franchise Bill be postponed. The Speaker consented to defer it for two days. The committee approved Gandhi's petition and got five hand-written copies made, with the help of an expert calligrapher. Durban merchants who owned carriages took three of the copies round the city, collected four hundred signatures in a few hours, and handed in the sheets at the House of Legislature. Another copy was shown to the press, drawing favourable comments, which forestalled any official attempt to hush it up.

As expected, the whites passed their bill. But Lord Ripon, Gladstone's Colonial Secretary, still had to approve it. Gandhi resolved to agitate for a veto. Such a campaign would require time, and a triple strategy. All Indians must be drawn into a working comradeship. They must be shown why the disfranchising law was dangerous. And their cause must be given publicity, not only throughout South Africa, but in Britain and India as well.

His own departure was out of the question. For his maintenance, as he would take no payment for public service, twenty merchants combined to retain him as their legal adviser with a guaranteed annual income of £300. Predictably, the Law Society of Natal tried to debar him from practice by procedural quibbles. The Chief Justice overrode the Society's complaints, but insisted on his removing his turban in court. This time he complied, rather to the Indians' disappointment. It was the first of his controversial retreats.

In July 1894 a new petition, with ten thousand fervently gathered signatures, went off to Lord Ripon. Gandhi heralded its approach with a letter to the Grand Old Man Dadabhai Naoroji, who now sat in Parliament as M.P. for Central Finsbury, returned by a majority of three in protest against a sneer by Lord Salisbury about 'electing a black man'. Dadabhai at this point was Gandhi's ideal of a patriotic Indian leader. A thousand copies of the petition were broadcast in all directions. The *Times of India* declared its support. So did *The Times* of London. Ripon (a Catholic, like the invaluable Mr Paul) did actually refuse the bill in the form in which it reached him. He explained that no part of the British Empire could impose a colour bar. The Natal Assembly retorted with a fresh bill to disfranchise Indians indirectly. But Gandhi had scored on the point of principle. The struggle for the vote continued.

Meanwhile he had been busy with a more original project. Natal's

Indians needed a firmer basis of solidarity than *ad hoc* meetings and protests. They needed an organization. Why not follow the example of Congress, back in India? Gandhi still knew very little about Congress. But he was aware of the increasing prestige of its name, and he was also aware that Dadabhai Naoroji had been one of its annually chosen presidents. Encouraged by these facts, he broached the subject of a 'Natal Indian Congress', a few weeks after the launching of the franchise campaign. That August it was formally set up, with himself as its secretary.

His ignorance was his strength. Not being equipped to copy the prototype, he invented a Congress of his own. The National Congress of India was an élite assembly that met once a year. The Natal Congress was active all round the calendar, while its subscription, though high (five shillings monthly, and wealthy members paid more), let in many of the less opulent. Its objects were startling in their scope. It coolly proposed to promote concord between Indians and Europeans; to increase knowledge of India; to introduce Indians to their own history and literature; and to do social, political, and charitable work among them. In a few months Gandhi had spun this ambitious programme out of a makeshift petition against a single bill.

Recruits came in at three hundred a month. Most of them could talk or understand Gujarati, so proceedings were conducted in that language, which of course was the Secretary's. While pressing on in politics, Congress also taught Indians to improve their living conditions, and reform evils which gave their enemies a handle—dirtiness, for instance. Qualified members looked after press relations, feeding items to the papers, and refuting attacks with accuracy and promptitude. A branch Educational Association provided a rendezvous for the English-speaking youths born in the colony. They aired grievances, listened to lectures on their motherland, got practice in public speaking, and made contact with fellow Indians.

The promotion of concord with Europeans made a more halting start, and on the whole continued to halt. At first Europeans did not notice that the Congress existed. When a court case drew attention to it, there was a newspaper scare about the Indian 'secret society'. This blew over, and tolerance temporarily reached a point where jokes could be made. A philanthropic employer was described as a 'proper Gandhist'—i.e. propagandist—of good race relations.

But few whites responded seriously. One journalist advised Gandhi to go home and work against caste and Untouchability instead.

The Secretary took this criticism to heart, but he was still many years from acting on it. He was endlessly busy, darting backwards and forwards, watching everything, keeping everything in motion and under control. He even assumed the burden of collecting subscriptions. It taught him how to turn a screw at the right moment. Once he refused the dinner offered him by a rich member until his host agreed to pay double; the confrontation lasted most of the night and ended in victory. He kept precise accounts, and devised economies, such as cyclostyling forms instead of having them printed.

A problem arose over the indentured labourers and wage-earners, who were too poor to join. Though Gandhi wanted to reach them, he could not see how. The answer came by chance. One day an indentured Tamil named Balasundaram staggered weeping into the Congress office, his clothes torn, his mouth bleeding. Even in his distress he remembered to pull off his head-scarf, a gesture of respect which Europeans demanded from the inferior Asian. Gandhi told him to put it back on, and then, with the aid of a Tamil clerk, got his story. It was simple. Balasundaram's master—a gentleman of high social standing—had personally beaten him and broken his teeth.

Gandhi obtained a doctor's certificate stating what the injuries were. Armed with this, he hustled the bewildered Tamil to a magistrate, and insisted that a summons be issued. His object was not revenge but release. If an indentured labourer quit his job without leave, he became a criminal, liable to a prison sentence. Gandhi told Balasundaram's employer what had been done, and practically blackmailed him into letting his victim go. A better master was found.

Here was the area of contact: social service. News of the affair spread among the labourers, who discovered that they were no longer without friends among their better-off compatriots. They began streaming into Congress headquarters, and the Secretary listened to them and gave advice. Again he had taken a stride beyond the precedents of the parent Congress—this time a huge stride, destined to be decisive for India itself.

Congress fought for other causes besides the franchise. The Natal Government proposed to enact that when an Indian's indenture expired, he should be forced to do one of three things: return to India, submit to a new indenture, or pay for freedom with an annual tax of £25. After strenuous protests the Viceroy of India, Lord Elgin, signified his objection to this impossible sum. However, he agreed to its replacement by a poll tax of £3, applying not only to a householder but to each of his dependants also. That burden, still crushing, remained unmoved for two decades. So the gain was small.

Yet the Indians were steadily learning to act for themselves, and their propaganda was having an effect overseas. Congress, the great Congress of India, passed encouraging resolutions. During the next three years *The Times* carried eight leading articles on the Natal Indians' grievances. Gandhi pushed ahead with further petitions; with an Open Letter to the Natal Council and Assembly, issued in December 1894; and with pamphlets. *The Indian Franchise,* an appeal to the British population throughout South Africa counter-ing various anti-Asian clichés, came out a few days before Christ-mas 1895. In parts of the British homeland it still has an eerie fitness. Some copies handled by Natal settlers have been preserved, scrawled over with such evergreen comments as 'Dam Rot'. Re-sponsible reviewers were more polite but hardly more inclined to agree.

4

Writing his Open Letter to the Natal law-makers, Gandhi took the offensive. Far from being apologetic for Indians, he trumpeted the glories of the country they represented. He himself, at last, was among the rediscoverers of those glories. He invoked authorities of recognized if unequal weight—Goethe, Schopenhauer, Max Müller, Sir William Hunter, and Andrew Carnegie (who had condescended to praise the Taj Mahal). His arguments reflected his reading, more copious now than ever before. Through history, philosophy, art, he was groping toward a synthesis of his present task and his permanent quest. The Absolute, like the Chief of Police in Chesterton's *The Man Who Was Thursday,* had given him his com-mission without showing its face.

As a seeker he still accepted invitations from white Christians, such as Mr Baker, who took him to a Protestant rally near Cape Town. On the way Baker dealt firmly with people who made trouble over his coloured companion. As always, an individual Christian's goodness was not lost on Gandhi. He liked the ones whom he met at the convention. But Christian exclusiveness repelled him. The metaphors used of Jesus failed to register. If God could have a son, why shouldn't he have any number of sons?

And yet on reflection, Gandhi saw that this type of criticism could be turned round against Hinduism. He considered its scriptures and asked himself: "What is the meaning of saying that the Vedas are the inspired Word of God? If they are inspired, why not also the Bible and the Koran?' To check the propriety of his question, he sampled the Koran. The impression persisted. Was any religion clearly right, even clearly preferable? Hindus seemed to him more unselfish than Christians, but Hinduism included such vilenesses as Untouchability. He had not been convinced—perhaps he had not even been reached—by the Brahmo Samaj's case for a 'true' pristine Hinduism of simple purity, which could be got at by dismissing everything ugly as interpolated. In reply to his inquiring letters the devout poet Raychandbhai advised him to study his ancestral religion deeply and patiently, and sent him books. His feeling was that it would suit him best when he came to know it. But he glimpsed many avenues of knowledge.

Throughout his hectic African months he had gone on contributing to *The Vegetarian* and keeping up this London connection. He tested a freak diet prescribed by A. F. Hills, and reported adversely. For a second time his integrity forced him to oppose that admired gentleman. An English friend put him in touch with Edward Maitland, the collaborator of Anna Kingsford—whose vegetarian book he had read—in a system of 'Esoteric Christianity'. Maitland sent him their book *The Perfect Way* and his own *New Gospel of Interpretation*.

There is a touch of mystery about Gandhi's response to these. He was more excited than he ever cared to recall afterwards. *The Perfect Way* is, in fact, the only book which can be proved from contemporary evidence to have struck him as being The Answer. It ought to be the key to his religious development. The most significant thing about it is that it is not.

Anna Kingsford supplied most of the ideas for it. She was one of those occasional mystics who go through the Catholic Church and out the other side, not into atheism, but into Catholic-flavoured occultism. Maitland made the curious claim that she carried on

Newman's thought. Her message in *The Perfect Way* is that Christianity is true, but not as understood by Christians, who foolishly treat it as historical. Actually its creed is a restatement of themes found in older religions and cabbalistic lore, mapping out the inner life of the soul. Scripture is allegory. The 'false doctrine of the exclusive divinity of one man' must give way to the 'true doctrine of the potential divinity of all men'.

In effect the Esoteric Christians were precursors of Jung. With more lucidity and honest research they might have made a serious impact. As it was, the band of disciples which Gandhi's interest placed him in was minute. But their case against Christian orthodoxy appealed to him, and their system gave generous room to the wisdom of India. Almost persuaded—apparently, for a moment, quite persuaded—he set up as Durban agent for the Esoteric Christian Union, and sold (or at any rate advertised) its literature. In November 1894 the *Natal Mercury* printed a letter from him, praising *The Perfect Way* as a sort of new Bible, and asserting that it solved the three supreme problems: 'Whence come we? What are we? Whither go we?'

Those questions stayed with him, not only in his private meditations but also, indeed much more imperiously, in his musings on India and Indians. But although he kept in touch with the sect for the few years of its activity, its alleged solutions were eased into the background or thrust down to subconscious levels. Esoteric Christianity had two fatal flaws. It was cliquish, and it was theoretical. Hence it could not satisfy Gandhi. In another book (one of dozens which he dashed through) he found a message that was strong where Anna Kingsford's was weak, and a master to put beside Raychandbhai. This book swung him toward a bleaker and sharper faith. Losing much, he gained what he needed most, a doctrine that fitted into his work and hallowed it.

What he read was Tolstoy's *The Kingdom of God is Within You*. He had already come across at least one essay by the same author, and Salt and Madame Blavatsky had given him other previews of the Russian's teaching. But here, he now discovered, was a prophet of genius; and ideas charged with literary power could lift his heart as sermons could not. Like so much of his reading, *The Kingdom* was a recent book, fresh and topical. It won him completely.

Tolstoy, he quickly realized, wrote as a foe of Christian orthodoxy, but in a very different spirit from the Esoterics. His starting-

point was Christ's precept 'Resist not evil' . . . the very text which
had stirred Gandhi. In his view it implied a total renunciation of
force. But all governments are power-structures using force, intern-
ally for oppression, externally for war. Therefore—Tolstoy argued
—they are unholy; and the churches, which prop them up with
ritual and special pleading, are fraudulent. Christ must be obeyed
because he teaches the truth, and his teaching leads to a kind of
pacifist anarchism. As for authority, it cannot produce good. 'The
possession of power corrupts men.' Human well-being must come
from 'inward perfection, truth and love', in self-abnegating closeness to God, the source of life.

Since the State and the class hierarchy are evil, the disciple of
Jesus must be a rebel, a conscientous objector, a subversive
character. He must go as far as he can toward seceding from an
unjust society. But he must be non-violent, and try to convert even
the ruling class. Calm resolution can be potent, even against a
mounted *gendarmerie*. 'There is one and only one thing in life in
which it is granted man to be free, and over which he has full
control. . . . That one thing is to perceive the truth and profess it.'
If enough apostles do, the transfiguration of mankind, its 'union in
the truth', may come very suddenly.

All this confirmed what Gandhi was already coming to feel, at
least in his more exalted moods, and arrested another drift toward scepticism. As before a westerner was expounding a Hindu
concept—in this case Ahimsa or non-violence—but with a clarity
that displayed its value as the Brahmins did not. Tolstoy indeed
carried it further. Ahimsa in India was seldom more than a negative
recoil from the horrors of violence, which Hindu militarists were
as guilty of as anyone else, when they had the chance. It meant
simply not injuring other creatures, and could easily decline into
cowardice. Gandhi in 1894 definitely did not believe in non-violence
on Hindu grounds; it took a westerner to convert him. Tolstoy's
Kingdom, by putting the idea in New Testament terms, showed
how rules of action might be deduced from it.

That disposed finally of Michael Coates. Gandhi had no further
use for the volumes lent him by the Quaker. Instead, with deepening fascination, he read more of Tolstoy, including a tract against
civilization in favour of peasantry and manual labour. Meanwhile
he was expanding his modest bridgeheads in the culture of India.
He studied the Upanishads, and a series of lectures by Max Müller,

lately published under the title *India—what can it teach us?* It was here (in the work of a European yet again) that he found the hints for some of his best-known future policies. Müller said, for instance, that the authentic India had to be delved for under the corruption of centuries, and could be met only by going out receptively into the villages. There alone it had lasted into modern times without being utterly disfigured. There alone the embers could be made to glow.

Each Sunday during these intellectual adventures, Gandhi had to yawn through a church service as the conscripted guest of a lady Methodist, who accused him of corrupting her little boy by encouraging him to eat fruit. Yet certain other churchgoers, who applied no pressure whatever, managed after all to influence him profoundly. His Tolstoyan rapture raised an obvious question. The dream of shaking off the grip of established society, of forming a free and apostolic community on a moral basis, might sound alluring. But were there any people who had actually done it? He learned in a strangely roundabout way that there were.

At Mariann Hill near Pinetown, sixteen miles out of Durban, the Trappist Order had a monastery and convent. Having read in Anna Kingsford that Trappists abstained from meat, he went to look, and described them in an article in *The Vegetarian* published on 18 May 1895. Nobody had prepared him for what he saw: a 'quiet little model village', he called it, a true republic in a beautiful setting high above sea-level. One set of buildings housed a hundred and sixty monks. Away over the farmland lived sixty nuns. Most of the Trappists were Germans. However, all races were equal. All the men laboured alike in the fields and workshops, palpably thriving on their diet. They observed vows of silence. Natives came to the monastery to learn handicrafts. Crosses everywhere reminded visitors of the spiritual basis.

Gandhi loved the place, and ridiculed tales he had heard from other Christians about the 'weakly, sickly, sad' papists. 'If this is Roman Catholicism,' he wrote, 'everything said against it is a lie.' He was past the point where the Catholic Church might have attracted him even briefly. But he had glimpsed a mode of life that fused the eternal with the practical. Later he was to imitate it after his fashion. The historic Ashram at Sabarmati is, in a sense, a daughter house of Marian Hill.

V

Commitment

1

Tracing Gandhi's first African years, and comparing them with his life elsewhere, one is conscious of a contrast. It is as if the lighting were different. In India or England, whatever his stature, he has a vivid human context. Other people stand out around him. In South Africa they do not; at least in their own right. The drama has only one fully realized character, under a constant spotlight. Gandhi is the master spirit, while most of his companions, with all their zeal and goodwill, are simply names.

To anyone who has met Indian businessmen, it will seem highly unlikely that Abdulla Sheth and the rest were as colourless as the record makes them. Yet Gandhi is 'there', so to speak, as nobody else is. The Natal Congress seems to have had no trouble with rival leaders or factions. In such a movement that absence is amazing. Clearly he exerted a spell long before he was adored as a saint. But the reasons lay in the membership as well as the founder. He had plunged into a faceless and depressed sub-world, the limbo of a trampled minority, powerless to generate forces of its own. The story from 1895 is largely the story of his waking that sub-world into life. The individuality which a few of his colleagues begin transmitting to us is still, in a sense, his own. For the first time but not the last he acquires a mythical air. He is a culture-hero, a Prometheus moulding men from clay. The South African picture is not of a continuum of events on the same plane, but of a series of transfiguring upsurges.

The Mohandas Gandhi of December 1895, who issued the 'appeal to the Britons of South Africa', was at last a successful lawyer. Commissions thrown his way by the Muslim traders had put him on his feet. His practice could support his family whenever he cared to bring them over, and with further progress it would supply a

67

surplus to finance public work. Also, of course, he could serve
Indians in his professional capacity. His talent for languages was
unfolding. He had picked up a smattering of Tamil, an asset in
dealing with the labourers. Also he knew some Zulu, the language
of a nation he had begun to admire, though his admiration was
from the outside: they impressed him chiefly as handsome and
nobly built. He was always slow to understand non-Indian races.

But non-Indians were taking notice of him, and perhaps even
understanding him. The Natal Congress's publicity had made him
known in England. His frequent reports to Dadabhai Naoroji, and
to the sympathetic historian Sir William Hunter, were getting discussed. Sir William edited the India section of *The Times,* to which
he contributed articles about Natal. On 27 January 1896 Gandhi
was named in that paper as one 'whose efforts on behalf of his
Indian fellow-subjects in South Africa entitle him to respect'. Not
that he had scored any solid victories. The new Franchise Bill was
passed on 13 May. But he had given an immense impetus to Indian
unity and morale. Furthermore, many onlookers were grasping his
main point—that as citizens of the British Empire, the Indians had
a right to equality under its laws.

His success as an organizer led to imitation. Indians in the Transvaal and Cape Town formed daughter Congresses. In his own
Durban home, as a domestic manager without Kasturbai, he did
not do so well. He lived in a semi-detached house called Beach
Grove Villa, in a European quarter facing the sea, next door to
Natal's Attorney-General Harry Escombe. The place was overrun with
guests and volunteer helpers. Bills were heavy, and the atmosphere
suffered from backstairs jealousies. Yet even here he could show
qualities of command. He made good use of an able subordinate,
his confidential clerk Vincent Lawrence, a South Indian Catholic
and Franciscan tertiary (who survived to be decorated by John
XXIII). Lawrence aided in the eviction of a less well-chosen assistant. Gandhi had brought over Sheikh Mehtab, the meat-eating
disturber of his boyhood, as a kind of steward, and let him stay at
the Villa under the impression that he was reforming him. One
day a messenger summoned him urgently from his office. They
caught Sheikh Mehtab *in flagrante delicto* with a prostitute. It
emerged that he had had her in the house quite often, and abused
his host's trust in other ways. Gandhi told him to leave, and, at a
threat of blackmail, sent for the police. He acted without hesitation,

without apology, and without regret. It was an instance of what Professor Parkinson defines as the 'surgical touch' which a leader ought to have.

His African involvement was now so deep that there could be no early departure. He decided to go back to India to do some campaigning, and then bring his family to Natal. Having appointed a quiet but competent merchant to be acting secretary of the Natal Congress, he sailed on 5 June 1896 aboard S.S. *Pongola*. During the voyage he pursued his study of Tamil with the aid of the ship's doctor, though he never got further than a fair reading knowledge. Also he met a second Plymouth Brother—the captain, no less. That devout seaman's arguments for salvation through faith rather than works only strengthened his own belief that religion and morality were the same.

The ship docked at Calcutta. Gandhi boarded a train for Bombay, but was accidentally delayed at Allahabad, and turned the chance to account by visiting a paper, *The Pioneer*. Its editor, Mr Chesney, listened to him without being won over, but undertook to give space to the South African question. This interview gave him bolder ideas. It sounded as if there might be a large number of Indians who could be roused to support their overseas brethren. Changing course, he hurried straight to Rajkot and his family. After a month's work at home he brought out another pamphlet, later nicknamed the Green Pamphlet because of its cover. He had ten thousand printed, and enlisted the neighbourhood children to distribute copies, paying them with stamps (used). The pamphlet was duly noticed in *The Pioneer* and then in several more papers. Versions of its contents, increasingly compressed and distorted, passed along the wires from one Reuter office to another.

Unaware of this last ominous process, Gandhi turned his attention briefly to Rajkot's concerns. During a plague scare he offered his services to the public health committee, and went round inspecting latrines, a lifelong interest of his—more comprehensible in India than in the West. The rich, he observed, were often the least sanitary and the least co-operative. The cleanest dwellings belonged to Untouchables, whom most of the committee members wrote off as hopeless cases and not worth inspecting.

Resuming his travels, he made a speech in Bombay—or rather had it made for him, because his voice failed to carry—and a speech in Poona. There he met two of the Congress notables, Gopal

Krishna Gokhale and Bal Gangadhar Tilak. By this time nationalism was beginning to grow. Gokhale was a moderate, Tilak an extremist. However, they joined in giving him their blessing. Tilak rather overawed him. Gokhale seemed more gracious and welcoming, and they took to each other instantly. A further speech in Madras was not only a success but an excited, emotional success, the first in Gandhi's career. Mentally he noted how he had produced this effect: by telling the story of the labourer Balasundaram. Madras was Balasundaram's home town. When he had finished, his listeners fought to buy the Green Pamphlet.

Next he returned to Calcutta and tried to organize a meeting in that city, with the help of an English journalist who liked the balanced way he presented his case. But his Durban friends cabled that the Natal Parliament would open in January in a hostile mood, and he ought to be there. Abdulla owned a ship, the *Courland*; a free passage was arranged for Mr and Mrs Gandhi, their two sons and a nephew named Gokuldas whom they took with them. S.S. *Naderi* was sailing for Durban at the same time. The two together carried not only the Gandhis but eight hundred other Indians, on their way to work in South Africa. In December the little steamers left Calcutta.

They ran into a storm near Madagascar. As the *Courland* groaned and crashed through the waves, her unseasoned passengers took fright. Anguished prayers rose to God under various names, in various languages. Gandhi moved tranquilly among them, giving what assistance he could and reporting to the skipper. He noticed how naturally they prayed together; the crisis blotted out sect. Perhaps it hinted to him that India's regeneration might be achieved through a permanent crisis. After a while the sky brightened and they settled into their old routines. But ahead, over the horizon, human beings were preparing a longer and crueller storm. When the ships approached Durban harbour a week before Christmas, they were forbidden entry.

The alleged reason, quarantine, soon wore thin. Natal's white militants were opposing the landing of any more Indians at all, regarding them now not as a source of cheap labour but as a pure menace. Ashore they were holding rallies with demands for repatriation, and besieging Abdulla with threats and bribes. Their wrath, moreover, centred on Gandhi himself, and his own neighbour Escombe was fanning it. Reuter had transmitted a garbled summary of the Green Pamphlet, asserting that it spoke of the Natal Indians as 'robbed and assaulted', 'treated like beasts'. The rumour ran that its author was personally importing the further eight hundred coolies to swamp the fifty thousand whites. Gandhi realized the trouble which his presence was causing, but refused to retreat. The passengers backed him and insisted on their right to land.

Days passed at anchor. During a Christmas party he made a speech of Tolstoyan intransigence, attacking white civilization as based on force. The captain (who had learnt to respect him during the storm) swallowed this, but asked him what he would do if his enemies assaulted him on disembarkation. Would he remain non-violent? 'I hope,' he replied, 'that God will give me the courage and the sense to forgive them.'

God did. After twenty-three days—well into the new year—the ships were allowed to dock. Escombe, shifting to his more dignified role as a member of the Natal Cabinet, tried to avert a clash. He advised Gandhi to smuggle his family ashore at night. But Abdulla's lawyer advised him otherwise, and furtiveness did not appeal to him. Kasturbai and the boys, he decided, should go by carriage to the house of Mr Rustomji, a Parsee well-wisher. He himself would descend the gangway in daylight, and walk.

When he did so he was spotted at once. 'Gandhi! Gandhi!' some youths began shouting. Demonstrators closed in from all sides, pelting him with stones, bricks, and rotten eggs, all kept in readiness. They ripped his turban off and kicked him and punched him. He was saved for a moment by Mrs Alexander, the police super-intendent's wife, who courageously used her parasol as a shield. At last her husband pushed through with an escort. They convoyed Gandhi two miles to Rustomji's house. Dusk was falling, and a mob gathered outside yelling for his blood. Alexander persuaded him to take refuge in the police station. He escaped (like Lloyd George on a similar occasion) disguised as a policeman, while Alexander diverted the crowd by leading them in a song with chorus:

> Hang old Gandhi
> On the sour apple tree.

Having been notified that the getaway was complete, he convinced them that their quarry had gone, and they dispersed muttering.

A report of the Durban uproar had already been sent to Joseph

Chamberlain, who was now Colonial Secretary. Chamberlain cabled the Natal Government asking for prosecutions. Escombe told Gandhi, who, however, declined to press charges. His willingness to forgive and forget made a good impression, and he managed to clear the air further in an interview with the *Natal Advertiser*. Nevertheless the affair had been ugly, frightening, and for Kasturbai —who was pregnant—a brutal introduction to her new home. It left Gandhi himself with misgivings about his flight in fancy dress.

But he had no intention of dropping the struggle. The family had not been settled in Durban long when two new bills were introduced in the legislature. One required that all traders must have a licence. While nobody could object to the letter of the bill, it was certain that in practice Europeans would get their licences easily and Indians would not. The other bill imposed an educational test on immigrants, in terms designedly adverse to Indians. Gandhi's deputy-secretary handed over his Congress in a thriving state, and the two bills were resisted. Both passed, but again the fight improved the community's morale.

To glance through Gandhi's writings in this period, his letters and petitions and speeches and articles, is to see at least part of the secret of his impact. Taken in a mass they convey, as no single item can, the essential effect: an effect of relentless, pervasive energy. He never slackens or misses a trick. He goes on and on, factually, lucidly, with a fearful staying power and meticulousness of detail. His strength does not come from religious ardour as usually understood—there is hardly a word of religion—but from dedication to his Truth, a dedication that will not let him rest.

A Congress drive for membership and donations raised over £4,000. At this point Gandhi wanted Congress to own property and have a permanent fund, and he arranged matters thus. Later he decided that wealth bred irresponsibility; public bodies should live in a sensitive day-to-day dependence on the public they served. Not for the first time or the last, he reached a religious position ('Take no thought for the morrow') by a practical path.

His household in 1897 hardly reflected this attitude. He was frankly well-off, with a growing professional income. A photograph shows him looking westernized. Kasturbai is charming and tastefully dressed. For a while there was a danger that his dominating energy would make him a mere supercharged philanthropist, a Lord Bountiful, rather than a servant of the community. His efforts over the next couple of years to reform the Indians' hygiene and drainage were much less welcome than his championship of their civil rights. Many resented him as a do-gooder. He forestalled criticism to some extent by learning to live simply and economically. His example enabled him to succeed in another enterprise, raising money for famine relief in India. At his call even indentured labourers scraped together a few pennies for the homeland. Also he did voluntary welfare work, helping two hours daily in a charity hospital maintained by Rustomji. Nursing had always suited his temperament since his father's illness. With engaging forethought, he taught himself midwifery and baby care, out of a book entitled *Advice to a Mother*.

In 1899 came what appeared to be a resurrection of Indian dignity.

The Boer War broke out. It faced Gandhi with a hard choice. Despite all he knew against the Boers, his sympathies in the crisis lay on their side. Yet he was loyal to the British Empire. Here he dissented from Tolstoy's total subversiveness. He believed that British rule was for the benefit of the ruled, and that racial discrimination was a local un-British perversion, which could be cured. All his campaigning was within the constitutional scheme and presupposed it. He had memorized the National Anthem, not such and easy tune for a Hindu as for an Englishman, and taught it to his children. While in Rajkot he had belonged to a committee preparing for Victoria's Diamond Jubilee, convinced that India's emancipation must come through the Empire. Of course he was disquieted sometimes. No adherent of Henry Salt's group could view British capitalism complacently. The Jubilee fuss repelled him as humbug, and the lines in *God Save the Queen* about 'scattering her enemies' offended against his principles. But with real enemies to be scattered, one clinching argument stood. He claimed the rights of a British subject for himself and others. How could he evade the duties?

With these thoughts in mind the future opponent of imperialism supported one of the most sordid of imperial wars. He proposed to raise an Indian ambulance corps. Most of the English, to whom Indians were untrustworthy poltroons, poured scorn on his plan. However, he got Escombe's backing, and Dr Booth, a medical missionary at the hospital where he worked, undertook to train recruits. After some wire-pulling involving the Bishop of Natal,

Gandhi persuaded the authorities to accept his aid. Boer victories had sapped their contemptuous confidence. They were prepared to risk having Indians with the army.

The corps consisted of 300 free Indians and 800 indentured, with 40 leaders. There was still opposition to placing them in the firing line, but in the Spion Kop emergency that objection was waived. They served honourably, making marches of twenty miles a day and over. When Lord Roberts's son was killed they carried his body from the battlefield. Relations with British troops were cordial. After six weeks the unit was disbanded in a regrouping. But it had given the Indians prestige and pride, and enhanced their solidarity further. The leaders received medals and the praise of General Buller . . . for what that was worth. White South African goodwill seemed to promise more solid rewards. The papers printed items congratulating Indians as, in the words of *Punch,* 'sons of the Empire after all'.

An idea took hold (as such ideas do in war-time) that Gandhi's volunteers had completed the work of the Natal Congress; that his people were accepted at last, and British triumph would usher in a new dawn for them throughout South Africa. When Victoria died Gandhi laid a wreath on her statue in Durban on behalf of the whole loyal Indian community.

2

Despite his moments of misgiving, he was disposed to believe in the new dawn. As the war trailed toward its close he got ready for a final return to India. He had groomed a successor, Mansukhlal Nazar, to direct whatever work was still to be done, and he expected this work to be so much lighter that if he stayed himself, he would be merely another lawyer with spare-time interests. Instead of that, his purpose was to practise at the Bar in Bombay and enter Indian politics. Gokhale, who had been so congenial in Poona, would be his guide. The Natal Congressmen let him leave, on condition that if they wanted him back urgently during the next year, he would come. The Gandhis departed in a flurry of farewell meetings and a cascade of gifts. Unwilling to take any payment for his services, he set up a public trust under Rustomji, and handed the gifts back into its keeping; not without protests from his wife—of which more in due course.

They sailed on 18 October 1901. After a stop at Mauritius, where they were the Governor's guests, they arrived in India without mishap. That December Congress was holding its annual meeting in Calcutta. Gandhi had never had a chance to attend these functions. Now he made it known that he wanted to move a resolution in support of the South African Indians. He travelled on the same train as Dinshaw Wacha, who was to preside at the meeting, and Sir Pherozeshah Mehta, who had succeeded to the honour once enjoyed by Dadabhai Naoroji of 'uncrowned king of Bombay'. Mehta summoned Gandhi to his compartment and assured him that the resolution would pass. The trouble was that it would carry no weight when it did. 'What rights have we in our own country?' he said. 'I believe that, so long as we have no power in our own land, you cannot fare better in the colonies.'

Gandhi was shocked. As with many who have lived abroad, his homecoming had a Rip van Winkle quality. Nothing had prepared him for the growth of disenchantment with Britain, or the doubts thereby cast over his African hopes. On the surface, all was calm. But the first explosion was less than four years away.

In Calcutta he had more adjustments to make. In spite of its increasing outspokenness, and the popularity of the fiery Tilak, Congress struck him as a poor thing compared with his own modest creation in Natal. To begin with, it still incongruously used English: the presidential remark which he afterwards remembered best was a quotation from 'Lead, kindly light'. Again, though these three-day rallies were national events, very little was done in between. Hence the December delegates came without the slightest notion of organization. They imagined that it meant chiefly shouting orders at a clueless rabble of volunteer stewards. Caste rules led to segregated kitchens and added chaos. The lavatories were few and foul. Untouchables could seldom be found to clean them, and caste Hindus would not. Gandhi caused a minor sensation when he mopped one out himself.

Through stink and muddle the proceedings lurched on. Gandhi approached his own nearest equivalent, the Congress Secretary Ghosal, and offered to help. Ghosal—an infirm, courteous veteran —handed him a stack of correspondence to sort, then discovered who this young-looking assistant was, and became apologetic. The assistant told him not to worry and buttoned up his shirt for him.

Dealing with the letters was instructive. Moving the resolution was an anti-climax. The committee that arranged the agenda got to it late at night after many others, when everyone was restless and eager to leave. Only Gokhale saved it from being sunk without trace. Gandhi nervously read it to the members, who, to his annoyance, endorsed it without attempting to understand it. At the plenary session next day, 27 December, he was given five minutes to speak. Mounting the platform in Parsee coat and trousers, he embarked on a carefully timed address. In the full tide of his argument the President suddenly rang a bell. Nobody had explained that the bell was simply a warning that he had two minutes left. He thought it was a signal to sit down, and so, with a botched conclusion, he did. The resolution was carried unanimously. But all committee-endorsed resolutions were. Few delegates had taken it in.

Gandhi had the blessing of Congress, duly minuted, with the full text of what he had meant to say; and that counted for something. The question was, how much? That winter he made his first contacts with some other institutions and individuals supposedly working for a new India. Having read a book about Keshab Chandra Sen, the late head of the Brahmo Samaj, he called on one of its officers in Calcutta. All he got was a ticket to a concert. This gave him a lifelong love of Bengali music but no enthusiasm for the Brahmo Samaj. Next he tried to see Swami Vivekananda, famous as the teacher of a patriotic philosophy based on reformed Hinduism and social service. Unfortunately the Swami was ill, and so a meeting which historical logic required failed to take place. He also visited a prominent Christian Congressman, Kalicharan Banerji. Banerji lectured him on original sin, which Gandhi (curiously) conceded, and on the vanity of Hinduism, which he would not concede. These damping experiences were followed by others. He looked in at a temple of Kali and was revolted by the blood of sacrificed sheep. He paid his respects to his old acquaintance Annie Besant, now in Benares, where she had founded a school. She too was ill, and the conversation collapsed before it started.

On his travels he usually went third class, and shuddered at the crowding, yelling, spitting, and general squalor in the cheap carriages. If the state of the masses depressed him, the state of the aristocracy seemed even worse. They lived in luxury and cynically paid for it with humiliation. He met several rajahs, and eyed the absurd costume they put on when presented to British proconsuls —jewels and silk pyjamas and dummy swords—which the British expected them to wear, while treating them as flunkeys. The fact was that in spite of the murmurs of discontent, the British regime was still all-powerful. It was close to its very apex of grandeur, Lord Curzon's viceregal durbar. At that function Curzon forbade the singing of 'Onward Christian Soldiers', not because his subjects belonged to other religions, but because of the lines 'Crowns and thrones may perish, Kingdoms rise and wane'. The Viceroy's opinion of Congress was that it was 'tottering to its fall' and that he could expect to assist in person at the obsequies.

When one's hopes are repeatedly disappointed, anybody who measures up to them and restores faith is apt to acquire a halo. Gokhale, at least, did not disappoint. He was Gandhi's host for a month in Calcutta and became confirmed as his tutor in politics. Gokhale was among the best of the moderates—honest, public-spirited, and devoted to India's freedom, meaning constitutional freedom within the British scheme. A professor of mathematics, he was unrivalled for his command of facts and figures and the smooth logic with which he could state a case. Even Curzon respected him. He supplied his guest with introductions, and approved the plan to work in Bombay, where he lived himself for most of the time. After a trial run in the courts at Rajkot Gandhi effected the move. He installed his family in a bungalow at Santa Cruz, where Bombay Airport now is.

But the year covered by his pledge to the Natal Indians was not yet up. Just before it expired they sent him a telegram: 'Chamberlain expected here. Please return immediately.' Again he left his wife and children, and went. A cousin, Maganlal Gandhi, accompanied him.

It appeared that the British, having got hold of the Boer territories, were not fulfilling the pledges which the Indians supposed had been given. Forebodings expressed before his departure were being realized. As for Joseph Chamberlain, his objects in going to Natal were (as Gandhi afterwards put it) 'to get a gift of thirty-five million pounds from South Africa, and to win the hearts of Englishmen and Boers'. Indians were not Englishmen or Boers and most of them had no money. The Colonial Secretary received Gandhi politely and promised to inquire into any grievances. But of course, he added, the Imperial Government could not dream of dictating to Natal.

As for the war-impoverished Transvaal, entry was now controlled on a permit basis. Fairly applied, this measure would have been sensible. In practice, whereas Europeans could get their permits by asking, Indians had to wrestle with a new Asiatic Department. To reach Pretoria Gandhi himself was forced to do a thing he detested —exploit personal connections. When he arrived the Asiatic Department appalled him. It was staffed by Sahibs from India and Ceylon, who had come over in the war bringing their attitudes to 'natives' with them. Gandhi's old friend Tyeb Sheth introduced him to the head of the Department. That official merely insulted him, kept him standing, and would not let him speak.

There was no help for it. He would have to stay in South Africa again, and resume the struggle. Accordingly he rented an office in Johannesburg, enrolled in the Transvaal Supreme Court, and broached the topic of his family coming over, though it was some time before they actually came. Johannesburg seemed noisy and restless after the quiet of Pretoria. But it was the centre of business and he would need to be there.

Whether in spite of or because of his devotion to Truth, he built up a second flourishing practice. His London study of Roman law, which had been a little superfluous at the time, now gave him an advantage, as the law he had to work with was Roman-Dutch. His income rose to five or six thousand pounds a year, out of which he paid four Indian clerks and a typist. As an employer he inspired loyalty and affection. Court cases brought a steadily deepening insight into Transvaal ways, teaching him, for example, the precise problems involved in persuading a white jury to convict a white defendant on the complaint of anyone who was not white. But he had not revised his priorities. He was practising law to serve the Indian community and from no other motive.

The issue here was more complex than the Natal franchise. Under British occupation the plight of Indians who lived or wished to live in the Transvaal grew worse than before. In Johannesburg, thousands were crammed into a slum-ghetto: the municipality, having provided no sanitation, kept trying to evict them on the ground that they were insanitary. Gandhi defended seventy cases of this kind, nearly all successfully. However, what was really in question was an Indian's right to be in the Transvaal at all. The

Asiatic Department was corrupt after the British manner of corruption, yet it had a rigid correctness which was also British. The Boers had been too lax to enforce their own laws. In any given instance the personality of the official would count for much, and an easygoing one might connive at evasion. But the British were never easygoing. They administered the law of the land as they found it, with a flawless impartiality that did not leave loopholes. A committee under Lord Milner sifted the Boer statutes to see if any ran counter to Imperial principles. The anti-Indian laws were ruled to be outside its scope and remained in force. They could be invoked against not only the poor and feckless but the educated and businesslike. European traders who had feared competition breathed more freely. In 1903 Gandhi had a conversation with Lionel Curtis, the Assistant Colonial Secretary of the Transvaal. Though Gandhi was the first Oriental whom Curtis had ever actually met, the Secretary had no hesitation in lecturing to him. 'It is not the vices of Indians that Europeans fear,' he explained, 'but their virtues.'

General Jan Christiaan Smuts, the Boers' brilliant young war hero, was co-operating with the new rulers. His philosophic acumen supplied the whites with a rationalization. This conflict, he argued, was between two cultures which could not mix, the Eastern and the Western. Indians' claims to civilized dignity were beside the point. Their alien culture, whatever its merits, threatened that of the West, which had a right to defend itself. Apparently the best defence was attack. For this, Englishmen and Boers marched shoulder to shoulder throughout South Africa. And then the despised rival culture counter-attacked. It began publishing its own newspaper.

3

In launching the weekly *Indian Opinion*, Gandhi's aims were both propagandist and educational. He wanted to give his people a voice. He also wanted to guide and inform them. The paper was not his own idea, but when a Gujarati printer suggested it to him, he adopted the scheme with enthusiasm and put up funds for it. Their first number came out in Durban on 4 June 1903. It was printed in six columns, messily but accurately. The intention was to publish material in English, Gujarati, Hindi and Tamil. Four languages were to prove too much of a burden, but English and Gujarati survived. The editor—unsalaried—was Mansukhlal Nazar, whom Gandhi had once earmarked for leadership of the Natal Congress. He had done journalistic work in India. However, a persistent diffidence in pronouncing on South African problems caused him to lean on Gandhi, who was very willing to be leant on, and soon assumed the major responsibilities.

One was the basic responsibility of getting the paper fairly afloat and keeping it so. He subsidized it out of his savings, and found himself spending £75 a month, a forbidding sum even now and in those days alarming. Complete solvency was beyond hoping for. As South Africa had at most twenty thousand literate Indians, there was a low ceiling on circulation. In the early stages Gandhi had between twelve hundred and fifteen hundred subscribers. At first he carried advertisements and accepted outside printing orders. Then he cut back on both, eventually dropping them entirely. The labour of touting failed to bring adequate returns. Urging that *Indian Opinion* was a public service and not a commercial venture, he appealed to the community to rally round. His staff did the same, with more zeal than they had shown when canvassing for advertising and printing orders. Subscriptions rolled in until with mounting political consciousness the figure passed three thousand. Furthermore he had been able to raise the price without reversing the trend. The deficit became manageable.

It was one more case of his backing into sainthood, or at least into that quarter. A saint might have taken the anti-commercial stand at the outset, as a matter of principle. Gandhi, by proceeding experimentally, reached a point where he saw that the saint would have been right and fell in line with him . . . only, when he got there, he was far richer in practical experience.

Readers' letters were many and voluble. Gandhi read most of them and learned much through doing so. While educating himself, he kept to his purpose of educating his readers. He was his own chief columnist. Some of his articles and paragraphs were topical comments with a distinct bite. On the constructive side, his favourite theme was self-reliance. Again and again he urged Indians to be brave, tenacious, upright. He held up Great Lives to them as models. Through his accounts of Nelson, Elizabeth Fry, Mazzini, Lincoln, the 'squalid coolies' glimpsed a larger and more heroic world. While his style could be a shade pompous, he learned the homely touch. In his Gujarati pieces he would quote proverbs, some of which sound oddly to a western ear. 'Hunger will drive a man even to join a musical band.' 'A squint-eyed uncle is better than no uncle.'

Journalism was an activity that made sense to Europeans. A few now began coming to him in a spirit of near-discipleship. As friends a few had come earlier. His Durban household before the Boer War had been as open as Indians' homes are apt to be, and among the guests were non-Indians, whose habits upset Kasturbai. But after the paper started, such relationships grew more lasting and fruitful. Gandhi's white admirers and sympathizers were people of the sort he had known in England. L. W. Ritch, the manager of a commercial firm, introduced him to the Johannesburg branch of the Theosophical Society. He still would not join, however. The joining was in the other direction. Ritch left his employers, accepted a job in Gandhi's office, and began studying for the Bar while helping with his public work.

Also, as in England, Gandhi was meeting people at a vegetarian restaurant. Johannesburg did possess one. Its owner was a German with ideas about water-therapy and no head for business. Gandhi paid some of his debts and made several contacts through the restaurant before its demise. Among his finds was a man from Lincolnshire, Albert West, a partner in a small printing concern, unmarried. West's adherence to the Indian cause resulted from an outbreak of pneumonic plague during 1904. Gandhi nursed the victims in the Indian ghetto, and acted as quarantine organizer and banker when the district was cleared, riding about on a bicycle. West noticed his absence from the restaurant and went to offer help with the nursing. Gandhi was grateful but declined, and suggested that the printer might make himself useful at *Indian Opinion* instead. Owing to the plague, he had been neglecting it. West agreed, settling for a salary of £10 a month, plus a half-share of certain profits which the business manager was then sanguinely talking about. He left for Durban the next day.

It was the first instance of the Gospel-like 'Rise up and follow me' in Gandhi's career. The sequel, however, was not vagrant holiness but a coolly damning report on the paper's condition. This was before the subscription drive and other events had put it on a firmer basis. Money was pouring out, debts were not being collected, the books were incomprehensible, and even the list of subscribers was in chaos. 'But', West wrote, 'all this need not alarm you. I shall try to put things right as best I can. I remain on, whether there is profit or not.'

Another restaurant discovery was Henry Polak, a twenty-two-year-old Jewish lawyer, who was impressed by Gandhi's efforts during the plague and asked permission to join him at his table. It transpired that he worked as a sub-editor for the *Transvaal Critic*. He had a candour and simplicity that endeared him, with momentous results. Shortly after their meeting, West's report on the paper arrived. Gandhi took Polak into his confidence and remarked that he would have to go and sort matters out. Polak saw him off at the station and lent him a book for the journey. It was Ruskin's *Unto This Last*.

Gandhi knew of Ruskin from Salt's pamphlet, but not first hand. On that long train ride to Durban *Unto This Last* joined the *Gita* and Tolstoy's *Kingdom* as his third formative book: in terms of immediate effect, the most potent of all. Published in 1862, it consists of four long articles bound together, with a preface and notes. Its main object is to give 'a logical definition of wealth'. True wealth, in Ruskin's view, does not mean the capitalist's power to compel people to work for him. It means abundant life. 'That country is the richest which nourishes the greatest number of noble and happy human beings.' He attacks the cut-throat individualism of the political economists, urging with prescient vigour that motives are more complex than they concede, and that people are not machines. The welfare of society requires a balanced, functional economy, with a moral foundation and a co-operative philosophy. In that spirit Ruskin puts forward some interesting suggestions about vocational training, full employment, and the just wage, slightly reminiscent of medieval guilds, but far ahead of Gradgrind's England.

Once again Gandhi responded to a case presented with literary power. He gave a fair account of his mental process: 'I believe that I discovered some of my deepest convictions reflected in this great book of Ruskin, and that is why it so captured me and made me transform my life.' In previous instances of the same kind, the 'convictions' which a book reflected or made sense of had been vague sentiments derived from his Hindu upbringing, and not always even assented to, at the conscious level. With Ruskin they

were nearer to being genuine beliefs of his own. But this time there
was a subtler self-revelation. He considered that *Unto This Last*
could be summed up in three maxims:

1. That the good of the individual is contained in the good of all.
2. That a lawyer's work has the same value as the barber's, in-
   asmuch as all have the same right of earning their livelihood
   from their work.
3. That a life of labour, i.e. the life of the tiller of the soil and
   the handicraftsman, is the life worth living.

The Gujarati version which Gandhi afterwards composed is entitled *Sarvodaya,* meaning 'general good' or 'the welfare of all'. But
in fact he misunderstood the book. The second maxim is not there,
the third only doubtfully. He read them into the text himself, out
of what he described as a 'dim realization' in his own mind. This
dim realization that dictated the three-point summary was an
amalgam of Tolstoy, Edward Carpenter's Simple Life doctrine, the
memory of Mariann Hill, the theory of the Ashram in Hindu
religion, and the theory of corporate property in Hindu law (which
had lodged in Gandhi's mind when he read Mayne).

It is clear that discontent with his cosy professional status had
been gaining on him for some time. To be a prosperous lawyer, even
if one devoted the proceeds to social service and crusading journalism, was not enough. But if it was not, then whatever *was* enough
would have to be very radical indeed. Within a few weeks of his
thirty-fifth birthday, in the midway of life where Dante saw his
vision, Gandhi saw his; or at least the beginning of it. For him the
logical consequence of *Unto This Last* could only be a kind of
agrarian communism. With that shattering directness which is a
mark of the type of genius he was growing into, he embraced the
logical consequence and embraced it on the spot. After a sleepless
night in a hotel he walked into the *Indian Opinion* office, disin-
terred West from the jungle of proofs and bills, and proposed to put
the paper on a co-operative basis. They would transfer their press
to a farm, and the staff would live there by their own labour.

As before, West agreed. They decided that each worker should
draw £3 a month, without regard for colour or nationality. About
ten were involved. Would they take the step? Not all would. The
opponents, however, were more or less expendable. The business
manager disapproved strongly; but West's adverse report had re-

duced his prestige. The writers of the Hindi and Tamil sections also demurred; but Gandhi was lukewarm about those sections in any case, and their end was in sight. Chhaganlal, one of his many cousins, had joined the staff and expressed readiness to try the new scheme. So did the head mechanic. Other employees, though reluctant to become rural co-operators, said they would go wherever the press went. Gandhi argued that the move would be economical as well as virtuous, and justified it to his readers on practical grounds.

He advertised for a site. Somebody offered him a small property at Phoenix, fourteen miles from Durban. He inspected it with West and found that it consisted of twenty acres, with a spring, and some orange and mango trees. They bought this and eighty acres adjoining, with more fruit and a tumbledown cottage. No other buildings were visible except a few far-off Zulu huts, and there were no shops except a shoddy general store near the railway station, itself two miles away. The total cost was a thousand pounds.

They carried out the transfer during October and November 1904. Rustomji, the Parsee philanthropist, supplied corrugated iron sheets and other materials. With the aid of some carpenters and masons—veterans of the Indians' Boer War effort—West and the staff built a shed 75 feet by 50 to house the press. The party camped out in tents, and had trouble with snakes. Gandhi stayed and worked with them most of the time. When dwelling quarters were put up, his own consisted of a living-room, two small bedrooms, a tiny kitchen, and a shower where the occupant pulled a string and got sprinkled by a watering-can through a hole in the roof.

Producing the first Phoenix number of *Indian Opinion* was a nightmare. Gandhi had obtained an oil engine to drive the press, and a wheel for hand operation in case it broke down. He had also reduced the format from newspaper size to foolscap, so that if all else failed, they could use a duplicator. The engine did break down. Furthermore, there seemed to be too few hands to keep the wheel turning—heavy work done in relays, four men together. The carpenters were sleeping and West was afraid to disturb them. Gandhi, however, had no compunction. He woke them up and they were willing. West sang a hymn and everybody took turns at the wheel. In the morning the engine did work, but that night of self-reliance was not forgotten. A time came when the staff dispensed with the engine and used the hand-wheel by choice.

Though Phoenix was never entirely stable, it survived as a community and grew more gracious. Gandhi could not be there himself as much as he wished. However, he housed Kasturbai and the boys there for longish periods. Several of his friends and relations tried their hands on the farm. Of these only Maganlal Gandhi stayed on, becoming a skilled compositor. West also stayed, except during a trip back to England—from which he returned with a charming bride from a Leicester shoe factory, plus a mother-in-law, and his sister Ada. They all settled at Phoenix. Ada, a versatile spinster, cooked and set type and looked after the children of other families. The mother-in-law did sewing and mending with inflexible cheerfulness.

Henry Polak was astounded at what he had inspired, and asked to join the farm as soon as it was established. He resigned from the *Critic* and worked for *Indian Opinion* at Phoenix, where his ease and sociability made him popular. However, when Gandhi's assistant Ritch went to England for his legal studies, Polak left the farm and replaced him at the Johannesburg office, signing articles with a view to qualifying as an attorney. He boarded in Gandhi's house as one of the family, and married on his advice, as indeed West had done. Gandhi's desire that others should live as he thought proper for himself extended to their sexual behaviour. When his own sexual ideal changed, the demands he made on others changed with it. The remarkable thing is not that he offered such advice, but that he got people to follow it with so little resistance or resentment. Polak continued faithful, and travelled to England and India for the Cause.

By fellow Indians Gandhi was affectionately called 'bhai', brother. But in his new role he was acquiring a new dominance, going outside the ethnic group. The change had its effect on *Indian Opinion*. One dissenter from his Phoenix experiment was the editor, Mansukhlal Nazar. Mansukhlal insisted on maintaining an office in Durban and editing the weekly from there. When this problem was unhappily solved by his sudden death, the next editor was not an Indian but an English Theosophist, Herbert Kitchin, an electrician by trade. Then Polak took over, with a deputy during his absences; and even the deputy was not an Indian, but the Reverend Joseph Doke, a Baptist minister. Yet the incongruously conducted paper gained in readership and public esteem. Other westerners drifted into Gandhi's circle. The most colourful was a German Jewish architect, Hermann Kallenbach. When they first

met, Kallenbach was a bulky, rich, free-spending bachelor, with a
handlebar moustache and a talent for boxing. Study of Buddha pro-
pelled him toward a sort of conversion. Gandhi warmed to the
German's 'strong feelings, wide sympathies and childlike simplicity'
(he had 'simplicity' as well as Jewishness in common with Polak).
Kallenbach cut his outgoings to one-tenth of what they had been.
Food reform was one of his interests, and master and disciple had
many congenial discussions.

Phoenix at its apex had an average resident population of half a
dozen families, European and Indian. It was a miniature republic
under Gandhi's spell, whether he was present or not. The English
members went through severe trials when they found snakes or
spiders in their bedrooms, and recalled that they were expected to
be non-violent and treat all creatures as sacred. Yet they passed
the test. Their home was a place of spiritually heightened atmosphere, the centre and power-house of a new life. If that meant
chiefly a new life for Indians; if they themselves, children of the
Imperial race, were Indians' servants here and not their overlords
. . . well, they were learning to see the world better by looking at it
upside down.

4

Success in moulding others is apt to depend on what one has
made of oneself. Gandhi's private character was partly a result of
his public activities. But it was also much more, and it reacted back
on them, raising him by way of Phoenix to a unique position. The
story of his advance toward sainthood is very much his own story,
not a mere illustration of Hindu hagiography. It is an odd mixture
of the splendid and the comic, the holy and the scandalous. To the
end of his days, any one of those elements was liable to come to
the fore.

The man who could absorb Ruskin, convert several journalists
and technicians, and persuade them to become rural co-operators,
all within a day or two, had of course undergone a preparation. To
shake off the bondage of plutocratic society, to take one's stand on
a frugal self-sufficiency, had appealed to Gandhi in theory for years.
He had digested the Simple Lifers' message. He had admired the
Muhammad of Carlyle's portrait, doing his own cobbling and darn-

ing. He had studied the works of Tolstoy in the same vein. And long before the encounter with Ruskin, he had made some attempts to put theory into practice. Charity might not begin at home, but austerity did.

Here as elsewhere his original motive for actually doing something was neither moral nor religious but strictly mundane. As in his student days, he wanted to reduce expenses. He still believed in saving for family needs, and the Cause made its demands on his pocket. His economy drive started in Durban in 1897. He tried washing his own clothes, using a book on *How to Launder*, and reading it to Kasturbai. Also he cut his own hair. Barristers watched for him in court with amusement: he would arrive wearing a collar that dripped with excess starch, or looking as if the rats had got at his head. Their grins never discouraged him. He learned to dispense with both the launderer and the barber, a double achievement that gave him great satisfaction. (Though he confessed that he 'could not make his friends appreciate the beauty of self-help'.)

Diet and hygiene kept their hold on his interests. About the same time, he read Adolf Just's *Return to Nature*, which advocates eating nothing but fruit and nuts, and regulating the bowels by earth treatment. Hitherto Gandhi had relied heavily on Eno's Fruit Salts. Now he took to wrapping earth poultices round his abdomen, and was pleased with what he regarded as the result. The full Adolf Just regimen did not appeal to him yet. But his vegetarianism remained active—indeed, too active. He not only propped up the German's restaurant in Johannesburg, but, after its collapse, financed another out of money entrusted to him by a client. This was one of the few downright silly acts of his life. The proprietor was a lady Theosophist, Miss Bissicks, and Gandhi had to make good his client's inevitable loss. While ceasing to sponsor such public ventures, he went on testing menus himself, with Kallenbach and others as co-experimenters. The trend was toward simplicity.

His concern for cleanliness extended to all around him and to himself. People called him Mahabhangi, the Great Scavenger, long before they called him Mahatma, the Great Soul. Each morning he spent thirty-five minutes washing. Fifteen were taken up with cleaning his teeth. The clue to that surprising fact is in one of his youthful *Vegetarian* articles, which explains the painstaking Indian method. A fresh brush has to be made each day out of a thorny twig, and the scouring goes on and on. By a typical transition, Gandhi's tooth-cleaning affected his religion. The Johannesburg Theosophists, unlike the Durban Christians, wanted to learn from him as a Hindu rather than preach at him as a heathen. They invited him to lecture. To keep abreast of their inquiries he had to search his own scriptures more diligently. So he copied out verses of the *Gita* in Sanskrit, stuck them on the wall, and read them while he scratched at his teeth.

Gradually he came to know most of the poem by heart. It flowed through all his thoughts and activities, till it became the light of his path. Tolstoy and Ruskin, the practice of law and the battle for Indian rights, all found their sanction in Krishna's Song. Its chapters on *karma-yoga,* salvation through action, were still rather unfashionable with Hindus. Most holy men sought union with God by other routes: by *bhakti-yoga,* the way of love and devotion; by *jnana-yoga,* the way of knowledge; or by *raja-yoga,* a combined method including bodily discipline. These were suitable to the hermit-saint, who was still rated above the man of action, largely because action under the conquerors was so apt to be futile. But a new day was dawning for *karma-yoga* in India, and Gandhi, though far off and out of touch, was a natural *karma-yogin.* 'Selfless action' in the task divinely appointed for him was his road to the eternal Truth.

He pondered the poem's teachings—on the absolute commands of duty, on never letting oneself be seduced by emotions or held back by attachments. Whereupon, like Arjuna, he was painfully faced with his own family.

It was the old issue raised in childhood by Harischandra and Rama: the claim of the ideal versus the counter-claim of others who may not share the ideal but still have to suffer for it. Too many admirers of the saints have slid over this difficulty. Can you let down people who love and trust you, in the name of integrity? Can you sustain your own brand of virtue out of the generosity of people who disagree? Can you turn somebody else's cheek? Apart from a few scattered words of regret, Gandhi seldom admitted that he saw any dilemma. His answer was Rama's and Harischandra's. But whatever his denials, he had to face the issue and advance by facing it. The escape route of the hermit was not for him, nor for his disciples. Always that problem stood before them, the problem of saints and revolutionaries, civil-rights campaigners and pacifists

—how to obey the uncompromising command, and live with it, yet live with other people too.

With one's wife and children, for example. Of all the supporting characters in Gandhi's story, Kasturbai is the one whose version would be the most worth having, and it is not to be had. Some day a novelist of genius may reconstruct it. Meanwhile the enigmatic little woman stares out from a series of photographs, always with the same expressionless expression, barely coming up to her husband's shoulder. Before 1896 his relations with her were as we have seen. When they came to Durban with Harilal and Manilal, aged nine and five, he still subscribed to the Hindu doctrine of the husband's dictatorship. That extended to every detail. Wishing his family to look respectable without looking European, he dressed them, as he sometimes dressed himself, in the style of the 'civilized' Parsees. The result was not bad. Kasturbai at twenty-eight looked very handsome in her rich silken sari. The boys went about in the Parsee coat and trousers. But Gandhi also required that they should wear shoes and socks, and eat with knives and forks. Their discomfort was acute.

When his special theories were added to these ambivalent habits, crises resulted. Two further sons were born in South Africa, Ramdas in 1897 and Devadas in 1900, the latter delivered by the father in person. All four had to be educated. Gandhi, however, concurred with Madame Blavatsky in rejecting the usual school programme. Also—in spite of his own response to literature—he rejected much of what is called culture, and inclined toward a Tolstoyan moral view of art. The effect was to narrow his range and therefore his sons' range.

He would not send them to any mission school, partly because of his dislike for the system, partly because he wanted them taught in Gujarati. The use of English to educate Indians was anti-patriotic, and at Rajkot it had slowed his own progress. He tried a governess without satisfaction. He tried sending Harilal to a boarding school in India, received reports so distressing that he almost disowned him, and brought him back again. The other three never went to school at all. Their father had notions of teaching them himself. But his priorities were such that he never found time to do this properly. College was out of the question. As adults they resented their academic lack, and Harilal revolted.

Their father's medical enthusiasms also affected them. Besides the do-it-yourself midwifery and baby care, he combated his sons' ailments with nature cures. Manilal had typhoid at ten. Gandhi refused to give him the eggs and broth advised by the doctor. When the temperature rose to 104, he wrapped the delirious child in a wet sheet. The fever passed, and Manilal convalesced on diluted milk and fruit juice for forty days (an appropriate period). Another time, when Ramdas injured an arm, Gandhi treated it with one of his earth poultices. While the boys were with him his confidence in such methods was buoyant, and they were dealt with accordingly. After they grew up his faith decreased somewhat. Manilal by then was the healthiest, but Gandhi confessed to a doubt as to whether he should credit the wet sheet or the grace of God.

In due course his household's simplicity and openness acquired a moral aura. Kasturbai had to serve as handmaid to his medley of lodgers, both in Durban and afterwards in Johannesburg. She did not retaliate with the nagging and meanness which were the usual weapons of Hindu wives; her forbearance was great and her resistance, when it occurred, was normally passive. But sometimes Gandhi went too far. Among other things, he insisted that she should regularly join him in emptying and cleaning the chamberpots. Once a Christian Indian clerk stayed with them, born of Untouchable parents. Kasturbai's upbringing as a caste Hindu made her almost incapable of handling his pot. Weeping and furious, she forced herself to carry it down the outdoor staircase. Her husband stood at the bottom, exhorting her to stop crying and do the job cheerfully. That was the last straw. 'Keep your house to yourself,' she snapped, 'and let me go.' Forgetful of non-violence, he actually dragged her to the gate. She told him to stop making a fool of himself in public; and he did.

They had other clashes. There was a bad quarrel in 1901 when they left Durban and were given expensive parting presents, including jewellery and a fifty-guinea necklace for Kasturbai personally. Gandhi was convinced that he must return the presents, and also convinced that she would not want him to. His idea of a tactful solution was to persuade the children and then confront his wife with a family lobby. She did not give way easily. If nothing else, she protested, couldn't the jewellery be saved for the boys' future brides? He answered that they should take care of themselves. Anyhow, if such sweeteners were needed, she could ask him for them whenever the need arose.

Her retort stuck in his memory. 'Ask you? I know you by this time. You deprived me of my ornaments, you would not leave me in peace with them. Fancy you offering to get ornaments for the daughters-in-law! You who are trying to make *sadhus* of my boys from today! No, the ornaments will not be returned. And pray what right have you to my necklace?'

'But,' said Gandhi maddeningly, 'is the necklace given for your service or for my service?'

'I agree. But service rendered by you is as good as rendered by me. I have toiled and moiled for you day and night. Is that not service? You forced all and sundry on me, making me weep bitter tears, and I slaved for them!'

The gifts, of course, went. When handing them over to the Natal Congress, Gandhi reserved the right to ask for them back under certain conditions, but he had no serious intention of doing so. He never regretted the step, and believed that his wife learned to 'see its wisdom'. Perhaps.

Their Johannesburg home was an eight-room house on the outskirts, thinly furnished. It received the impact of Ruskin. Deciding to bake his own wholemeal bread, and grind his own flour to bake it with, Gandhi bought a hand-mill. It was turned by an iron wheel which required two operators. He did his share himself, and so did his sons, and Polak and Mrs Polak. Kasturbai usually seemed to be busy somewhere else. Besides this exercise, the boys walked to their father's office with him daily. Such teaching as he had time for was imparted mainly during these walks. He spoke in Gujarati, not English—a policy which stung Polak into one of his rare protests. Surely the boys could at least be given a conversational competence in a language it would be so useful to know! However, the claims of India prevailed. Their English, picked up casually, was never better than fair.

To his guests and boarders the head of this household was an agreeable host. They enjoyed a quality in him that is almost absent from his writings and speeches—his humour. Gandhi's authentic jokes were few, but he created an atmosphere in which laughter occurred and jokes seemed to have been made. Even his earnestness, like his mother's, was apt to be fun. The Polaks conformed to family practice by calling him 'Bapu', Father, as many more were to do after them. A little incongruously, he now wore lounge suits (favouring a dark blue with a faint stripe); but the turban was superimposed. In this costume he presided over evening readings from the *Gita*.

Study of the poem led him to further disavowals of the common prudences and amenities. The house itself was not his—as an Asiatic he could not own it—but he surrendered his life insurance, and wrote to Laxmidas, back in Kathiawar, that he was giving up saving in general. For his kind and patient brother the blow was cruel. His improvidence was disgracing the family and directly hurting Laxmidas, who had come to rely on remittances sent by him in return for past help. Mohandas did not mend matters with further self-righteous letters beginning 'Respected Sir'. Contact almost ceased. Laxmidas died while Mohandas was still in South Africa. The brothers were reconciled in time, but only just.

Gandhi was being driven to ask a more profound question. Did his family fit in at all? How was one to divest oneself of possessions, when wife and children were like possessions only more so? Kasturbai had taunted him with wanting to make her sons into *sadhus*, holy beggars. In *The Light of Asia* Buddha forsook wife and child to become that very thing. Buddha's path was not for him. Though his marriage had been a trap, he accepted its consequences and had no notion of breaking it up. Yet he might take a hint. In the same poem, liberation is promised to the man who 'so constrains his passions that they die'. Slowly, but in accord with the logic he had learnt in England, Gandhi pressed through to the fundamental issue. Kasturbai was a fixture and he would not desert her . . . but should he sleep with her?

The sexual vow that completed his long apprenticeship was approached by the usual experimental road. Until about 1900 his relations with Kasturbai were normal and indeed masterful. Naturally, not without mental queries. He was well aware that Hinduism taught the virtue of *brahmacharya*—self-control and, especially, sexual restraint. The respected Raychandbhai had talked to him about this. He had read Madame Blavatsky on the celibacy of the higher type of Theosophist, and noted the relevant verses of the *Gita*. But no religious teaching set him in motion along that line. Nor was he impelled, as some have supposed, by guilt over his father's death. His characteristically prosaic motive was to avoid having any more children.

As a student he had followed the Allinson-Hills debate—contraception versus control—and inclined toward control. But when family planning was the only reason, he found that it did not work. He tried putting Kasturbai in a separate bed. That arrangement was no hardship to her, and she never made advances, but he still did. Meanwhile the demands of his career were rendering the need for limitation more urgent. If the memory of Kaba's death influenced him, it was probably in this phase, by holding up an image of sense at war with duty. From 1901 onward he succeeded a little better. However, it was not till 1906 that a chance happening brought him into haven.

A Zulu rising broke out in Natal. Or so the authorities viewed it. Gandhi liked the Zulus, but, as with the Boers, a question arose as to whether Indians could agitate for citizenship if they did not show willingness to perform civic duties. He raised a party of twenty-four stretcher-bearers and gave up his Johannesburg house, though not his office. Kasturbai and the boys stayed at Phoenix during his month or so of service. He was given the rank of sergeant-major (a strange thought) and the whole corps was put in uniform. His stamina was boundless; he could march forty miles a day, and get his men to do likewise. As it turned out, the rising was minimal. A chief had advised his tribe not to pay a new tax, and run an assegai through the tax-collector. Most of the work consisted in nursing Zulus who had been flogged or shot, often by mistake, during the restoration of order. Some had hideous wounds, but the white staff would do nothing. Idle soldiers watched the Indians at their task, jeered at them for taking such trouble over niggers, and abused the patients.

The atrocities started Gandhi reflecting, and long marches through empty country gave him time for reflection. He could not lead two lives. Total dedication to service was the only way. This implied a firm commitment. His mother had taught him the efficacy of vows. A vow had kept him steady in England against temptation, even against what seemed to be reason, and he was glad. The logical step now was to embrace *brahmacharya*. He must go beyond a mere fitful abstention from certain acts to a positive resolution of self-mastery, as Hindus understood it and as the *Gita* expounded it.

On returning to Phoenix that summer he discussed *brahmacharya* with Maganlal, West, and other residents, though not with Kasturbai, to whom he had never broached the topic. They understood him and he made up his mind. She, when faced with an accomplished fact, acquiesced. Their relation could cease to be

physical as far as she was concerned. Her husband took the vow.
One or two of his followers did also.

The effect on him was a sense of freedom. Whatever the difficulties ahead, he stood on solid ground. His mood was creative,
not restrictive. Gandhi never had any use for privation as an end in
itself. In an article written after he went back to India, he made his
view plain:

> It is better to enjoy through the body than to be enjoying the
> thought of it. It is good to disapprove of sensual desires as soon
> as they arise in the mind and try to keep them down, but if for
> want of physical enjoyment the mind wallows in thoughts of
> enjoyment, then it is legitimate to satisfy the hunger of the body.
> About this I have no doubt.
>
>   (*Navajivan,* 9 May 1929.)

His aim in fact was not to mortify passion but to get rid of it, as
part of a sublimation of the personality. Ordinary sensual existence seemed to him 'insipid and animal-like'. *Brahmacharya,*
meaning full self-control, could be a step toward a higher humanity
deserving the name. As negative sexual abstinence he never
approved of it, and it was always his impression that would-be
holy men who confined it to that were liable to fail.

His own motive, at the stage of taking the vow, was still not
religious but moral and psychological. As the Indians' leader he
felt obliged to conduct himself in a certain way. It was still around
the earthly battle, not any heavenly command, that his ideas took
shape. His *brahmacharya* was like the discipline of an athlete, his
sexual continence like the continence which trainers expect of
boxers before a fight. The extension of it which presently weakened
his position, and exposed him to justified attack, was not puritanism but a mistake of a subtler kind.

The struggle to keep the vow himself led him on from one
measure to another. For years he reduced desire by diet. He went
over to Adolf Just's fruit and nuts, varied by fasting. On a hint
from Raychandbhai he gave up even milk. As long as he stuck
to these rules he had less and less trouble, but when he had to un-
bend for health reasons, his senses grew unruly again. Physical
means were not enough. He at last examined *brahmacharya* as a
religious concept in Hindu scripture, and sought divine aid. With
that spiritual enlargement he opened the door to Hinduism's sexual

idiosyncrasies: its mixture of prudery and erotic frankness, its mystique of the female, its techniques for redirecting the human libido. But not yet, not in South Africa.

There, Gandhi's vow had a swift public sequel, his invention of the political method that made him famous. Its effect on his home was gradual but beneficial. With Kasturbai the storms passed. For some time she suspected that the vow applied to herself rather than to women in general, and he had to keep reassuring her that if she died he would not remarry. But they no longer quarrelled. He learned to value her firmness and loyalty, especially during an illness (she was anaemic) when she backed up his refusal to let the doctor give her beef tea. The family was de-fused. It was sober-spirited, a little sad.

In a letter to Manilal about three years after the vow, Gandhi wrote:

> As soon as a boy reaches the age of discretion, he is taught to realize his responsibilities. Every boy from such age onward should practise continence in thought and deed, truth likewise and the not-taking of any life. . . . It should be his enjoyment. . . . Let me tell you that when I was younger than you are my keenest enjoyment was to nurse my father.
>
> Of amusement after I was twelve, I had little or none. If you practise the three virtues, if they become part of your life, so far as I am concerned you will have completed your education—your training. Armed with them, believe me you will earn your bread in any part of the world and you will have paved the way to acquire a true knowledge of the soul, yourself and God. . . . Remember please than henceforth our lot is poverty. The more I think of it the more I feel that it is more blessed to be poor than to be rich.

This was hardly a letter to draw a son any closer. Except with Harilal, the danger of actual estrangement might be over. But Gandhi, that most social of men, had a share in the solitude of the gods.

VI

Truth-Force

1

He looked back upon the past decade as largely an overture to his vow. Yet the vow itself was an overture to something else, requiring exactly the sort of braced dedication that he had had in mind when taking it. This new thing which came into the world through Gandhi was Satyagraha—variously but inadequately translated 'passive resistance', 'civil disobedience', and 'non-violent non-co-operation'.

South Africa's white leaders provoked it, thus lighting a fire which was to spread across the Indian Ocean in a setpiece of Imperial suicide. But nobody foresaw such a result; not Gandhi himself or West or Polak; and certainly not the Asiatic Department official who made the first move. He was Lionel Curtis, the same with whom Gandhi had had that unhelpful talk in 1903. He had subsequently announced a plan to tighten the Transvaal permit system, as a check on further immigration. Every adult male Asian already resident was to register or re-register and take out a fresh permit, bearing his signature (his thumb-mark if he could not write), and —in spite of Muslim scruples—a photograph. Illegal entrants after this new registration would be easier to catch.

The Indians complied, and the process was completed early in 1906. Curtis, however, was still dissatisfied. On his advice the Transvaal Government drafted an Asiatic Law Amendment Ordinance laying down further conditions. Gandhi heard the first rumours of this during his Zulu service. When he returned from Phoenix to his Johannesburg office, he found a copy of the government gazette dated 22 August, giving the text of the Ordinance. He began translating it into Gujarati for *Indian Opinion*. As he studied the meaning carefully clause by clause, he realized that it was almost a declaration of war.

96

It decreed that all Transvaal Indians, of both sexes and all ages from eight upwards, should report to the Registrar of Asiatics and take out a certificate. When applying, they would have to give a number of personal details. The Registrar would record these, note any distinguishing physical marks, and collect a full set of finger-prints. Any Indian who failed to report before a certain date would forfeit his right of residence, and become subject to fine, imprison-ment or deportation. This penalty applied to minors as well as adults. After the registration, any Indian unable to produce his certificate at a policeman's order would be liable to a fine or jail. The police could ask for it anywhere, at any time, without warning and without giving reason, and enter private houses to do so. Further, it would be asked for whenever an Indian had any busi-ness with a government department, even getting a bicycle licence.

A peculiarly shocking feature was the taking of fingerprints. In 1906 a full set could not be demanded from anyone but a criminal. Gandhi verified the law on this point, and then summoned a meet-ing of prominent Indians. As he analysed the Ordinance for them their anger mounted, especially when they grasped that women and children were included. One said: 'If an official told my wife to go through all that, I'd shoot him on the spot.' Gandhi urged them to keep calm. However, he accepted that they were facing a crisis. The Government's aim was to establish the principle that Indians were second-class people, living in the Transvaal on sufferance and not by right. If the Ordinance passed, measures of the same type would follow in the rest of South Africa. The end would be slavery or expulsion.

'Therefore', he went on, 'we are responsible for the safety, not only of the ten or fifteen thousand Indians in the Transvaal, but of the entire Indian community in South Africa. The fate of Indians in Natal and the Cape depends upon our resistance . . . India's honour is in our keeping. For the Ordinance seeks to humiliate not only ourselves but also India, our motherland.'

His friends agreed. Within a few days they issued a call to a mass protest meeting. It was held in the old Empire Theatre, Johannes-burg, at 2 p.m. on 11 September 1906. Indians closed their shops in order to attend. Out-of-town delegates poured in and crowded the house. Gandhi, from the stage, estimated his audience at three thousand. As he rose to address them he was none too sure what to expect. With the aid of interpreters, he explained the Ordinance so that all could understand, whether their language was Gujarati, Hindi, Tamil or Telugu. Then a resolution was moved under his sponsorship, declaring that Indians should refuse to obey the Ordinance, and be ready to suffer the penalties.

Speaker after speaker leapt up to support it. The atmosphere became charged. The spark for an explosion was supplied by Sheth Haji Habib, a merchant with many years of honest trading behind him. The venerable Sheth cried out passionately that they should do more than vote. They should swear, with God as witness, that they would stand by their resolution and never submit. He took this oath himself before sitting down, and called on the rest to join him.

In a gathering where religion had potency, his gesture could not fail to impress. Resolutions, as such, were not taken too seriously; they had been passed before, and then amended or forgotten. Haji Habib had lifted the proceedings on to a different plane. While he was still speaking, Gandhi thought swiftly, very mindful of his own recent broodings on the solemnity of a sacred vow. Haji finished, a few more spoke in approval, and by then he knew what to do.

Asking the chair's permission to comment, he pointed out that an oath in God's name was not to be undertaken lightly by any believer. It could only be justified by a true crisis, a make-or-break moment of decision. The first question was whether such a crisis confronted them. In his view, it did. So the oath was a proper step. But did they realize what would happen if they took it and kept it? Unlike a resolution, it could not be imposed by majority vote. Each would have to decide for himself and be prepared for the consequences. If enough of them could stand firm, then yes, the Ordinance would founder . . .

We shall go on till we succeed. It is quite possible that some of those who pledge themselves may weaken at the very first trial. We may have to remain hungry and suffer from extreme heat and cold. Hard labour is likely to be imposed upon us in prison. We may even be flogged by the warders. Or we may not be imprisoned, but fined heavily and our property attached and held up to auction for non-payment. Though some of us are wealthy today, we may be reduced to poverty tomorrow. We may even be deported from South Africa for good . . .

Our wisdom therefore lies in pledging ourselves, knowing full well that we shall have to suffer things like these . . . Provided the entire community manfully stands the test, the end will be soon. But if many of us fall back under stress of trial, the struggle will be prolonged. At the same time I can boldly declare, that so long as there is even a handful of men true to their pledge, there can only be one end to the struggle, and that is victory.

His remaining words might have sunk into anti-climax, but they did not. He spoke briefly of his own position: he was ready to lead the way, and would never violate his pledge, even if he were left alone.

Reading his speech, one would imagine the audience breaking in with cheers. Actually they listened in a complete hush. Gandhi's style—as always—was quiet, lucid, with no rhetorical changes in pitch or volume. It carried his hearers past applause. The meeting was heroic and sacramental. At last, with raised hands, the whole three thousand unanimously took the oath in God's name. If the Ordinance became law they would defy it.

Next day there was an accidental fire and the theatre burned down. Its end, Polak remarked, was fitting. Nothing further could have taken place on that stage without sacrilege.

2

A mass campaign of non-compliance, without violence, was a political novelty. The delegates hurried hither and thither through the Transvaal persuading others to take the same pledge. But meanwhile, their chief had to invent a technique as he went along. He even had to invent a name for the movement. After trying 'passive resistance' he decided that a new one was needed, preferably not borrowed from English, and offered a book prize in *Indian Opinion* for the best suggestion. Modifying a term proposed by his cousin Maganlal, he arrived at 'Satyagraha', meaning 'Firmness in Truth' or Truth-Force. 'Satya' has connotations of deity and love. A person practising the method would be a Satyagrahi.

Even after the competition he sometimes talked of 'passive resistance'. The phrase had been applied to the conduct of British Nonconformists opposing an Education Act. But he grew to dislike it. To Europeans, he found, it implied weakness and sullenness and mere nay-saying. The scene in the theatre had not been like that at all. Nor was the movement, as it took shape, and advanced open-eyed toward the inevitable clash with authority. It was courageous, ardent, affirmative.

Satyagraha was destined to develop into a reasoned system of un- armed action, offered not merely as an expedient to use where force was impossible, but as a weapon superior to force. The main conception was Gandhi's. To suppose that he simply applied Hindu non-violence to politics, with or without a hint from Tolstoy, is to fall far short of comprehension. It must be stressed again that Hindu non-violence—Ahimsa in its traditional sense—was hardly more than a vague gentleness, and could easily become passivity toppling into cowardice. Even the Jains, who laid the most em- phasis on it, never made it an instrument for attaining an end. Hindus occasionally practised a kind of sit-down strike known as *dhurna,* but it was pure obstructiveness, and Gandhi always re- jected it as a precedent. Nor did Tolstoy get much further than praising some youths who refused military service. Gandhi was the pioneer. Through the embattled decades he grasped more and more fully what Satyagraha implied, and sharpened his definitions. But its essence never altered. So much of it was there from the begin- ning that the beginning is a proper place to clarify it.

The starting-point of a Satyagraha campaign is the radical wrongness of a situation. Correct action against evil requires correct insight. The Satyagrahi must reach a precise understanding of what is wrong, and what factor in the situation embodies the evil so starkly that a stand must be made there. Thus Indians in the Trans- vaal, however downgraded, might comply with registration laws of a more or less reasonable kind; it was the 1906 order that went too far, and brought all iniquities to a head. To identify this critical issue may not always be easy. To achieve the correct insight (Gandhi maintained) you must observe non-violence of the mind, getting rid of hate and passion and prejudice; you must seek the truth in a spirit of love. Otherwise you will not find it, or not retain it when found. Your insight and the resulting action will be incorrect.

At the heart of the situation, however obscured by myth or propa- ganda, is the truth. It is not only truth-in-this-instance but Truth with a capital T. In achieving his correct insight the Satyagrahi encounters the Absolute. That encounter supplies his marching orders. 'Here', he says, 'is the point of no return and no appeal. Here I *must* stand, I can no other.' The hackneyed phrase 'the Moment of Truth' is in this case apt.

Having won through to a reality free from illusion, he draws strength from the meeting. Gandhi—like Haji Habib, after his fashion—saw it as a meeting with God. Talking in 1931 to the Swiss pacifist Pierre Ceresole, he sketched his belief as it had then matured: 'Truth is God, and the way to find him is non-violence. Anger must be banished, and fear and falsehood. You must lose yourself. . . . Purified, you get power. It's not your own, it's God's.'

When Truth shines unclouded before him, the Satyagrahi asserts it by a fearless refusal to submit to the Wrong or co-operate with it. This usually involves public acts of dissent and disobedience, and may extend to setting up new institutions, political or economic. He keeps to his non-violence, not only on moral grounds but so as to hold firm in his own mind. To allow violence to possess him would be to lose his correct insight, and slip back through hatred into error. ('In war', as has been observed, 'Truth is the first casualty.') Non-violence means a clean break with the normal habits of mankind, a rebirth into light.

Satyagrahis, Gandhi decided, can employ such weapons as boycotts and strikes. But when authority moves against them they must submit to its blows without retaliation, and go to prison or death without rancour, indeed with joy and courtesy. Full responsibility falls on each one, as a soldier of non-violence. Satyagraha implies self-reliance, not raising funds for other people to spend, not wire-pulling through committees. It calls for colossal self-control.

The Satyagrahi—in theory—not only consents to suffer at the wrongdoer's hands, but conquers through suffering. Martyrdom is part of the method. In his agony he is driven back on the unwavering divine Truth at the centre of his soul, and that contact makes him invincible. Yet his victory is not the opponent's defeat. It is the opponent's conversion. To endure blows long enough is to unnerve the arm that strikes them, and win over the directing mind. Victory does not mean that one side triumphs at the other's expense, but that both sides are reconciled in a new harmony, with the Wrong cancelled.

That is the technique which was born in a Johannesburg theatre, and carried to such amazing lengths. Obviously it raised some grave queries . . . as it does still.

For a start, could its high moral tone be squared with law-breaking? Here was one of the paradoxes that caused Gandhi to be attacked as a hypocrite. The ideas of his own country supplied few hints. Hindu political thought, in fact, is strangely amoral. Its texts hardly attempt to apply ethics to the detailed conduct of public affairs. The model rajah tends to sound like a Machiavellian despot; his subjects' duty is to conform to his arbitrary decrees. Gandhi, British-conditioned, believed in the reign of law as a moral concept. But—he insisted—some laws can and should be broken, in the name of a higher law with which they conflict.

His was the Christian view summed up by his fellow-lawyer Thomas More, who perished on the block as 'the King's good servant, but God's first'. Gandhi indeed unconsciously echoed More in an early campaign poster: 'Loyalty to the King demands loyalty to the King of Kings.' The death of the great Lord Chancellor for defiance on a single point (royal control over the Church) is a partial illustration of Satyagraha. Gandhist disobedience was never mere anarchy. The struggle in any given phase was on a narrow front and highly specific. In 1906 and the next few years he was not fighting for a nebulous justice, but for the right of Indians to live at peace in the Transvaal. He organized his assertion of this around the planned and dramatized infringement of one law. Except in so far as they were demonstrating against this, his Satyagrahis were law-abiding. Their action might lead to controversy, publicity, the drawing-in of wider support; it might prompt the re-study of the whole status of Indians; but until circumstances altered, he did not allow Satyagraha to be extended to other anti-Indian laws—to issues not raised when the oath was taken. He thought such a step would be dishonest and confusing. A major problem when he came to apply the technique in India was how to maintain this concentration, this sharpness of focus, in pursuit of an ill-defined aim like national freedom. Once but only once he solved it completely, in a superb and redemptive moment on the beach at Dandi.

Whatever the moral bearings of Satyagraha, it rested on certain presuppositions. Gandhi's followers were Indians, and a sceptic might query how far any other race would have responded. The Hindus among them, as he well knew, had the ideal of Ahimsa in their religion, however little it amounted to. Hindu and Muslim alike accepted that a real Absolute, God or Truth or whatever one called it, did exist.

As Gandhi made assumptions about his own troops, so he made assumptions about the enemy. He retained a faith in Britain and British ways that was rather touching and not entirely misplaced.

He believed that the Empire's representatives, and Boers like Smuts who made common cause with them, would never go to the extremes of repression. The Indians would never be simply slaughtered. And there he was right . . . or nearly so. Englishmen like General Dyer, who did simply slaughter them, were exceptional. But under a Nazi government, or even a government of Dyers, could Satyagraha have made any headway? Gandhi's method left no resources in reserve. It ruled out everything that even savoured of warfare. Campaigns had to be conducted not only non-violently but openly, without craft, without conspiracy, without long-term planning; since all of these imply using secrecy to get an advantage, and belong to the world of conflict and untruth.

After Gandhi's death a President of India, Rajendra Prasad, conceded that the successes of Satyagraha had been partly due to the self-imposed restraint of the authorities it was used against. Gandhi never made that admission. He claimed that his method could win anywhere because it could convert anybody. This was a rash claim. With Satyagraha, moreover, there was bound to be an uncertainty as to what 'victory through conversion' meant. Did it mean that the opponent would confess his error and surrender with a good grace? Or did it mean that he would offer one of those peacemaking formulae which supposedly grant what both parties really want, without giving either what he actually asked for?

Gandhi was criticized on this point by Mary Parker Follett, the American writer on administration. Miss Follett, an advocate of the second type of settlement, attacked him on the ground that he aimed at the first. In so doing, she argued, he pursued the same end as the man of violence. Conquest by suffering was morally the same as conquest by force. The answer in theory is that where Satyagraha is right at all, there is, by definition, no room left for formulae. The 'crunch' has come, and one side or the other must yield. In practice Gandhi was not so definite. Sometimes he held out for total success, sometimes he accepted offers. His meditations on Satyagraha did not always tell him which course expressed its spirit. Indeed, his less docile followers muttered that he was apt to choose wrong. One campaign would be thwarted by his willingness to drop a vital demand, and the next by his obstinacy on some petty detail.

However, when the Johannesburg Indians took their oath, all such troubles lay in the future. Whatever weaknesses time might disclose, Gandhi had launched an extraordinary movement. Many people were to ask him where he got the idea. To his Baptist friend Joseph Doke he mentioned the Sermon on the Mount, and Tolstoy's expansion of it. Neither of these could have taken him all the way. The *Gita* helped with the moral psychology; yet since the whole point of Krishna's discourse is that Arjuna must engage in violence instead of abstaining from it, the *Gita* too is insufficient. (Gandhi wrestled with that dilemma for thirty years.) Thoreau's essay on civil disobedience had some effect, but he did not read it till after the struggle had begun. At other times he spoke of Socrates, of Jesus—by personal example rather than teaching—and of the prophet Daniel. As a prototype the last is the best, together with his three famous companions (*Daniel* chapters 1, 3 and 6).

None of Gandhi's alleged sources would have given him enough. There remains an intriguing query about another which would, namely Shelley's poem 'The Mask of Anarchy'. That brilliant, staccato outburst is an appeal to the English workers in the year of Peterloo and the Six Acts. In conjunction with Tolstoy—almost, indeed, by itself—it could have supplied the entire technique.

> Rise like lions after slumber
> In unvanquishable number,
> Shake your chains to earth like dew
> Which in sleep had fallen on you—
> Ye are many—they are few. . . .
>
> Let a vast assembly be,
> And with great solemnity
> Declare with measured words that ye
> Are, as God has made ye, free. . . .
>
> Let the tyrants pour around
> With a quick and startling sound,
> Like the loosening of a sea,
> Troops of armed emblazonry. . . .
>
> Stand ye calm and resolute,
> Like a forest close and mute,
> With folded arms and looks which are
> Weapons of unvanquished war. . . .
>
> And if then the tyrants dare
> Let them ride among you there,

Slash, and stab, and maim, and hew,
What they like, that let them do. /

With folded arms and steady eyes,
And little fear, and less surprise,
Look upon them as they slay
Till their rage has died away.

Then they will return with shame
To the place from which they came,
And the blood thus shed will speak
In hot blushes on their cheek. . . .

And that slaughter to the nation
Shall steam up like inspiration,
Eloquent, oracular;
A volcano heard afar.

Gandhi knew of Shelley through his reading of Salt, Howard Williams, Anna Kingsford. At a later date he knew this very poem, because he quoted it. But had he read if before 1906? Did a Freudian lapse of memory occur, owing to disapproval of Shelley's sexual principles? At any rate, if we consider Gandhi alongside not only 'The Mask of Anarchy' but also *Prometheus Unbound,* he unexpectedly emerges as the only true realizer of the poet's visions. Shelley died at thirty leaving those visions in the air. But when Gandhi was sixty, the imaginary scene in 'The Mask of Anarchy' became a fact at the salt works of Dharasana.

3

The first *Satyagraha* was less dramatic. *Indian Opinion* publicized the drive for pledges, with hopeful results. But the pledges as such were not illegal, and therefore brought no counter-measures. The Black Ordinance itself, as Indians called it, had yet to become law. The signs indeed were ominous. Smuts was talking of 'eradicating the Asiatic cancer', and Botha, the other prominent Boer soldier-politician, proposed to 'drive the coolies out of the country within four years'. Nevertheless, Gandhi still felt bound to avert the storm if he could.

In Britain a Liberal Government was preparing to give South

Africa—meaning the dominant white minority—home rule. Provisionally, however, the Transvaal was a Crown Colony under Botha's premiership. London could still overrule Pretoria. Hence there were two possible levels of appeal. Gandhi began by leading a deputation to talk with Patrick Duncan, the Transvaal Colonial Secretary. The party included Haji Habib, the proposer of the oath. There was no restraining Haji, whose ability to stay non-violent was limited. He shouted that any policeman trying to fingerprint his wife could expect instant death. Duncan was distressed, and said something about re-examining the clauses relating to women. Otherwise, he insisted, Botha was adamant.

In due course the Ordinance was passed. The clauses mentioned by Duncan had been withdrawn. This change removed the most hated insult, but did not affect the principle or weaken the threat to every breadwinner and his dependants. As in Natal, Gandhi made a bid for an Imperial veto. He went to England accompanied by an educated Muslim. They visited Dadabhai Naoroji—still full of life at eighty-one—and through his good offices they managed to meet Lord Elgin, now Colonial Secretary. While in London Gandhi also had talks with members of the Indian National Congress; with Lord Morley, the Secretary of State for India; and with several MPs. Among these last was the Irish leader Redmond. Neither knew it, but the simultaneous rising of their two countries was less than thirteen years away. Gandhi's old helper Ritch was studying law in England. He agreed to organize a standing committee for future lobbying. This committee was launched at a hundred-cover dinner, in keeping with what was then a British convention. The Indians thought the custom barbarous, but observed it for the sake of public relations.

They sailed for South Africa without having got a definite answer. Their ship put in at Madeira. Here a cable from Ritch informed them that Elgin was advising the King to withhold assent from the Ordinance. It soon transpired, however, that Elgin was merely shifting the burden. So long as Britain governed the Transvaal, royal assent could hardly be given to a bill imposing racial discrimination, because British maxims of government ruled it out. But from 1 January 1907 the South Africans would be on their own. Then, Elgin assured them, they could enact their Ordinance again and no one would interfere.

They did. It careered through all its stages in the Legislature on a single day, 21 March. On 1 July it was to have the force of law. All Indians were required to register by the end of that month.

Gandhi had created an *ad hoc* body to conduct the opposition. Formed before his new word was invented, it was called the 'Passive Resistance Association'. Afterwards this was altered to 'Satyagraha Association'. Money and membership came from the existing local Congress of Transvaal Indians. But some held back, and some argued that the oath was no longer binding, because the original Ordinance had not been passed; the one which had gone through, though almost word for word the same, was technically a different Ordinance. Gandhi noted these symptoms of wavering, and held new meetings to readminister the oath. His journalism grew more excited and pugnacious.

On 1 July the permit offices opened. Volunteers picketed the approaches, and dissuaded Indians from going in. They wore badges (perhaps the first step toward the political badgemanship of the CND era). Every man who seemed disposed to register was politely given a leaflet, or, if he could not read, a brief lecture. A little intimidation occurred, but Gandhi acted quickly to stop it. Generally the atmosphere was good humoured. Skirmishes, however, were not long in coming. Here and there the police manhandled the pickets, or charged them with causing an obstruction. Those who were hit remembered not to hit back, those taken to court were acquitted.

When July ended it looked as if they were winning. Only a few hundred had registered. The campaign had built up a spirit of comradeship which exerted its own pressures. Several of those who did register arranged to do it furtively in houses and shops, a subterfuge that leaked out and did them no good.

On 31 July two thousand resisters gathered in front of the Pretoria Mosque. To save expense all such meetings were held in the open, and everybody not on the platform sat on the ground. A politician named William Hosken, who was acting as intermediary between Gandhi and Botha, picked his way through the crowd with a message from the Prime Minister. He urged that the Indians had made a strong enough protest to save their honour. They should now submit gracefully to the Government and public opinion. General Smuts (who had succeeded to Duncan's responsibility for the matter) would listen to any suggestions they cared to make, so long as they accepted the main intent of the law.

Gandhi interpreted the speech, adding, it must be said, his own comments. Hosken withdrew amid the cheers of all present, after which they proceeded to the business of rejecting his invitation. The star speaker this time was another Muslim, Kachhalia Sheth, who had worked his way up from humble beginnings, and earned Gandhi's respect by his self-acquired legal knowledge. Kachhalia stirred the crowd with the same religious fervour which Haji Habib had introduced in the theatre. His face reddening, his veins swelling, his body shaking, he passed his hand over his neck and roared: 'I swear in the name of Allah that even though I am hanged I will never submit to this law. Let everyone present here take the same oath.' The melodrama seemed so overdone that Gandhi could not help smiling. Later, when he saw what Kachhalia was made of, he felt sorry. The Sheth had meant it.

Midnight went by with the vast majority of Indians unregistered and facing arrest. They were launched on a civil-rights campaign that was to last nearly seven years and carry them to social maturity. It was waged without permanent funds, and with only the loosest organization. Directives came chiefly through *Indian Opinion*. The number of its subscribers rose to the peak figure of 3,500, and since many copies were read aloud to groups, its message reached a far greater number. Gandhi's own articles were the most important items. The experience convinced him that whatever else he could do without, he could not do without a paper. He expounded Satyagraha quite openly. The Asiatic Department officials, puzzled to know what was going on, became his most faithful readers.

Faced with his challenge, the authorities could not stay idle. After extending the time-limit without result, they began considering whom to arrest first. That distinction went to a curious person, Rama Sundara. He was a Hindu living in Germiston, nine miles from Johannesburg, who enjoyed a local fame on the strength of his talent for giving recitations. Some of his neighbours spoke of him reverently as a Pandit or scholar. Others were envious, and it was they who prompted the Government to pick on him. They predicted that the arrest of this well-known figure would cow the Germiston Indians into taking out permits. Rama Sundara was duly arrested. A reputation hitherto confined to his home town immediately spread all over South Africa. The trial was a public demonstration verging on comedy. During his month in prison he was allowed unlimited visitors and food parcels. The case induced nobody to register, even in Germiston, and he came out a popular idol to be feasted and garlanded.

Unfortunately Rama Sundara did not live up to his role. He lost interest in Satyagraha and left the Transvaal. Gandhi afterwards heard that he was a labourer of bad character who had skipped his indenture. The lesson was valuable, and it was lucky they had learnt it so soon. Every movement has to endure the collapse of its heroes. The same lesson was later reinforced by the small group of Johannesburg Chinese. They helped the Satyagrahis because the Ordinance applied to them too. Then one of them absconded with their fighting fund, and most of the rest, though not all, dropped out.

In spite of disillusion the pseudo-Pandit had served his purpose. He had broken the ice. After his experience, plenty of Indians were willing to go the same way. Still the Government moved with caution. It was not till well on in December that the real blows began to fall. Then, however, Gandhi and several hundred others were summoned to show reason why they should not be deported. They made no attempt to do so and were ordered to leave by 10 January 1908. On that day, as they had not gone, they were summoned to court again. All pleaded guilty to disobeying the order, none made any defence. Gandhi himself came up for sentence in the Johannesburg court where he had made a name as a counsel. Since the Satyagrahis in Pretoria had just been given three months' hard labour, plus a fine or further imprisonment, he requested a heavier punishment.. The Bench had the sagacity to refuse. He got only two months without hard labour. Though the sentence avoided a glaring martyrdom, it was enough to inspire a protest march of Indians carrying black flags. The police broke this up and flogged the demonstrators.

Gandhi's jail term—the first of a memorable series—was most instructive. He soon got over the shock and loss of nerve due to emotional reaction, and looked around him inquiringly. With four other Satyagrahis, he was locked up in the 'black' part of a racially segregated prison. The dirtiness of his uniform disgusted him. There was trouble over food, as the Negro diet supplied in that wing was almost uneatable for Indians. After an argument the governor stopped the mealie-meal porridge and provided bread. On the whole, this first taste of jail was not too unpleasant to Gandhi personally. He had some of his books, and borrowed others from visitors and the prison library. They included the Bible, *Gita* and Koran; more of Carlyle, more of Ruskin, more of Tolstoy; Bacon's essays and Huxley's lectures. One of his discoveries was that a cell can be a good place for reading.

His worst suffering came from the influx of further Satyagrahis and the miseries inflicted on them. Within a short time he was joined by Leung Quinn, the Chinese leader, and Thambi Naidu, a Tamil shopkeeper with an intense patriotism for an India he had never seen. The Tamil's gifts as a linguist, and his readiness to take on any job from usher to chairman, had made him conspicuous in the movement; now he was paying the price. Fourteen more followed. Meanwhile a wave of arrests was sweeping over the Transvaal. Some were provoked. Indian hawkers, for instance, ostentatiously lost their licences so as to go to jail for illegal trading. There was almost a holiday mood . . . at first. But the bloom wore off. The swarms of inmates overcrowded the cells and made them fetid and filthy. Several fell sick, many were forced to sleep outdoors.

Towards the end of January Gandhi received a visit from Albert Cartwright, the pro-Indian editor of *The Leader,* who was trying to mediate. Through him, Smuts offered a draft agreement to break the deadlock. The certificate system should go on, but the details would be revised to appease Indian susceptibilities. Then, if Indians would register of their own free will, he would reconsider the Black Act.

Gandhi was suspicious, and asked for changes in the draft. But after consulting his colleagues he consented to negotiate. On 30 January he travelled to Pretoria under police escort for an interview with Smuts. The General welcomed him with a show of affability. 'I will repeal the Act,' he said, 'as soon as most of you have undergone registration.' Gandhi would be set free at once, the rest of the Satyagrahis before long. They could hold meetings, provided these were purely to explain the arrangement. He dismissed his released prisoner with a smile, and his secretary furnished the fare back to Johannesburg.

It was night when Gandhi arrived. He collected as many activists as he could and laid the offer before them. Under the premature impression that Satyagraha had won, he favoured acceptance. Indians, he argued, had never challenged the Government's right to control immigration. They could not object to registering for that purpose, so long as the monstrous Act was withdrawn.

Some of his hearers were far from happy. They wanted the Act withdrawn before they registered. Was Smuts going to keep his word? Gandhi's reply was to state a new rule of Satyagraha: that you should always trust your adversary. This proposition set off the first mutiny he had ever confronted outside his own household. A Pathan sprang up and asked him if Indians would still have to be fingerprinted. He answered that an opting-out clause was envisaged. However, he himself would submit, and urge the rest to do likewise. Yes, he had earlier concurred with their view that the demand was an outrage not to be borne. But circumstances had changed. Fingerprinting would now be a badge of honour.

For the Pathan, this was too much. 'We have heard', he yelled, 'that you have betrayed the community and sold it to General Smuts for £15,000.'

The accusation was a blunder. Gandhi brushed it aside as not worth refuting, and had the audience with him again. He ended by saying that he would set the example by giving his own ten prints at the head of the queue.

Up to a point, events justified his faith. The new permits turned out to be a decided improvement. On 10 February he went to lead the registration, and his troubles began. A policy destined to a bad end had a bad start.

He called in at his office on the way. Another Pathan named Mir Alam was hanging about outside with some cronies. Mir Alam was a client of his, a mattress-maker, over six feet tall and powerfully built. Today he looked sullen. Gandhi glanced up into his face and greeted him warily but politely. A number of colleagues assembled, including Thambi Naidu and Essop Mia, the chairman of the Satyagraha Association. They set off together, aware that they were being followed. Shortly before they reached the permit bureau in Von Brandis Square, Mir Alam quickened his pace and caught up with them. He now had seven companions.

'Where are you going?' he said.

Gandhi confirmed that he meant to register and give a complete set of fingerprints. As he spoke, one of Mir Alam's party lifted a cudgel and struck him a fierce blow on the head. Gasping 'Hey Rama!'—'O God!'—he sank to the pavement. The Pathans closed in, hitting him again and again. Thambi Naidu and Essop Mia tried to protect him, and were hurt themselves. Policemen ran up while the scuffle was still in progress and dragged off the assailants.

Gandhi, battered in the face and ribs, was carried fainting into a near-by office.

Three minutes' walk away his friend Joseph Doke, the Baptist minister, was chatting with Polak near the permit bureau. A young Indian rushed toward them shouting, 'Coolie he hit Mr Gandhi; come quick!' They hurried after him and found the street crowded with Indians. Doke fought his way through, collected Gandhi, and took him to his own manse. A doctor was sent for. The Registrar of Asiatics also arrived, much disturbed, and agreed at Gandhi's insistence to fetch the forms, so that he could still be the first to register. Mrs Doke made him comfortable and their small daughter charmed him by singing 'Lead, kindly light'. Since he had heard it quoted at the Congress meeting it had become his favourite Christian hymn.

This affair, characteristically, put to him in practical terms a familiar poser which for most advocates of non-violence remains theoretical—what they would do in the case of a crude assault, against themselves or anybody else within reach. (In England the protagonists have usually been 'a great hulking German' and 'your sister'.) Gandhi in fact had not defended himself, and the Satyagrahis with him did little more than get in the way. He refused to take part in the prosecution of Mir Alam, who was jailed on the testimony of witnesses. But his son Harilal asked him point-blank: 'What should I have done, if I'd been there?' and he answered, 'Fight.' Satyagraha never meant total pacifism, still less passivity. 'Where there is a choice only between cowardice and violence,' Gandhi wrote, 'I would advise violence.' That crucial sentence occurs in an article of his in the paper *Young India* for 11 August 1920.

The assault brought him some sympathy from Europeans. Smuts himself sent a message. But expressions of goodwill, if not accompanied by support for his cause, never interested him much. Over the past months he had had especially depressing encounters with clergymen, who turned up at his office with kind words, and ended by either trying to convert him or urging him to surrender. The unusual thing about Doke was that he turned up in the same way during December, and simply offered to help—which he proceeded to do, despite the annoyance of his flock. As Kasturbai and the boys were at Phoenix, Gandhi stayed with the Dokes for ten days of convalescence. Toward all his dubious-looking callers they showed an impartial courtesy. When Satyagraha entered its next phase, the minister edited *Indian Opinion* with gusto and encyclopaedic competence.

Not many were like him. However, Gandhi's seasoned European disciples—West, Polak, Kallenbach, Kitchin—were all carrying on. Also he enjoyed the unstinted devotion of his two office typists: first a Scottish girl; then her successor Sonja Schlesin, introduced by Kallenbach, Jewish like himself and Polak. Sonja was young and bouncing and on the plump side, but dedicated almost beyond belief, scornful of fatigue and danger, and fully equal to running the whole movement when its leaders were in prison. She made herself indispensable to Doke at *Indian Opinion*. Gandhi's middle-aged reminiscences of Sonja, who remained single, were to verge on the imprudent. Her advent was a foretaste of a problem he was a long time solving.

But few Europeans had thrown themselves into the ranks beside the Indians, and few were to do so in the campaign's later stages. Most white support was sympathetic rather than militant, a little chorus of liberal dissent against the clamour of mass opinion. Hosken had formed a committee that kept communications open between the two sides. People of kindred outlook included Albert Cartwright and another editor, Vere Stent of the *Pretoria News*, who had formed a good impression of Gandhi during the Boer War; a handful of clergymen; Olive Schreiner, author of *The Story of an African Farm;* and Emily Hobhouse, who had scandalized her aristocratic relations by being pro-Boer, done relief work in Kitchener's concentration camps, and won the respectful friendship of Smuts—which she retained.

Fortified in some degree by the knowledge that these allies existed, nearly all Indians followed Gandhi's lead and registered voluntarily. The outcries and menaces of extremists, mostly Pathans like Mir Alam, were overridden. Clearly it was time for Smuts to carry out his promise. But nothing happened. Apart from a minor administrative change, the Black Act remained in force.

4

Gandhi was shocked. The sceptics could now say, 'We told you so.' They added that after this fiasco he would find it hard to get

Satyagraha moving again. But although he spoke of 'foul play' he kept his head, insisted that a revival was feasible, and wrote to Smuts asking for elucidation. Cartwright and Hosken also tried. The General, it appeared, had shifted his ground. In January he had offered to repeal the Act if 'most' Indians registered. Soon afterwards he had implied in a speech that 'most' meant 'all'. That in itself was not fatal, because the gap was narrow. But now he was claiming that repeal had never been promised. Cartwright's recollection tallied with Gandhi's, but the discussion had been so informal that there seemed to be no way to pin Smuts down. Perhaps, even, a genuine misunderstanding had taken place; perhaps a qualifying phrase had been uttered and forgotten. However, the farthest Smuts would go was to offer repeal if Indians in the Transvaal would consent to immigration controls making the entry of any more—especially the educated kind whom the whites were afraid of—almost impossible. In other words they were to barter away the rights of their fellowcountrymen outside. Neither Gandhi nor his colleagues could accept such a bargain.

During the useless correspondence, he worked up the community for another round of Truth-Force. He held meetings and poured out articles. The next move, as he sketched it, was to be bolder. All the Indians who had trustingly registered were to hand in their new certificates to their leaders. An ultimatum demanding repeal would be sent to the Transvaal Government. If no undertaking was received by a certain date, the certificates would be burnt.

The response was lively, and the ultimatum was dispatched. Its polite but firm tone consolidated white opinion behind Smuts. Boers and English were outraged at Indians addressing them in the language of equals. Every member of the Transvaal Assembly rallied to the defence of civilization.

At 4 p.m. on 16 August 1908, when the ultimatum expired, most of the Indians in Johannesburg gathered in the grounds of the Haminia Mosque. Satyagraha's officers were beginning to learn showmanship. On the platform stood a huge cauldron, two thousand returned certificates, and a tin of paraffin. Just as the meeting started, a cyclist rode up with a telegram containing the Government's long-delayed answer. This was a flat 'No' which roused the audience to a frenzy of cheering. Gandhi made a speech about the negotiations, and then said that anybody who wanted his certificate back could have it. Of course nobody did. The speech was punc-

tuated with shouts of 'Burn them! Burn them!' Afterwards Mir
Alam (who had served his sentence for the assault) strode to the
platform, clasped Gandhi's hand, and gave him his own old permit
to be burnt with the new ones. It was the clinching gesture. Gandhi
had been proved right and his critics wrong. Without swerving
from his deadpan appeal to facts, he had reawakened Satyagraha
completely. The certificates vanished into the cauldron; the paraffin
was poured over them; and Essop Mia applied a match.

This time the event was taken up by the popular press in England.
The *Daily Mail* drew a comparison with the Boston Tea Party.

The second struggle was like the first, only more so—longer,
more embittered, and more inventive. Gandhi set up headquarters
in his office, at the corner of Rissik and Anderson Streets. The
whole campaign was organized from two sparsely furnished rooms,
decorated with pictures of Jesus and Annie Besant. At first the
authorities tried to damp it down by masterly inactivity. But he
manœuvred them into a position where inactivity would be merely
inept. Even before the burning, he had taken a step which he had
refused to take in 1907. He had broadened the front.

In doing so he was not departing from the rules of Satyagraha.
A tough Immigrants' Restriction Bill had been passed by the
Transvaal Legislature in the midst of the registration dispute. As
this was a by-product of the Black Act itself, and as the main emphasis had shifted to the right of entry, it was judged to be a proper
target for the Indians' defiance. They fought it by a test immigration. Out of several volunteers a Parsee named Sorabji was chosen,
an educated young man whom there was no tenable reason for
keeping out. He gave Pretoria due warning and entered the Transvaal from Natal at the border post of Volksrust. Everyone expected
that he would be stopped and put in the jail there. But the immigration officer, at a loss, let him through to Johannesburg. Then
he was summoned to appear in court, given a week to leave, and,
on his refusal, sentenced to a month's imprisonment with hard
labour.

Promptly a procession of further immigrants began to stream
after him. They included Gandhi's son Harilal and some old Natal
friends, such as the trader Rustomji who had once sheltered his
family. Meanwhile Indians already in the Transvaal were busy
with new devices for getting themselves into the hands of the police.
More hawkers traded without licences, and men who were not

hawkers took up that occupation so that they could do likewise. Arrest followed arrest till Volksrust and other jails were crammed. All Satyagrahis were given hard labour. The prisoners were separated and made to do stone-breaking and similar jobs, out of doors, in cold weather. Several died. But others, the moment they were released, broke the law again by leaving the Transvaal and re-entering. Some served as many as five terms in succession, and at one stage 2,500 of the 13,000 Transvaal Indians were in prison simultaneously. Those not in prison were harried by unofficial methods. Kachhalia Sheth, who became chairman of the Association that Autumn, was hounded to bankruptcy by white creditors trying to squeeze him into surrender. But faith in the leader was absolute. Even the disreputable Sheikh Mehtab (who was still in South Africa) joined the army of Truth. As a hawker put it to Doke: 'Mr Gandhi, he know. If he say go to prison, we go.'

In October Gandhi himself was arrested and sentenced to two months' hard labour at Volksrust. Doke wrote an eloquent description:

He looked thin and unkempt. . . . Two children, greatly attached to him, accompanied their friend on his return march to the Fort . . . (but) his face was 'steadfastly set to go to Jerusalem', and he saw nothing but that.

I wonder what he saw in that long march. Not the immediate Jerusalem, I imagine—the place of crucifixion. . . . The Fort, with its cells and its hateful associations. Those long files of prisoners. The white-clad, brutal native warders, swaggering along with their naked assegais. The lash for the obdurate, and the criminal taint for all. A city whose secrets may not be told: from whose dens children emerge criminals, and criminals infinitely worse than when they entered.

No, not that; it is another Jerusalem which he faces steadfastly . . . a new Jerusalem, whose beautiful gates are open to all nations.

As a prisoner Gandhi went out to work with thirty Satyagrahis, digging in hard soil. The season was growing hotter. He was soon blistered and exhausted, while others were weeping, limping, fainting. Once more he had to bear the responsibility. He had not only incited them but taught them to embrace punishment with ardour. And this was the reality, this was what his ideals were imposing on them, even if they did profess to be willing. All he could do was to tell himself very firmly that he could not have advised differently.

This imprisonment was followed by another in February 1909 lasting three months, first at Volksrust and then at Pretoria. Harilal also was arrested, and a warder at Pretoria mistook the father for the son. Despite a marginal greying of the hair, it did not occur to him that a Gandhi still so young-looking could be the arch-villain in person.

But Gandhi's jail treatment during the second campaign was not calculated to keep that error alive. He was put in a solitary cell, and at first had neither books nor enough light to read them. The warders abused and hustled him when he washed, and in the lavatory, where they watched him and called 'Sammy, come out!' Also he had a bad night in another cell with some Negroes and Chinese convicted of crimes of violence. Two of them seemed to be contemplating a homosexual assault, and his ignorance of their languages made the ordeal peculiarly nightmarish.

However, he obtained permission to read again, and even Smuts sent him books. He got through about thirty during these two terms. Besides continuing with Tolstoy he studied some Hindu religious works, and Emerson, and Thoreau. Salt's *Plea for Vegetarianism* had introduced him to Thoreau as a name at least, and in 1907 he had discovered the American's essay on Civil Disobedience and summarized it in *Indian Opinion*. The occasion of the essay was Thoreau's refusal to pay his taxes in protest against slavery and the Mexican war. It was hardly a protest to be ranked beside Gandhi's: Thoreau was taken to prison, but a friend paid the taxes for him and he came out. Still, his point was made. Gandhi naturally found the essay exciting, and explored Thoreau's writings further.

Under the stress of experience, his understanding of Tolstoy was deepening. In 1909 and '10, at the very end of the Russian's long life, they exchanged some letters. Tolstoy spoke of him as the 'Transvaal Hindu', a 'touching' correspondent close in spirit to himself, and gave a blessing to his work as 'the most important now being done in the world'. The aged novelist's message of nonviolence and love impressed Gandhi as much as ever, although, not being a frequent reader of fiction, he never made his acquaintance as a novelist. In prison he did read *Dr. Jekyll and Mr. Hyde*. Another of his prison books, Carlyle's *French Revolution*, confirmed his convictions by its portrayal of violence in practice, and also led him to suspect that Europe had no cure for the troubles of Indians. With such thoughts in his mind he served his three-month sentence, and emerged unsubdued to resume leadership.

In June 1909 he sailed to England again. The chief motive was that Smuts and Botha were there, negotiating the union of the South African colonies into a single Dominion. Gandhi hoped to put a word in. Impeccably dressed, top hat and all, he went about London talking with everyone he could get hold of. Besides finding time to admire the rising Suffragette movement, he met Morley again, and Lord Crewe, the Colonial Secretary. Lord Ampthill consulted Botha and Smuts on his behalf, but reported that they were set on a racist policy and would offer only minor concessions. Ampthill also contributed a preface to a book published in support of the mission—the first Life of Gandhi. Joseph Doke was the author. Sub-titling it 'An Indian Patriot in South Africa', he depicted his subject as a political figure with religious interests, not as a religious figure with political interests.

More important than Gandhi's talks with Morley and Crewe were some contacts with Indian revolutionaries, 'anarchists' as he called them. Their arguments turned his attention seriously to his own country's future. The outcome was a pamphlet, *Hind Swaraj*, 'Indian Home Rule'. He wrote this in Gujarati on the voyage back in November, thirty thousand words in ten days on the ship's stationery, using each hand alternately to rest the other. It was serialized in *Indian Opinion*. A copy went off to Tolstoy.

But *Hind Swaraj* would belong to the next phase of Gandhi's life. It had no bearing on his unfinished business in South Africa. When he returned to the slow ordeal, he learned that Smuts was trying a 'Niggers Go Home' policy. The Transvaal was deporting Indians back to India—though many had not come from there, had never even seen India. The measure caused a near-panic, as it was meant to do, but still no general surrender. As an anguished and bewildered shipload was about to embark at Durban, Gandhi, who was in the town, suddenly spoke to one of his co-workers named P. K. Naidu.

'Will you escort these poor brothers to India?'
'Why not?' said Naidu.
'But the steamer is starting just now.'
'Very well, I'm ready.'

'What about your clothes and food?'

'The suit I have on will be enough, and I can get food on board.'
Naidu had never been to India himself.

The deportations were doubtfully legal, and Gandhi managed
to check them by court action. The battle slackened. With an adroit
shift in tactics, Smuts was teaching his police to thwart Indians by
not arresting them too readily. Many were set free, many weakened.
The hard core of Satyagraha dwindled to less than a hundred. But
it held firm, and the Black Act remained unenforceable. Notorious
resisters went on being pulled back into jail at intervals. In the
Diepkloof Convict Prison some of them went on hunger strike, then
a novelty.

Again Gandhi had to come to grips with the problem of suffering
inflicted in virtue's name. His few dozen stalwarts, constantly in
and out of prison, were unemployable. The plight of their wives
and children was desperate. Hitherto he had cushioned the effect
of jail terms with cash grants to dependants. But this new crop of
chronic victims could not be so easily dealt with. Most of them
were in Johannesburg where the cost of living was high; and in
keeping with his convictions about money, no large fund had been
allowed to accumulate. Satyagraha required a haven, where families
could dwell in safety together with subsistence assured.

Phoenix might have served if it had not been so far away. The
solution came from Kallenbach. He owned a farm of 1,100 acres
near Lawley, twenty-one miles from Johannesburg, and on 30 May
1910 he gave the Satyagrahis the use of it without charge. The
property was on level open ground, overlooked by low hills. Its thousand fruit trees provided in season enough oranges, plums and apri-
cots to feed as many residents as might be expected. It had two wells
and a spring. Under the name of Tolstoy Farm it became a second
Phoenix.

Gandhi—who had transferred most of his legal practice to Ritch
—was able to stay there himself a great deal of the time, and to
keep his own family there. The men dressed in western labourer's
clothes and, as before, did as much as possible for themselves. They
built accommodation for seventy people out of timber and corrugated iron. Remembering his happy glimpse of the Trappists, he
arranged for Kallenbach to learn sandal-making at Mariann Hill,
and then teach it at the farm. Carpentry flourished, also under the
direction of Kallenbach, and so did home bakery and other activi-

ties. Gandhi personally sewed some jackets for Kasturbai and assured everybody that she actually wore them.

The main difference from Phoenix lay in the number of children and adolescents. Quite by accident Gandhi became involved in education. For once his own sons got a kind of schooling, together with the orphans of Truth-Force (though some of these were so disreputable that Kallenbach tut-tutted at their being put with the Gandhi boys). He still preferred character-forming to academic instruction, and used few textbooks. His pupils worked in the orchard and garden. Besides elementary training in the three R's, history, and geography, he gave them some religious teaching with due regard to the various beliefs of their parents, summing up the tenets of Hinduism, Islam and so forth as best he could. He read them stories from the *Mahabharata* and discovered and recommended *Gulliver's Travels*. Prayer—'the key of the morning and the bolt of the evening', as he once described it—was always practised punctiliously.

The school was mixed, not only because it would have been hard to run otherwise, but on theoretical grounds. He was determined that the sexes should learn to co-exist sensibly. Boys and girls worked together, bathed together and slept together: not in couples, however, but in groups, and normally with a chaperon near. On the whole the experiment succeeded. Once, when two girls did complain of improper advances, Gandhi persuaded them to let him cut their hair short. A cropped head would mean 'hands off'. Everybody entered into the spirit of the gesture. At Tolstoy he showed a courage and clear-headedness in this respect that temporarily deserted him later, when his own sexuality revived and sapped his faith in human nature.

He was happy not only about the boys and girls but about diet and everything else that interested him. He experimented with fasting, and mud poultices, and feeding typhoid patients on bananas and olive oil. This was the time when he gave up milk and lived almost entirely on fruit, a course in which he persisted for five years. It suited him. He still thought nothing of walking forty miles in a day, with a bag of chocolate-coated almonds (his favourite sweet) to appease any pang of hunger. The Indian Messiah of the 1920s used to look back on this kibbutz idyll, with the down-at-heel heroes coming and going, and speak of it wistfully as his finest hour.

5

A modern racist regime would have suppressed Tolstoy Farm, probably on moral grounds. But Smuts and Botha left it alone. That was a tactical mistake. Its quiet prosperity steadied the waverers through a dreary phase and helped them to regain their nerve. In 1911 it was plain that although the conflict was muted, although there was even talk of a 'provisional settlement', there was not going to be any mass capitulation.

At this juncture the Indian Congress leader Gokhale stepped in. He was deeply concerned. A year or two before, he had convoyed Polak on a speaking tour through India, raised £5,000 for Satya-graha, and persuaded the Viceroy's Council to suspend the recruitment of indentured labour for South Africa—or at any rate, recommend suspension. Now he was anxious to pin down the provisional settlement and get Gandhi back where he belonged. With British approval, but not without difficulty, he reached Cape Town on 22 October 1912. The Union authorities could hardly snub him once he was there. They offered him hospitality, they exempted him from the colour bar on railways, they even (grudgingly) let Indians decorate the stations. In Johannesburg Kallenbach erected a triumphal arch.

The ageing Gokhale was unfortunately too frail for the ambitious programme proposed by Gandhi, but he made a number of speeches which were well received. South Africans who despised their local Asians were more disposed to listen to one from outside. They hailed him, somewhat ambiguously, as a Coolie King. After visiting the Union's larger cities, he went to talk with Botha and Smuts in Pretoria. Gandhi judged it tactful not to accompany him, but supplied him with a written statement. Armed with this, he met the ministers in a two-hour session, and reappeared full of optimism. The Black Act would be repealed, and, in Natal, the £3 tax on labourers who had served their indenture would be abolished. He sailed on 17 November. Gandhi stayed on the boat as far as Zanzibar undergoing a copious briefing on Indian politics, into which Gokhale expected to initiate him within a year. At a subsequent meeting in Bombay Gokhale told the audience: 'Gandhi has in him the marvellous spiritual power to turn ordinary men around him into heroes and martyrs.' He meant it; but he left this wonder-worker pondering a private warning that the spiritual power was not unalloyed with a domineering quality, which frightened people into accepting burdens too heavy for them.

The mediator had failed to extract any promises in writing. Gandhi, having been through all this before, was sceptical. What in fact ensued was that Asiatic matters were transferred from provincial to Union jurisdiction. The Black Act, as such, vanished from the statute book, but the position of Indians was scarcely improved, and the £3 tax remained. Nothing more happened. On 14 March 1913 it became clear that nothing more was intended to happen. Instead of relaxing, the whites hit the Indians again from a new quarter. The Supreme Court ruled in a test case that Hindu, Muslim and Parsee marriages were invalid. Therefore Indian wives were concubines without status, liable to deportation, and the children were illegitimate. In the face of the resultant outcry the Government upheld its judges.

Without that ultimate insult Satyagraha, already in uncertain abeyance because of the 'settlement', might well have smouldered into extinction. Instead it erupted. Another of Gandhi's special tactics was born. 'The beauty of non-violent war', as he once remarked, 'is that women can play the same part in it as men.' He suddenly found himself heading, or rather swept along by, a cohort of furious and exalted maenads. Apparently the Government had quite failed to foresee the effect of telling thousands of Indian women that they were living in sin and that their children were bastards. Young mothers and the consorts of solid merchants began demonstrating in the hope of being arrested. Kasturbai herself, stigmatized as a mere mistress and not to be outdone, at last offered Mohandas her active services. When that point was reached, there could be no doubt. The time had come for him to take a fresh initiative. He asked Smuts for the instant implementation of the promise about the Natal tax, coupling this request with a threat to broaden Satyagraha again. If no satisfactory answer came, he would advise Indians liable to the tax not to pay it, and labourers working under indenture to go on strike. The new action would if necessary be Union-wide.

No answer did come, satisfactory or otherwise. At once a group of women crossed over from the Transvaal into the Natal coalfield, where many Indians worked. In response to their impassioned appeals at the first pits they came to, the miners walked out.

And finally the nerve of the opposition began to crack. South Africa's mining magnates were already embroiled with their white labour. A coloured strike, hitherto unheard-of, was a portent to horrify. The coal-owners summoned Gandhi to Durban and tried to shake his account of the broken pledge. Botha and Smuts, when queried, denied having given it, but a colleague who had been present significantly declined to confirm their statements. Then Gokhale—in the midst of another speaking tour on the African crisis—cabled from India that he had no doubt whatsoever.

The women agitators were rounded up by the police, whereupon the strike spread farther through an outraged community. Coal-owners began to talk of flogging, and cut off the light and water supply in company houses. Gandhi exhorted the strikers to quit their homes as pilgrims. Albert Christopher, an Indian Christian, opened a camp near Newcastle where they could take refuge with their families. About four thousand people assembled, bringing only a few necessities in pathetic bundles on their heads. They slept out on the veldt high above sea-level, living chiefly on rice, bread and sugar donated by sympathisers. None had second thoughts. With the long-delayed entry of the women and industrial workers, Satyagraha was soaring at last.

On 28 October Gandhi struck camp and shifted his improvised republic to Charlestown, the starting-point of that hideous coach ride twenty years back. Hundreds more joined him there, with stories of terrorism and violence against the strikers left in the coal-field. On 6 November, having warned Smuts's secretary by telephone and got a contemptuous answer, he advanced the more able-bodied to Volksrust: 2,037 men, 127 women, 57 children. Sonja Schlesin and Kallenbach (who was having to cope with absurd challenges to duels) stayed in Charlestown looking after the other women and children, and the older men. The army led by Gandhi was to invade the Transvaal and make for Tolstoy Farm. Either they would all be arrested, he reasoned, or they would reach Tolstoy and make it their headquarters. While he was trying to explain this to a Volksrust border official, the entire mass—ragged, poverty-stricken, shining-eyed—surged forward cheering. Policemen scattered and the Indians, in a do-or-die mood, were through.

They tramped on to Standerton, still following the ghost of the iniquitous coach, and covering twenty-five miles a day. Panic spread before them. Gandhi was twice arrested, and twice released on bail because no one else could keep the column under control. To the marchers he was 'Bapu', Father, as among his own sons and guests. The women and children had to halt, but nearly all the men were with him on 9 November when he left Standerton and headed for Greylingstad. Polak had joined him, and was appointed deputy leader in anticipation of yet another arrest. This in due course occurred. Then Polak was served with an order to shepherd the marchers into three special trains drawn up at Balfour, for shipment back to Natal and prison. By the exasperating logic of Satyagraha such a reverse was a victory, and Polak complied, exerting the little pressure that was needed.

Within a few days the cells were packed again. Gandhi's joyful martyrs included women condemned to hard labour, and forcibly vaccinated as threats to public health. Old men, boys and young girls endured the test; some died, smiling. Polak and Kallenbach were hauled in to stand trial with Gandhi. All three testified against each other and thereby obtained three-month terms in Volksrust. Albert West hung on at Phoenix. But as thousands more miners downed tools in sympathy, and were joined by fifty thousand indentured labourers, Phoenix became a rendezvous and West too was jailed. The authorities gave the mine compounds the status of temporary prisons, and the strikers were fenced in with wire netting. Mounted military police tried to drive them back to the coal-face, using rifles and whips, but without success.

Smuts had gone too far. Suppression was reduced to absurdity and worse. Another stalemate was out of the question, because of opinion overseas. The Viceroy of India, communicating through a distressed British Cabinet, was asking peremptorily for negotiations. On 18 December Gandhi was set free. At a meeting in Durban shortly afterwards he appeared in Indian dress without concessions to Europe—as a sign of mourning for the dead strikers, he said. His feet were bare and he had shaved his moustache.

In January 1914 came his last move, and it was decisive. Having announced a second mass march, he cancelled it when the white railway workers struck on their own account. Satyagrahis, he declared, would not take advantage of an opponent's accidental difficulties. The moral impact was overwhelming. Messages of congratulation poured in from England, India, even South Africa.

Partly because of the gathering wrath abroad, partly because of an appeal from his valued friend Emily Hobhouse, Smuts agreed to parley again. The Government set up a commission on Indian grievances. The main demands were for the end of the £3 tax, the recognition of marriages, the easing of immigration and residence controls, and the rundown of the indentured labour system. All these demands were met. The Union Parliament passed an Indians' Relief Bill, Gandhi and Smuts adjusted various details between them, and in an exchange of letters at the end of June 1914 they metaphorically shook hands. The General accepted a parting gift —a pair of sandals made by his adversary in prison—and wore them on his farm each summer, till he returned them as a compliment on Gandhi's seventieth birthday.

Truth-Force had triumphed. That was the judgement of most vocal Indians (though some of the Muslims had reservations), and of well-disposed foreigners, such as Gilbert Murray. But had it?

In 1931 the two protagonists met again. Recalling their conflict, Smuts observed: 'I did not give you such a bad time as you gave me.' 'I did not know that,' Gandhi replied. The remark is illuminating. He was so utterly wedded to his concepts as not to recognize that there had been a real fight involving the hurting and humbling of an enemy. He persisted in thinking that the end was a conversion. Here he was wrong. The prevailing white attitudes had not altered. Smuts indeed had acquired a soldierly respect for him which was to grow into admiration. But even Smuts, on Gandhi's departure from South Africa, wrote to a private correspondent: 'The saint has left our shores; I hope for ever.'

By confining the attack to a narrow front, on Satyagrahi principles, the 'saint' had broken through to his objectives. But he had also excluded the only kind of campaign that might have made a difference to South Africa. Apart from his joint action with a few Chinese, he had never attempted to enlist a non-Indian people. Therefore he had never directly challenged white racist supremacy as such. Myriads of Negroes were all around him; he liked them, he knew them to be oppressed; yet he never made them his allies, because the particular laws which he was combating did not apply to them. Satyagraha in South Africa was purely a minority movement, and the end left a question mark overhanging its claims. Several discriminatory laws still stood, and afterwards, when the Indians had to rely on second-rate leadership, most of the ground gained was lost. Smuts's son even claimed that they had been beaten.

But their champion, setting out for his homeland in a state close to apotheosis, had no misgivings. In his farewell speech at Johannesburg he flung bouquets in all directions, praising everybody concerned, including the supposedly reformed General. He sincerely believed in his moral revolution, and saw immense possibilities ahead. Kasturbai, sitting beside him as consort to the guest of honour, listened and seemed to acquiesce.

On 18 July they sailed, taking the boys and Kallenbach. Gokhale was in England, and they intended to go there first and return to India with him. Kasturbai wore a white sari with a flower design and looked tired. Her husband, also a trifle haggard, had gone back to his European suit. He realized that India had become a strange land to him, and that the future was obscure. But he travelled light, for ever free from expensive tastes and a clutter of possessions, trusting in divine guidance. He might have said, quoting that beloved hymn (indeed he probably did say)—

> I do not ask to see
> The distant scene; one step enough for me.

An odd incident happened on the voyage. Kallenbach had a weakness for binoculars, and owned a pair costing £7. In Gandhi's view this toy was a moral encumbrance. One day, in their cabin, he pressed the point so hard that they quarrelled, like medieval Franciscans disputing over poverty. Both were unhappy that the binoculars should generate so much heat.

'Why not just throw them in the sea?' he exclaimed.

'All right,' said Kallenbach.

'I mean it.'

'So do I.'

Gandhi tossed them through the porthole.

VII

When the Pupil is Ready ...

1

India was profoundly changed. The restlessness which Gandhi had noted during his last visit had been more than a mood. By 1914 its significance and effects were patent.

About the turn of the century, educated Indians had begun shedding their sense of inferiority. They dared to question the virtue of British rule and even its necessity. When Gandhi finally started homeward, they had progressed from grumbling unease to articulate demands for power. There was no upsurge among the masses, but there was a threatening ferment among the thoughtful.

Indian nationalism—groping, divided, but now at last a reality—was a resultant of several forces. The British themselves, who had inflicted such deep humiliation, were also fostering India's recovery from it. Few of them saw that they were doing so. Yet the benefits of the Empire were preparing its fall, as surely as its sins were. In the quarter-century before 1914 Britain was building an India with a capacity for statehood. The country was free from war, and united by railways, a far greater mileage than independent China possessed. With a more mobile populace, the barriers of caste and language were cracking. Medical services, on however mean a budget, had at least loosened the stranglehold of disease. So also with famine, which the authorities were learning to combat by distributing local surpluses and spreading purchasing power through public works.

The regime gave India central rule and an efficient civil service. It gave India homogeneous laws and education, even though the education was Anglicized. Therefore, in spite of itself, it gave India nationalism—or at any rate a field for nationalism to flourish in. Admittedly the best of the old Hindu political talent had gone into eclipse with the decay of the villages. These were now sunk in utter

127

depression, with their crafts ruined and their·debt-ridden peasants unemployed at least four months of the year. But on the other hand, the Government had accepted some industrialization. By 1914 India had a million factory hands, not a vast number, but not negligible. Most of the firms were British-owned, paying huge dividends wrung from workers in frightful conditions. Yet even these meant a growing urban life with new energies, soon to expand strongly with the industrial boom brought by the war. Furthermore, some were not British-owned. Names like Tata and Birla were heralding the rise of a native capitalism.

The Congress chiefs whom Gandhi had met spoke for the thrusting middle class, which the rulers had nurtured for their own ends, but did not know what to do with. It was liberal in outlook and not too much concerned about caste origins. Indian business men and professional men were seeping into the lower strata of administration. Elective city councils, set up as early as 1883 by the enlightened Lord Ripon, gave many of them their start in politics. Like their fathers, most of them admired libertarian England and swore by John Stuart Mill. But the bitter contrast between that Utopia in the distance and the despotism of its agents around them was always before their eyes. Cautiously, but more boldly as time went on, they appealed to the English at home against the English in India. Their appeals went unheard, or nearly so. Indian parliamentary debates emptied the House. The Indians, however, kept trying.

Their own shadow-parliament was Congress. It continued to meet annually in various places. Its demand for more democratic legislative councils had had some marginal effect on official policy. It was less successful in speeding the intake of Indians into the Civil Service, which remained predominantly British, and almost solidly so at levels that mattered. As long as this was the trend, the Government showed no outright enmity toward Congress. Confined to liberal hands, nationalism could scarcely be nationalism at all. The liberals were rootless. While professing to speak for India, they distrusted the masses (especially the rural masses) and lacked sympathetic contact with almost everybody who had not gone to the same schools. Their secular view of politics weakened whatever hope they had of wide influence over a religious population. Even within their own circle, there were few with clear notions of what they wanted or what the progress of India implied.

The liberals could hardly have expected to be the unchallenged vanguard indefinitely; and they were not. From about 1894 onward another voice was heard in Congress and also outside it—the voice of a nationalism that was authentic and fervent. This did not aim at gently nudging the British toward a transfer of power, but at getting rid of them, and founding a nation on a basis of Hindu culture. Its prophet was Bal Gangadhar Tilak, known as the Lokamanya or 'Respected of the People'. When Gandhi met Tilak in 1896, at the same time as he met Gokhale, the Lokamanya remarked in an Olympian tone on the visitor's ignorance of Indian politics. Though it was Gokhale who remedied that failing, it was Tilak whose heir Gandhi became—partly by implementing his programme, more by reacting against the way it was implemented by Tilak himself.

Tilak's party was not simply an extremist wing of the liberal body. It reflected a new growth in Hinduism, and the partial merging of the earlier revivalist movements into a more Gangetic stream. The spiritual basis of Congress, so far as it had any, was the Brahmo Samaj. Brahmo teaching (especially in Bengal, the heart of thinking India) had enabled a good fraction of the intelligentsia to westernize without breaking away from Hindu culture entirely. However, there had been splits and secessions, and the pallid Brahmo rationalism was losing attractiveness. Swami Dayananda's Arya Samaj, with its militant Vedic faith, showed more staying power yet could not broaden its appeal. The trouble with both these bodies was their desire to trim Hinduism into shape. The reformers tended to be cliquish and priggish. When they saw the masses clinging to orthodoxy, with its charivari of myth and taboo and ritual, they drew away. So much the worse for the masses, who were dragging India down! Some who did want to bridge the gap flirted with Theosophy. In Annie Besant's hands this was moving leftward and branching out. But few could embrace it as the answer.

What the wiser sort of Hindu desired to see was a patriotic religious renaissance. For many years Hinduism had been so chaotic as to rule this out. But the British regime promoted religious unity as well as political. Also, there was the challenge of Christianity. It spurred Hindus to pull their own religion together. The materials of a new cohesion—the shared scriptures, the common ceremonies and devotions—were ready to hand throughout India. Western scholars were providing a firmer intellectual basis.

The renaissance came. It was this, to a very large extent, that laid the groundwork for the true nationalism which Tilak fathered and Gandhi transmuted. In Hindu philosophic tradition, great importance attaches to the special relation between the *guru* or master and the *chela* or pupil. 'When the pupil is ready,' the saying goes, 'the master appears.'

2

The process of making India ready can be traced as far back as 1875, when Keshab Chandra Sen was head of the Brahmo Samaj. His western leanings were strong, his attacks on Hinduism outspoken. That March, however, at Dakshineswar near Calcutta, he talked with a Hindu mystic. Thenceforward he mellowed toward his own world. Still liberal, still pro-Christian, he no longer insisted that India must bow to England. 'I am a child of Asia,' he wrote. 'Her sorrows are my sorrows, her joys are my joys.' Several of his colleagues visited the same mystic with the same result.

But the impact of this remarkable person was not to be confined within the intellectuals' debating clubs. His name was Ramakrishna and he was grotesquely unlike an intellectual. At the period of his Brahmo contacts he was about forty. As a youth—a dreamy, emotional youth—he had become a priest at the Dakshineswar temple. After prolonged and agonized aspiration he saw a vision of Kali, the terrible goddess: not however as the patroness of the Thugs, but in her kindly aspect as Divine Mother. He went on to have many more visions, living in ecstasy through the whole history and mythology of Hinduism, and identifying himself with its characters. Friends took the unlettered seer in hand. They put him through a course of spiritual discipline and taught him Vedanta. Like Gandhi he took the vow of *brahmacharya*. As a mystic he attained the supreme goal of realized union with the One, and claimed to have resolved the argument over whether God is personal or impersonal, because 'God the Mother' was above that plane altogether. After traversing his own religion he tried others, and had visions of Muhammad and Christ.

Then it was over. Until his death in 1886, Ramakrishna was simply a shrewd, cheerful teacher, a fascinating talker in crisp Bengali, a courteous host. While lucidly sane, he was convinced that his experiences had all been valid. The effect on his hearers was disturbing yet compelling (as it is in the Gospels, where Christ speaks of himself as only a madman would, yet is manifestly not mad). Ramakrishna's genius lay in having reawakened a moribund order of things by realization. He had proved that the divine realm was 'there', so to speak. His quest had convinced him, and enabled him to convince others, that far more of popular Hinduism was true than the intelligentsia cared to admit . . . if only you looked at it in the right way. His own way was novel partly because it was affirmative, even joyous. Furthermore it confirmed several religions besides Hinduism. When he died, some Indians were already fore-shadowing a Gandhian practice by holding ecumenical prayer meetings, with readings from Hindu, Muslim, Parsee and Christian scriptures.

One reason why his teaching carried conviction was that it had practical effects with a distinctive flavour. He gathered a group of young disciples, to their parents' annoyance, and trained them to behave radically. They were given a special warning against the love of money—hence, against the liberal equation of progress with capitalism. For Ramakrishna the timely path of sainthood was the service of God in Man. He did not live to form any society for that purpose. But he did use his personal influence on behalf of the poor, once exerting pressure by fasting.

His chosen successor was Swami Vivekananda. Vivekananda was a well-read sceptic who had sampled the Brahmo Samaj without liking it, and then yielded to Ramakrishna's spell. After the seer's death he organized the disciples. A stalwart but critical patriot, he saw religious rebirth as the key to national rebirth. Hinduism would be the same popular faith, but re-stated, cleansed of superstition, and imbued with a social conscience. Touring the sub-continent in 1892, he swam to a rock off Cape Comorin at the southern tip, and looked back in imagination over India in her misery. 'We have to give back to the nation its lost individuality,' he said, 'and raise the masses'. His task was to 'find the common bases of Hinduism and awaken the national consciousness to them'. The result would be a spiritualized Socialism. 'I cannot believe in a religion that does not wipe out the widow's tears or bring a piece of bread to the orphan's mouth.'

Vivekananda translated the poetry of his master's visions into the prose of Vedanta. He pictured a reborn India evolving a world religion which would be 'the sum of all, with more beyond'. On a trip to America he made a profound impression. William James was among his admirers, and so, incidentally, was Sarah Bernhardt. At home he drove the disciples into action, especially in the neglected villages. He founded the Ramakrishna Order, the first in Hinduism to be dedicated to social service. Its monks undertook charitable and medical work, opened schools for Untouchables, and campaigned against the subjection of women.

Through Vivekananda Hindu reform grew broader and richer. His followers learned to be religious, patriotic and forward-looking at once. Orthodox Hinduism had been obsessed with the dismal Yuga myth, according to which the world is doomed to grow worse and nothing can be done about it. The earlier reformers had got as far as resuscitating what they said was the pure primitive Vedic faith, but it remained a static ideal, not leading anywhere. Vivekananda too claimed to be disinterring the ancient inheritance in its proper splendour. But he preached his true Hinduism as dynamic, an engine of human progress.

The Swami was that rarity among Hindus, a perceptive student of history. In 1896 he forecast a world upheaval ushered in by working-class revolutions, and, with clearer insight than the Marxists themselves, pointed to Russia and China. His fatal illness in 1902 came early, tragically frustrating the visit of Gandhi, who got no closer than reading one of his books. It was left to others to carry resurgent Hinduism into politics. This was the task which Tilak's party began, though they fell short of the full conception. While exploiting the new energy and pride, they damped down the self-criticism.

Tilak was a Maratha Brahmin from the Bombay area, an excellent Sanskrit scholar, an embittered and forceful personality. His forebears had been powerful and the British had forestalled their advance to greater power. His talents were oddly mixed with a kind of tactical bigotry. In trying to activate Hinduism as a mass movement against the foreigner, he was prepared to take it much as it was, resisting reform. In that spirit he promoted the cult of Kali as Ramakrishna had done, but in her fierce rather than her gentle aspect. He made the first attempts to organize peasants and factory workers, but with anti-Muslim as well as anti-British slogans. He founded festivals honouring Shivaji, a past Hindu fighter against the Muslims, and Ganpati, a god with an elephant's face. His conduct sometimes bore the stamp of that Hindu political amorality which had forced Gandhi to work out his own rules. Whereas Gandhi arrived at Satyagraha, Tilak stayed a shade too close to the Maurya handbooks of statecraft, which proclaim jungle law and the end justifying the means. He trained volunteers to fence with sticks, condoned terrorism, and came near to condoning murder.

But as his title of Lokamanya implied, he commanded respect. He was not afraid to go to jail for sedition—as he did, in 1897 and again ten years later. Also, he made a contribution to Indian political thought that paved the way for Gandhi as much as any single thing.

He wrote a commentary on the *Bhagavad Gita*. No Brahmin could fault it as unorthodox. Yet it transformed the current view of the poem by stressing its passages on the virtue of action. Gandhi of course had done the same for himself in his English and African isolation. But few other Hindus had. Now, under Tilak's tutelage, many caught up with him and passed him. The *Gita* became the gospel of militancy, which would-be patriotic leaders were expected to study and expound. Though Tilak wrote guardedly, his readers knew that he construed the dispirited Arjuna on the battlefield as a symbol of India, and Krishna's call to arms as a summons to rise. The poem's doctrine of selfless action, governed not by one's desires but by one's role in the scheme of things, became a command to act for *Loka samgraha*—the welfare of the world. Ruthlessness itself found a sanction. Krishna is very ruthless indeed, and his portrait includes hints, dangerous in the hands of a Tilak, that the champion of the world's welfare can be beyond good and evil.

One of the merits of the *Gita* was that it supplied a text for Vivekananda's hope of progress and renewal, even within the orthodox frame. Krishna says: 'Whenever and wherever *dharma* decays and unrighteousness prospers, I shall be born in successive ages for the purpose of destroying evildoers and re-establishing the supremacy of the moral law.' The *Gita* in fact admits that the world generally grows worse, but injects the idea of having a revolution from time to time, under divine auspices, to restore what has been lost. The revolutionary then has God on his side. For Tilakites the moral was plain.

It is a matter of profound psychological interest that this mystique of transfiguration, as one might call it, is not confined to Hinduism. Tilak and Vivekananda both proposed to reinstate the authentic, holy and ancient India, the India of heroes and saints and flourishing village-republics—not in a spirit of romantic nostalgia, but as a new beginning. In so doing they conformed to an archetype. Such a programme occurs again and again in revolutions, with far more potency than the liberal idea of progress. In the history of Israel, in Rome and Germany, in the utterances of Luther and Rousseau and even Lenin, it is repeated: the vision of the resurrection of a long-lost glory or promise, as the point of departure for a fresh start, with intervening corruption swept away. The Zionist wants to restore the Jews to their Promised Land, Luther wants to restore the Apostolic Church, Rousseau talks of bringing back the Natural Man. The roots of this mode of thought undoubtedly lie deep. The theme of a reversion to origins and a fresh start appears in primitive rituals of rebirth.

On the need for a fresh start for India, however conceived, Tilak and Vivekananda were in accord. One of the fieriest of the Tilakites was Aurobindo Ghose. After the death of Vivekananda, the Swami's brother joined a brother of Aurobindo to launch a paper called *The Yugantar,* meaning 'New Era'. It was the first frankly subversive organ to appear on Indian bookstalls.

There were people not yet old who could remember the Mutiny.

3

In 1904, when the impervious and climactic Curzon was still Viceroy, the shocks began. Japanese victories in the war with Russia sent a tremor of excitement south-westward. Asia, the militants exulted, was not finished after all. Then the Viceroy himself obliged them with an opening. Bengal was administratively clumsy, and he announced a plan to cut it in two. Partition as such might not have aroused any anger. But the scheme was to split the province into a mainly Hindu part and a mainly Muslim part. This meant divide-and-rule, the first step on the course of communal politics that was to lead to Pakistan.

Before the Mutiny the British regime had been, if anything, mildly pro-Hindu. But as the Hindus recovered their nerve, it swung the other way. Curzon—setting a precedent which his successors were to follow—proposed to stiffen the outnumbered Bengali Muslims by giving them a separate political structure which the Hindus could never hope to dominate.

The Congress line was to reject religious politics in favour of a secular state, the word 'secular' connoting not hostility to religion but neutrality. Congress therefore denounced the Bengal partition. Tilak denounced it too, not only because of its divide-and-rule aspect, but because it would set up half Bengal as a fortress against universal Hindu ascendancy. His chauvinism gave the Muslims a ground for fear, and the Viceroy an excuse. But when the measure was pushed through, in October 1905, Tilak and the liberals were able to combine in a programme of opposition. The Arya Samaj rallied to the Hindu cause. Aurobindo attempted terrorism. Surendranath Banerji, a journalist, twice President of Congress, led a boycott of British goods and a Buy Indian campaign with the battle-cry of Swadeshi, 'one's own country'—the Indian equivalent of Sinn Fein. Students made bonfires of British cloth.

Rabindranath Tagore, disillusioned with his once-adored English, emerged from the school which he was running and made one of his massive interventions in politics. He became a star anti-partition speaker, and tried to aid home industry by assisting co-operative societies and the revival of weaving. Set to a tune composed by him, a patriotic song taken from a novel achieved the status of an Indian Marseillaise. This was 'Bande Mataram', Hail Mother, meaning the Motherland (not, as worried Englishmen thought, Kali).

In 1906 Congress endorsed Swadeshi and passed its first resolution demanding Swaraj or Self-Rule. The venerable Dadabhai Naoroji presided. His speech, read for him by Gokhale, was answered by twenty thousand voices roaring 'Swaraj!' But some Muslims were already retorting with a Muslim League of their own. They had Britain's blessing, which grew warmer when the Aga Khan petitioned Lord Minto, the new Viceroy, to make the political separation of the communities a general policy. Moreover the Congressmen themselves could not hold together. Gokhale approved the boycott, but condemned Tilak's violence and the murders of officials to which it was leading. Pherozeshah Mehta, who had opened Gandhi's eyes to the profundity of Indian grievances, nevertheless took the same stand. The following year the Congress meeting broke up. Moderates and extremists pelted each other with their sandals and the extremists walked out. Tagore withdrew to his school.

In 1908 the Government began a series of concessions, known as the Morley-Minto reforms after the Secretary of State for India and the Viceroy. Provincial legislative councils were to have majorities of elected members. Middle-class liberals saw a wider prospect before them, and became more docile. Tilakites retorted that as the reforms envisaged separate Muslim electorates, they spelt divide-and-rule in another guise. In any case the councils had no power to make laws. They were advisory only, and Morley disclaimed any intention of preparing the way for a parliamentary system. But the moderates won. The extremists were weakened by the absence of their chief, who was in prison, and the suppression of *The Yugantar*. After a last bid to capture Congress, Aurobindo took refuge in scholarly retirement in the French city of Pondicherry.

The next Viceroy was Lord Hardinge, the same conciliatory statesman who pressed Smuts to settle with Gandhi. In 1911 George V and Queen Mary visited India. Amid liberal applause the King announced the cancelling of the Bengal partition and the transfer of the capital from Calcutta to Delhi. The object was to suggest that a new leaf was being turned. As war approached, Indian politics were superficially quieter.

Nationality, however, was gaining in other ways: not only through the religious revival, but through art, vernacular literature, and a sudden rush to catch up in science. Young men with a future, such as G.D. Birla of the millionaire industrial family, no longer regarded alien arrogance as a cross to be borne for ever. Congress was seeking a rapprochement with the Muslims, and they, annoyed at Britain's diplomatic softness toward Italy when that country attacked Turkey in 1911, were inclined to listen. One very able Muslim, Abul Kalam Azad, had started a paper to oppose separatism and weld the communities into a patriotic alliance. The revolt against Curzon had died away, like the concurrent Russian revolt against the Tsar; but in India as in Russia, there were the makings of another.

4

Gandhi had been only fitfully in touch with all this. But Tilak's remark about his political innocence was no longer true. The distant association with Dadabhai Naoroji had been followed by the much closer link with Gokhale. For anybody restricted to a single informant, Gokhale, on balance, was probably the best. He had emerged from the testing years as the most eminent of the moderates. His great mental powers, fine oratory and fluent English had won respect for the Swadeshi campaign. He was on good personal terms with Morley and sincerely anxious for the reforms to work, yet above suspicion of selling out. In 1905 he had founded a society with a special interest for Gandhi, the Servants of India. The Servants were volunteers who renounced office-seeking and approached public affairs as a vocation. Their relief work among famine victims and Untouchables, and their pioneering trade-unionism, made Gokhale's Society a lay counterpart of the Ramakrishna Order.

Gandhi, like his compatriots at home, had been impressed by the defeat of Russia in the Far East. While deploring the bloodshed he praised the Japanese in *Indian Opinion* for their self-sacrifice and courage and magnanimity, their 'resolve to do or die'. A few months afterwards he was commending the anti-partition campaign, with a touch of scepticism already about the liberals' dream of permitted progress. The best hope, he believed, lay in the British people rather than their governments. But the 1909 pamphlet *Hind Swaraj* was his first contribution to the debate. Prompted by his talks with Indian extremists in England, it moved away from them into a moral realm that was very much his own.

In it he resolved a dilemma. Most of the Congress patriots thought of their country's progress as modernization. India would achieve Home Rule by becoming more civilized—in effect, more like England, even if that only meant learning from the English how to defeat them. But Gandhi had drawn his philosophy from the Simple Life heretics who held civilization to be a curse. How could he, or India, have it both ways? The momentous leap which he alone had the boldness to take consisted in saying 'No' to the West. Not a 'No' of blind hate, but a reasoned 'No'. India's salvation did not lie in becoming more like England, it lay in becoming more like India. And this implied reconstituting the Simple Life on a vast scale, as the true expression of India's soul.

The prod which incited Gandhi to take this leap came from his fellow journalist G. K. Chesterton, who thereby made his greatest contribution to history without knowing it. Chesterton was not then the literary Catholic of later years, but a leftish all-round writer, a Little Englander and Old Pro-Boer. Also he was yet another member of Henry Salt's circle. By the time Gandhi read him he had revolted against the Simple Life as a fad, but retained most of what was best in its spirit. On 18 September 1909 an article of his about Indian nationalism appeared in *The Illustrated London News*. Gandhi, who was in England then, pounced on it and sent off a Gujarati version (the mind boggles) to *Indian Opinion*, with some excited comments of his own.

Chesterton's theme, expressed with his habitual verve, was that Indians had every right to be patriotic, but that they were perverse and misguided in the way they went about it. They had every right to seek national fulfilment through their own institutions, which might well be preferable to those of the West, but in trying to become civilized and pseudo-English they were attempting what they should not, and what was perhaps not worth doing.

When a respected and popular Englishman said this, why should an Indian hesitate? After a slight further sorting-out in a discussion at the Hampstead Peace and Arbitration Society, Gandhi combined Chesterton with the Carpenter-Tolstoy scheme of thought to concoct his own brand of nationalism. *Hind Swaraj* or *Indian Home Rule* (it appeared in both languages) takes the form of a dialogue between 'Editor', himself, and 'Reader', a westernized Indian revolutionary. 'Editor' praises Congress and the leaders of national revival. But he goes on to condemn modern civilization and all its works, political, technological, even medical. The Mother of Parliaments is a prostitute, machinery is anti-human, newspapers are corrupting, railways spread disease which doctors take our money for not curing.

'Editor' sounds like a complete nihilist. But presently constructive ideas emerge. Instead of copying the West, India should ask herself what she really is, where her true calling lies. The key to the recovery of her lost glory is in her ancestral village culture, her almost forgotten cottage industries such as spinning and weaving, and so forth. Her genius is for co-operation; the Hindu-Muslim conflict is artificial. By using her proper weapon of Satyagraha—expounded as Truth-Force or 'Soul-Force'—she can win genuine Swaraj. The essential point is not to drive the English out, but to cure them of their present attitudes and manner of life. If they are converted they can stay on in India as partners of her renascent peoples, sharing in a higher and holier culture, talking Hindi, abstaining from meat, and letting their railways rust.

Gandhi was reverting to his old London milieu, but giving its lessons a novel application. As in the past he was using Europe to bring India into focus, thereby advancing beyond the range of un-aided Indian minds. Those minds were slow to catch up with him. Even Gokhale shook his head over the pamphlet and said it read like the work of a fool. But Gandhi was firm. He not only demanded that Indians should seek their salvation in the Simple Life, he seriously proposed that their rulers should. In a letter to Lord Ampthill he assured that nobleman that since India was being exploited by British capitalists, the remedy was for Britain to discard modern civilization. There would then be no capitalists to do the exploiting.

This doctrine was neither Gokhale's nor Tilak's. It was not even very close to Vivekananda's. Gandhi had much in common with the other Hindu reformers and activists, yet no school or party could annex him. As a faraway theorist he would have counted for nothing. *Hind Swaraj* made little headway in India, and was banned for a time without thereby acquiring an aura. A movement to put him up for the Congress presidency in 1911 was stillborn. But when he turned homeward he had one colossal advantage, even over Tilak, even over Gokhale. While the others had been making speeches and burning shirts, he had led an actual Indian revolt all the way to success, by a method which a disarmed people could employ.

He was to capture India not as a sage or mystic but as a holy doer, an apostle of action, the trail-blazing *karma-yogin* of the new dispensation. Krishna's message as taught by Tilak pointed to no one else so decisively. The pupil was almost ready for the master. Meanwhile, Krishna's words about his own divine manifestations hung in the air. In *The Yugantar* an article had applied them openly to the present time.

> When righteousness was on the wane and unrighteousness was springing up in the sacred land of India . . . God, by becoming incarnate again and awakening his favourite disciple Arjuna to duty, re-established the kingdom of righteousness in India. At the present time righteousness is declining and unrighteousness is springing up in India. A handful of alien robbers is . . . robbing the wealth of India. . . . Fear not, oh Indians, God will not re-

main inactive at the sight of unrighteousness in his kingdom. He will keep his word. Placing firm reliance on the promise of God, invoke his power, and he will descend in your midst to destroy unrighteousness.

He will descend in your midst. The words are virtually those of one of the Jewish prophecies of a Messianic advent, on the eve of the Christian era.

'The saint', General Smuts wrote, 'has left our shores.' When the saint touched India's shores, wearing the laurels of the first Indian victory over the West, in what light was he likely to be regarded?

VIII

....*the Master Appears*

1

His homecoming was roundabout, and the war made it more so. He landed at Southampton with Kasturbai and Kallenbach on 4 August 1914. Gokhale was in Paris and could not join them. However, Indians in London gave them a reception at the Hotel Cecil. Among those present was Mohamed Ali Jinnah, the rising political prodigy of the Muslims.

On the war issue, Gandhi's attitude was the same as in the previous conflicts. Some Indians were frankly pro-British and others frankly seditious. He wanted Home Rule himself, but nevertheless decided to do his bit. Indians could hardly let the Empire down and still hope to convert its rulers. Polak, who had stayed in South Africa looking after the implementation of the settlement, protested by cable at this departure from non-violence. Gandhi replied (with more realism than some pacifists) that anyone living in a country at war is involved in the war. You cannot contract out, you must simply do your best under the circumstances. His own best was to organize another ambulance corps. About eighty Indians enlisted, mostly students. They trained at the Regent Street Polytechnic.

Two notable things happened to him in England—his first meeting with F. W. Pethick-Lawrence, the future Secretary of State who was one of the obstetricians at the birth of free India, and his first meeting with Sarojini Naidu, an effulgent woman and gifted poet, later President of Congress. Mrs Naidu looked in at his Kensington lodging and was amused to find 'an open door framing a living picture of a little man with a shaven head, seated on the floor on a black prison blanket and eating a messy meal of squashed tomatoes and olive oil'. They liked each other instantly and she helped in clothing his ambulance corps. However, it was not a success. A dispute with his superior officer was followed by an attack

141

of pleurisy which his diet made worse. Gokhale was back over the Channel now, and they had discussions about the war with Kallenbach as a third. But Gokhale returned to India, and when Gandhi's illness lingered, his doctors advised him to do the same. Kallenbach, being of German birth, was unable to go. Eventually he found his way home to South Africa.

The Gandhis reached Bombay on 9 January 1915, amid acclamations. Their first concern was with family matters. Their sons had sailed from South Africa separately, with Maganlal and others from Phoenix. Uncertain where to send them, Bapu had entrusted the whole party to Charles Freer Andrews, an English missionary who had come from India at Gokhale's instance to aid in the struggle and the negotiations that ended it. Andrews taught at Shantiniketan in Bengal, the school founded by Rabindranath Tagore. Gandhi learned in Bombay that Maganlal and the rest were there.

Satisfied that they were in safe hands, he did not go at once. He paid a courtesy visit to Lord Willingdon, the Governor of Bombay, and then went to see his relatives in Kathiawar. After doing this (pausing en route to complain about the conduct of some railway officials) he travelled southward again to Poona. There Gokhale and the Servants of India gave him a heartening welcome. They suggested that he should join the Society. He said his own wish would be to have a place of his own in Gujarat—a colony on the lines of Phoenix or Tolstoy. If he did, they replied, perhaps the Society could sponsor it.

On 17 February Mr and Mrs Gandhi at last arrived at Shantiniketan. Tagore was away. They had only been there a day or two when Gandhi was shocked to hear that Gokhale had dropped dead, a martyr to overwork in the public cause. He attended the funeral and returned to Shantiniketan on 5 March. This time Tagore was present; and so they came face to face—the hero of South Africa, and India's Nobel prize-winner, a literary giant so peerless that he was called simply 'The Poet'—together in Tagore's private kingdom.

Shantiniketan means Abode of Peace. The school was two miles out of Bolpur in a dry upland plain, a region of paddy-fields and thorn bushes and hot winds. Tagore had founded it in 1900 as 'a home for the spirit of India'. At Gandhi's advent it was an oasis of sweetness and light, with its own dairy farm, its own hospital, even its own post office. Rabindranath presided—the greatest member of a great family, fifty-three years old, bearded, handsome and patrician. Though he had seen through the English he still opened his arms to western culture. He could be scathing toward his own nation, yet he was deeply patriotic. Like William Morris he had turned from the poetry of legend and impersonal beauty to the poetry of people. He genuinely loved villagers, and his songs were genuinely popular. He led the renaissance of vernacular literature, while his brother, at the Calcutta School of Art, led the renaissance of Indian painting.

In March 1915 he was composing the lyric sequence *A Flight of Cranes*. His hundred and twenty-five pupils sang and acted and danced and wove garlands. The Poet was their Gurudev, Celestial Master. The boys from Phoenix lived among them under Maganlal's charge, still keeping Phoenix rules. Into this scene strode Gandhi, ecstatically welcomed. Promptly he began making suggestions. Why did they employ cooks and dish-washers? The teachers and boys should learn to cook for themselves, look after their own kitchens, empty their own garbage. This proposal appealed to the boys, and when some of the teachers demurred, Tagore gave his casting vote. They should try it.

As long as Gandhi was on the spot, the experiment worked. Tagore told the boys benignly that it contained the key to Swaraj. If he thought so, it is a mark of the contrast between these two patriots that in fifteen years he had never tried it himself. After Gandhi left, he made no effort to keep it alive. Soon all that the school retained of it was an annual Gandhi Day, when the staff and students did the work, and the servants rested.

In some respects the two were alike. The Poet's faith in the peasantry, his longing for a village rebirth, put him closer to Gandhi than to most of the Indian politicians. They had certain loathings in common—child marriage, for instance. Nor was the visitor a Philistine. He had kept his love of music and poetry. Writing to Maganlal in advance of his arrival, he had advised him where to shop for a sitar. Yet when he moved in on the gracious flower-bedecked school, its whole character altered. As a wise American woman once remarked, 'Tagore was like the mountain and Gandhi like the cataract going down to the people below.'

Gandhi had never found a *guru* in the full sense. Tagore, despite his title of Gurudev, did not qualify. But the Poet made a magisterial contribution to his career. He conferred the status of a Mahatma on him.

'Saint' is not a precise equivalent. A Mahatma is someone who embodies the indwelling spirit of all life in a specially high and noble form. That is why he is a 'great soul'. He has risen above the human mass but is still of it. He is not only holy, but also a sign of hope for others—if not in this life, then in future lives. As such he radiates, so to speak; he dispenses blessing. It is good to be with him.

Gandhi himself applied the title to one or two people he esteemed, such as Gokhale. But it came to him a little stained with misuse. Theosophists believed that Mahatmas were mysterious masters of wisdom who guided the world's destinies from caves in Tibet. Superstitious Hindus thought of them as wonder-workers. Both were right to this extent, that Mahatmaship is a concept that looks beyond everyday experience. Great Souls are not simply men with high IQ's, or a talent for power or philanthropy. Nor are they institutional figures. They need not be priests or monks, they need not even be Brahmins. In the *Gita* Krishna uses the word when speaking of his true devotees, and the Kshatriya Arjuna can become so. Several of the profoundest sages of the Upanishads are also Kshatriyas. Gandhi's rank as a Vaisya did not exclude him from the honour.

At least one admirer saluted him in this way while he was still in South Africa. But Tagore launched the cultus. He was already referring to 'Mahatma Gandhi' in correspondence that February, and he spoke in a poem of 'the Great Soul in beggar's garb', an allusion to the simplicity of dress which Gandhi was beginning to practise. A belief was current that any twentieth-century Mahatma would have to identify himself with the downtrodden millions. Vivekananda had written that a Mahatma must be one whose heart bled for the poor. If it did not, he was no Mahatma.

Gandhi never enjoyed being called so. He insisted that he was only a seeker. But the title stuck to him. The masses embraced him as a Great Soul before they knew him as a politician. Therefore, he acquired the ability to sway them as no one else could; and therefore, he became the most indispensable politician of all.

2

While the seed of a Messianic cult had been sown, the early months of 1915 produced no visible plant. Both of Gandhi's mentors were dead—not only Gokhale, but Raychandbhai—and their passing left him at a loss. The African struggle had given him no Indian role that he could see with any exactitude. Outside Gujarat his name meant little among the educated, except in the largest cities. It had spread by rumour among the poor. But he did not yet know that.

A remark of Gokhale's had impressed itself upon him: that he should travel about observing India for a year, and keep his mouth shut. He would have to learn before he could lead. It became clear that this could not be done under anybody else's aegis. The suggestion that he should join the Servants of India was aired again and dropped. Some of the members now admitted frankly that they were opposed to him. In any case, Gokhale's advice implied more than developing a few contacts with a set of unusual people. Gandhi had to become attuned again to a world overwhelmingly different from his African milieu of farm and city and veldt, with its simple goods and evils.

To quote Jawaharlal Nehru, 'India contains all that is disgusting and all that is noble'; and in its complex life, where the maddest contradictions can co-exist, the two may be one. East of Suez (in the words of another well-known authority) the best is like the worst. The logic of Europe, which had shaped Gandhi's mind, did not function so smoothly in a land where men could believe with equal correctness in no God or one God or three hundred million gods; where the wisest could not agree whether the universe existed, but were certain that they themselves did not; where any hard-headed lawyer or engineer might wander off in the evening to contemplate the Absolute under a telegraph pole. Nor was it a region of dream or metaphysical mist. It was gaudy, intense, cruel—a country full of tigers and snakes, with twenty thousand of its inhabitants killed annually by wild beasts; a country of heat, earthquakes, monsoons, floods, epidemics, famine deaths in myriads; and above all of human beings in huge polyglot swarms, dark and brown and yellow. India had the world's longest epics and the world's most crowded trains and the world's most tumultuous festivals.

It was at a festival that Gandhi had the first inkling of the role he was being cast in. April 1915 was the time of Kumbha Mela, a sacred bathing ceremony at Hardwar, drawing over a million pilgrims. The Servants of India sent volunteers to look after their needs. Gandhi came to help, with Maganlal and the Phoenix party. The baseness of Hindu piety shook him. As an act of atonement for the benighted conduct around him, he made a vow, which he observed ever after, not to eat more than five different articles of food during any one day. In the immediate situation at Hardwar, he tackled some of the latrine work. But he found himself unable to do much in person, because his fame with the masses, due to what was already a kind of oral saga about South Africa, had made him an object of pilgrimage himself. He had to sit in a tent receiving a queue of visitors. They came chiefly for *darshan*, which is an important factor in Hinduism, and one of the secrets of a Mahatma's influence. The word means 'blessing' and more, a spiritual tonic. Since, in Hinduism, no clear line can be drawn between the 'religious' and 'non-religious' (or for that matter between gods and mortals), *darshan* can be derived from great people or occasions that are not explicitly holy. The agnostic Nehru dispensed it. But Gandhi, however unwilling, was better qualified to do so. The stream of pilgrims at Hardwar was the vanguard of an army which finally drove him to exclaim 'The woes of Mahatmas are known only to Mahatmas!' and take refuge in a day of silence each week.

He could keep silence when he imposed it on himself, but not by request. In spite of Gokhale he talked in public during 1915. People invited him and it was hard to refuse. Sometimes he appeared as guest of honour at banquets, with Kasturbai beside him; he praised her as his 'helpful partner' and she said nothing. Many of his admirers were disappointed. They expected an epic warrior larger than life. They saw a slight figure, not above average height, with projecting ears and a floppy turban. His voice lacked resonance. It had stirred his Transvaal audiences when it carried a message, but now its power was checked by the handicap of having nothing to say.

Vallabhbhai Patel, a barrister destined to be one of his ablest lieutenants, first saw him in this year. Patel—solid, moustached, intensely efficient—was playing bridge at an Ahmedabad club when the alleged hero entered. He took stock of him, was not impressed, and returned to the game. Respect did not dawn till later, at a conference on peasant taxation.

Gandhi's attunement, in fact, was progressing slowly. His spiritual status was not yet translated into a programme. On the war issue he sounded out of key. At a dinner in Madras that April, he defended his support for the British war effort by talking of the British ideal of liberty. Three years later he was to defend it by saying that Indians should fight so as to win respect. In old age he was to defend it by saying that at this period he had not yet found his feet. From the outset, however, defence was necessary. His stand proved unpopular. Most of the Indians who did join the colours were fine soldiers, but only a small percentage came, and many others were restive. Tagore, horrified at the slaughter, was turning against the war and the West itself. Tilak was out of prison, and had shifted from a brief conciliatory stance to new threats. Annie Besant felt justified in forming an Indian Home Rule League and persuading the nonagenarian Dadabhai Naoroji to be its president.

These were activities which gave Gandhi no scope as yet. His own vision of Home Rule was meaningless to the politicians, and even to Mrs Besant. As a Mahatma he might have been expected to win the heart of this high-priestess of Theosophy. She entertained him at Adyar with a complimentary banquet, but he was so unlike her notion of what a Mahatma should be that they never got on too well. By the time her League was launched he was finally in motion along his own track, experimenting as always, without a master.

His new starting-point had been a decision to give up all thought of practising again as a lawyer. Whatever his divine Truth would demand of him, it would demand on a full-time basis. Satyagraha was his unique contribution to the world. Hence, he reasoned, his task was to plant the Satyagrahi mode of living in India, and find how to apply the method to Indian problems. If a point of entry could be discovered, the results might be swift. He never subscribed to the doctrine of gradualism. In Carlyle's essay on Muhammad, which he had read and re-read, there is a sentence about the Hero and his Time. The Hero has always come, says Carlyle, 'as light-ning out of Heaven: the rest of men waited for him like fuel, and then they too would flame'. Tolstoy, also, believed in sudden transitions.

Gandhi's first positive move was in the matter of clothing . . . that recurrent motif. In South Africa, at the end, he had made an effective entry wearing Indian dress. On his return he had taken to wearing a *dhoti*—an ample kind of loincloth—instead of trousers. This, with a shirt, cloak, and white scarf, made up the costume of

Kathiawar. He soon shed the scarf and cloak when travelling, and tried to blend into the crowd of the poor. Though he always denied that he chose his clothes for public-relations purposes, their value from that point of view was incontestable.

In May 1915 he ceased from merely hovering. A logical course for the founder of Phoenix and Tolstoy Farm was, after all, marked out by a Hindu custom which Vivekananda had revived. Gandhi announced that he was starting an Ashram or lay community. After some hesitation about the best site for it, the choice was made for him by some friends in Ahmedabad, who offered to finance him. A lawyer let him a large bungalow in Kochrab, near the city. Here in his own Gujarat, on 20 May, he settled with a group of disciples —twenty-five men and women, some of them veterans of South Africa who had elected to stay with him. They dedicated themselves to poverty, chastity and service. Since the main object was to spread the lessons of South Africa, and work out how to apply them in India, they agreed to call their home the Satyagraha Ashram. But Gandhi's mind was already forming a more specific aim: the rebirth of the cottage industries which the factory goods of Britain had ruined. Hand-spinning and hand-weaving in particular might themselves become a species of Satyagraha, a non-violent challenge to economic oppression, in keeping with *Hind Swaraj*.

By a paradox, most of the funds for this anti-capitalist colony came from capitalists. Ahmedabad textile magnates were open-handed. So were Bombay shipowners. Such are the ironies of patriotism. Communists were later to argue that the whole mighty Gandhian enterprise which branched out from this Ashram was a big-business fraud, a plot to capture the national movement by exploiting a man held in religious reverence. He who pays the piper calls the tune. However, Gandhi's divine Truth seldom fitted so neatly into anyone else's Truth. One of his early actions refuted facile cynicism in the only decisive way: by showing that this particular piper could stick to his own tune, even if it meant that he had to forgo payment.

The crisis arose over caste. When starting the Ashram he made it clear that he wanted to bring in an Untouchable. If a worthy candidate came forward, admission would be instant. His backers acquiesced, or seemed to, but chiefly because they did not think any Untouchable ever would be worthy. India's outcaste people, the descendants of tribes enslaved but not absorbed by the Aryans, actually were distinct from the rest at their social and economic roots. Yet the contemptuous loathing felt for them by caste Hindus was not like the snobbery of Victorian gentry toward the lower orders in England, or the lesser breeds overseas. It arose from the doctrine of *karma*. A person's condition in this life is the just consequence of his conduct in previous lives. Hence his condition is both sacrosanct and deserved. The *Gita* itself was (and still is) perverted to support that belief. In Gandhi's India it was a stubborn obstacle to reform, and the treatment of Untouchables was its worst single effect. People born so low in the scale—outcastes with no social rank at all—must have been perfectly villainous. There was little reason to sympathize, or to think they could have improved much in their present penal incarnation.

This was why they were shunned as unclean, given the foulest work, barred from the temples, and generally degraded. The politest name for them was 'depressed classes'. The belief created its own truth, by debasing its victims to a point where they really were outside normal society, and could not exist by normal rules. Charles Andrews, the clergyman friend of Gandhi and Tagore, used to tell how he once entered a cottage to ask for water. He was in Indian dress. The woman he spoke to screamed with horror. She was an Untouchable, and although she had done nothing, the neighbours would beat her and her family for defiling the supposed high-caste Hindu.

Gandhi wanted to flout the taboo as a matter of policy. Not that he rejected *karma* or caste. He was close enough to orthodox Hinduism to accept both. But caste, for him, meant the four-tier system of the *Gita*—a simple functional scheme based on mutual respect. There, Untouchability had no place. He abhorred it as a disease, a perversion. Many of his indentured workmen, the vanguard of the last battle with Smuts, had been outcaste themselves. India could never be properly free if a fifth of the population had to toil on under this loathsome burden.

Hence his wish to effect a token break in his own Ashram. Nevertheless he moved with caution. It would be fatal to admit some plausible sponger whose behaviour justified the bigots. His long-ago drain inspection in Rajkot had convinced him that Untouchables were cleaner, if nothing else, than their karmic superiors alleged. But he doubted whether a thoroughly safe applicant would appear quickly. So he was surprised to get a letter from a prominent citizen, only about three months after the Ashram opened, recommending a 'humble and honest' family of Untouchables who desired to join it.

Now that the issue was put squarely, most of his co-ashramites were prepared to welcome the newcomers. The family consisted of three: a young man named Dudabhai, his wife Danibehn, and their small daughter Lakshmi. They took up residence in September. Though Dudabhai lacked formal education, he had been a teacher of sorts in Bombay. He was intelligent enough not to submit passively to his status or the insults that went with it. His life was one of studied patience varied by outbursts, and he needed careful handling. But on the whole he was an acceptable recruit. So were Danibehn and Lakshmi. The respectable, however, thought otherwise, and an explosion resulted. There was trouble with the landlord, whose servant had charge of the well, and was loudly afraid of being contaminated. There was talk of a social boycott. More ominous yet, the funds from pious Hindu industrialists dried up. They realized too late that their protégé had meant what he said.

Maganlal, who managed the Ashram's finances, reported that he had no finances left to manage. Gandhi proposed to move to the Untouchable quarter of Ahmedabad and live by manual labour. They were saved from having to try this desperate step by one of those incidents familiar to readers of the lives of the saints. Sheth Ambalal Sarabhai, a rich Muslim mill-owner whom Gandhi scarcely knew, drove up in his car one morning and said he wanted to help. Would his infidel cash be accepted?

'Most certainly,' Gandhi answered. 'And I confess that I am at the present moment at the end of my resources.'

'I shall come tomorrow at this time,' the visitor promised.

Punctually he reappeared and sounded his horn. Gandhi came out. Without leaving his seat in the car, Ambalal handed over a sheaf of notes and vanished in a cloud of dust. The gift amounted to thirteen thousand rupees, enough for months.

Seemingly Gandhi had compounded his sin. Having slapped the orthodox by admitting Untouchables, he had slapped them again by acquiescing in dependence on Muslim money. Actually his stand strengthened him, even with many of the orthodox, who were shaken into second thoughts and a fresh interest in his experiment.

The failure of Hindu funds turned out to be temporary. His worst ordeal was within the Ashram, where the objections, though few, were hurtful. Kasturbai herself and another woman resented the new inmates. Danibehn, with whom they shared the kitchen, had an unpleasant time. Maganlal's wife walked out altogether, taking her invaluable husband with her. But Gandhi was adamant. The more he pondered Untouchability, the more determined he grew to fight it. Satyagraha in India would mean this, whatever else it meant. He told Kasturbai that if she persisted, she would have to go. He adopted Lakshmi as his daughter. Kasturbai began adjusting herself to the change in her husband which India was producing without either of them seeing exactly how. He was no longer just a morally passionate lawyer. He was . . . well, a Mahatma, perhaps? Anyway a holy man as he had not been before.

Holiness continued to have its painful side for the family. While the Mahatma could cheerfully bring in somebody else's daughter, he was quite willing to expel his own son. Manilal Gandhi, who had a small savings account, made a loan to Harilal Gandhi, who was in difficulties in Calcutta. Manilal's standing had been insecure for three years because of a passing affair with a married woman. Now his father accused him of virtual embezzlement, on the ground that an ashramite's savings were Ashram property, and after a miserable scene, packed him off to work under an alias. He left with only his train fare and a scrap of pocket-money. Having undergone a year's penitential labour, first as a weaver and then as a publisher's assistant, he received a parental order to go back to Natal and edit *Indian Opinion*. This became his career, and he only returned home for occasional visits.

'All India is my family,' Gandhi once remarked. Noble sentiments can have disturbing corollaries.

3

Outside the Ashram his admirers waited for him to do something. Throughout 1915 he still seemed to be doing very little. Indeed, to the casual observer he had a dreadful air of incipient respectability. On 3 June the King awarded him the Kaisar-i-Hind gold medal for public services in South Africa. The same Honours List included a knighthood for Tagore. Gokhale's advice to keep quiet for a year was restraining Gandhi politically if not otherwise. But when he did break his silence, he broke it with a crash.

India's reviving unrest came into the open at the December meeting of Congress in Bombay. Gandhi sat on the committee which arranged its agenda. He had a share, though an unobtrusive share, in a shift to the left. For eight years Tilak's nationalists had been shut out. Attempts by Annie Besant to heal the breach were blocked by Gokhale, who feared that Tilak would capture the organization. But now, with Gokhale dead and anti-British feeling returning, the majority favoured Mrs Besant's conciliatory line. Congress agreed to admit anyone as a delegate if elected by an association at least two years old, which included constitutional achievement of Home Rule among its aims. As the Tilakites were content to be constitutional for the moment, they could re-enter under this clause, stronger than before the schism. Indian students of the generation born around 1890 had nearly all swung toward Tilak, and they were now old enough to matter.

Unity was being advanced in another way, in another part of the city. The Muslim League held its own annual session in Bombay at the same time. This gesture was Jinnah's idea. He proposed a Congress-League alliance to campaign for Swaraj. Several Congress personages attended the Muslims' deliberations. They included Mrs Besant, Sarojini Naidu, and Gandhi himself. He renewed an old acquaintance with the League's President for that year, Maulana Mazharul Haq, who invited him to call whenever he should be in Patna. The invitation was to prove providential.

Mrs Besant, meanwhile, was on the brink of a triumph outside politics. She aspired—not altogether absurdly—to a position of acknowledged leadership in the realm of the intellect. This prize had eluded her through the sixty-eight years of her life, as indeed it had in her previous lives as Hypatia of Alexandria and Giordano Bruno, which had both been cut short. The present incarnation was at last looking more hopeful. Her school at Benares, started in 1892, had been enlarged and granted university status. At a three-day function in February 1916 it was to be refounded as the Hindu University Central College, in the presence of the Viceroy, and an array of rajahs and maharajahs and their magnificent ladies.

Would Gandhi address the gathering on 6 February? He promised to do so. Thus, just as his year of caution expired, he was presented with a mighty audience and a mighty occasion.

The moment came. Lord Hardinge, having done his viceregal duty at the foundation ceremony, sat in a place of honour. All around on the platform spread the jewelled and gorgeous ranks of the nobility. Facing them were the students and other guests. A maharajah presided. Gandhi rose to speak wearing a plain cloak, short *dhoti,* and turban. Almost at once it became alarmingly clear that he was going to do as he had done in the very first speech of his public life, to the Indian worthies of Pretoria. Instead of uttering platitudes about culture and progress, he was exhorting Indians to self-criticism. With a sinking heart the foundress listened as the dreadful sentences rolled on.

I venture to suggest to you that we have now reached almost the end of our resources in speech-making and it is not enough that our ears be feasted, that our eyes be feasted, but it is necessary that our hearts have got to be touched and that our hands and feet have got to be moved.

He lamented that he was forced to speak English, a 'foreign language', in an Indian institute of learning.

Suppose that we had been receiving education during the past fifty years through our vernaculars, what should we be today? We should have today a free India, we should have our educated men not as if they were foreigners in their own land, but speaking to the heart of the nation; they would be working amongst the poorest of the poor, and whatsoever they would have gained during the past fifty years would be a heritage for the nation.

A few of the audience applauded. But he had no intention of leaving them in the dream of an India that might have been. He turned relentlessly to the India that was—the filth in the temples, the dirty habits of the people, the vile conditions on the railways, where (among other scandals) students who spoke English and wore Norfolk jackets thought themselves entitled to grab the best seats. Were Indians fit to rule themselves?

Worse was to come. He spoke of the dignitaries on the platform.

I compare with the richly bedecked noblemen the millions of the poor. And I feel like saying to those noblemen: 'There is no salvation for India unless you strip yourselves of this jewellery and hold it in trust for your countrymen in India.'

Some of the students shouted 'Hear, hear!' But already murmurs of protest were audible. Gandhi continued unaffected.

Whenever I hear of a great palace rising in any great city of India, be it in British India or be it in the India which is ruled by our great chiefs, I become jealous at once and say, 'Oh, it is the money that has come from the agriculturists . . .' There cannot be much spirit of self-government about us if we take away or allow others to take away from the peasants almost the whole of the results of their labour. Our salvation can only come through the farmer. Neither the lawyers, nor the doctors, nor the rich landlords are going to secure it.

He passed from the tactless to the unmentionable: the anxiety felt for Lord Hardinge's safety, the posting of detectives in the streets of Benares. India, he said, was living in a dangerous atmosphere of frustration and fear. This had produced an army of anarchists—the Tilakite bomb-throwers, inactive for the moment, but unrepentant. He himself was a kind of anarchist, but in a different spirit.

If we trust and fear God, we shall have to fear no one, not maharajahs, not viceroys, not the detectives, not even King George.

Now the audience was muttering and rumbling. Groups were forming on the floor, arguing among themselves. As the hubbub mounted, Mrs Besant made a frantic bid to avert disaster. She asked Gandhi to stop. He turned politely to her and then to the chairman, but the words that passed among them were almost drowned. Shouts of 'Sit down!' mingled with rival shouts of 'Go on!' In a lull the speaker could he heard saying something about India's road to self-government. He was calling for moral regeneration, for trust and love, for a readiness to shoulder blame where it was due. Freedom was not a thing to be simply granted. India would have to earn it and take it. . . .

Uproar again, beyond redemption. The pattern of the platform disintegrated as guest after guest walked out. At some point it became apparent that Gandhi had given up, and that the chairman himself had left the assembly to its fate. Afterwards Mrs Besant issued a series of statements endeavouring to disown Gandhi without disagreeing with him. The police told him he was *persona non grata* in Benares, and he departed.

By all the rules of democracy there could be only one verdict on this affair. Gandhi was a political suicide without a future. India, however, was not a democracy, and the rules did not apply. As reports of the speech spread outside, the public reacted differently from the princes. Even in Benares Gandhi made a convert who outweighed a hallful of critics—a twenty-year-old student named Vinoba Bhave. He read the speech in a paper, wrote to Gandhi, and joined the Ashram. Vinoba's progress in discipleship was gradual and little publicized. But his gifts were such that he was to be spoken of, in the crises of mid-century India, as the Mahatma's only credible heir.

Vinoba was not alone. After Benares Gandhi's sheer uniqueness began to exert a fascination, especially, and significantly, over some of the young. It was in 1916 that he met G. D. Birla of the industrial family, then aged twenty-two. Exasperated at British pride and contempt, Birla had flirted with the extremists, and was not predisposed to favour the prophet of Ahimsa. Nor could anybody in his position feel much sympathy for cottage economy and the Simple Life. But Gandhi's 'greatness and generosity' (to quote his own words) captured him against his convictions. Within a few years his money and his houses were at Gandhi's disposal.

For several months after Benares this quickening of personal interest did not show in politics. The sole issue on which the Mahatma took any action was a matter carried over from South Africa, the winding-up of the indenture system. In March the Viceroy gave a promise to end it which he condemned as too vague. He began an agitation that included a threat of Satyagraha, and, as in the Transvaal, a deadline. The Government honoured the pledge before his time limit expired. This was fortunate, as he had no notion how to apply his technique in such a case. Satyagraha in India was saved from a false start.

Otherwise his demeanour during the rest of 1916 was wary. He reverted once to the provocative style, in a challenge to the Muir College Economics Society at Allahabad: the economists heard with bewilderment that he had never read Adam Smith, that he preferred the scriptures because economics should have an ethical basis, and that progress through industrialization was a mirage because big business was anti-moral. However, he spoke more often on one of his less blatantly outrageous Benares themes, the need for a revival of Indian languages. By vernacular education, he argued, the ground that took sixteen years to cover in English could be covered in ten, and knowledge confined to an élite could be made free to all. As a lingua franca he proposed Hindi. Such talk was more radical than it sounded. It aligned him with the creators of Hindu nationalism, and with Tilak against the Anglicized liberals.

Tilak was himself again, excited by the Easter Rising in Ireland. That April he launched his own Home Rule League, in a relation with Annie Besant which she described as 'working-together-separately'. On 1 May, at a political rally in Belgaum, he called for a united front of extremists and moderates. Gandhi came, and addressed the audience in Hindi. Naturally he also came to the Congress meeting in December, which was held at Lucknow. The occasion was triumphal, with 2,301 delegates and many visitors. The re-entry of the Tilakites restored Congress's all-embracing character, and the Muslim League, again holding its session in the same town at the same time, brimmed with fraternity. A joint programme, the Congress-League Scheme, was recommended by Mrs Besant, Jinnah and Tilak, who was now not so aggressively Hindu. It provided for democratic reforms and a rapid march toward Swaraj. Congress conceded separate Muslim electorates. The programme was approved and submitted to the new Viceroy, Lord Chelmsford, with a request for firm undertakings.

Two men among the dozens who spoke with Gandhi were to become part of his life. They were a weirdly contrasted couple. One was Jawaharlal Nehru, the son of Motilal Nehru, a wealthy lawyer prominent among the Congress moderates. Jawaharlal was twenty-six, a product of Harrow and Cambridge, a Brahmin and a patrician. Both the Nehrus had been influenced by Theosophy. Jawaharlal's conscious impression of Gandhi was of someone 'very distant and different and unpolitical'. Yet the spell had started to work. While Nehru Junior's brain allied him with the progressives and in due course the Socialists, his heart—as he finally realized—linked him irrevocably to the Mahatma.

The second figure of destiny was a peasant, poor and thin, exactly like millions of other peasants. He pushed his way to Gandhi through the turmoil of Lucknow and said: 'I am Rajkumar Shukla. I am from Champaran, and I want you to come to my district.'

IX

Mahatmaship in Practice

1

To Gandhi Champaran meant nothing. However, it was soon to mean much. At the end of Rajkumar Shukla's road lay his first Satyagraha in India. Furthermore it was this campaign which first made him think seriously about getting the British to hand over power—perhaps not at once, but some day—and using Truth-Force to persuade them.

Before he went to Champaran, his conception of the change from British Raj to Swaraj was no more than a vague vision of mutual enlightenment. He had not committed himself to revolution. Nor had he yet employed Satyagraha as a full-scale revolutionary strategy. In South Africa it had been the weapon of a minority against a few specific laws. His experience there did not show whether it could be expanded for a national rising with unlimited aims. That idea had been hinted to him, indeed, at an early stage. During his London visit in November 1906 he had met a Bombay barrister, Shyamji Krishnavarma, who insisted that the British should quit the country and that if they did not, Indians should refuse all co-operation. Gandhi noted the far-sighted Krishnavarma's proposal in *Indian Opinion*, but without pursuing it.

Listening to Rajkumar Shukla at Lucknow, he gathered that the trouble was grave but could not entirely grasp what it was. Champaran was a district of Bihar which had indigo plantations. The peasant was an indigo worker. After some incoherent talk about grievances he rushed off to fetch a lawyer, Brajkishore Babu, who came to Gandhi's tent to elucidate. But Brajkishore, who wore a black alpaca coat and trousers, failed to carry conviction as the spokesman of an oppressed peasantry. Suspecting some private motive, Gandhi advised him to move a resolution in Congress, and stressed that he could say nothing himself without studying the problem (whatever it was) in person.

157

Rajkumar immediately pressed him for a promise to come. He agreed to fit Champaran into a future tour, and left for Cawnpore. To his consternation Rajkumar followed him, still pressing. He returned to the Ashram, right across India, and there too Rajkumar appeared. Gandhi said he was going to Calcutta in a few months; Rajkumar could meet him there. On his arrival at the address he had given, the indomitable peasant was squatting outside. He dealt with his Calcutta business and they boarded a train for Patna, the capital of Bihar, which they reached on 10 April 1917.

Gandhi assumed that his companion had friends in Patna, who would explain the situation and organize his visit to Champaran. It transpired, however, that Rajkumar's plans were nebulous in the extreme, and he found himself without trustworthy guidance in a strange city. The peasant at last decided that all would be well if they went to another lawyer, Rajendra Prasad. He was not in. Gandhi dashed off a note to Maganlal, now fortunately back at the Ashram:

> The man who has brought me here doesn't know anything. He has dumped me in some obscure place. The master of the house is away and the servants take us both to be beggars. They don't even permit us the use of their latrine, not to speak of inviting us to meals. I take care to provide myself with a stock of the things I need and so I have been able to maintain complete indifference. I have swallowed a good many insults and the queer situation here does not trouble me. If things go on this way I am not likely to see Champaran.

Such was his first contact with Rajendra Prasad, who, because of him, was to become President of India.

But he recalled that he had a card of his own to play, his long-standing invitation from Maulana Mazharul Haq, the Muslim leader. A message brought the Maulana hurrying over in his car. Soon Gandhi was aboard a train to Muzaffarpur, where he knew someone else—J. B. Kripalani, a former lecturer at the Government College (destined like Prasad to a high place in politics). He wired that he was on his way, and although the train pulled in at midnight, his friend was waiting at the station with a crowd of students. Arrangements had been made for him to stay with a Professor Malkani. Writing of this episode later, Gandhi remarked: 'It was an extraordinary thing in those days for a government professor to harbour a man like me.' Even the quieter nationalists were perilous company.

His journey across the dusty, poverty-stricken land of Bihar ended in a collision with brutal realities. Meeting a group of lawyers next morning, he learned all he needed. Rajkumar was vindicated.

Champaran lies beside Nepal and the Himalayas, a country of mango groves and legend. Its area is about 3,500 square miles, its population a couple of million, mainly Hindu and almost entirely rural. The only towns are Motihari and Bettiah. In 1917 Champaran was a preserve of English planters who, for more than half a century, had owned most of the arable land and imposed an almost feudal regime. Every hearth, every oil mill, every wedding, was subject to special levies called *abwabs*. These were illegal in theory but condoned in practice. An *abwab* would be raised when a Sahib wanted an elephant or a new car. The English could hire labour at will, paying men $2\frac{1}{2}d.$ a day, women $1\frac{1}{2}d.$, and children (as soon as they were big enough to handle a hoe) $\frac{3}{4}d.$

Under a contract system known as *tinkathia*, the tenants had to plant three-twentieths of their holdings with indigo, and hand over the indigo harvest as a part of their rent. It went into dye factories belonging to the English. *Tinkathia* had contributed to futile waves of unrest that swept over Champaran at intervals. However, the worst grievance dated from the years just before the war, when new synthetic dyes were driving indigo from the world market and making it an unprofitable crop. The landlords protected themselves before the tenants found out. They offered to end the indigo contracts in exchange for an increase in rent or a lump sum. After the first glad acceptances the tenants did find out, and the intake of pseudo-compensation threatened to dwindle. But the planters had a tight grip on the district and plenty of money to hire agents. Peasants who demurred at the new agreements were coerced into signing. They were beaten up, or arrested on faked charges; their houses were looted, their cattle stolen; tradesmen became afraid to supply them. From 1912 to 1914, with the aid of special registrars furnished by the Government, Champaran's landlords secured thirty thousand revised tenancies, with rent increases in the order of 60 per cent and cash payments totalling £90,000—as recompense for relinquishing a crop that was worthless anyhow. Meanwhile they assured outsiders that their tenants were happy, and that such trouble as occurred was stirred up by agitators from Bengal.

A few of the tougher peasants took legal action or organized petitions, and in 1917 they were still struggling. Hence the lawyers' involvement. Some merely exploited the situation for profit. Others genuinely wanted to change it, and these were the sort who met Gandhi in Muzaffarpur. Rajendra Prasad caught up with him here, and so did Brajkishore, making a better impression than in Lucknow. But Gandhi noticed that even they charged fees which the poorer victims could never afford.

Court proceedings, he told them, could achieve nothing with an intimidated populace. The peasants must be freed from fear. He was satisfied as to the urgency of the case, and willing to undertake a campaign, but only with the lawyers' help. They assumed that he meant professional help, and were aghast when he brushed this aside and made it clear what he did mean. Were they prepared to be sent to jail, for instance? They hadn't pictured that precisely. 'The idea of accommodating ourselves to imprisonment', one of them put it, 'is a novel thing for us.' What else? They would have to be ready to drop their practices when required and work as clerks or interpreters, unpaid. That too was a disturbing prospect. In a conversation lasting till midnight it grew apparent that the first fear which Gandhi had to overcome was the lawyers' own. At last they promised to work with him, on the basis of an informal rota which would always give him as many assistants as he wanted.

In keeping with his rule since the Abdulla case, he started by collecting facts. As the Sahibs' point of view was itself a fact, he called on the secretary of the Planters' Association, and on the commissioner of the Tirhut division which included Champaran. The secretary said he had no business interfering, the commissioner advised him to get out of Tirhut at once. These interviews established one fact at least—that he might go to prison sooner than expected. Not caring to be arrested before he even reached Champaran, he got on a train with a contingent of lawyers. They dismounted at Motihari and had to battle through a mob. To these remote peasants a politician would have meant nothing, but the rumour of a liberating Mahatma drew them to the station in hundreds.

Gandhi set up headquarters in a house and received all comers. Within a few hours somebody reported that a peasant had been illtreated in one of the villages. Next morning, 16 April, he set out to investigate with two companions. In rural India the traveller must get used to a variety of transport, and Gandhi made this journey on the back of an elephant. He swayed uncomfortably along with the hot west wind tossing sand over him, talking to his surprised fellow-riders about the need to rescue Bihari women from purdah. After nine miles they dismounted at a place where they had another inquiry to make. A police sub-inspector toiled up on a bicycle with a request to return. Leaving his companions to pursue the inquiry, Gandhi mounted a bullock cart, transferred to a light carriage, and finally arrived back in Motihari. Here the police handed him a notice to leave Champaran. He answered that he would not—thereby launching Satyagraha—and was summoned to stand trial next day. In anticipation of prison he spent the night writing letters, sending Maganlal directions about the Ashram, and composing a statement to the Viceroy.

Even this brief delay had put the authorities in a difficulty. Word had spread through the district, and when the sun rose the streets of Motihari were full of demonstrating peasants. They surged round the courthouse with an incredible air of not being afraid. Gandhi was the only person they would listen to. He bore himself toward the officials with courtesy, and they were forced to rely on their own prisoner to keep the crowd under control. His presence had a magic which would have been far less potent, at this stage, in a place where he was known as a politician or reformer. The point of the occasion was that he was not so known. Nor did he come representing any organization. Congress, to the peasants, was an irrelevant name; to the English it stood for sedition; so he had agreed with his co-workers that it should not be mentioned. The confrontation of Mahatma and peasantry was a purely Messianic moment. God had descended in their midst to destroy unrighteousness.

The alarming potentialities for the British Raj soon began to emerge. Neither the District Magistrate nor the prosecutor could decide what to do with Gandhi. The expulsion order had been served on him—improperly—under Section 144 of the Penal Code. Despite the prosecutor's attempts at postponement, he insisted on pleading guilty to disobeying the order. He read a statement declaring that he had come by invitation on a fact-finding mission and intended to proceed, 'not for want of respect for lawful authority, but in obedience to the higher law of our being, the voice of conscience'.

The magistrate, badly needing a pause for reflection, said he would give judgement after a two-hour recess, and requested the prisoner to put up bail for the two hours. When the prisoner declined, he could think of nothing to do but let him go without bail and defer judgement again. Rajendra Prasad, Brajkishore and Mazharul Haq were now in Motihari. So was Polak, who had come over from South Africa. Several other lawyers were with them. Gandhi asked the group what they would do if he went to jail. The question took some of them aback. They had come to advise him. If he went to jail there would be no one to advise, so they would go home. And leave the peasants to suffer? he asked. They held a worried confabulation among themselves. Here was a Gujarati who could hardly even follow the local dialect, yet he was willing to go to prison for the sake of the peasants. He had caught the peasants' professed champions in a moral trap. When they told him they would stay, he exclaimed gaily that the battle was won, and drew up a schedule showing the order in which they should get arrested.

They were not driven to that extreme. Sir Edward Gait, the Lieutenant-Governor of Bihar, instructed the magistrate to drop the case and allow Gandhi to carry out his plans. The officials were to give him whatever facilities he required. His act of defiance had succeeded. But now he trod carefully, discouraging all moves for further publicity or political action. The onus of trouble-making was thrown on the planters. They inspired an abusive press campaign. The manager of the Motihari dye factory wrote to *The Pioneer* denouncing Gandhi as a crank and fanatic with megalomaniac delusions. But whenever the attacks were specific, Gandhi strengthened his position by the restraint and accuracy of his replies.

Meanwhile, in a house rented for the purpose, he was spending day after day taking down depositions from peasants. Half a dozen lawyers assisted. At the outset they tried to live in the style to which they were accustomed, with servants and individual kitchens. Gandhi laughed at these luxuries, and they sent the servants home. His stringency made it possible to finance the whole venture out of cash gifts from Bihari sympathisers (not the peasants; he refused to accept money from them). Masses of people poured in with the interviewees, seeking the Mahatma's *darshan*. Reluctantly, he stopped work and went on view for them at fixed times. He co-operated, indeed, with everybody. He let C.I.D. men watch the interviews, went out on little tours, and visited planters to hear their side of the case, even persuading one or two to state it rationally.

On 29 April W. A. Lewis, a civil servant at Bettiah, wrote to the District Magistrate about Gandhi's activities. This letter is perhaps the earliest documentation of the new Messianism among the peasants.

> They credit him with extraordinary powers. He moves about in the villages asking them to lay their grievances before him, and he is transfiguring the imaginations of masses of ignorant men with visions of an early millennium. I put the danger of this before Mr. Gandhi, and he assured me that his utterances are so carefully guarded that they could not be construed as an incitement to revolt. I am willing to believe Mr. Gandhi, whose sincerity is, I think, above suspicion; but he cannot control the tongues of all his followers.

More than ten thousand depositions were taken and filed. By June the enraged planters were exerting so much pressure on the provincial government that Gandhi was again asked to leave, though not ordered. Again he refused. Sir Edward Gait sent for him and he left half-anticipating another arrest. But after four long talks, the Lieutenant-Governor agreed (at the instance of the Viceroy) to set up a commission of inquiry, with Gandhi as spokesman for the peasants. The abrupt South African reversal seemed to have repeated itself. Gandhi brought the same tireless energy and mastery of detail to the conference table. The commission found in the peasants' favour, recommending that *tinkathia* should be abolished and that the planters should refund a percentage of the money they had extorted. In spite of the planters' protests, Sir Edward sponsored a bill giving these recommendations the force of law.

A query arose as to the size of the refund. Gandhi proposed 50 per cent, but when the planters, perhaps hoping for a deadlock, offered 25, he let this figure go through without haggling. His view was that the principle mattered more than the amount. Simply because the landlords had been compelled to disgorge, their *imperium in imperio* had suffered a blow from which it would not recover. He was right. Indigo planting ceased, and most of the planters withdrew, selling their land piecemeal to the tenants. Synthetic dye would have put them out of business sooner or later, and they were relieved at such an easy escape.

The Mahatma could claim a classic victory. The only civil disobedience had been his own, and its effect confirmed a long-cherished belief that even individual Satyagraha could be potent.

But the entire exercise had been Satyagrahi in spirit. Now, to safeguard the gains, he had to solve a psychological problem: how to build up the peasants' inchoate will to protest into a lasting intrepidity and responsibility. Since there was not to be a drawn-out struggle as in South Africa, the right method was to give Truth-Force a constructive form, a Champaran equivalent of Phoenix and Tolstoy Farm.

This programme kept him in Champaran till mid-August, and brought him back at the end of September and again in November, with Rajendra Prasad deputizing for him between. His watchwords were education and self-reliance. On the second he was uncompromising. Against Prasad and the rest, he had rejected the help of his friend Andrews; he condemned the lawyers' weakness in wanting an Englishman's support. 'You must rely on yourselves to win the battle,' he said. His aim was to teach the peasants to win future battles when he was not there. Picking out six villages, he opened a primary school in each. Educating the next generation, in itself, might not produce any quick advance in morale. But he made his schools into community projects, with the villagers giving the staff their board and lodging, so that parents as well as children became involved.

Finding teachers who would work for no more than a subsistence was a greater problem than persuading villagers to accept them. Gandhi appealed for volunteers. A number came forward, some from as far off as Bombay. Among them was Mahadev Desai, a fellow-Gujarati. In him Gandhi recognized a potential disciple of at least equal calibre to Polak and Maganlal, and said, in effect, 'Leave all and follow me.' Mahadev became his secretary and amply fulfilled his expectations. He also sent for a few of the ashramites, including his son Devadas, and Kasturbai—or Kasturba as she could now be called for reasons of seniority (*bai* is a polite suffix for a woman of no very definite age, *ba* means mother). Kasturbai spoke only Gujarati, and was barely literate in that. Some of the other women were hardly better qualified. However, he told them that the children needed training in cleanliness and good conduct rather than grammar, and they would have no trouble picking up the local version of Hindi. His judgement was sound. The women without academic background got the best results. Moreover they could make contact, as he himself could not, with the peasants' wives and daughters.

This last point was important. Besides their school duties, Gandhi wanted his volunteers to improve village sanitation and medical care. Among the older villagers, skin disease was the norm rather than the exception. Accordingly he equipped every school with staff of both sexes, so that the whole population could be reached. A doctor from the Servants of India supervised this part of the scheme. The teachers were allowed to use castor oil, quinine, and sulphur ointment. For anything further they consulted the doctor, who made regular rounds of the villages, not only attending to patients but organizing improved drainage and scavenging and the cleaning of wells. Gandhi also sketched a project for cattle-breeding and better dairies.

The peasants' response was mixed. Many were hostile or apathetic. Others plunged ardently into village schemes. Gandhi had had a car put at his disposal, and where the absence of roads prevented him from making full use of it, the peasants would sometimes level out a track. Once the impulse for teamwork came from sabotage. The school where Kasturbai taught was a hut of bamboo and grass, and a vengeful planter burned it down. Within a short time a local crew put up a less vulnerable schoolhouse of brick.

To Gandhi, with his theoretical faith in village culture, the sight of real villages at close quarters was a revelation. Everywhere, thanks to deficiencies in the diet and water supply, he saw the lame and the prematurely senile, and the goitred giggling imbeciles who were a speciality of the district. When he noticed some dirtily dressed women, he asked his wife to find out why they did not wash their clothes. Kasturbai put this question to one of them, who led her into a bare hut and explained that the sari she had on was her sole garment; she could not wash it in the hut, and she had nothing else to change into. This and similar stories appalled Gandhi. He was made cruelly aware of ignorance and filth and lack of resource, sweated labour and soul-killing idleness, sheer vacant misery without end. The retreat of the planters and the virtues of an honest Lieutenant-Governor could yield a certain relief but no solution.

Any other rural enthusiast might have been dashed. Not he. His reaction to the gulf between ideals and realities was simply to design bigger bridges. The tasks which he proposed for Truth-Force began to grow vaster and more radical. Its improvised extension as village welfare began to blossom into a whole patriotic philosophy, a constructive programme.

'In Champaran,' he said later, 'I declared that the British could not order me about in my own country.' The remark had a moderate sound which was deceptive. No Indian had ever made that declaration before—at any rate with impunity. But once made, it implied that the British had no right to order any Indian about, in a country which was indeed his own and not theirs. Most of the visible achievement in Champaran faded away. The volunteers could not stay for ever, and in 1918 Gandhi himself regretfully had to give up further action. The schools closed down, the cattle-breeding never started. But the dizzying infusion of hope spread through Bihar. It shook off its backwardness and became one of the most awakened of the provinces. Its masses turned to the Mahatma with a faith and yearning which could only be satisfied through a more apocalyptic rebirth.

2

Gandhi had installed himself in a special status before the politicians had grasped what was happening. People spoke of him now with the honorific suffix *ji*, as Gandhiji or even Mahatmaji. But two things remained to be seen. First, could he step out of the country of indigo and elephants, and work with urban reformers who had ideas of their own? Second, could he enlist large numbers of Indians under British rule for his own brand of civil defiance?

During the main struggle in Champaran, while asking the Congress leaders to stay out, he had kept them posted privately and never lost touch. On 3 November 1917 he was at Godhra presiding over the first Gujarat Political Conference. Tilak spoke, but Gandhi stood out in public estimation as chief popularizer of the Congress-League scheme in that part of India. His own address, in Gujarati, contained some sensible warnings about India's future parliament. It would be no cure-all. It would progress by trial and error. But so long as British autocracy continued, Indians could not do even that. 'The nation today is in a helpless condition; it does not even possess the right to err. He who has no right to err can never go forward.' Gandhi pressed the claims of Satyagraha as India's special weapon. Through the discipline and independence of spirit which it promoted, Swaraj could be gained.

The following month Congress met in Calcutta. Annie Besant,

released in September after a spell of internment, presided. Tilak's influence carried increasing weight. Congressmen were showing interest in Satyagraha, and a desire to test it—notably the younger sort such as Jawaharlal Nehru, who had been concerned, during Mrs Besant's incarceration, in a project for 'passive resistance' on her behalf. Some, however, were still cautious. The respected Punjabi reformer Lala Lajpat Rai distrusted an Ahimsa which seemed to him too much like the rationalized spinelessness of the Hindu past.

Gandhi attended, but he had other preoccupations. During his last Champaran tour, two letters from Gujarat had arrived. One was from local politicians anxious for his help in the Kheda district. The crops had failed, but the Government's tax assessment was based on the assumption that they had not. Hence the peasants were receiving demands which they could not meet. Gandhi replied that as in Champaran, he would need to make inquiries himself. The other letter was from Anasuya, the sister of Ambalae Sarabhai, Ahmedabad's leading textile manufacturer. Conscience-stricken at the exploitation of labour, she was supporting a wage claim by the city's thousands of weavers . . . and her brother was not only the chief employer, but the saviour of the Ashram during the Untouchable crisis.

After nibbling at both problems in spare moments, Gandhi went to Bombay early in February 1918. Bombay was the capital of the province which then included Gujarat, and he meant to begin investigating the Kheda complaints. However, he met Ambalal Sarabhai, who seemed as eager to have him in Ahmedabad as Anasuya was. So he returned to the Ashram. It had been shifted eight months previously from Kochrab to Sabarmati, across the river from the city.

The origin of the labour dispute lay in a recent outbreak of plague. The mill-owners had paid their weavers a bonus—sometimes as much as 70 per cent of wages—as an incentive to run the risk of staying. With the danger past, they proposed to cancel it. But meanwhile prices had shot up. The workers asked that the plague payment should be replaced by a cost-of-living bonus of 50 per cent. Gandhi persuaded the parties to accept arbitration, and tried to get away to Kheda. But Anasuya summoned him back. Negotiations were breaking down. Small work stoppages had occurred, and the employers had seized the excuse to withdraw from the arbitration board. Their offer was 20 per cent, and they were talking of dismissing all workers who turned it down.

He studied the situation with his usual minuteness. Finally he suggested a 35 per cent increase, which the mill-owners, whose profits were soaring, could well afford. But on the 22nd the dead-lock was complete and the workers found themselves locked out. He discussed strike action with their leaders. If they struck, he maintained, they should be firm but orderly. They should abjure violence, even against blacklegs, and try to support their families by odd jobs rather than begging; there were no funds for strike pay. When the leaders agreed to observe these rules, he addressed a mass meeting under a banyan tree beside the river. Ten thousand workers took a pledge not to return till they got their 35 per cent.

The Ahmedabad strike was not the first in India. A mass walk-out had occurred in Bombay as far back as 1908, in protest at the jailing of Tilak. Nor was it Gandhi's first contact with industrial workers. His memory of the Natal miners was vivid, and he told their story to encourage the weavers. But this clash arose from a new unrest which was a greater factor in Indian society than the author of *Hind Swaraj* had foreseen. The war had given a fillip to industrialization, and government policy, for the moment, favoured it. Factory-owners were planning for expansion with a fresh confi-dence. The rural poor were drifting into the cities for work, as the English had done a century or so before. Like the English, they sank into a morass of slums and dirt and debt and corruption. Like the English, they were goaded into organizing and fighting.

Gandhi entered the field at a stage resembling the Luddite period. His outlook might have been expected to turn his interests away from the mills, and make him the prophet of an Indian Luddism. It did not. He ranged himself with the strikers as an able and effective commander-in-chief. Every afternoon at 4.30 they gathered at the banyan to listen to the Mahatma and sing militant songs of their own composition. One of their slogans was 'Be not afraid, for we have a divine helper'. The helper was God, not Gandhi, but the chief's Messianic halo was shining as brightly among the city proletarians as it had among the peasants. He issued daily leaflets. They marched through the streets with banners in-scribed EK TEK—Keep the Pledge. Their unexpectedly peaceable bearing swung public opinion in their favour. Gandhi kept sounding out the employers, but they met his advances with a pitiless paternalism that rejected any mediation. 'Our relations with the labourers,' they told him, 'are those of parents and children.' He knew what the existence of the 'children' was like, because he had made a point of visiting working-class homes; and the employers knew that he knew.

On 12 March Ambalal and his colleagues proclaimed that they would open their mills to all workers willing to settle for 20 per cent. Now that it was possible to go back, some wanted to go. Their weakening led to threats against them, which Gandhi had to veto sternly. Agents of the employers were sowing mistrust by a whispering campaign. The strike showed signs of crumbling. Meetings were less buoyant and much more thinly attended, families were hungry. For Gandhi, Truth was his mainstay: a vow once taken could not be broken. But on the 14th, when his cousin Chhaganlal called some strikers to a meeting scheduled for the next morning, they replied: 'What is it to Anasuyabehn and Gandhiji? They come and go in their car; they eat sumptuous food, but we are suffering death-agonies; attending meetings does not prevent starvation.'

Their remarks were reported to Gandhi just before he addressed the meeting. On impulse, he said: 'I cannot tolerate for a minute that you break your pledge. I shall not take any food, nor use a car, till you get your increase or leave the mills altogether.'

This announcement ushered in his much-publicized use of fasting as a form of Satyagraha. He had fasted before at Phoenix and Tolstoy, sometimes as self-discipline, twice as a penance for his own negligence when his young charges misbehaved. These gestures shook the inmates considerably and, he thought, beneficially. The public fasting which he first practised at Sabarmati was an outgrowth of that experience. In theory he was setting an example, showing that he would not flinch from the extremest consequences of his responsibilities, so as to shock and shame those who loved him into facing theirs. In practice he was taking a course that might be hard to distinguish from coercion. The response to his Ahmedabad gesture made him aware of both aspects. Anasuya burst into tears. The strikers implored him to forgive them for wavering; many offered to fast themselves. The mill-owners complained that they were being morally blackmailed. Ambalal was increasingly at odds with his wife as well as his sister. Appeals began pouring in on him from all over India. However, he still appeared unbending, and he stiffened the others. They besieged Gandhi demanding that he should end the fast. They even offered to pay the 35 per cent if he would promise to take food, go away, and never come back.

But the peril to the Mahatma's life broke the deadlock. It unleashed a new tide of activity. If the strike was to go on, the strikers and their dependants had to be kept alive too . . . and perhaps, a proof that they could not be starved into submission would turn the scale. The barrister Vallabhbhai Patel, who had represented them on the arbitration board, tried to find municipal jobs for them. Maganlal Gandhi managed to give some of them employment carrying sand from the dry river-bed for Ashram building operations. They filed back and forth, and Anasuya led the procession with a basket on her head.

As Gandhi tactfully put it, 'the hearts of the mill-owners were touched'. Conferences were held at Anasuya's house. On the 18th an agreement was reached, with a face-saving compromise which in fact conceded the 35 per cent. Gandhi broke his fast. The final scene was an unlooked-for and pathetic harlequinade. The employers invited the workers to a celebration which included a distribution of sweets—that is, confectionery and candied fruit. It was held outdoors in the same place as the strike meetings. The sweets were to be doled out under the famous banyan. With the workers fresh from strike discipline, it never occurred to Gandhi that any problem of order would arise. But this candy distribution was the one point where he lost control. Neither the Mahatma nor the strike committee could keep the recipients in line. They broke ranks and scrambled and fought, scattering sweets over the ground and trampling them into inedibility. The attempt was abandoned. Gandhi and his helpers retrieved as much as they could, and handed it out quietly next day at Sheth Ambalal's bungalow. Then the explanation emerged. It was sobering. News of the feast had leaked out to the city's famished beggars. Swarms of them mingled with the workers unrecognized. It was they whose rush to grab had thrown the crowd into chaos.

In later years Gandhi wrote of this incident with a rare bitterness, assailing both the poverty which drove men to such degradation and the philanthropists who offered them alms instead of work. He might have added that when mill-hands and beggars could not be told apart, it was an interesting comment on the paternal care alleged to exist at the mills. His three and a half weeks as a labour activist had disturbed him. He had been sure throughout of his duty to change the employers' minds. Even the best of them were 'philanthropists' of the sort he condemned. Yet he accepted their money for his Ashram, and sincerely believed in love and persuasion. The inescapable fact that he had fasted *against* them, and split the household of his revered friend Ambalal, weighed on his conscience.

In the Ahmedabad strike Gandhi had seemed to be rising as a champion of the Left. Actually it stopped him from becoming so. To make a policy of leading one section of Indians against another —even against the pernicious pupils of western capitalism—would have meant too sharp a rupture with his habits of mind. Instead he devoted himself to national rebirth and tried to infuse it with his own spirit. He never engaged so deeply again in the battles of industry. But he did not desert the workers of Ahmedabad. For the rest of his life his word was potent in the mills and restrained the worst abuses of power. He adjusted disputes, brought labour and management together, and guided the growth of a trade-union body, the Textile Labour Association. Today this by-product of his work, in a sphere always thought of as peculiarly un-Gandhian, is among his most durable monuments. It has a hundred thousand members (with better pay and conditions than those in rival unions) and a wide range of activities, social, cultural, educational and civic. In the Ahmedabad of the 1960s it is still possible to meet veterans who recall, with rapt looks, how Gandhiji once touched them or spoke to them. Above the entrance of the Association's main office is an immense gilt plaque portraying him in the unusual role of a leader of industrial workers.

But his brand of unionism never took root outside Gujarat. It remained largely a might-have-been. With a foreshadowing precipitancy, as soon as the strike was over, he turned his back on the city and hurried to the peasants of Kheda.

3

He already knew that the crisis was genuine. Most of the peasants in the six hundred villages of the district owned their land and paid tax on it. The last harvest had been below 25 per cent, a failure so serious as to border on famine, and entitle them to a remission of tax. The Government refused on the ground that the harvest was above 25 per cent. Protests in the provincial legislative council were turned down insultingly. The Reverend Mr Andrews made no headway with an appeal to Lord Willingdon, the Governor.

Aided by volunteers, Gandhi persuaded most of the peasants to sign a pledge. It set forth their grievance and informed the Government that they would not pay. Thus in March 1918, India witnessed Satyagraha on a fairly large scale. The papers gave it lavish publicity. Visitors and donations streamed in. But unlike the strike, this was a slow grinding affair that lasted for months. The war was in its most anxious phase, and British officials had some excuse for severity, but the form which it took was mean. Cattle were confiscated and sold, standing crops were attached. These measures threatened the peasants with starvation. Some surrendered and paid, others were so furious that Gandhi had trouble keeping them non-violent, especially as he insisted on 'civility' toward the collectors as well as mere abstention from hitting them.

To restore the resisters' nerve he staged an ingenious token counter-attack. In theory Satyagrahis never broke any law but the law they had pledged themselves to break. Even in the Transvaal, however, that rule had been stretched. Now the Mahatma argued that attachment of crops was a kind of looting in which the State had exceeded its rights. The orders could be defied. With maximum fanfare a group of volunteers led by Mohanlal Pandya, himself a lawyer, removed the onion crop from a field that had been attached. They were duly arrested, but their action had snapped the spell. When they went to jail a cheering procession escorted them. For ever after Mohanlal Pandya was nicknamed Dungli Chor, the Onion Thief, an accolade surely without precedent.

The Kheda campaign was brought to a close by an ungracious government retreat. Without making any public announcement or even informing Gandhi, who heard indirectly, the chief collector instructed his staff to drop their demands against the poorer peasants, and insist on payment only from those who could evidently afford it. Most observers hailed this outcome as a victory. Yet it was a feeble end, without that sense of turning over a new leaf which Truth-Force was supposed to bring. Gandhi's main source of satisfaction was that established politicians and other educated people had come out to join him among the masses. Vallabhbhai

Patel was with him again, having virtually shelved a lucrative practice at the Bar. So were Anasuya and Mahadev Desai.

Meanwhile Home Rule propaganda, especially Annie Besant's, was seeping into the Gujarati countryside. The villagers' response to Gandhi's appeals on the tax issue gave him faith in his power to rouse them for other causes. But they soon taught him not to presume too far. The sequel to his qualified triumph was an almost total fiasco.

Russia's defeat had removed a check to a possible Turkish push eastward. In April Lord Chelmsford summoned a viceregal War Conference in Delhi, with a view to strengthening the Indian forces. He could hardly invite Tilak or Mrs Besant, but Gandhi, he considered, was on the borderline. In a note he speculated whether the Mahatma's 'restless activities' might be 'diverted into a useful channel'. If left alone he caused unrest, but could he be sent to Mesopotamia? Finally an invitation went off. Gandhi, in Kheda, could not make up his mind how to take it. He disliked the exclusion of the Home Rulers, and also of Shaukat and Mohamed Ali, two Muslim brothers who had been detained for political reasons. Hindu-Muslim unity was bulking large in his thoughts. He decided that if he went to the War Conference, he could and must use it to affirm his solidarity with Islamic India. But he was not happy, and Andrews urged that Britain's secret treaties made it incompatible with his principles to take part.

Hence the Viceroy's request threw him into a dilemma where his Absolute deserted him. When Gandhi tried to juggle several ideals in a complicated context, he could end by producing an effect that was less than idealistic. He went to Delhi still hesitating. Chelmsford received him in private audience and argued that if he admitted (as he did) that the Empire had been, on the whole, a power for good, he should help it in its need. This was a well-judged appeal that brought him to the conference table. The Viceroy asked if he would support a resolution on recruiting, and he complied. His speech consisted of one sentence. But even with that he managed to create a stir, because he spoke it, by permission, in Hindustani —a language never uttered before at such a meeting. Afterwards he wrote Chelmsford a letter. With a curious notion of potential contamination, he looked round for a 'pure' messenger to convey it, and chose a Protestant missionary.

In the letter he protested at the snub to Tilak and the others, and added that his own support was conditional on visible progress toward Swaraj. Not that he would stress this himself—he would prefer silence till after the war—but his fellow-countrymen were impatient. 'Nothing less than a definite vision of Home Rule, to be realized in the shortest possible time, will satisfy the Indian people.' As for his own activities he declined to suspend them, and claimed that Champaran had been a contribution to the war effort, because it had revealed the real justice of Britain.

Back in Kheda, and before the tax battle was quite disposed of, Gandhi embarked on the course to which a muddle of loyalties had committed him. The peasants were stupefied to see their non-violent apostle in the role of a recruiting sergeant. This time he was not enrolling stretcher-bearers but soldiers. His arguments were various. One was that Indians were despised as cowardly, and could blot out that reproach if they learned to use arms. Another was that a mortal blow to the Empire would destroy their hopes of a progress into partnership. If they rallied round, Britain would be grateful and grant India Dominion status. Kheda could raise ten thousand men, whose sacrifice on the battlefield would immortalize themselves, their villages, their country. The women should encourage them, etc.

It was no good. The villagers saw through his rationalizations. For Satyagraha they had supplied his team with volunteer help, transport, and food. For the recruiting drive they would not lift a finger, or lend him their carts even when he offered to pay. He was reduced to trudging about the district with a handful of loyal but depressed disciples, carrying their own food in satchels. Villagers turned up at his meetings, but mainly to heckle. They asked how a preacher of Ahimsa could exhort them to fight, and what the Government had ever done for them. Little support came from other national leaders. Annie Besant held aloof. Tilak sardonically offered to bet that he could raise five thousand soldiers, if Gandhi could extract a promise that they would be put on the same footing as British soldiers, with the same prospects of promotion. Authority itself was far from appreciative. The District Commissioner had unluckily read one of his leaflets which contained a painful attempt to have it both ways: 'Among the many misdeeds of the British rule in India, history will look upon the Act depriving a whole nation of arms as the blackest. If we want the Arms Act to be repealed, if we want to learn the use of arms, here is a golden opportunity.'

By dogged persistence well into August, sometimes walking twenty miles daily, he succeeded in collecting a few names. But the combination of physical and moral strain was too much. His second bout of war work on behalf of King George ended like the first, in a breakdown. At this period his diet was at its simplest. It consisted chiefly of lemons and peanut butter. He was still vowed not to drink milk, partly because Raychandbhai had told him it was an aphrodisiac, partly because he was disgusted at the cruelty used in Indian milking. His distresses began with a mild onset of dysentery. On 11 August he meant to rest at the Ashram with no food. However, a Hindu festival was in progress, and Kasturbai gave him some soup and rice. The dishes were refilled in the Indian fashion till he had eaten more than was prudent. Soon the dysentery returned. He was expected back at his former Satyagraha headquarters in Nadiad, and managed to drag himself there, but then collapsed in pain and weakness. His distrust of doctors (it was part of the Simple Life cult; Shaw had it too) now rebounded on him. He refused medicines and injections, and grew rapidly worse. Ambalal Sarabhai, who bore no grudge over the strike, took him to his own house and then back to the Ashram.

For months Gandhi lay ill, with long spells in which he could not read and could scarcely talk, and sometimes listlessly imagined that death was imminent. The end of the war removed his most pressing worry, and he started to mend. But his mixture of principles and fads slowed down his convalescence. He tried a water treatment. He allowed a crank from the Brahmo Samaj to pack him in ice. The ice-doctor restored his appetite, and coaxed him into taking a stroll, but then forfeited his obedience by advising a diet of eggs. Having developed a fistula, Gandhi went to Bombay with Kasturbai to consult a more orthodox practitioner, Dr. Dalal. They arrived on 13 December and stayed at Mani Bhavan, a house in Laburnum Road belonging to Revashankar Jhaveri, a relative of the Dr Mehta who had helped Gandhi in his student days and introduced him to Raychandbhai.

Dalal was blunt and decisive, and inspired trust. He forecast a full recovery if the patient would consent to injections of iron and arsenic, and also take milk. Gandhi no longer opposed injections, but he held out against milk. The doctor asked why, and he explained about the ill-treatment of cattle. Suddenly Kasturbai spoke.

'In that case,' she said, 'you can't object to goat's milk.'

Dr Dalal seized on her idea as a way out. 'Goat's milk will do,' he said.

In Gandhi's eyes this was an evasion. But his spirits had revived, he badly wanted to resume public life. He followed the prescription. On 21 January 1919 the doctor operated on his fistula. Health came gradually back. Ever afterwards he kept on with the goat's milk, pricked by conscience, but unable to give it up.

4

Despite the martial aberration, his place in India was now secure and unique. The best contemporary witness to his cult is a book called *Mahatma Gandhi: His Life, Writings and Speeches,* published in Madras in December 1917 and re-issued with enlargements the following year. Its preface by Sarojini Naidu takes his Mahatmaship for granted. The editor describes him:

> He is the latest, though not the least, of the world's apostles. He seems for ever robed in vestments of shining white. Infinitely gentle, to the inner ear, is his footfall upon earth. His accents have the dewy freshness of the dawn.

Plainly we are outside the world of ordinary politics. Even the warmest partisan would hardly have written thus of Lloyd George or Clemenceau.

The account of his career ends with the statement that his 'most pregnant act in India' has been the foundation of the Ashram, the 'nucleus of a great new order for the perfecting of the individual and the uplifting of the nation'. History has borne out this judgement. The Satyagraha Ashram was the birthplace of modern India. After Gandhi's recovery its role became increasingly clear.

The move to Sabarmati was due to plague in Kochrab. When Gandhi acquired the site it was an empty waste beside the river, without trees or buildings. Near by was a prison as a constant reminder of Satyagrahi duty. The ashramites, now numbering about forty, built their new home while living under canvas and contending with snakes and rain. When finished, the Ashram looked very much as it does today.

Pilgrims see a cluster of plain, single-storey whitewashed buildings, with trees here and there, and plenty of open space. Lacking

the slightest claim to architectural beauty, the Ashram is a place
where you can wander and breathe (barefooted, as in all such
precincts in India). A broad flight of steps goes down to the river.
As you look across, the industrial city is on the other side, but from
this angle it is not obtrusive. Beside the steps on your right is a
patch of sand with a tree overhanging it. Here the ashramites
assemble at dusk, to sit cross-legged for the singing of evening
prayers. Beyond the prayer ground is Gandhi's bungalow. His room
is very bare with a barred window. It adjoins a veranda where he
worked and talked with his guests. All the dwellings are like his—
not cramped, but austere, with almost no furniture except mats and
water-vessels and cots made of cords stretched over a frame. Meals
are eaten squatting on the floor in a refectory, with girls from the
Ashram school serving. One of Gandhi's rules was that food and
water should always be handled, and therefore polluted, by Untouchables. Thus no one could live with him who would not give
way at least slightly on the orthodox taboo. The school where these
young people are taught, and the workshops and other parts of the
establishment, lie farther back away from the river.

While the Christian world has no institutions quite like this, it
has some which resemble it, retreat houses and so forth. To know
them is to suspect that the holy peace which impressed visitors in
Gandhi's time was by no means typical of Ashram life seen from
within. In fact it was not; nor was it meant to be. Sabarmati was
a social laboratory. The medley of people which it housed grew
steadily larger and more bizarre. Children and ancients, gentle
mystics and ardent patriots, Sanskrit scholars and lady handicraft-
teachers, shared their meals and collaborated and quarrelled. To
all of them Gandhi and Kasturbai were Bapu and Ba, Father and
Mother.

The ashramites were meant to be the vanguard of Bapu's Utopia
—an India rejecting urban capitalism and most of modern civilization, even in what seemed its beneficent aspects; a wise, classless,
busy India, that would dissolve Imperialism by recovering its own
soul, and converting the conquerors to its own simplicity. Politicians
who came to him for guidance—as, after 1918, more and more
did—were told to stop trying to influence the English by aping them.
Instead they should put on Indian costume, and go out among the
peasants talking with them in their own languages. In that way
Gandhi himself had come to know the abiding horror which now

drove him on: the sight of village India cowed and destitute because of a system that was not necessary but man-made, and could only be changed by the resurrection of its victims.

The resourceful Maganlal was the Ashram's manager, and Bapu's deputy in his absence. As for the rest, there was no question of the Father having favourite children. However, his eye lingered on Vinoba Bhave, whom he had put to work teaching in the villages and studying Hindu literature. Vinoba was a mathematician and linguist, but he also had a Gandhian practical streak, and ran a class in corn-grinding. His discipleship was total, and he wanted 'Bapu' to be more than a courtesy title in his case. Reading a report of his labours in February 1918, Gandhi remarked that the pupil was surpassing the master, and wrote in reply: 'Your love and your character fascinate me. . . . A real son is one who improves on what the father has done. . . . If ever I become another Hiranyakashipu, oppose me respectfully like Prahlad.' (The legend of the tyrant Hiranyakashipu and his son Prahlad was one the Mahatma often quoted. Prahlad refused to admit his megalomaniac father's claim to be greater than God, and withstood every torture till rescued by divine intervention. This was perfect Satyagraha.)

At Kochrab the ashramites had been classified into controllers, candidates and students. The last included the children who were accepted for Gandhian education, given in Gujarati, with English as a second language and a strong vocational bias. At Sabarmati the distinctions were blurred, but they persisted. Besides studying and teaching in the neighbourhood, ashramites worked on the land, and planted and tended fruit trees. On admission as full members they took fourteen vows. So long as Gandhi was present, his liveliness and sense of humour kept most of them cheeful. But the list of their obligations was daunting.

They were pledged to Truth; Ahimsa; Chastity; Control of the Palate; Non-Thieving; Non-Attachment; Poverty; Swadeshi; Fearlessness; Rejection of Untouchability; Use of Vernaculars; Manual Labour; Khadi; and Study of Politics in the Light of Religion. Some of these are amply illustrated in Gandhi's own life, but others require comment. 'Control of the Palate', for instance, meant more than a mere abstention from gourmet meals and alcohol. It covered what C. S. Lewis calls the gluttony of delicacy, an undue and fastidious concern with food even in small amounts. Orthodox Hindus, with their complex culinary rituals, were prone to this. A faithful ashramite would simply eat what was set before him—vegetarian, of course—and not care. 'Non-Thieving', again, looks like a platitude. But behind it was a belief very like Proudhon's, that property itself is theft. Any economic exploitation counted as stealing. Any marked inequality in one person's favour implied that others were being deprived. Therefore an ashramite could not, for example, hire labourers to work for him.

Three of the vows had even deeper significance. For Gandhi, Swadeshi went far beyond its 1906 'Buy Indian' meaning. His disciples preached not only the use of national products rather than imports, but the use of local products rather than what came from a distance. India's ancient village-republics had been almost self-sufficient, each with its carpenter and its potter and its smith and its barber. To Gandhi this neighbourly do-it-yourself system was the key to right living. His definition of Swadeshi was 'that spirit within us which restricts us to the use and service of our immediate surroundings, to the exclusion of the more remote'. Given the will to revive the village economy, British power would be turned back and India would be on the road to Swaraj.

Hence Gandhi's famous advocacy of the spinning wheel and the handloom. When he wrote *Hind Swaraj* he had never seen either. One of the earliest assignments of the Ashram controllers was to reinstate both. Weaving came first, with the introduction of a few country looms. No instructor could be found, but Maganlal, whose talents included a mechanical knack, succeeded in mastering the technique. Then some ashramites went outside and learned to use fly-shuttle looms of the Madras type. At the end of 1916 the Ashram had three country looms and three fly-shuttle; in 1917 four more of the latter were added. Gandhi learned to weave himself, and worked three hours at a stretch.

But Swadeshi eluded him, because the weaving depended on machine-spun yarn from unsympathetic mills. His discovery of the wheel or *charkha* did not come till late 1917, when a widow named Gangabehn Majmudar reported that she had met some Muslims at Vijapur, in Baroda, who still had dusty old wheels in their lumber rooms. They undertook to spin if they were guaranteed a market and supplied with the raw material—cotton slivers. For a while Gandhi made do with slivers sent him by Umar Sobani, a friendly mill-owner. Then he acquired the services of a carder. He learned spinning himself in Bombay, while Maganlal organized it at

Sabarmati. Maganlal invented an improved wheel. Further improvements superseded the traditional design entirely. The old wheels were upright and cumbersome. The modern type, still made at the Ashram and employed throughout India, lies flat in a case and is compact and portable.

Homespun cloth is known as khadi or khaddar, and the ashramites' khadi vow was a pledge to wear nothing else and to spin themselves, not an easy requirement. This plain, rather thick fabric became the uniform of the national movement, the 'livery of freedom' in Jawaharlal Nehru's phrase. Once Gandhi summoned all his flock to a bonfire of foreign cloth, in the manner of the Bengali campaign. Among the articles produced was a splendid sari belonging to his wife, a present from Gokhale. It was hand-woven, but from foreign yarn. The Mahatma gazed at it sadly for a moment, then threw it on the flames with his own hands.

As usual we are not told what his wife said. The expressions on those firelit faces were not unrelated to the vow of Chastity and the interpretation he put on this. It was here, rather than in his derided but defensible economics, that his insight faltered.

The Ashram was not like a monastery or convent, a house of celibates of the same sex. It included both, and it included married couples. Bapu and Ba were the prototypes. Bapu's *brahmacharya* had cancelled the physical bond between them. The question was whether all his disciples should do likewise. He laid it down that they should. Here he diverged from moralists in the Christian tradition, the best of whom have always allowed that there can be such a thing as married chastity—sexual partnership rightly fulfilled and ordered. Chastity to Gandhi meant abstinence: not repression, which he never approved, but sublimation.

He insisted that the Ashram's ideals could not be attained, Satyagraha could not be fully practised, by men and women in marital relations. If he had argued that the responsible head of a family may not feel free to do or die as required—may actually be deterred by worry over his dependants—the point would have been valid. But that was not how he did argue. His axiom was that marriage meant diversion of energy and division of loyalty. In a commentary on the vows, he wrote:

> A man whose activities are wholly consecrated to the realization of Truth, which requires utter selflessness, can have no time for the selfish purpose of begetting children and running a house-

hold. . . . If a man gives his love to one woman, or a woman to one man, what is there left for all the world besides?

In other words, the hundred-per-cent Satyagrahi must be above sex. Anyone else, however devoted, is relegated to second class as a part-time follower, not a leader. Gandhi goes on:

What about people who are already married? Will they never be able to realize Truth? Can they never offer up their all at the altar of humanity? There is a way out for them. They can behave as if they were not married. . . . If the married couple can think of each other as brother and sister, they are freed for universal service. . . . Their love becomes free from the impurity of lust and so grows stronger.

The main blame for this frankly false psychology must rest on Hinduism and Hindu marriage as Gandhi knew it—an institution of whose depressing nature the fetter clamped on himself in childhood was only one aspect. Among the many splits and discontinuities which have confused Indian culture, those in the sexual field are the most obvious. Through the millennial vistas of Hindustan we glimpse vagary after vagary—fevered amorousness and ruthless mortification, erotic licence and exaggerated fidelity, stylized *Kama Sutra* gymnastics and the crudest sadism, salvation through lust and magical power through restraint. . . . Hindus at one time or another have thought of almost everything, except perhaps balance. However, the ecstasies tended to evaporate and the dregs to remain. One of the less remembered concerns of the Brahmo Samaj was an attack on the debased vice which disfigured nineteenth-century India. By Gandhi's time, most marriages at whatever age were no better than bargains, sordid and graceless, with at best a poor sort of fruition. When Hindus began to write novels the misery of the matrimonial system was their commonest theme.

What Gandhi heard of marriage at second hand undoubtedly appeared to confirm his experience. In its usual sense it was an entanglement, with few redeeming features. As Father of the Ashram he reasoned from his own case. The one safe rule, anywhere, was that wedlock should involve as little as possible, except on a spiritual plane. When the aim of sexual intercourse was to produce children, and no economic objection existed, it was a proper act. Otherwise it was lust and dissipation—better than morbid self-denial, but not good, a waste of energy. Inside the Ashram dissipation was wrong and parenthood a distraction. Therefore it could not be justified at all. Human beings could opt for sex *or* service, but not both.

For those whom it suited, the way of sublimation was valid, a way of charity and freedom. But Gandhi's palpable error was to deny that there could be another. The shortcomings of Hindu society had pushed him into a false dilemma. To solve it he adopted a rule which could apply only to a few, and applied it to everyone. He never grasped that a sexual companionship might be ennobling and generous. Myopia in this quarter was his tragic flaw, all the more tragic because he was free from vulgar prudery. Once he came very near to refuting himself. John Hoyland, an English friend, recorded a confession of his about Kasturbai:

> I learned the lesson of non-violence from my wife. . . . Her determined resistance to my will on the one hand, and her quiet submission to the suffering my stupidity involved on the other hand, ultimately made me ashamed of myself and cured me of my stupidity in thinking I was born to rule over her; and in the end she became my teacher in non-violence. And what I did in South Africa was but an extension of the rule of Ṣatyagraha which she unwillingly practised in her own person.

If a sexual relation taught him Satyagraha, even back-handedly, how could he regard sexual relations as necessarily leading away from it? But he did. As a result, however heroic his achievement, there was the shadow of something pallid and life-denying close to its heart; while his feebler disciples, incapable of being heroes, proved their Gandhism by being prigs.

He could have tolerably said 'No' to much else, if he had said 'Yes' to this. Sometimes he seemed insensitive to what is called culture; but he was putting first things first, and culture was a mockery to the hungry millions. He opposed meat-eating and smoking; but he had medical arguments for doing so. He opposed alcohol; but in India, alcohol did not mean the pub or the café, it meant Gin Lane and Skid Row. If these had been the sum total of his negations, he would have been simply a resolute leader with strict priorities and a mild crankishness. It was his notion of chastity that gave the lesser denials the flavour they had. That other genius from the same school, Bernard Shaw, was also a rejecter of many things and largely the same things. Yet Shaw never gave the same impression, and the chief reason is summed up in his recognition that Candida's husband might be more and not less effective as a reformer through being married to her.

The Mahatma's mistake was to bring its own retribution. Orthodox *brahmacharya* was a practice for ascetics, who could live as hermits away from women. But Gandhi made women his allies and co-workers. Their emancipation in India was to be mainly his doing. The more freely they mingled with the men, the plainer the difficulty grew. He himself was not exempt. Gifted and charming ladies surrounded him, and as Tagore observed, he differed from his mentor Tolstoy by being fond of them. Before his illness he was already in the throes of an affectionate correspondence with Esther Faering, a young Danish missionary who made him ill-fitting vests, and annoyed her superiors by persistently going to the Ashram.

Sabarmati was not Phoenix. The glare and colour of India, the reversion on doctor's orders to a less austere diet, reawakened his impulses. Then his failures in the self-purgative task made him liable to moods of shame. These sapped his confidence, and, on account of the weight which 'purity' had assumed in his thoughts, persuaded him that the correct method of training for improved leadership was to put himself through exercises in re-sublimation. He carried this theory through to a most curious triumph. But the path was long, rough and tortuous. It was not only with vision and courage, but also with a disturbing misconception, that he entered the gigantic struggle which filled the rest of his life.

For in 1919, when he was not far short of fifty years old, he at last sighted the White Whale.

X

Violence and Non-Violence

1

The inflammatory fact about post-war India was that it could not return to normal. At some stage—nobody quite knew when—the norm had been lost. By themselves, Congress histrionics and Home Rule Leagues would not have shaken the British Government. But the attempted revolution in Ireland, and the actual revolution in Russia, put Indian unrest in a more menacing light. On 20 August 1917 they helped to extract from Edwin Montagu, the Liberal Secretary of State for India, an assurance that British policy envisaged 'not only the increasing association of Indians in every branch of the administration, but also the granting of self-governing institutions with a view to the progressive realization of responsible government in India as an integral part of the British Empire'. Furthermore, 'substantial steps' would be taken as soon as possible.

This apparent pledge of Dominion status raised some hopes. Lord Chelmsford's War Conference was meant as a gesture in the same spirit. But as Gandhi complained, the leaders of the campaign for Swaraj, without whom all talk of self-governing institutions would be pointless, were not invited. The most substantial steps actually taken were in the opposite direction. The Government invoked its emergency powers to re-intern Tilak, to lock up some lesser politicians without trial, and to tighten the censorship. Gandhi's *Hind Swaraj* was again banned, and so was *Sarvodaya*, his Gujarati version of Ruskin. Queries were raised about the proper use of these powers. Sir Sidney Rowlatt, an English judge, looked into the matter. On 19 July 1918 his committee issued its report. This drew attention to alleged terrorist plots, and advised that the powers should be retained in peace-time. A prospectus for reforms based on Montagu's statement was published almost concurrently,

184

but in that context it fell flat. Indian nationalists denounced Rowlatt and did not warm to Montagu.

India emerged from the war haggard, wretched and apprehensive. The extortion of taxes and forced loans, the unchecked profiteering and price increases, had thrust down the populace toward destitution. The world influenza epidemic, coming on top of a pneumonia epidemic exclusive to India, had killed at least thirteen million of them—a figure comparable to the battle losses of all Europe put together. Soldiers were mutinous and factory hands desperate. In December a Bombay mill strike began, which spread till it involved 125,000 workers. The Punjab simmered with grievances due to methods of raising men and money during the war. Congress met at Delhi in a ferocious mood (to the distress of Annie Besant, whose ardour in propaganda was not matched by her willingness to accept the consequences). It appealed to Woodrow Wilson's slogan of self-determination, and demanded the lifting of the restrictions.

Delhi's retort, early in February 1919, was to embody the Rowlatt recommendations in a Bill. If this became law, cases of sedition could be tried without a jury, and suspects could be interned with no trial at all. Another Bill made it clear that 'sedition' extended to such offences as having a nationalist leaflet in one's pocket, for which the penalty was two years' imprisonment. Gandhi realized what was intended when he was still lying weak and weary at Mani Bhavan, in a tree-shaded residential street of Bombay. But his mind was lucid enough. Champaran had disposed him to think that the British Raj must be challenged sooner or later; the Rowlatt Bills stung him to challenge it at once. He might still have hesitated and pondered, but his Bombay friends would not let him. The mill-owner Umar Sobani pressed him to act, and so did Shankarlal Banker, who was Sobani's associate in his other business, the *Bombay Chronicle*.

Was this a case for Satyagraha? Gandhi came to the portentous conclusion that it was. A regime which had been full of evil, but never strictly intolerable, had brought its iniquities to a sudden head by a measure which he was bound to resist. On 9 February he sent a letter of encouragement to Shrinivas Shastri, an Indian member of the Imperial Legislative Council, who was opposing the Bills. 'If we succumb,' he wrote, 'we are done for.' In a telegram to the Viceroy he denounced the Bills as symptomatic of a 'deep-seated disease in the ruling class'. He made his way painfully to a debate of the Legislative Council, the only one he ever attended. Shastri and other Indians spoke out, and Lord Chelmsford looked as if he were listening; but it was obvious that the debate was purely formal, and that the Council's built-in majority of officials could carry the Bills and meant to do so.

Already Gandhi had gone to Ahmedabad to discuss resistance with Vallabhbhai Patel. He suggested a Satyagraha pledge on the tested model. This was drawn up at a meeting at the Ashram on 24 February. About twenty signatories were present, including Patel, Sarojini Naidu, Anasuya, the two publishers, and B. G. Horniman, the editor of their *Chronicle*. The pledge bound them to defy the Bills if they became law, and also to disobey 'such other laws as a committee to be hereafter appointed may think fit'. A Satyagraha Sabha (Association) was formed in Bombay with Gandhi as president. The Transvaal drama was seemingly about to be re-enacted. The *Chronicle*, supplemented by Sabha bulletins, filled the role of *Indian Opinion*, and the pledge was administered at meetings. Six hundred people in Bombay signed it.

But 1919 was not 1906. The anti-Rowlatt agitation could not rely on the same unity. Gandhi with his religious appeal, his work among peasants, his insistence on talking in the vernaculars, was an essentially popular leader such as India had not hitherto produced, and did not know how to regard. Up to now he had been in complete control of his own activities. Even when the intelligentsia helped, as in Kheda, they submitted to his orders. But in Bombay they were in their own urban element. They clustered round with ideas which were not his, putting the Sabha under a strain. The more militant distrusted non-violence. The more cautious wanted to soften the tone.

These divergences might have been contained, if it had not been for a second factor distinguishing Rowlatt from Smuts. How were the Bills to be resisted? In 1906 Indians had been ordered to do a certain thing, and Satyagraha meant, primarily, refusing to do it—a clear-cut programme. The further steps, such as hawking without licences, had been tactical incidentals for keeping the campaign on the boil. But in 1919 no such government decree was proposed. Until the authorities actually invoked Rowlatt to arrest somebody, Satyagraha could only be offered in the second way. The incidentals would be the whole campaign. Gandhi might declare what shape they should take, but his choice would be open to dispute.

Therefore, at its inception as a weapon against the British Raj, Truth-Force entered a phase of blurring and broadening. As a national leader Gandhi had to wrestle with two problems: how to keep the intelligentsia in step, and how to give Satyagraha the logic, precision and moral rectitude which it was in constant peril of losing.

With the Rowlatt campaign he seemed, at the beginning, to have more success in the second respect than the first. The moderates held aloof from his Sabha, and no top-ranking Congressmen joined him. An early fiasco was averted by a Madras lawyer, C. Rajagopalachari, who secured him an invitation to speak in that city. He was still shaky, but he made the journey. It was eased by his love for southern India. The Tamil and Telugu labourers in South Africa had been among his staunchest fighters. In going to Madras he was keeping a spiritual rendezvous with a host of small, dark, patient friends, from Balasundaram onward. Mahadev Desai, now firmly attached as his secretary, went as well. Mahadev showed a valuable perceptiveness, drawing the shy Rajagopalachari into the limelight and advising Gandhi to cultivate him—a process which was duly begun, and led to Rajaji, as he was called for short, becoming the first Indian Governor-General of the Dominion of India.

Gandhi's public appearances in the Madras area had nothing superficially stirring about them. His voice did not carry, and his speeches had to be read by Mahadev. He could not even stand for long. But the matter and moment were more important than the style. With Rajaji's quietly determined backing, and his aid as an interpreter, the tottering convalescent guiltily sipping goat's milk rallied an army of supporters. The response convinced him that he could ignite most of British India, at least in so far as it was articulate, if he could hit on the right formula.

On 18 March the main Rowlatt provisions passed, with the certainty of becoming law within a few days. Whatever he was going to do, he would have to do quickly. He went to bed in Madras with his mind labouring over the problem. After a few hours' restless sleep, he was jolted awake by an intense dream. In the borderland between one state and the other the inspiration abruptly shone. At breakfast Rajaji was confronted with a hypnagogic image as the first shot in the war of independence. Gandhi had decided to proclaim a national *hartal*: that is, a protest strike. For one day all Indians should stop work and devote themselves to prayer and fasting. 30 March would be a suitable date. He still could not picture what would happen after that, but he was sure about the *hartal*.

The fact that the answer had come through an inner voice, rather than conscious reflection, was not lost on him. After all, it was a logical deduction from Satyagraha theory that the contact with God should give insight as well as strength. Henceforth Gandhi listened for the inner voice as a guide toward those grandiose clarifications he was always seeking. In 1919 at least, it had a true ring of authority. While Congressmen deprecated and wavered, ordinary citizens by the hundred thousand began preparing for the Mahatma's day as if it were a festival. In every city the police braced themselves for . . . they did not quite know what.

2

Gandhi's appraisal of his mighty opponents was part sagacity, part delusion. He was still much affected by the way he had acquired most of his knowledge of them—through meetings in London with kindly intellectuals, through studies and negotiations that had taught him to believe in British constitutionalism. The outbursts in *Hind Swaraj* expressed a perfectionist's mood rather than a reformer's working principles, and even there he had affirmed British virtues. In South Africa it had been axiomatic with him that racist laws were a departure from the Empire's true justice, and that he had only to insist on this doggedly enough to swing South Africa back on course. Non-violent action had grown to take new forms, sometimes bordering on rebellion; but it still pre-supposed a certain restraint on the authorities' part, a certain openness to conviction. Four years in his home country had battered his faith but not destroyed it. The English stood condemned by their own standards. Nevertheless, most of them did accept those standards. They could surely be made to see their error and concede India's rights.

It was true after a fashion, but a half-truth. Gandhi was one of many Indians who had difficulty adjusting themselves to the difference between the Englishman at home and the Englishman in the tropics; between the bowler and the pith helmet; between the gentleman and the Sahib. Always a real contrast, this was now growing more acute. Forster had not yet written, nor had Orwell, but he might have pondered on his own experience in 1892 with the agent. The affluence, freedom and decency of England were made possible largely by the fact that these were denied to India. When the Englishman was transplanted to an alien soil and a dreadful climate, he was apt to undergo changes which made him well qualified to safeguard that discrepancy.

In the words of a brilliant if wayward Hindu historian,* the English in India lost their nuances. By 1919 the quality of their life was not only coarser than at home, but becoming more so. Their clubs were strongholds of sneering racial arrogance. Their united front had stiffened into amoral solidarity; Englishmen backed each other right or wrong. To those who knew them best, Gandhi's trust in solving problems by reason and merit might well look naïve.

Yet the façade was flawed, and the flaws intensified the evil. The overlords were sun-sick and out of tune. Even their love life was strained and ugly. Even their light reading inclined towards pornography. Indian servants ministered to their tastes with obsequiousness and secret contempt. Strangest of all, they were showing symptoms of cowardice. They starved the public services to finance internal security. They carried weapons everywhere and forbade anyone else to carry them, apart from the police and troops. It was not unknown for an Englishman to keep his hand on a revolver in his desk drawer throughout every interview with a native, however harmless. Some were afraid to turn their backs on children.

Most of them still believed that they were in India for the Indians' good. With a fair number, this was true. With others, it was an instance of what Gandhi called an amazing capacity for self-deception. But in either event the Hindu mind no longer seemed to be reacting comprehensibly, with frank appreciation or frank ingratitude. The English did not know where they were. They judged all Indians by the 'loyalists', place-seekers and flatterers who surrounded them, and then found that the analogy did not hold. Their tempers shortened, their will and ability to do good correspondingly declined. And the war had made them tougher. Whatever the gutless politicians might promise, the English on the spot had no intention of relaxing. Even the old zeal for building up

* Nirad C. Chaudhuri.

Anglicized natives by education was losing ground to a widespread resentment that natives should be educated at all.

India had no chance of obtaining real reforms, let alone Swaraj, through a mass conversion of civil servants and soldiers and businessmen. Major change would have to come via Westminster and its Viceroy, as a thing imposed. In those quarters Satyagraha could not be brought to bear directly. Its conversions, if any, would be made at long range through awakened British opinion. Gandhi indeed could do this if anyone could. But concrete results in that political stratosphere would also require negotiation. It remained to be proved that his understanding of British minds and methods was broad enough.

With the immediate target of non-violent action—the entrenched officialdom—his problem was strategic and tactical rather than moral. Most of the English at this level could not be persuaded. They could only be pushed toward acquiescence in a surrender dictated from above. Here too the Mahatma was the fittest person to take the lead; but here too he had his limitations. He found it hard to admit that Englishmen were ever quite as mean, obstinate and vicious as they were liable to be. It was typical of his outlook that he always ascribed the granting of the Champaran commission to the goodwill of Sir Edward Gait, whereas in reality it had been forced on Sir Edward by the Viceroy. With such mirages before his mind's eye he was too liable to revert to the futile and disconcerting pose of a missionary.

His very first blow, the summons to a *hartal,* had a religious character. The English were totally unmoved. The impact on Indians, however, was potent. Delhi observed the stoppage on 30 March (in other cities it had been postponed for a week), and the huge demonstrations were marked by an unheard-of phenomenon —Hindus and Muslims fraternizing. Swami Shraddhanand, a leader of the Arya Samaj, spoke by invitation in the Great Mosque, and a composite procession streamed through the streets. The police and troops signified the moral effect on English hearts by opening fire. In the bazaar district Swami Shraddhanand stood outfacing the Gurkhas with his chest disdainfully bared. Nine people were killed, thirteen taken into hospital. Five of the dead were Hindus and four were Muslims. A government report noted this intercommunal unity with alarm. It upset the theory of implacable hate which had been a mainstay since Curzon.

On 6 April the rest of the country followed. Thousands of villages took part as well as the towns. The effect on economic life gave Indians a galvanic sense of their own power. Gandhi was overjoyed. He observed the *hartal* himself in Bombay, where Mani Bhavan had become his headquarters. An immense crowd gathered around him on Chowpati Beach, a spacious crescent of sand in a bay near the house. Like many Indian crowds it was amphibious, over-lapping the water. After a while it splashed into parade formation and marched through the city without incident. Gandhi and Mrs Naidu (not only a Hindu but a woman) spoke in one of the mosques.

For the civil disobedience which was to go on afterwards, Gandhi had offered his followers two suggestions. One was that they should defy the detested salt laws by making tax-free salt at home. As events were to show, this was a stroke of genius. But India was not ready for it, and it was not related closely enough to the Rowlatt Act. His second proposal was that Satyagrahis should sell prohibited books and seditious papers. They preferred that idea, and made a start on the evening of the 6th. Headed by Gandhi in a slow-moving car, they strode through Bombay handing out copies of *Hind Swaraj* and *Sarvodaya* printed for the purpose. Purchasers usually gave them more than the price, which was four annas. One man paid fifty rupees for a single copy.

Next day at Mani Bhavan, Gandhi began publishing a small weekly which existed solely to be illegal. To make sure there was no mistake, he sent over a copy to the Commissioner of Police with a covering letter pointing out that the paper was unregistered. The police, however, did not rise to the bait. They ignored the paper, and argued that as the books which had been hawked were reprints, the ban on the original editions did not apply to them. Nobody was arrested. The day sank into anti-climax. A meeting to recruit workers for Swadeshi and improved Hindu-Muslim relations aroused hardly any interest. While the Mahatma's *hartal* had been a universal triumph, his personal leadership was at a momentary impasse.

But the pause was no breathing space. Elsewhere in India the movement was taking a different and ominous course. It was becoming what he had not yet envisaged, a major disturbance. On the issue of large-scale popular action he had never taken a clear line. In South Africa the Indians had been a minority. He still thought in terms of idealistic pledge-signers in compact, manageable groups. At a Madras rally he had spoken of an 'attempt to revolutionize politics and restore moral force to its original station', quoting President Wilson. Answering a right-wing critic, he had maintained that Satyagraha was not an aid to Communism but the best antidote. However, when the anarchic millions did respond, he cheered them on without trying to supervise. Now the result was plain. In Bombay, under his control, the agitation was moving too slowly; but in the Punjab, out of his control, it was moving too fast.

The situation there had been tense for some weeks, owing to the pre-Rowlatt unrest. His *hartal* strengthened a rebelliousness already active. Riots occurred, shots were fired, Europeans assaulted. British nerves were strained by rumours of an Afghan invasion. Two Congress leaders, Dr Satyapal (a Hindu) and Dr Kitchlew (a Muslim), begged Gandhi to intervene. On 8 April he boarded a train for Delhi. The police intercepted him. An inspector explained that Sir Michael O'Dwyer, the Lieutenant-Governor of the Punjab, objected to his visit. Nothing personal, but he must keep out. The police also knew, though they did not tell him, that telegrams were flashing up and down the hierarchy debating what to do with him. Deportation to Burma had been suggested but dropped. Ignoring his protests that his sole object was to check the riots, they escorted him back to Bombay, and, in the hope of avoiding trouble, set him down at a small station where he was not expected.

The precaution was futile. Reports of the police action, exaggerated into actual arrest, were spreading through India. In Bombay itself he was soon discovered and treated to an uproarious welcome, which ended when mounted police armed with lances charged and trampled the crowd. When he went to the Commissioner to complain, he was met with the news that his alleged arrest was inspiring a wave of arson, sabotage and hooliganism. Even the Ahmedabad workers were showing their wrath at the Mahatma's treatment with a desolating forgetfulness of his non-violent teaching. Civil disobedience, the Commissioner angrily told him, had got out of hand . . . as anyone could have foreseen that it would. On his own principles he should call it off.

Gandhi was shocked, and went off to lecture his followers on the duty of non-violence. The movement could not continue unless they kept the rules. Instead, he heard, they had been throwing stones and obstructing traffic and assaulting Englishmen. From Bombay he hurried to Ahmedabad, where the news was worse. On the 13th he summoned a meeting at the Ashram for the next day, at which he denounced his false disciples. 'In the name of Satyagraha we have burnt down buildings, forcibly captured weapons, extorted money, stopped trains, cut off telegraph wires, killed innocent people, and plundered shops and private houses.' He announced that he would fast for three days in penance, and then went to make inquiries in Kheda, with similar results. A letter came from Tagore, saying gently and reverently what the Police Commissioner had said bluntly: that in the absence of moral self-control, civil disobedience could not be kept within bounds. Swami Shraddhanand, whose courage and devotion were amply proven, also raised queries. So did Horniman, the sympathetic editor of the *Bombay Chronicle*.

Farther north the disaster was exceeding all bounds whatever, though not in the way the Poet meant. Gandhi's exclusion from the Punjab had ended any hope of his pacifying that area. At Amritsar, the holy city of the Sikhs, the police arrested and deported the two Congressmen who had invited him. During the *hartal* Amritsar had been fairly peaceable. But now a crowd protesting at the deportations—still more or less non-violently—was fired on with many casualties. Hindus and Muslims affirmed their indignant brotherhood by publicly drinking out of the same cups. With some, indignation reached breaking point. They set fire to buildings and murdered several English bankers. Miss Sherwood, a schoolmistress, was assaulted. Stray terrorism and arson occurred in other parts of the Punjab, with lurid anti-British talk, though not much action.

On 11 April Brigadier-General Reginald Dyer, a middle-aged professional soldier born in Simla, arrived in Amritsar to take command. He issued a proclamation forbidding public gatherings. But he issued it in English only, and made no serious effort to ensure that it was read everywhere. At one o'clock on the 13th, when all had been quiet for two days, he learned that a mass meeting was being called for half-past four at Jallianwala Bagh. Whether this was done in defiance or ignorance he did not know or try to discover. Nor, in the hours available, did he station troops at the ground to prevent the meeting. He said later that he spent the entire time 'thinking the matter out'.

At Jallianwala Bagh, over ten thousand people of the holy city assembled. 'Bagh' means a garden, but the meeting place had long ceased to be that. It was an oblong patch of cluttered waste land, about the size of Trafalgar Square, used for fairs and other public events. Walls closed it in on all sides. The only proper entrance was at one end. This led on to a platform of ground higher than most of the Bagh, which spread away below. Elsewhere the walls had four or five narrow gaps in them. By one route or another the citizens streamed in. None had firearms. A speaker began addressing them from a rostrum in the centre.

Dyer, however, had thought the matter out to some purpose. He suddenly appeared through the main entrance on the higher ground overlooking the rest. With him were twenty-five Nepalese Gurkhas and twenty-five Baluchis, all carrying rifles. Two armoured cars remained in the street outside solely because he had found that the passage was too narrow for them. Without warning the crowd to disperse, he gave the order to fire. The trap was almost perfect, and penned in a sufficiency of human targets for ten minutes of shrieking panic. There was a rush to scramble over the lowest wall, which was five feet high. Here the corpses fell in heaps. The soldiers fired individually and in no great hurry, making nearly every bullet tell, and aiming wherever the crowd was thickest. Altogether they discharged 1650 rounds and inflicted over 1500 casualties, including 379 dead. The wounded were left where they fell. Dyer's interpretation of his duty was that he should give help if it were asked for, but not go out of his way to offer it.

His avowed object was to produce a moral effect. The echo of Gandhi in that phrase was doubtless unintentional. To quote him further, 'I thought I would be doing a jolly lot of good.' He was not alone in his satisfaction. An English subaltern spoke with relish of the spectacle of a 'seething mass of sweating niggers' being mown down. On the 15th Sir Michael O'Dwyer proclaimed martial law throughout the Punjab, with a special censorship which prevented news from getting out. Dyer followed up his own gesture with a series of decrees. Any Indian passing along the street where Miss Sherwood was attacked must creep on all fours.* At the sight of a British officer, Indians on animals and vehicles must dismount, Indians with umbrellas must lower them, and all Indians must salaam. Any who neglected to do so were flogged at an outdoor whipping post set up for the purpose. Elsewhere in the Punjab, men were seized almost at random for public stripping and beating;

* The soldiers he posted to enforce this famous order went one better. They made the Indians drag themselves on their bellies.

prisoners and women were tortured; peasants were bombed from the air. By these and kindred methods, the authorities crushed a revolutionary plot which never existed. It took them eight weeks.

On the afternoon of the massacre Gandhi had been in Ahmedabad exhorting Indians not to use violence against the English. During the ensuing days his thoughts flowed on, undeflected, to a conclusion which he announced at Nadiad. In launching Satyagraha when few outside his own circle knew what it meant, he had been guilty of a 'Himalayan blunder'. As mere chaotic defiance it would not work. A Satyagrahi must be a responsible citizen, with a precise awareness of what the issues are and what he is doing. He must show obedience to the law in general before he can claim a right to break this or that law in particular. Above all, he must cultivate Ahimsa in thought and deed.

Though Gandhi thought that his arrest, or semi-arrest, had been the main cause of the explosion and his own powerlessness to check it, his tone toward the English was unembittered. He kept in touch with the Viceroy's secretary about his efforts to restore peace. Before leaving Gujarat he sought out the families of the one or two English victims of violence there, and did his best to compensate. Back in Bombay on 18 April he suspended the campaign. Opponents laughed, even supporters felt let down. Neither side could shake his belief that the move was morally correct. Strategically, it was a *reculer pour mieux sauter*. Like Lenin he had decided that the key to future success lay in creating a vanguard—a corps of leaders and trainees, who would absorb his ideas thoroughly, and guide civil disobedience properly when the moment for resumption arrived. The Ashram alone could not provide enough. At Mani Bhavan he issued a call for volunteers.

Not many came, and not many of those who did persevered. Learning and living a positive philosophy was less exciting than strikes and parades. But after the Punjab terror, the potentiality was there. Indian readiness for hard work in the national cause was simply a matter of time. All over the sub-continent people were listening, whispering, comparing notes. Later the same year, Dyer happened to travel from Amritsar to Delhi in a sleeping compartment with several other officers. One upper berth had an Indian in it, but the General, not noticing or not caring, held forth loudly about his pacification of the city and his clemency in not burning the whole place down. At Delhi he stepped out on to the platform wearing pink striped pyjamas and a dressing gown, without a glance at the mute eavesdropper. It was Jawaharlal Nehru.

3

Gandhi made it his business to get the facts about the Punjab himself. He again tried to go there, in spite of the danger from two quarters—Englishmen angry with him for launching Satyagraha, and Punjabis angry with him for calling it off. The latter could only send threats of assassination which he ignored. But the former could deny him entry, and did. The Lieutenant-Governor blamed him for all the trouble. The Viceroy refused to overrule O'Dwyer's objections.

However, information was leaking out through the special censorship. By the end of May its cumulative effect was so frightful that Tagore wrote to Lord Chelmsford renouncing his knighthood, and allowed Gandhi to publicize the text of his letter. It was the Poet's finest hour. The censorship was lifted partially in June, completely in August. Gandhi's friend Andrews went to the afflicted province and sent back reports which induced him to renew his own efforts. On 17 October he at last reached Lahore. No assassins appeared; the crowd which greeted him at the station was wildly enthusiastic. He was charmed by Punjabi hospitality, and not so deeply preoccupied as to overlook the beauty of Punjabi women. Several Congress leaders were in the city, among them Motilal Nehru, now far along the road from moderation to subversion.

The Government had appointed a committee under Lord Hunter to sift the evidence and publish the facts. Indian politicians carried out an inquiry of their own. The chief members of their unofficial committee were Motilal Nehru, the Bengali C.R. Das, and Gandhi, who drafted the report. It was a conscientious and damning document. While the Congress investigators co-operated with the Hunter Commission as little as they could, Gandhi was invited to testify before it. Hunter and others questioned him about the nature of Truth-Force. An Indian member, Sir Chimanlal Setalwad, adroitly exposed two flaws.

> Sir Chimanlal: However honestly a man may strive in his search for truth, his notions of truth may be different from the notions of others. Who then is to determine the truth?

Gandhi: The individual himself would determine that.

Sir C.: Different individuals would have different views as to truth. Would that not lead to confusion?

G.: I do not think so.

Sir C.: Honestly striving after truth is different in every case.

G.: That is why the non-violence part was a necessary corollary. Without that there would be confusion and worse.

Sir C.: Must not the person wanting to pursue truth be of high moral and intellectual equipment?

G.: No. It would be impossible to expect that from every one. If A has evolved a truth by his own efforts which B, C and others are to accept, I should not require them to have the equipment of A.

Sir C.: Then it comes to this—that a man comes to a decision, and others of lower intellectual and moral equipment would have to blindly follow him.

G.: Not blindly.

The unsatisfactoriness of the answers was palpable. If Satyagraha was to avoid the evils imputed—conflict among the decision-makers, dictatorship over the followers—there would need to be a long process of definition and education before it could be employed again. The Mahatma's volunteer corps was languishing. But tools of a more promising kind were now in his hands. During April B. G. Horniman, whose editorial tone in the *Bombay Chronicle* vexed the Government, had been deported. The directors, Umar Sobani and Shankarlal Banker, asked Gandhi to take his place. This proposal fell through when the paper itself was suspended, but they offered him another publication, *Young India,* an English-language weekly. An associate of theirs was running a Gujarati monthly, *Navajivan.* This too, converted into a weekly, was put under the Mahatma's control. At his request the publication of both was transferred to Ahmedabad, where he could operate his own press unhampered by the fears of commercial printers. Thus he acquired his equivalents of *Indian Opinion.* Both achieved a circulation of forty thousand, without advertisements. As free-speaking media of enlightenment about Satyagraha and much else, they were to carry the best of his journalism. The best could be very good.

With the two papers to produce, there could be no question of his remaining silent between crises. He had to have a policy. Like many of his compatriots he had been driven by the Punjab affair to want an early end of the British Raj. A chasm had yawned and it would never be closed. But could it be bridged? If tempers cooled, could power be transferred gradually and amicably? The issue of the promised reforms was now crucial. Britain had moved slowly, distracted by the peace treaty, Ireland and other problems. But the programme devised by Montagu and Chelmsford was being embodied in a parliamentary Bill. Indian politicians had to make up their minds about it.

Gandhi noted some hopeful signs. The Punjab authorities were yielding somewhat to public clamour. Hundreds of their prisoners, detained without trial, were emerging from the cells. Though the Rowlatt Act remained in force, it stood as an enabling measure only. The Government had had second thoughts about using it. So long as Indians showed that they could not be bullied, it did not seem too irrational to trust the British again and try to work with them.

The Government of India Act of 1919 set up a new constitution on a basis described as Dyarchy, the Rule of Two, namely Britain and India. An All-India Assembly with an elected majority would sit in Delhi. But real sovereignty would remain with the Viceroy and his Council. In the provinces, most of the government departments would be entrusted to Indian ministers, responsible to councils elected on a propertied franchise. The voters, however, would amount to only 2.8 per cent of the population. Also the British governors would retain a veto, and control finance and the police. The royal proclamation announcing these changes included promises of amnesty for many political prisoners, and increased Indian participation in the Civil Service.

Could a nationalist accept Dyarchy without betraying Swaraj? Did the Act mean a step or a stoppage? Moderates were willing to give it a chance. But C. R. Das dismissed its proposals as 'inadequate, unsatisfactory and disappointing'; and Das was a rising man, a leader of the Calcutta Bar, known as the Deshabandhu or Friend of the Country. His views carried weight. Jinnah and Tilak concurred. Annïe Besant, who had recently been scared into a moderation so frantic that she defended Dyer, now swung back and assailed the scheme as perpetual slavery. Motilal Nehru—who had joined her Home Rule League, and cut down his practice at the Bar to run an amateurish but popular political daily—was also more than dubious.

Congress met that December at Amritsar, a choice of locale

which a would-be conciliatory Government did not forbid. Gandhi arrived in the last of his pro-British moods. The Punjab atrocities, he argued, must not be allowed to unbalance Indian judgement: 'Both sides were mad.' It would now be becoming to make a gesture of trust. At Amritsar he stayed with Pandit Malaviya, the head of Mrs Besant's Benares college, who had forgiven him for the disaster of 1916. Through Malaviya he soon found how widely at variance he was with the dominant Congressmen. His reaction was an uncharacteristic loss of nerve. He wanted to slip away, but they would not let him. At a session attended by 7,031 delegates, he had a seat on the platform. Besides his habitual Indian dress he wore a white homespun cap, reminiscent of Transvaal prison caps. This was the original of the Gandhi Cap which became a badge of nationalism.

It was clear from the outset that his vogue among the rank and file threatened a split. Much more Hindustani was being spoken. Crowds could be heard chanting 'Mahatma-Gandhi-ki-jai'—Victory to Mahatma Gandhi. Motilal Nehru, who presided, had experienced that spell in his own family. When the Satyagraha Sabha was formed, he had opposed it, being especially put off by the Gandhian mystique of jail-going. Then he had been startled to learn that his son Jawaharlal wanted to enrol in the Sabha and, if necessary, go to jail. Tension in the prosperous home at Allahabad went on for days. Motilal surreptitiously slept on the floor, to see just how unpleasant a cell would be, if Jawaharlal were ever put in one. Finally he begged Gandhi to talk to the young zealot himself. Gandhi advised caution, and quietened Jawaharlal almost as easily as he had roused him.

So the President knew that a motion rejecting the Montagu-Chelmsford plan would be a tricky thing to press against Gandhi's opposition, even if it were backed by the united prestige of the Congress magnates. The debate was unhappy and largely bogus. Every speaker had to compete with the real debate on the platform behind him, where the magnates were passing notes back and forth, in quest of a compromise which Malaviya was pressing for. Tilak suggested that they should agree to hoist Dyarchy into the saddle so as to give India a practical demonstration that it was no good. But that line was too devious for Gandhi. When a synthetic resolution was drafted which he did approve, and Tilak had to be won over, he dramatically tossed his cap at the great man's feet in token of obeisance, and entreated him to consent. Tilak said he would if

Das did, and Das gave an indication which was enough for Malaviya. To the vociferous relief of the audience, the Pandit shouted
that a formula had been found.

In the upshot Congress thanked Montagu and pledged collabora-
tion with Dyarchy, so long as this was understood to be a stage on
the way to parliamentary government. Lord Chelmsford, however,
was censured for being too soft with Dyer. Other resolutions demanded the repeal of the Rowlatt Act, and condemned excesses in
the Punjab, Indian as well as British—a stroke of impartiality due
to Gandhi. He regarded this meeting as his real entry into Congress
politics. The leaders took sympathetic note of his ideas about spinning. They also asked him to draw up proposals for a new constitution for Congress itself. He accepted the job, on condition that
Tilak and Das would associate themselves with his work in a committee of three. As they were too busy they had to be represented
by deputies, who never in practice came. Thus, without losing the
prestige of the big names, Gandhi virtually reduced the committee
of three to a committee of one. Its report was unanimous.

4

But behind his victory the forces of change were already gathering. He had already made moves in another quarter which could
overturn the whole structure that Congress had obligingly built for
him. He had prepared a weapon which, if events compelled him to
use it, would destroy his own formula.

The disturbing factor was Muslim. The Delhi *hartal* had re-
invigorated his passion for inter-communal partnership. His views
were realistic. He recognized that Hindus and Muslims were unlike,
and could not be lumped together as Indians who merely belonged
to different sects, like Anglicans and Methodists. What he wanted
was not blending (intermarriage, for example, struck him as
hazardous) but creative reconciliation. The Tagores and Rammohan
Roy had desired the same. He maintained, with some justice, that
communal clashes were artificial. The incidents which set them off
were petty and preventable: Muslims slaughtering cows at a
festival, Hindus bellowing hymns outside a mosque.

He had gone further than most of the Hindus in public life to
fraternize with Muslims and promote their interests. His plea to

Chelmsford in 1918 on behalf of the Ali brothers was only the first in a series, and the brothers' popularity spilled over on to their champion. They were former theological students, charming and courageous, who had taken to journalism and been jailed for sedition. The elder, Shaukat, was tall and fat and heavy; he was 'the big brother'. Mohamed made up for his smaller size by being quicker-witted. The Government released both in time to attend the Amritsar Congress. This move was one of the reasons for Gandhi's flash of optimism. As a known friend of Islamic India he had addressed Muslim gatherings—at a college, at a Muslim League rally, and in the Bombay mosque. October 1919 brought a proposition with graver implications. He was invited to a conference in Delhi on the Caliphate.

Up to this time the Muslims' stance in politics had been equivocal. Some belonged to Congress, some to the League, some to both. In spite of the Congress-League pact, their fear of Hindu power made them doubtful allies. Many were pro-British in what they imagined to be self-defence. But a crisis abroad was making them less amenable to the British Raj, and offering the Mahatma an opportunity which he was glad to seize.

With the Treaty of Versailles safely signed, Lloyd George and his colleagues were discussing the terms to be imposed on Turkey. As the Sultan was Caliph or head of all the faithful, and Muslim misgivings during the war needed soothing, the Premier had given assurances on his future status. One of the Caliph's most sacred tasks was to protect the pilgrim routes to Mecca, a duty which he could not perform without free access and independence. But as the peace settlement drew nearer, it transpired that Britain meant to deprive Turkey of the Arabian provinces and portions of Asia Minor, and to set up Sheikh Hussein, conjured out of the desert by Lawrence, as a puppet Caliph in charge of the Holy Places.

The Delhi conference which drew Gandhi in was part of a protest agitation conducted chiefly by Jinnah and Abul Kalam Azad, the Muslim leader in Congress—Maulana Azad as he was called, the title being a compliment to his learning, like 'Pandit'. Swami Shraddhanand of the Delhi *hartal* was also present, representing a strong though unorganized body of Hindu sympathy. On 24 November Gandhi presided. The Caliphate, or Khilafat as they spelt the word, was not of much interest to him in itself. Indeed, he gave far too little consideration to such details as the rights of the Arabs.

But his mind was fixed on the Muslims of India. The intended treaty was a betrayal, a blow at their religion. Here was a major moral issue, genuine and not contrived, on which Hindus could make common cause with Muslims.

Furthermore, the Muslims of the Khilafat Committee were eager to attract Hindu support. They were so eager that in Gandhi's eyes they overreached themselves. They proposed, as a *quid pro quo*, to stop their ritual killing of cows. On that notorious topic, Gandhi occupied a middle ground between orthodoxy and rationalism. He did not make the cow a fetish, yet he said there was holy virtue in reverence for an animal. At Delhi, however, he brushed the Muslims' offer aside. If their cause was right, it was right, and he was not going to soil it by driving bargains. Cows faded from the agenda.

Manifestly the Muslims could take no action while the Turkish treaty was still being drafted. They could only petition. The problem was what to do if their pressure failed and the treaty took the form predicted. Some speakers suggested reviving Swadeshi in its 1906 version, and boycotting British textiles. It seemed a feeble riposte. Indians were too dependent to make such a ban complete. A sceptic pointed out that almost every person at the conference was wearing or carrying something British.

On the platform, Gandhi groped for a slogan. It darted into his head almost as spontaneously as the *hartal* idea. Non-co-operation. Perhaps he recalled Krishnavarma, whose project for freezing the English out he had mentioned so long ago in *Indian Opinion*. The term had also been used by a contributor to *Young India*. But whatever the source, non-violent non-co-operation was a legitimate extension of Truth-Force and one that suited the case. The bad treaty would not be a law which civil resisters could break, it would be the outward and visible sign of a bad government. The right method of defying such a government was to dissociate oneself from it. For example, Indians with titles could give them up; Tagore had shown the way. Indians in government service could resign. Non-co-operation would not be so intense and fiery as direct civil disobedience, but it would be less liable to provoke clashes, and therefore less dangerous as a mass technique.

When laying his scheme (expressed with some awkwardness in Hindi-Urdu) before the conference, Gandhi was careful to stress its hypothetical nature. He put in phrases like 'in case of a betrayal'.

His Congress plea for co-operation soon afterwards was not inconsistent. He was keeping the weapon in reserve, hoping it would never be needed. The Muslims' initial response was cool and they did not embarrass him by talking about it. In *Young India* during January 1920 he was enlarging on the blameless topic of 'purifying politics'. But the Government—despite the efficiency of the detectives who shadowed him—could scarcely be expected to follow his train of thought. If, after the Amritsar Congress, he whisked the concealed sword out of its sheath and proclaimed non-co-operation, he would brand himself in official opinion as either unstable or dishonest; anyhow, not trustworthy. The role of a revolutionary would be the only one left open to him.

As the first months of 1920 passed, it grew increasingly plain that this was likely to happen. On 19 January he took part in a Khilafat deputation to the Viceroy, without result. Another deputation including Mohamed Ali set out for London. Meanwhile a sub-committee of three debated policy. The three were Gandhi himself, Maulana Azad, and the lately liberated big brother Shaukat Ali. Gandhi pressed the claims of non-violent non-co-operation. He realized that Islam was a martial faith. But what else could the Muslims do? An unarmed people could not stage a violent revolt. Their only other option was to walk out on the British infidel and migrate to a Muslim country. That, Azad and Shaukat Ali admitted, would be absurd. (It was not so absurd that nobody tried it. In the course of the year, peasants by the hundred thousand sold their land and made for Afghanistan, now accessible again after the easy repulse of the dreaded attack on India. Their Afghan co-religionists threw most of them out. Deaths were numerous, and the survivors straggled home ruined.)

Non-co-operation was looming as the incvitable retort to the humbling of the Sultan. April saw Gandhi still behaving pacifically. He appeared beside Tagore at a Gujarati literary conference. He built up the Ashram as a khadi sales centre, and rejoiced at a breakthrough in the world of fashion when Tagore's niece wore a khadi blouse and sari to a public function. In the same monch, however, he was elected president of Annie Besant's Home Rule League, which she herself had abandoned. On 14 May the publication of the Treaty of Sèvres disclosed the Turkish peace terms. They were as exorbitant as expected. This treaty was to prove a dead letter, but the fact was neither foreseeable nor much to the point. The terms showed Lloyd George's intentions, and his inability to carry them out was no mitigation.

Later in May the Hunter Commission published its findings on the Punjab. The report, in Gandhi's words, was a 'laboured defence of every official act of inhumanity', and a full and final revelation of British contempt. It confirmed the horrors, yet drew the weakest of conclusions. Dyer had 'committed a grave error of judgement which exceeded the reasonable requirements of the case'. His conduct was based upon an 'honest but mistaken conception of duty'. The General was deprived of his command, and Montagu disowned him. But the House of Lords passed a vote of approval, his admirers gave him a sword of honour and twenty thousand pounds, and he withdrew into comfortable retirement. As for O'Dwyer and the minor persecutors, they came through unscathed.

The union of embittered Muslims and embittered Hindus was now accomplished. Britain had affronted both. While feelings rose, clouds thickened over the economy. The first half of the year had brought two hundred strikes involving more than a million workers. The second half was to bring a slump.

For the moment the Khilafat Committee was more representative of Muslims than the Muslim League. On 30 June (after much heart-searching, for reasons both theological and practical) a conference at Allahabad adopted non-co-operation. As Gandhi made it a rule of Satyagraha to warn one's opponent, he wrote to the Viceroy: 'I have advised my Muslim friends to withdraw their support from Your Excellency's Government and advised the Hindus to join them.' Chelmsford rejoined that non-co-operation was 'the most foolish of all foolish schemes'. By this time he was convinced that the Mahatma was a rebel.

Montagu was less sure, and they exchanged letters on the subject. The Secretary still dwelt on Gandhi's talent for calming things down. The Viceroy saw no merit in that, if he stirred them up in the first place. British attitudes to him were still in process of formation. During the Champaran phase there had been a tendency to view him as a dreamer exploited by agitators. On this ground Montagu had sought to flatter him out of the political struggle as being above it. He replied: 'I am in it because without it I cannot do my religious and social work.' By mid-1920 the Champaran authorities' doubts over what to do about him were recurring in Delhi when Delhi could not afford them.

Moreover, he had seen through the rulers' arrogance to their underlying nervousness. In *Young India* he made it an argument for his own methods.

> I make bold to say that the moment Englishmen feel that although they are in India in a hopeless minority, their lives are protected against harm not because of the matchless weapons of destruction which are at their disposal, but because Indians refuse to take the lives even of those whom they consider to be utterly in the wrong, that moment will see a transformation in the English nature in its relation to India.

On the face of it he is merely expounding the theory of non-violence and victory by conversion. Yet he conveys it through the image of a wronged Indian magnanimously sparing his cringing oppressor.

Non-co-operation was to start on 1 August. During the previous night, Tilak suddenly died in Bombay. Gandhi, notified by telephone, exclaimed : 'My strongest bulwark is gone.' Their approaches to politics had been vastly different, and Tilak, though mellowing toward Muslims, had been tepid about the Khilafat. But the bond of patriotism counted for more. As Gandhi stood by the funeral pyre on Chowpati Beach, Tilak's mantle descended almost visibly on his shoulders. The death of the Lokamanya left a gap which only the Mahatma could fill. He made his first move in non-co-operation as the sole credible chieftain of resurgent India.

It was a quiet move. Writing to the Viceroy on 1 August, he returned his Kaisar-i-Hind medal. He had nearly done this at the crisis of the Champaran conflict. Now he did it. The British Government, he declared, had been going 'from wrong to wrong, in order to defend its immorality'. Guilt attached to Delhi as well as London. After the Khilafat betrayal, the Punjab crimes, and the light treatment of Dyer and the rest, he could retain neither respect nor affection for such a government.

Besides the gesture with his medal, he got non-co-operation endorsed at the Gujarat Political Conference. The resolution strengthened his hand for coping with Congress, which was to meet in special session at Calcutta on 4 September. There, as at Amritsar, most of the veterans were against him. His only firm ally at that level was Motilal Nehru, who was ready to lead an exodus of barristers from the courts. But when the delegates assembled, a glance was enough to show who was likeliest to win. Congress had turned Gandhian. Its pseudo-English veneer had worn off. The hall was full of lower-middle-class Indians in miscellaneous national costume, sitting on the floor talking Hindustani. Jinnah, a tall thin figure, elegant and resentful in a suit, looked almost as odd as Gandhi a few years earlier. The right-wing moderates who might have made a stand had seceded from Congress to form a separate Liberal Party. The proportion of Muslims was unusually high, and they were in a fierce mood.

Lala Lajpat Rai presided, and Gandhi moved his resolution. Non-co-operation was to be a phased strategy. First came the relinquishing of titles and honours. Then students were to quit government colleges; lawyers were to desert British courts; candidates for the new legislative councils were to stand down, and voters to stay away from the polls; foreign cloth was to be boycotted. Congress should start its own colleges and courts, and keep India supplied with cloth by organizing Swadeshi on a colossal scale, including, of course, hand-spinning and hand-weaving. These last activities alone were to engage the masses. The rest of the programme was middle-class. It owed a little to Sinn Fein.

The weakness of the Mahatma's position was that if all this was to be done merely to compel British rethinking about the Khilafat and the Punjab, it seemed excessive. Motilal Nehru transformed the situation. The proper aim, he declared, was Swaraj itself. The others were necessary, but secondary. At this point in the noisy debate it became uncertain who was dominating whom. But presently—by a small majority in the committee, and a big one in the full assembly—Gandhi found himself elected to lead non-co-operation with Swaraj as its goal. Conversion to the principle of Indian freedom was, he agreed, the only British change of heart which would be adequate. He forecast that with an all-round effort, that change would come within a year.

Thus Indian nationalism adopted Truth-Force, or at any rate, its technique. Motives were various. For Gandhi himself the method was inherently best, even if other choices were open. In *Young India* he had just published his classic statement that he preferred violence to cowardice, but believed the non-violence of the brave to be better than either. Congress, however, lacked his faith. He carried the vote not because of any deep-seated Ahimsa but because constitutionalism and terrorism were both bankrupt. In the light of recent events, the bulk of Congress was no longer receptive to the idea that British reforms spelt British retreat, even potentially. As for violent revolt, the younger Nehru simply observed that for an unarmed people it was impossible, and therefore they had no other way but Gandhi's to attain liberty. This was a pragmatic view which did not go very far. But his own sympathy for Gandhi had been increased that June by some nightmare glimpses of rural India, and many besides him were soon to be caught up into the Satyagrahi cosmos. It was a foretaste of things to come that Congress should have been persuaded to endorse the spinning wheel and the cottage loom. The grounds appeared to be strictly practical. Yet the Imitation of the Mahatma (to adapt a Christian phrase) was already at work. The practical decision opened the door to the whole khadi mystique.

Non-co-operation faced an early and severe test at the elections to the provincial councils. They posed a well-known dilemma. Should a revolutionary join such bodies and use them to promote his ends, or should he keep clear? At Amritsar, under Gandhi's influence, Congress had opted conditionally for the first choice. At Calcutta, again under his influence, it shifted to the second, adjuring its members to keep out of British-sponsored politics whether central, provincial or municipal. It thereby aroused a voluble critic. Annie Besant had finally approved the Amritsar line, and with her talent for being on the opposite side from Gandhi she was sticking to it. In November, the month of the elections, she published a counterblast—a sheaf of articles by herself and colleagues entitled *Gandhian Non-co-operation: or Shall India Commit Suicide?* Her version was that the policy had been railroaded through unrepresentative Muslim meetings, and then forced on Congress by fanatics who howled her down. Gandhi was wrecking reform just when it was at last dawning. His programme meant chaos without victory. He 'began as a dove of peace, but has become a destroyer'. Mrs Besant's charge of anarchism established the pattern of right-wing Indian opposition to Gandhi. Left-wing opposition had yet to take shape.

The boycott of the elections, however, proceeded. Congress candidates loyally stood down—even C. R. Das, who had favoured participation—and in some places the ballot boxes were empty. But the success was ambiguous, because the non-Congress Indians who did become members were all docile, and made the councils so. The main result was to confirm the breach. Congress was a separate institution and not a party within Dyarchy. The Government recognized a challenge, but refrained from action, confident of its strength and 'the sanity of the classes and masses alike'. Here was the first British admission that the masses could affect politics at all.

Skirmishing was over. It was time to sound the charge. Congress held its regular December session at Nagpur, with fourteen thousand delegates in attendance, among them a massive bloc of Muslims and over a hundred women. Again there were mutterings at high levels. Gandhi was accused of aspiring to a moral dictatorship. But again his presence dissolved the opposition, and the doubters were more nearly won over. In a rapture of excitement, Das moved and Lajpat Rai seconded the main resolution. It reaffirmed the entire programme, with the addition that at some undefined stage Indians might be called upon to stop paying taxes. This would be outright civil disobedience, and by myriads . . . but not yet. A Tilak Memorial Swaraj Fund would be launched to finance the battle, with a target of ten million rupees. Gandhi was to be in supreme command; and the aim, in keeping with his Calcutta prophecy, was Swaraj within a year.

Congress regrouped itself into a mass fighting force by adopting the new constitution he had composed for it. Drawing on his Natal experience, he provided for a Working Committee of fifteen members, to function as an executive all the year round. It was to be responsible to a policy-making All-India Congress Committee of 350, resting on a broad organization open to almost anyone for a tiny subscription, with every office elective. He himself had no official position at all. But his future strength in Congress was to arise in part from this very fact. Because he usually held no definite post, he was not subject to too many rules. Besides the other changes, there was a change in the definition of Congress's object. This was now said to be Swaraj by 'peaceful and legitimate means' (the word 'constitutional' was deleted) 'within the British Empire if possible, or outside it if necessary'.

That clause killed the alliance with Jinnah and the Muslim League. In September, he had grudgingly told the League that non-co-operation in some form seemed unavoidable. At Nagpur, the suggestion that India might quit the Empire was too much for him. He made a speech saying so. But he was ill at ease, and made the gaffe of referring to 'Mr Gandhi', at which the assembly roared 'MAHATMA Gandhi!' Cold and cultured and westernized, Jinnah did not take kindly to the new breed of Congressmen. They were disreputable; like the troops who first sang the *Marseillaise*. Having talked himself into total inefficacy, he deserted Congress for ever. Henceforth he confined his attention to the League. In the shadow of Nagpur the League did not count for much. His revenge, a ghastly one, was a generation away.

XI

What Sort of Revolution?

1

'Swaraj in one year'—that was the Mahatma's slogan. But what did it mean?

To a *Times* reporter at Nagpur he spoke of 'parliamentary government of India in the modern sense of the term for the time being, either through the friendly offices of the British people or without them'. That definition, however, soon led to trouble. As the campaign rolled forward there was a fresh demand for his own *Hind Swaraj,* which was duly rushed through the press; and this book dismissed the Westminster model as not worth copying. Confronted with his printed gibe that the Mother of Parliaments was a prostitute, Gandhi had to explain that he was not now working for his ideal Swaraj, but for a transitional step.

This was not a makeshift reply to an awkward question. He had been saying the same privately for two years. But it failed to shed light on remarks he let fall at other times. Swaraj was 'self-realization', 'the capacity of the people to get rid of their helplessness', 'the ability to regard every inhabitant of India as our own brother or sister', and 'abandonment of the fear of death'. C. R. Das tried to sum it up as not primarily a system of government but a state of mind. Gandhi acknowledged that the state of mind would express itself in institutions, but he refused to be tied down. On one occasion, he said Swaraj meant 'not a change of government but a change of heart'. On another, he said it was indefinable.

Such haziness of outline seemed to violate the laws of Truth-Force. What would constitute victory? What would count as British conversion? The logic of Gandhi's position lay in his magisterial 'If', which Congress took too lightly. Swaraj could come in a year *if* the response to his call was satisfactory; and however vague he might be about Swaraj, he was explicit about the conditions.

Congress—the new-style democratic Congress—must plant itself everywhere, in villages as well as cities. Indians must learn discipline and non-violence. Hindus and Muslims must shed their mutual distrust. There must be a drive to get the spinning wheel into every home, and end the use of foreign cloth. The fund-raising target must be reached. Hindus must relax their social ban on Untouchables. The traffic in drugs and liquor (from which the Government derived a huge revenue) must be checked. With enough people pursuing these aims, Swaraj would define itself in the process. Answering S. E. Stokes, an Englishman who applauded the movement but shuddered at the likely sequel of a British withdrawal, Gandhi quoted his favourite hymn: 'One step enough for me.'

A fairly precise idea did underlie his programme. The clause which put it all in focus was the one about Congress. The sovereign importance he attached to the new constitution was often overlooked. Yet he said plainly, more than once, that he envisaged 'the mere fact of fully working it out' as enough to bring Swaraj. He meant his popularized Congress to be a state within the state, a citadel of dissent against the wrongful regime. Under its aegis, a transformed self-reliant society would take shape. Regenerate Indians would set up their own schools, their own courts, their own cottage industries, their own police. As they became less and less dependent on the regime, they could cut down their co-operation further and further. Also, the existing police and the soldiers could be weaned away from British service.

'There can be no Swaraj', Gandhi wrote, 'without our feeling and being the equals of Englishmen.' Equality could never be won by exerting pressure through Dyarchy. 'Let us not mistake reformed councils, more law courts and even governorships for real freedom or power. They are but subtler methods of emasculation.' What he proposed was that the British Establishment in India should be forced to live with a Counter-Establishment, not aggressive, not vengeful, but simply growing. It would grow in size and freedom of action until (to use Marxist language) quantitative change piled up into qualitative change. Sooner or later, the beam would tip. The Sahib would recognize that his power had vanished, and make amends.

It was a bold vision, and perfectly communicable. Yet for some reason Gandhi did not communicate it with anything like enough clarity. He talked about it in bits and pieces, as if his hearers were already aware of it as a whole. Most of them were not. For most, 'Swaraj in one year' remained a myth rather than a programme. But, as such, it was potent. To convey the feeling that spread among Indians, St Paul supplies apter words than Marx. The trumpet was sounding and they would all be changed: in a moment, in the twinkling of an eye.

Some of the first blasts were a little muted. The Tilak Fund, intended to provide the sinews of non-violent war, was launched in Bombay without much fanfare, at an indoor meeting in Mani Bhavan. During January 1921 the Duke of Connaught was arriving to open the new legislative councils, and non-co-operators had to devote time and effort to organizing a boycott of the ceremonies. Meanwhile not very much had come of the planned renunciation of British-conferred honours. The Government was showering titles and medals on Indians who did co-operate. Only a few dozen of those who already had them followed Gandhi's lead by handing them back.

The major offensive was begun, not by the decorated and middle-aged, but by the boys and girls of Bengal. In response to an appeal from Das, three thousand Calcutta students went on strike. The academic walk-out spread through the province and throughout British India. Lecturers returning after the Christmas vacation faced almost empty classrooms. One college lost 280 out of 300 registered. Gandhi delivered and printed a congratulatory address 'to Young Bengal'. He published an article by a Punjabi student quoting Shelley's *Prometheus Unbound,* that most Gandhian of all long poems, where the perceptive student found a motto for Satyagraha:

> To suffer woes which Hope thinks infinite;
> To forgive wrongs darker than death or night;
> To defy Power, which seems omnipotent;
> To love, and bear; to hope till Hope creates
> From its own wreck the thing it contemplates;
> Neither to change, nor falter, nor repent;
> This, like thy glory, Titan, is to be
> Good, great and joyous, beautiful and free;
> This is alone Life, Joy, Empire, and Victory.

Behind the students' revolt there was in fact a bitter record of woes and wrongs patiently borne; and they seized the chance to defy Power with an enormous gasp of relief. Most of them belonged to the social class which was still supposedly being groomed for equality. Yet nearly every one, in person or in his family circle, had witnessed the hollowness of the claim. The students employed their fluent English to exchange stories of English officers kicking their uncles out of railway compartments, English managers wrongfully dismissing their fathers, English ladies insulting their mothers. As soon as Gandhi raised his standard they flocked to it.

Some left their books altogether to help him and Congress as full-time workers. He urged them to learn spinning and go out among the villagers. Others re-enrolled at a chain of new centres improvised by Congress, with an Indian course of studies and vernacular teaching. Gandhi founded a National University of Gujarat in Ahmedabad, a National College of Bengal in Calcutta. These institutions, sketchily financed out of the Tilak Fund, attracted some outstanding teachers. The head of the Calcutta college was the twenty-five-year-old Subhas Chandra Bose, who resigned from the Civil Service to take the post, thus embarking on a brilliant and tragic career.

But it was manifest that no amount of talent would induce the Government to recognize rebel degrees. The students who joined the new colleges, the students who followed the Mahatma, and the students who lay on the steps of examination halls to deter pro-British examinees from entering, were alike throwing away their parents' savings and all too often breaking their parents' hearts. In Gandhi's presence such agonies had a way of happening. They drew a protest from Tagore, who spoke with a stronger voice than the parents. He favoured the type of education which the movement was sponsoring. But he disapproved of the student exodus before a complete new system was ready, and of the narrowly national attitude he thought it implied. Though he had taken the lead himself, fifteen years earlier, in an anti-British boycott, non-co-operation struck him as negative.

Gandhi replied to the Poet's criticisms with profound courtesy, arguing that the loss was nothing to worry about, and the moral stand was far more important. His own opinion of 'literary training', especially when the medium was English, was no higher than it had been when he denied it to his sons. As for the British colleges, they were factories for the making of 'clerks and interpreters', meaning slaves. To the Poet's charge that non-co-operation was negative, he retorted with a leap into metaphysics. The Upanishads offer us the word *neti* (not so) as the best description of the Supreme Reality, that which most positively *is*. Similarly India's colossal No, looked at in another way, would be a colossal Yes.

For some weeks the actual magnitude of the No remained doubtful. Many of the less Promethean students were drifting back. But the stalwart stayed out, rendering service, as Gandhi said, of the highest order. Congress meanwhile was urging the lawyers to fulfil their part of the programme and quit the courts. Popular tribunals were formed to dispense 'Swadeshi justice'. In this case no mass response occurred, but as with the students, the movement had a solid success in terms of quality. Among the several hundred who came were some of the highest in the profession. Those who undertook Congress work had to subsist on their savings, or on minute stipends out of the Tilak Fund. Gandhi's friends and comrades—Motilal Nehru (who brought Jawaharlal), C. R. Das (now a warm convert and most annoyed with Tagore), Rajendra Prasad from Bihar, Vallabhbhai Patel from Gujarat, Rajagopalachari from Madras—all threw away their rich practices and joined him. Their altered status as his lieutenants meant a sharp break with the comforts they were accustomed to, even in the matter of costume, since he insisted on khadi. However, he welded them into a staunch and devoted team. Besides the lawyers it included Lala Lajpat Rai from the Punjab, and also three Muslims, namely Maulana Azad and the Ali brothers.

Over the years Gandhi had become a shrewd judge of character. He could pick capable men, and was not afraid to give them responsibility. Now he began performing prodigies of generalship. He calmly proposed to recruit ten million members for Congress, and actually did recruit six million. He stuck to his ambitious target for the Tilak Fund, equivalent to £750,000, and before the year was far gone he had reached and surpassed it. As shock-troops of Swaraj he enrolled a National Volunteer Corps, drawn largely from the students. His volunteers pledged themselves to work non-violently for India's unity and the redress of India's wrongs, to uphold Swadeshi and wear khadi, and to endure prison or physical attack without resentment. All they got from the Fund was a bare subsistence, less than £1 a week, though many had wives. They fanned out through the country wearing Gandhi caps and—after a while—civilian uniform, a knight-errantry of Truth-Force. Life altered wherever they passed.

Village after village started up out of apathy. The resurrection was gay, with music as well as speeches. Gandhi was a great believer in music at meetings. So far, all he asked villagers to do was to spin and weave. But the spinning wheel supplied what no Indian politician had hit on before, an instrument by which the educated could make contact with the uneducated. Where the wheel went it was understood, and much more could follow. His troops promoted literacy as well as handicrafts. They campaigned against dirt and drink and Untouchability and purdah, and planted the seeds of future Satyagraha. In the quiet sanity of the poor the more volatile city-dwellers discovered reserves of strength, waiting to be mobilized; and the hideous months of seasonal unemployment supplied what few mass movements can command—spare time at the grassroots level. As early as July 1919 Gandhi had noted the fact, and written: 'I propose to utilize this spare time of the nation even as a hydraulic engineer utilizes enormous waterfalls.'

Up and down India extraordinary figures stepped out of the shadows. One of the truest of all Gandhists was the Pathan chief Abdul Ghaffar Khan, a Muslim from the wild north-west, gigantic and gentle and vowed to poverty. Having become a disciple during the Rowlatt crisis, he had set himself the fantastic task of teaching non-violence to the feuding tribesmen of the frontier, and with many he was succeeding.

The gospel of Swaraj shone into swarming rural colonies of darkness and squalor, into unspeakable industrial slums. Flushed with hope, Hindus and Muslims suspended their mutual sniping. Cow slaughter was stopped and the peace of mosques was respected. While the Christians of the missions hung back, the ancient Christian community in the south (founded, according to legend, by the Apostle Thomas) gave the movement a leader named George Joseph. But the ferment was upheaving India beyond the range of Gandhi's evangelism. As before in the Punjab, he intensified unrest which was there already. Strikes blazed up all over the country —four hundred during the year, extending as far as the tea plantations of Assam. His attitude to these was friendly but cautious. He supported strikers who had a genuine grievance of their own, but discouraged striking as a gesture of sympathy or political protest, because he thought labour insufficiently educated and in danger of being exploited by demagogues: a view which he expressed openly, without worrying whom it might offend. While the strikers struck, a religious and economic struggle convulsed the Sikhs. The national

stir tossed up myths and misconceptions. Thus, although the Khilafat had not been lost sight of, millions now connected it with the
Urdu word *khilaf,* 'against', and imagined that the agitation was an
agitation 'against' the Government. That belief made the Khilafat
a popular cause with peasants who had never heard of the Sultan
of Turkey.

Whatever shapes non-co-operation took—flamboyant or unobtrusive, fierce or absurd—the trend was always onward. By early
March the Government had become anxious. It was not that the
mild Hindu was displaying hate. Thanks to the doctrine which
directed him, the element of hate was small. Instead he was doing
something deadlier to British morale, standing upright and looking
purposeful. Delhi began to impose restraints. Das and others found
it harder to travel, some of the minor leaders were put in prison.
Among these latter was Ghaffar Khan. His field was the frontier,
and one British contention was that non-co-operation would betray
India to a fresh Afghan invasion. Arrests, however, did not seem to
do any good. Unable to credit that Gandhi meant what he said,
officials nervously assumed that he was covering up some darker
conspiracy. Congress workers with nothing to hide were dogged
by relays of feebly disguised policemen. They smiled. Owing in
part to its own fume over Afghan spies and Bolshevik agents, the
British Raj faced a more serious menace than either: loss of
prestige.

                                    2

Gandhi himself sat in the eye of the cyclone. At fifty-one he had
the same wiry energy as ever. Yet in the pauses of campaign
tours, his life was rhythmic and remarkably tranquil. At the Ashram
he never allowed politics to upset his routine, or encroach on his
religious observances. He got up at four and went to bed at half
past nine, supplementing his sleep with cat-naps, which he could
take at will. The day always included two short walks and a prayer
meeting before sunset, when friends of various faiths sat with him
cross-legged singing hymns, reading from the scriptures (chiefly the
Gita), and listening to his reflections. Praying alone he used a
Hindu rosary, or repeated the invocation to God under the name
of Rama, which he had learnt as a child.

For the rest of the time he usually had to cope with a deluge of visitors. Most of these came to consult him, though he was always ready to listen to advice and criticism. He planned his time-table meticulously, measuring out each interview with a heavy old-fashioned watch that hung at his waist. 'People call me a dictator', he is said to have remarked once, 'but this watch is the only dictator here.' By not letting himself be overwhelmed, he managed to attend to interests outside the campaign. One was the organization of a daughter ashram at Wardha, in the Central Provinces. That April he sent Vinoba Bhave to take charge of it.

There was nothing bogus about the personal magic that drew people and held them. His ardour, his faith in human beings, his expressive gestures, his good temper and sparkle, his gift of being efficient without being repellent—these won nearly everybody who met him. With Indians of traditional outlook, his austere life was an even greater asset. He gained from the belief of Hindus that asceticism confers powers above normal humanity; he gained from the reverence of Muslims for chastity (which surprises the superficial, but was a prime reason for the respect shown to another leader, General Gordon).

Gandhi's personality, rather than his campaign, achieved the first tiny breakthrough toward British recognition of the new thing he stood for. Chelmsford's term as Viceroy ended, and on 2 April a successor arrived. This was Lord Reading, the former Rufus Isaacs, a self-made statesman of varied talents, and a target for anti-Semites. As Attorney-General he had been smeared in the Marconi scandal. His subsequent elevation to Lord Chief Justice inspired Kipling to write the venomous poem 'Gehazi'. With that accolade from the Laureate of Empire, Lord Reading took up his duties. He made a point of sending for Gandhi. During May they had six talks totalling thirteen hours. Gandhi wore his hand-woven cap and white *dhoti*, with bare legs and feet. The Viceroy found him unimpressive to look at but compelling to listen to. The Mahatma stressed that his movement was religious, and designed to 'purge Indian political life of corruption, deceit, terrorism and the incubus of white supremacy'. Lord Reading made what he could of this, and went so far as to countermand a proposed prosecution of the Ali brothers. He afterwards wrote about the visitor in a letter home:

He is direct, and expresses himself well in excellent English with a fine appreciation of the words he uses. There is no hesitation about him and there is a ring of sincerity in all he utters, save when discussing some political questions. His religious views are, I believe, genuinely held, and he is convinced to a point almost bordering on fanaticism that non-violence and love will give India its independence and enable it to withstand the British Government. His religious and moral views are admirable and indeed are on a remarkably high altitude, though I must confess that I find it difficult to understand his practice of them in politics. . . . Our conversations were of the frankest; he was supremely courteous with manners of distinction.

It is interesting to see Reading, a Jew, warming to qualities in Gandhi such as Jews tend to possess and value. He might have employed almost the same words to describe one of the Zionists who were founding pocket Utopias in Palestine. But the Hindu masses saw their leader quite differently. When he toured among them, personifying and guiding the struggle, he was inescapably the Great Soul. He was not only a source of benediction but a wonder-worker, and not only a wonder-worker but—perhaps—a deity. India's saviour might surely be an incarnation of God himself, an avatar, like Krishna or Rama. One day when he was in Bihar, his car had to stop because of a puncture. He climbed out with the other passengers and strolled by the roadside. Not knowing who he was, an old woman told them she was 104 years old, and was waiting to see the Mahatma. Gandhi asked why. 'He is an avatar,' she answered. It was no good arguing. Another worshipper painted a nauseating portrait of him in the guise of Krishna.

Outright deification was rare, and did not yet present a problem. But the Mahatma cult did. If he was not actually God, he might well be God's superhuman agent. 'Often', he was to write, 'the title has deeply pained me, and there is not a moment I can recall when it may be said to have tickled me.' Though he could not suppress the cult, he tried to weaken it. Instead of the battle-cry 'Mahatma-Gandhi-ki-jai', he suggested 'Hindu-Musulman-ki-jai' (Victory to Hindu-Muslim unity), 'Allah-O-Akbar' (God is great), or the ever-green 'Bande Mataram' (Hail Motherland). His audiences applauded and went on shouting 'Mahatma-Gandhi-ki-jai'. Sophisticated Congressmen, who pooh-poohed the notion that he was a special sort of being, could be seen aping his personal habits as if he were.

For seven months of that year he spent most of the time on tour, often in murderous heat or stifling humidity, visiting places where no politician had ever trod. He went by car, by train or on foot, never sparing himself in the effort to reach at least an appreciable fraction of the seven hundred thousand villages of India. His three daily meals were always the same—three slices of bread or toast, two oranges, a bunch of grapes or a handful of raisins, and sixteen ounces of goat's milk. The Ali brothers often accompanied him, and he looked frail beside them. But his appearance did not save him from the overwhelming and clamorous welcome of Indian villagers—the singing, the garlands, the music, and above all the trampling rush to get close enough to receive *darshan*, that blessing from his mere presence which made his Mahatmaship a dynamic force. When travelling by rail he was besieged wherever he halted. At one obscure station the local people swore that if the train did not stop, they would lie down on the track and let it run over them. About midnight, amid uproar, the train was sighted. It did stop. Gandhi was asleep, but he staggered up and showed himself. The din died away and the crowd knelt on the platform, weeping.

He endured these onslaughts with incredible stamina, but deplored them. They were 'the tyranny of love'. Compassion carried him through the graver encounters, and quips helped in handling the sillier sort. 'If I had no sense of humour,' he wrote in *Young India*, 'I should long ago have committed suicide.' At least his status enabled him to command silence for his speeches, and these were what mattered. He addressed groups of all sizes, indoors and out of doors. Sometimes he faced mass meetings of a hundred thousand or more. In the absence of microphones, most of these people could not hear. They were content if they got a glimpse of him, and some walked twenty miles in the Indian sun to get it.

As an orator he was markedly less mobile than he was in private. Standing on one spot tired him (the only lasting effect of his illness) and he preferred to speak sitting down. His voice had no spellbinding music, but sounded, as always, fervently sincere. It ran on in level lucidity with pauses for questions. He could be pungent, but seldom used ridicule, and he could be felicitous, but seldom went out of his way to charm. He still appealed firmly to facts and reason, and did not try for laughter or frequent applause. His audiences were held by a kind of awe. Every meeting had the air of a great occasion—an initiation, solemn yet happy, into a new courage and fellowship. Afterwards the children would gather round him and bring out his sense of fun. He called them 'our future leaders'.

Besides speaking, he kept up his journalism. The routine of running *Young India* and *Navajivan* was delegated to Mahadev Desai. Gandhi, however, contributed campaign articles which were reprinted in papers throughout India. He was never abusive or inflammatory, and when the Ali brothers were, he made them apologize. But his tone toward the British system, as distinct from the people who kept it going, was as outspoken as any patriot could wish. 'Satanic' was one of the adjectives he favoured. Collections of his writings and speeches were published in paper covers under the titles *Swaraj in One Year* and *Freedom's Battle*. His name now appeared on books as 'Mahatma' Gandhi, not 'M.K.', though he remained 'M.K.' in the weeklies under his control.

His mind darted everywhere. He gave talks to students on 'What Students Can Do' and to merchants on 'What Merchants Can Do'. In all towns and in many villages he looked after the formation of Congress branches. Whenever he could (which was often) he extolled the spinning wheel. As an Indian flag he designed a red, white and green tricolour with the redemptive *charkha* in the middle. For this propaganda, the most promising subjects were naturally women. Gandhi addressed them as 'my dear sisters', and they showered him with bracelets and jewellery for the Cause. He had no plans to unleash them for direct action as in South Africa, but he was unwearyingly emphatic about their rights. In pursuit of his other aims, he posted National Volunteers to picket the liquor shops, and presided in April over a conference of Untouchables, urging them to throw off their bondage. He declared in *Young India* that if he had to be reborn, he would wish to be reborn as an Untouchable, so as to share their wrongs and help to free them.

Through all his actions ran the theme of Indian unity—not a monolithic unity based on his own religion, but a secular unity with a place for all. The chief prerequisite was Hindu-Muslim rapprochement. Concessions like cow protection were good, but there was much less to be said for mere levelling and assimilation. Hindus should keep their shape, Muslims likewise. In the same spirit Gandhi sketched his further dreams when opening one of the national universities. Indian scholars, he said, should explore all the varied life of the sub-continent, ransacking the treasures of the past to disclose the sources of national strength. What their labours should promote was not fusion on the American model but synthesis, a co-existence of cultures. It should be a co-existence of classes and races also. Society should flourish without conflict or oppression, rooted in Ahimsa.

To intellectuals as to peasants, Gandhi offered an image of Swaraj which was far more compelling than any westernized progress into a doubtful future. It seemed to his hearers that the crust of alien corruption was cracking and the buried splendour of India was showing through, still there under all disfigurements, immortal and recoverable.

3

To be stirred, however, was not to be hypnotized. By July some of the non-co-operators were growing restive. British institutions functioned everywhere without check. For weeks Gandhi had been advising patience, and predicting that the constructive programme would be the key to success. His more critical followers ventured to wonder how. At Nagpur, Congress had given him an ace to hold in reserve—civil disobedience in the form of a tax strike. But he showed no sign of playing it, and as his method excluded secrecy, he could not be hatching a surprise of some other kind. S. C. Bose landed in Bombay after a trip to England and talked with him at Mani Bhavan. Lloyd George's Government, beset by crises domestic and foreign, looked vulnerable. Yet Bose saw no sign that the measures taken and foreshadowed by Gandhi would ever shift it. He left dissatisfied.

On 8 July the Khilafat Committee met in Karachi. The Turkish situation had become more confused, but not so as to appease Muslim wrath. The Sultan had fallen abjectly under British control. Mustapha Kemal, the leader of the nationalists resisting the treaty, was menaced by a Greek invasion with British backing. Indignation ran high. Swayed by the Ali brothers, the Committee called upon Muslims to stop enlisting in the police and the army, and, if already in, to desert. Five hundred doctors of Islamic law supported the appeal. It included a threat to proclaim a republic at the end of the year, forcing the pace of the Gandhian transition. The Moplahs, a Muslim tribe on the Malabar coast, did not wait. That August they declared a holy war against infidels generally, killing some Europeans, and also many Hindu landlords and money-lenders.

Moplah violence pained Gandhi profoundly. He wanted to reason with the fanatics in person, but the Government would not let him go. The revolt was slowly and bloodily stamped out. Enemies exploited it to discredit his whole campaign. The same season brought the first full scale attack on him by a fellow-countryman, in the shape of a book entitled *Gandhism Exposed*. The author, under the pen-name Argus, repeated Mrs Besant's charge that he was subverting society just when Dyarchy was opening the road to reform. India was being sacrificed to a Swaraj that nobody could define. Non-co-operation was effective enough to be dangerous without being effective enough to win. The spinning wheel was a fraud, the popular tribunals were kangaroo courts. Gandhi's disciples were lining their pockets out of the Tilak Fund, and misleading the superstitious by letting them think he was an invincible god.

Gandhi, however, had by no means lost the initiative. His reaction to the fire-eating of the Khilafat Committee was to murmur 'hasten slowly' and insist that the masses were not ready for civil disobedience. But as he had carefully explained as far back as the fifth issue of *Young India,* 'He to whom Satyagraha means nothing more than civil disobedience has never understood Satyagraha. . . . Swadeshi is Satyagraha.' From July onward he was busy with the Swadeshi part of his programme. After that month no Congress member was to be allowed to wear imported cloth. He hoped to make India independent of textiles from other countries by the end of September.

On 31 July, in Umar Sobani's yard in Bombay, he put the match to a bonfire of foreign finery. It delighted the crowd but worried Charles Andrews. The reverend gentleman wore homespun himself, but protested that the flames had destroyed objects of beauty and value which might have been given to the poor. Gandhi replied that the objects hurt India. It would dishonour the poor to own them. Also he was diverting the citizenry's destructive passions from human beings to inanimate things. For the next few weeks, holocausts of the same kind were a feature of his tours. He would ask all the men at a meeting to strip off their imported garments and put them on a heap to be burnt. The result would be a wild flurry of shirts, coats, trousers, underwear, even shoes and hats. When this had died down, at least one person might turn out to be totally naked.

Gandhi had long since shed imported garments himself. But when given the opportunity for a further step, he took it. A problem arose because many Indians could not afford enough homespun to replace everything they wished to discard. 'Let there be no prudery about dress,' Gandhi wrote. For men, a loincloth was sufficient. In September he began going about for much of the time wearing only that. He was identifying himself with the poorest. Some of his associates were shocked.

As he thrust the spinning wheel more and more into the fore-front, his conception of it grew more and more exalted. He continued to press the practical case—that it would give families work and income in the dead months, and loosen the grip of British capitalism. But the mystique gathered strength. Spinning was a means to self-reliance and self-respect. It was a bond between all who did it. It was an aid to meditation that steadied the mind and cleansed the soul. 'When millions take to it as a sacrament,' Gandhi wrote, 'it will turn our faces Godward.' After meeting some temple prostitutes he proposed it as a method of rehabilitation. He put in half an hour at the wheel daily himself, and maintained that spinning would prepare the masses for the discipline of non-violent action.

When Tagore returned from a stay in Europe, Gandhi invited him to spin and set an example. He thought the idea naïve. In an article in a Calcutta magazine he praised the Mahatma most eloquently, but jibbed at his cult among the people, as he found it to have developed or rather narrowed.

> An outside influence seemed to be bearing down on them, grinding them and making one and all speak in the same tone, follow in the same groove. Everywhere I was told that culture and reasoning power should abdicate, and blind obedience only reign.

Tagore asked if 'spin and weave' was an adequate message for the *guru* of a nation to offer. He drew a parable from the birds outside his window, which sang as well as eating.

On 13 October Gandhi answered with an article in *Young India*. As Tagore had called him the Great Soul, so he saluted Tagore as the Great Sentinel, rightly on the alert for India's safety. He acknowledged the need for far more in life than his present programme embraced. But he passed to one of the most sublimely conclusive retorts in the history of journalism.

To a people famishing and idle, the only acceptable form in which God can appear is work and promise of food as wages. God created man to work for his food, and said that those who ate without work were thieves. Eighty per cent of India are compulsorily thieves half the year. Is it any wonder if India has become one vast prison? Hunger is the argument that is driving India to the spinning wheel. . . .

True to his poetical instinct the poet lives for the morrow and would have us do likewise. He presents to our admiring gaze the beautiful picture of the birds early in the morning singing hymns of praise as they soar into the sky. These birds had their day's food and soared with rested wings in whose veins new blood had flowed during the previous night. But I have had the pain of watching the birds who for want of strength could not be coaxed even into a flutter of their wings. The human bird under the Indian sky gets up weaker than when he pretended to retire. For millions it is an eternal vigil or an eternal trance. . . .

I have found it impossible to soothe the suffering patients with a song from Kabir. The hungry millions ask for one poem— invigorating food. They must earn it themselves. . . .

I do indeed ask the poet to spin the wheel as a sacrament.

4

Gandhi read and answered Tagore at Mani Bhavan, under mounting stress. In September the Government had begun to close in. The Ali brothers were arrested for attempting to detach Muslims from the armed forces. On 4 October a Congress meeting in Bombay approved all they had done. A manifesto was published over the signatures of Gandhi, Motilal Nehru, Sarojini Naidu and most of the other leaders, saying that Indians ought not to remain in the employ, civil or military, of 'a system of government which has brought India's economic, moral and political degradation'. Next day the Working Committee endorsed this manifesto. On a visit to Trichinopoly Gandhi courted arrest by repeating one of Mohamed Ali's speeches verbatim.

On 1 November the brothers were sentenced to two years' imprisonment. Congressmen clamoured for civil disobedience.

Gandhi was reluctant. The textile phase of the campaign was far behind schedule. But the year which was to bring Swaraj had only a few more weeks to run, and Indians were spurred on by events in Ireland, where Sinn Fein had achieved the equivalent. Four days after the Ali sentence, the All-India Congress Committee authorized provincial branches to prepare for a refusal of land-tax. Gandhi announced that he would make an experimental start in Bardoli, a district in Gujarat with 137 villages and about eighty thousand inhabitants.

In *Young India* he defined civil disobedience as rebellion without the element of violence. To write this was to admit that he was rebelling, or about to rebel. Still he was not arrested, though there was much debate in Delhi as to whether he should be. The prevailing view was that arrest would make him a martyr, whereas if he were left free and failed to deliver Swaraj, he would lose his influence. Fears persisted, however, that non-violence was a camouflage disguising plans for an armed revolt. One spokesman for this theory was Sir George Lloyd, Willingdon's successor as Governor of Bombay. Some colour was given to his belief by an occurrence on his own doorstep.

On 17 November the Prince of Wales (afterwards Edward VIII) was due to arrive for a state tour of India. The Congress Working Committee proclaimed a national *hartal*, and called for boycotts of the ceremonies wherever the Prince went. When he landed in Bombay the pro-British element, headed by wealthy Parsees, defied Congress and staged a welcome. Opponents attacked them in the streets, and riots broke out. Several policemen were beaten to death separating the factions. Gandhi, who had come to superintend a peaceful protest, issued desperate appeals which did not save him from a torrent of abuse. With murder and arson still raging, he wrote: 'The Swaraj that I have witnessed during the last two days has stunk in my nostrils.' He began a fast and the turmoil gradually died down. A deputation representing all sections of the community waited on him at Mani Bhavan, gave pledges of good conduct, and persuaded him to eat some grapes. But fifty-eight Bombay citizens had been killed and four hundred injured.

The Mahatma miserably inferred that civil disobedience would produce much the same result. He said God had brought him to the city to warn him, and postponed the Bardoli tax strike. Andrews called and found him, for once, really shaken. He looked haggard and emaciated. His tone at this time was responsible for a rumour that he had gone to the Prince of Wales and prostrated himself. This legend was still current ten years later. When he came across it in a London newspaper, his comment was: 'I would bend the knee before the poorest scavenger, the poorest Untouchable in India, for having participated in crushing him for centuries. But not before the King, much less the Prince of Wales.' As for Congress, it was not deterred from snubbing the royal traveller with *hartals* and boycotts. The most popular young man in the world drove through disorganized cities and half-empty streets.

Official patience was running out. In the first week of December the long-anticipated wave of arrests began. The victims included the Nehrus, Das, Lajpat Rai, Azad, and the English sympathizer Stokes. Many non-co-operators practically forced the authorities to take them. The National Volunteers were outlawed, and rounded up in droves. None of the accused defended themselves in court, because a defence would have implied acknowledging the court's jurisdiction. Their cases, therefore, were quickly disposed of. In two months the number of political prisoners rose above thirty thousand. Efforts were made to keep them apart from ordinary criminals. But they soon knew what jail was like. These intelligent Indians were taught to see Imperial justice in terms of vile food, brutish inefficiency, flogging, graft, and an utter absence of any intent to reform the prisoner. Nor did the lesson help the Government by wearing them down, because Gandhian philosophy lightened the burden, in more ways than one. Rajagopalachari wrote cheerfully to the Mahatma about the delights of being cut off from politics and newspapers.

> What an ideal condition which I know you are envying. . . . It took me till now to get rid of the boils. I am now quite free from the trouble. . . . Your eyes would flow with delight if you saw me here in my solitary cell spinning, spinning not as a task imposed by a tyrant faddist, but with pleasure.

The few leaders still at liberty could not share Rajaji's peace of mind. Congress held its annual meeting at Ahmedabad in a tense and aggressive mood. The year of Swaraj was almost over, and Indian moderates, taking their cue from Mrs Besant, were sneering. Maulana Hasrat Mohani, the President of the Muslim League, urged the non-co-operators to take further measures. The logical aim of their programme, he observed, was the creation of a rival Government. It might achieve this if the existing Government did not interfere; but the existing Government manifestly was interfering. Therefore, he proposed proclaiming an Indian republic and marshalling the forces around it. Gandhi rejected the idea, but accepted a resolution investing him with 'sole executive authority'. He emerged as dictator of Congress . . . on the understanding that he would resume preparations for civil disobedience.

Events heaved up toward a climax. There were strange moments when it seemed that he had, after a fashion, won. Jinnah, Pandit Malaviya (who had stayed aloof from the struggle), and the former Congress President Sir Sankaran Nair, were trying to arrange a truce. The Viceroy offered to set most of the prisoners free and confer with Congress. Gandhi could fairly have claimed that such a move amounted to recognizing his state-within-a-state as more than a political association. But he held out for specific concessions which Reading would not grant—the legalization of picketing, the release of the Ali brothers. Then, in January 1922, there was talk of a constitutional conference on Dominion status. Gandhi sketched a scheme for a constituent assembly elected by Congress members. The mediators convened an all-party meeting in Bombay to air the suggestion. Lord Reading would not touch it, and the onus was shifted back to Gandhi.

Through January he sat inactive at Sabarmati, preaching the virtues of self-control and self-sacrifice. He gave no important orders and was apparently waiting for a voice from heaven. All eyes were upon him, and not in India alone. Over the past few years, growing numbers of westerners had been corresponding with him and writing articles on him. While many were hostile or at least critical, so much praise had accumulated that in this month a Bombay publisher compiled a volume of tributes culled almost entirely from Anglo-American sources.

Such admirers gave him no guidance in his silent torment of decision. Indeed they were out of date. One of them had quoted Tagore as saying that Indian nationalism could not go radically astray in the Mahatma's hands. But now Tagore made a public statement voicing his apprehension. He believed in Ahimsa if it really sprang from the depths of a people's moral being, but it could not be imposed as a technique on millions whose lives had been conditioned otherwise. Once in motion they would be out of control again.

This was daunting. Furthermore, Gandhi had scruples about the position of Indian landlords. Wherever the zamindar flourished, he collected his rent and the land-tax together in a lump sum, and passed on the Government's share. Peasants who withheld their money would thus deprive not only the British, but many compatriots who happened to be part of the British Establishment. The prospect of Indians in conflict with Indians revived the distress Gandhi had felt over the Ahmedabad mill strike. Bardoli, which was a district of peasant proprietors, did not raise this complication. But it would soon come up if disobedience spread.

While he meditated, his hand was forced. The peasants of Guntur, a district in Andhra, began a tax strike on 12 January. In Guntur as in Bardoli there were no zamindars. The issue lay directly between Indians and the Government. Most of the peasants joined in, and Gandhi had no choice but to bestow a provisional blessing. On the 29th, fully briefed and mobilized, the resisters of Bardoli resolved to start. He approved. On 1 February he sent Lord Reading an open letter saying he would authorize civil disobedience in that district within a week, unless various demands were met.

The letter was an odd document, only fully comprehensible in the light of Mohani's speech to Congress. Stating his price for calling the action off, Gandhi made no conditions about the Punjab, or the Khilafat, or Swaraj. Instead he asked for the release of all prisoners and 'absolute non-interference with all non-violent activities'. In other words, he wanted Reading to let him go on building up his Counter-Establishment with an advance guarantee against hindrance of any sort—even if he persuaded the troops to desert to him; even if he enabled three hundred million of Britain's customers to dispense with her products; even if he declared a republic with himself as President. His courteous, diffident language was the vehicle for an audacity which would almost have excused his cult as a god.

The Viceroy of course declined. Gandhi wrote again reaffirming his stand. British officials waited for an attack which no one knew how to deal with. Some suspected that it could not be dealt with, that Bardoli was checkmate. Taxes might be extorted, there or in Guntur, at bayonet point. But if Bardoli's lead were followed and the stoppage became general, the Raj would be on the road to bankruptcy. And Gandhi let it be supposed that he foresaw some such trend. 'When the Swaraj flag floats victoriously at Bardoli,' he had declared in a sanguine moment, 'then the people of the district next to Bardoli, following in the steps of Bardoli, should seek to plant the flag of Swaraj in their midst. Thus in district after district, in regular succession, throughout the length and breadth of India, should the Swaraj flag be hoisted.' Lord Reading sent Whitehall an ominous report. Villages all over the north were simmering, cities rumbled with working-class discontent, millions of Muslims were embittered and sullen.

On 8 February a bit of India would become free. For how long? For a day? for a week? for ever?

It was not free for any time at all. On the 5th, nearly a thousand miles from Bardoli, the lunacy of a mob dragged down the whole edifice. The incident happened at Chauri Chaura in Gorakhpur. A body of police disrupted a procession of non-co-operators. Driven back by weight of numbers, the policemen took refuge in the town hall. Hooligans set fire to it and pounced on them as they ran out. Twenty-two were battered to death and incinerated.

Gandhi sank under the news. The lesson of Bombay was atrociously confirmed. India's masses had not absorbed his teaching. Civil disobedience would lead to violence as its inevitable sequel, and unhallowed means could not bring victory, only, at most, a diabolical pseudo-victory. He fasted five days in penance and summoned members of the Working Committee to meet at Bardoli on the 12th. They gloomily yielded to his importunity. All plans for direct action were dropped. The milder forms of non-co-operation could go on, but the main stress henceforth would be on Swadeshi and the constructive programme.

He explained his decision in an article in *Young India*. God, he said, had been abundantly kind to him, plucking him back from the brink with another warning. Though tempted to press on, he had recognized the origin of that prompting.

'What about your manifesto to the Viceroy and your rejoinder to his reply?' spoke the voice of Satan. It was the bitterest cup of humiliation to drink. 'Surely it is cowardly to withdraw the next day after pompous threats to the Government and promises to the people of Bardoli.' Thus Satan's invitation was to deny Truth and therefore Religion, to deny God. . . .

The drastic reversal of practically the whole of the aggressive programme may be politically unsound and unwise, but there is no doubt that it is religiously sound. . . .

I must undergo personal cleansing. I must become a fitter

instrument able to register the slightest variation in the moral atmosphere about me. My prayers must have much deeper truth and humility.

He closed the article with a hope—one of his few lapses into mere wishful thinking—that the constructive programme would achieve everything without civil disobedience.

At Bardoli he threw away his ace and momentarily lost his bearings. But in the act, he enrolled himself among the immortals. The idea that he was an unworldly mystic miscast in politics, and that the mysticism wrecked him, is not borne out by his speeches or writings before the fatal February. These show no trace of any conflict. While the motif of applying religion to politics is present, the tone is never unworldly. All the evidence confirms his own version. He sustained a blow which came like a command from outside, a divine rebuke. In Bombay his Absolute had begun troubling him. Now it struck with a crushing impact. For the first time (it is worth stressing that this actually was the first time), a course which he admitted might be politically correct—might even gain the political objective—was vetoed at a higher level.

The revelation of Truth-Force was complete, and its inventor had not been found wanting. He rose from his abasement with the unique glory which still haloes him. Here and here alone in the human record is a revolutionary who could have launched his revolution, could very likely have carried it through, yet refused because it would be the wrong sort of revolution. Rather than lead his people along the old paths of bloodshed and terror and cheated hope, Mahatma Gandhi, the Great Soul, was willing to fail.

XII

Things Fall Apart

1

To his immured lieutenants, the greatness of his conduct was not instantly apparent. He had cancelled the operation without even consulting them. Long letters from Motilal Nehru and Lajpat Rai led a chorus of protest. Motilal, after all, had persuaded Congress to entrust Swaraj into Gandhi's keeping. Lajpat Rai had seconded the resolution at Nagpur, and his name, in witness of unwavering faith, had headed the recent anthology of tributes. They felt cruelly let down. So did many. Subhas Chandra Bose, who was in the same prison as C. R. Das, found him transported with rage and grief. The shocked bewilderment which Bose shared reverberated through Congress and breached the Hindu-Muslim front. Why, the critics complained, had Gandhi never warned them of such a possibility? And if every forward step, anywhere in India, was liable to be prevented by unrelated events anywhere else, what was the use of planning at all?

The Mahatma's replies reflected a contrast in his nature which the campaign had sharpened. Still sweetly reasonable in discussion, he could be ruthless in action. He told the chief prisoners that they were 'civilly dead' and had no claim to advise him. But having ruled them out of order as policy-makers, he put them in the picture as colleagues.

It was easy to show that some of their charges were unfair. For instance, he had given a warning at the time of the riots in Bombay. One of his most conciliatory letters went to the junior Nehru. He had not heard from Jawaharlal directly, but his assistant secretary, a young Punjabi named Pyarelal Nayyar, passed on a bitter outburst against his leadership and the spinning wheel. Gandhi answered this, gently recalling his own South African experience. When in jail he had always lost touch with events outside. So it was

231

with the Nehrus. Chauri Chaura had not been a sudden or isolated incident. It was simply the clinching proof of a latent anarchy which a whole series of incidents, from Bombay onward, had led him to suspect. 'The cause', he wrote, 'will prosper by this retreat. The movement had unconsciously drifted from the right path. We have come back to our moorings, and we can again go straight ahead.' As for the spinning wheel, Jawaharlal should not despise it. It was the *karma yoga* of the age.

To judge from this letter, Gandhi imagined that non-co-operation could proceed as before. Certainly his tone in *Young India* was as firm as ever. He spoke of a fight to a finish, and said Indians could not compromise whilst the British lion 'shook his gory claws' in their faces. But Bardoli had thrown the ranks into too much confusion. The upward curve had turned and was bending down. Lord Reading judged that the Mahatma's magic was gone. On Friday 10 March, at half past ten in the evening, a police car drew up at the Ashram. An officer walked to Gandhi's bungalow with a polite request to consider himself in custody, and to come along when he was ready. After praying and singing a hymn with a group of ashramites, the prisoner strode buoyantly to the car and was driven the short distance to Sabarmati jail. He took two blankets, a spare loincloth, and a few books including the *Gita*. Kasturbai was allowed to ride with him as far as the prison gate. Next morning she sent some food and more clothes.

He had already called upon the people to stay calm. They did. In 1919 the report of his arrest had caused turmoil. In 1922 there were no serious demonstrations. According to some, the reason was that his influence was stronger, his teaching better understood. According to others, nobody at this precise juncture had the will to demonstrate. Probably both these explanations had truth in them.

Gandhi was tried in a small, heavily guarded courthouse in Ahmedabad on 18 March, before Mr Justice Broomfield. The charge was sedition, on the basis of three of his more challenging articles in *Young India*. The publisher, Shankarlal Banker, was tried with him. At the preliminary hearing Gandhi pleaded guilty, and gave his occupation as 'farmer and weaver', a gesture of identification with the masses which he had first made when giving testimony in another case two years before. Technically he was a barrister still. But he had not practised for a decade, and he was soon to be disbarred. When he entered the courtroom for the actual trial, wearing his loincloth and looking insignificant, the public benches were jammed with well-wishers who scrambled to their feet in his honour. Among them was Sarojini Naidu.

The Advocate-General of Bombay read the indictment and stated the Crown's case. Gandhi replied with a short speech offering no defence, and enlarging on his plea of guilty.

> I have no desire whatsoever to conceal from this court the fact that to preach disaffection towards the existing system of government has become almost a passion with me. . . . I knew that I was playing with fire. I ran the risk, and if I was set free, I would still do the same. . . . I am here, therefore, to invite and submit to the highest penalty that can be inflicted upon me, for what in law is a deliberate crime, and what appears to me to be the highest duty of a citizen.

Then he read a written statement, tracing the series of disillusionments which had turned him from a supporter of the Empire into a rebel. He went on:

> I came reluctantly to the conclusion that the British connection had made India more helpless than she ever was before. . . . She has become so poor than she has little power of resisting famines. Before the British advent, India spun and wove in her millions of cottages just the supplement she needed for adding to her meagre agricultural resources. This cottage industry, so vital for India's existence, has been ruined by incredibly heartless and inhuman processes as described by English witnesses. Little do town-dwellers know how the semi-starved masses of India are slowly sinking to lifelessness. . . . No sophistry, no jugglery in figures can explain away the evidence that the skeletons in many villages present to the naked eye. . . .
>
> Many Englishmen and Indian officials honestly believe that they are administering one of the best systems devised in the world. . . . They do not know that a subtle but effective system of terrorism and an organized display of force on the one hand, and the deprivation of all powers of retaliation and self-defence on the other, have emasculated the people and induced in them the habit of simulation. . . .
>
> It has been a precious privilege for me to be able to write what I have in the various articles tendered in evidence against me.

He asked again for the severest penalty.

Mr. Broomfield bowed to him, and spoke.

The determination of a just sentence is perhaps as difficult a proposition as a judge in this country could have to face. . . . In the eyes of millions of your countrymen, you are a great patriot and a great leader. Even those who differ from you in politics look upon you as a man of high ideals and of noble and even saintly life. . . . But you have made it impossible for any government to leave you at liberty.

The only case remotely like a precedent was that of Tilak, and the Judge followed this by sentencing Gandhi to six years' imprisonment. He added that if the Government later saw fit to reduce the term, no one would be better pleased than himself. Then he sentenced Shankarlal Banker to one year and a fine of a thousand rupees. Gandhi thanked him and the court stood adjourned.

India's Messiah had risen from political death. The 'farmer and weaver' had reverted for a confounding moment to his old profession and indicted the Empire. When Mr Broomfield was gone, half the courtroom fell weeping at Gandhi's feet. He took his leave with a benign smile. As the news spread, his reputation began to mount again. The authorities saw their mistake too late. But they did learn from it. This was the last time they ever put him on trial. After 1922 they imprisoned him without trial.

2

His cell was in Yeravda Prison at Poona, a gloomy place, but not too badly appointed. For several reasons his sentence was welcome. It came as a relief and a species of holiday. It gave him a chance to exemplify his mystique of going to jail gladly. Also it destroyed—for a while at least—the more preposterous part of his cult.

Many Indians had taken it for granted that their Mahatma had superhuman powers, and that if the English tried to lock him up, he would in all likelihood fly out of the window. Such expectations were not confined to the unlettered. Hindu minds are apt to admit ideas which western minds on the same level (wisely or unwisely) refuse. Hence their respect for Annie Besant, long after her belief in occult conjuring tricks had discredited her at home. This has always been so. Kautilya, the Machiavelli of ancient India, mingled sophisticated maxims of statecraft with recipes for making spies invisible. One of Gandhi's most cultured opponents, assailing his views on education, reproached him for hindering the work of Indian scientists just when there was a good hope of their developing their own X-rays and radio through yogic techniques, without the need for apparatus. Faced with the crude prophecy that a distinguished politician would take to the air, Hindus could scoff as loudly as Englishmen. Yet some had an unsettling suspicion that perhaps, after all, he might.

By going to prison like anybody else, and insisting on normal treatment, Gandhi pricked an undesirable bubble. Indians would now be more inclined to work for their own freedom, less prone to rely on a Mahatma's miracles. With that thought as solace, he settled down for a spell of reflection and reading.

At first he was disappointed. The Yeravda staff made him uncomfortable. They put difficulties in the way of his getting books and a spinning wheel. They kept him apart from other prisoners, except an African with whom he had no language in common. They forbade him to sleep outdoors (a hardship in hot weather) and supplied no pillow—he rested his head on the clothes he was not wearing. The warders went through the offensive ritual of a daily search. All this was petty and unpleasant. When he saw how badly his son Devadas was upset by a visit, he asked the ashramites to dissuade Kasturbai from coming.

However, most of the rigours soon relaxed. A spinning wheel was allowed in, and Gandhi not only used it but taught the African. He drew up a programme of study and got through a hundred and fifty books. These included the immense *Mahabharata,* which he succeeded in finishing, and numerous works on Hindu philosophy. He also probed further into other religions, took up Tolstoy and Ruskin again, and (with a fleeting revival of interest in the esoteric) sampled the German mystic Boehme. His general reading included Scott, Ben Jonson, William James's *Varieties of Religious Experience,* Wells's fashionable *Outline of History,* Shaw's *Man and Superman,* and, at last, Kipling, as represented by *Barrack-Room Ballads.* Also he returned to the attack on Goethe's *Faust,* which he had read before and found opaque. This time he foreseeably enjoyed the scene where Margaret, in her distress, works at the spinning wheel. Besides reading he made a fresh attempt to master Tamil, and wrote some chapters of a book on Satyagraha in South Africa. Another project was his autobiography, which he had started in 1921 during a lull. But this was postponed.

Outside Yeravda the nationalist movement was slipping into fluidity. Reaction, confusion of purpose, the lack of any clear-cut achievement, diverted attention from the solid gains. Obsessed with the One Year slogan, Congressmen had made no plans for a second year. When Gandhi went to prison, Kasturbai broke her usual silence with a touching appeal to Indians to press on with the tasks her husband had set them. But she mentioned only spinning and the khadi campaign, giving no guidance otherwise. In June 1922 Motilal Nehru was released, and the All-India Congress Committee appointed a commission to look into the prospects of civil disobedience. Its findings bore out Gandhi's judgement: the country was not ready.

Optimists cherished a dream that the Mahatma would be delivered by a Swaraj Parliament. He shared it himself, briefly. But although he had to forget it, he did leave prison sooner than he expected. The diet and discipline sapped his health. In January 1924 he was seriously ill. The doctor diagnosed appendicitis, and he was rushed to Sassoon Hospital in Poona. The clerk admitting him put his name down as 'Mahatma Gandhi'. Colonel Maddock, the English surgeon, obtained his permission to operate at once. Before anaesthesia he asked to see an officer of the Servants of India Society. They drew up a statement, which he signed, praising the hospital staff and warning Indians against any demonstration if he should die. This eased the surgeon's apprehensions during a midnight appendicectomy that was cursed with bad luck. A storm cut off the electric current. One of the nurses held a flashlight close to the body, but it went out. The job had to be completed by the light of a hurricane lamp. Completed it was, however. The result softened Gandhi's prejudice against western medicine. Maddock became a lifelong friend.

His recovery was slow, complicated by an abscess. The Viceroy wondered what to do. A return to jail would revive the danger of martyrdom. Congress, moreover, was in no state to be urged to the charge again by a free Mahatma. On 5 February Colonel Maddock brought Gandhi the news that the rest of his sentence was remitted. The following month he was well enough to go to Bombay. He recuperated at Juhu on the coast north of the city, in a bungalow belonging to Shantikumar Morarji, the wealthy son of a fellow citizen of Porbandar.

Today Juhu is a rather splendid seaside resort. Hotels and villas nestle in a forest of palm-trees fringing a picture-postcard beach. In 1924 it was less frequented. Gandhi, however, had no yearning for solitude. He shared his convalescence with various friends, inviting any who felt unwell to join him in experimenting with mud-packs and other forms of nature-cure. They humoured him, he knew he was being humoured, and it was a happy time. Every day he strolled through the palms on to the splashy sands, paced back and forth among the children and coconut-sellers and marooned jellyfish, and watched the breakers of the Arabian Sea, the uncompromising sunsets. About four in the afternoon he said his prayers there and received visitors. On that side of the palms lay healing and renewal; behind them, the country he had to rediscover. Anxious to make a start, he resumed the burden of *Young India* and *Navajivan* on 3 April, too early for his own welfare. Motilal Nehru and C. R. Das came to Juhu and brought his politics up to date. They told a depressing story.

First, the Hindu-Muslim alliance was broken. The Khilafat Committee, unnerved by Bardoli, had virtually succumbed to events in Turkey. There Kemal had routed the Greek invaders and extracted a better treaty. The Sultan, however, was deposed in the process. For a while a nephew had held the Caliphate in a purely religious sense. Then that institution had been given its death-blow —ironically, by an Indian Muslim. A message of support from the Aga Khan had been resented in Turkey as foreign interference, whereupon Kemal took advantage of public feeling to end the Caliphate altogether. The news of this final step had been in the papers in March for Gandhi to read. If he still felt any doubt as to its implications, Motilal dispelled them. With the Caliphate issue defunct, the basis of inter-communal partnership was gone. A revived bitterness traceable to the Moplah rising had already produced riots.

Congress retained a few outstanding Muslims such as Maulana Azad, and could count on the goodwill, if not the enthusiasm, of the Ali brothers. But there was more plausibility now in the charge that it was a Hindu body illegitimately claiming to speak for all India. Worse, it no longer spoke for even Hindu India. The hard core of dues-paying membership was less than a quarter of a million. While the tonic effect of 1921 had not worn off entirely, Indians were bored with non-co-operation. Most of the barristers and students were back in their former places. A few national colleges plodded on. So did a half-hearted Swadeshi movement. Swaraj, however, had receded over the horizon. The immediate political question was not how to defeat Dyarchy but how to live with it, and on this, Congress itself had split. Some wanted to go on boycotting all councils, central, provincial and municipal. Others wanted to enter them.

So the Government had no cause for alarm. In its hands was a subtle and formidable new weapon, the 1921 census. This could be invoked to scout all notions of Indian unity, present or potential. It included, with other proofs of ethnic division, a table of 222 distinct languages allegedly spoken in the sub-continent. Careful readers were picking out some curious facts. Comparison with the census of 1901 revealed that Indians had somehow invented 75 more languages in twenty years. Among the dozens of dialects supposed to exist along the borders, one was said to be spoken by only three persons, another by two, another by one. It was not made clear who the 'one' talked to. But careful readers were rare, and the '222 languages' were ready to be hauled out as a bludgeon against nationalism for years to come.

Das and Motilal Nehru approached Gandhi at Juhu not only as purveyors of information but as champions of a new policy to which they hoped to convert him. At the 1922 meeting of Congress they had favoured ending the council boycott as sterile. Voted down, they had launched their own Swaraj Party to contest elections. It attracted S. C. Bose, Vallabhbhai Patel's brother Vithalbhai, and many of the more progressive Congressmen. The Swarajists demanded Dominion status. But their short-term aims were more equivocal. Like the Communists of that period, they wanted to get inside the machine so that they could obstruct it, discredit it, and change it—a strategy for a professional élite. In the 1923 elections they had done well, especially in Bengal. But several Congress leaders, such as Vallabhbhai Patel and Rajagopalachari, were No-Changers unwilling to shift from Gandhi's line. Jawaharlal Nehru differed from his father by leaning toward the No-Changers, though he showed the first signs of his future skill at formula-finding in the moves to avert a total break. Motilal and Das laid the conflict before the Mahatma, and asked if he could see his way to endorsing them.

He could not. He had faith in his own methods, and disliked theirs. But he would not confirm the breach by throwing his weight behind the No-Changers. Instead, he gave his blessing to a pact recognizing the right of both groups to freedom of action. As for himself, he would consider what course to take. On 28 May he went back to Sabarmati.

3

For the next six years Gandhi made the Ashram his home again. He did not forget its daughter house at Wardha, which he visited each December. There, however, he was the guest of Vinoba Bhave, who was already developing a distinctive style. At Sabarmati he was 'Bapu' in his own kingdom.

These were the years of legend-making, when, as in other cases, immortality grew out of failure. While Gandhi was in jail Tagore had come to the Ashram and given a talk on the nature of a Mahatma. His verbal sketch of a person whose life goes outward without limit, acting for the whole world, fitted the absent leader so obviously as to leave no doubt that the Poet still saw him in that role. The Bapu of 1924 was greater, not less, than the Bapu who had vanished into a police car. But he stuck to the old congenial title, even signing it to letters, and encouraged the ashramites to call him by it; though they often added the honorific and called him Bapuji.

His wife said 'Bapu', and continued to be 'Ba' herself. His return had not been marked by any emotional reunion with her—nor by conspicuous coldness either. Few people ever noticed their greetings and partings, until the last parting of all. She had a way of being simply there, small, hard-working and level-headed. She set an example by spinning, as her husband wished. Younger women hovered adoringly round him, and she never said a word. Yet Ba was no doormat. Her housekeeping was imperious, she did not conform to Bapu's diet, and she made it quietly clear that he could not dictate to her.

The Ashram had grown. It housed over a hundred inmates, a number which went on rising to an eventual peak of 230. They were a medley. The women, generally speaking, were there because their husbands or male relatives were. But the variety of motives among the men was wide. Hardly any were coming now in a monastic spirit. Vinoba, an ascetic himself, catered for the ascetics at Wardha. Gandhi attracted social workers, scholars, minor politicians, students, and cranks. The sole common factor was his personal spell. Many were temporary residents who did not take the vows. There was much tension and argument, and some rivalry for his favour, which he damped down with tact. In admitting applicants he was not fastidious. He harboured atheists and bigots. He even harboured believers in violence. Some of the ashramites were quite evidently deranged. A visitor asked why he wasted his time on them. He replied: 'Mine is a mad house and I am the maddest of the lot. But those that cannot see the good in these mad people should have their eyes examined.'

As ever he enjoyed playing with the children, especially at a sort of blind-man's-buff of his own invention. He made sure they were taught to swim in the river. Photographs that show him pulling faces and rubbing noses with babies are not mere public-relations imagery. He appealed to the children as kind and simple, and drew out the best in them. It pained him to hear a child deceived even in fun. After they grew up, they sometimes found it hard to realize that the famous Mahatma was the same gentle person. Teachers at the Ashram school were forbidden to use the cane; the law of non-violence applied here. One teacher who had his doubts got Gandhi's leave to try corporal punishment. The ashramites were amazed, but presently they understood. The teacher achieved nothing and reverted to non-violence with more conviction.

While Bapu was always Bapu, his informality saved him from becoming an object of awe. He joined the potato-peelers in the scullery, and did his share of the other chores. When an inmate was ill he would drop in, chat, and provide little luxuries. Coffee was an instance. Normally this was not served. Kasturbai, however, kept a supply for herself, and when a patient had a craving for it, Gandhi brewed him a pot.

On certain points he was strict. No beggars were allowed in the Ashram. All inmates were expected to spin if they could, and to do manual labour. Lapses from the moral standards implied by the vows were exposed ruthlessly and publicly. Bapu was a stickler for such virtues as punctuality and cleanliness. He had no patience whatever with the slovenly. A Congress district secretary from southern India, well-meaning but slipshod, turned up with what he supposed to be a pathetic tale. He hadn't kept his Committee's accounts very carefully, and now they were holding him responsible for a thousand rupees which he had lost track of. Gandhi almost threw him out. He protested that he was penniless, without even the fare home. Gandhi told him to walk.

The Mahatma's tyrannous watch hung always beside him. His own punctiliousness showed in the way he handled his large correspondence. He kept well abreast of this and dealt with much of it in person, using his left hand when his right was tired, as he had taught himself to do in South Africa. Either way, his writing was ugly but legible. Probably no man with so much paperwork was ever more economical with stationery. He used postcards whenever possible, took notes on the backs of incoming letters, wrote outgoing ones on torn half-sheets and undistributed leaflets, and folded scrap paper to make envelopes. He wore every pencil down to a stump, and once, when a just-viable stump was lost, refused a replacement and made his secretaries grovel about till they found it.

Behind his care there was more than a mental habit. The spectres of India's poor made him psychologically incapable of waste. That dreadful haunting was as urgent as ever. At Sabarmati the talkers came and went. Only the poor, in Christian phrase, were always with him.

Their unseen presence guided him during the first weeks of readjustment and rethinking. By founding the Swaraj Party, Das and Motilal Nehru had widened the chasm again between the politicians and the masses. Even their party's name raised a query. Who was Swaraj for? Whose concern was it? Gandhi could not allow that it was primarily a politicians' affair, or that an élite had any right to make use of the people as a mere dumb source of support. The proper course was the course which he had chosen himself— to go out among the masses, to serve them and understand them and teach them, awakening the dormant subconscious of India. Swaraj was for them, it was their concern. In 1921 they had been stirred, but not mobilized. He had tried, and glimpsed an abyss of chaos. His duty was not to join the new party but to turn the chaos into a cosmos.

As he reviewed his constructive programme, it began to acquire a deeper coherence. He began to see it as a method of rebuilding the nation 'from the bottom upwards' (his own words) to a point where a transformed society would be ready to march behind its leaders. This would be in essence a Non-Violent Society. His mind was running on his Counter-Establishment again, but with a more profound logic and a less hurried tempo.

In the social order, Ahimsa implied getting rid of group conflict and coercion, and fostering harmony instead. When that principle was worked out, all the items of the constructive programme fell into place and fitted together. Thus a Non-Violent Society would be free from the enmity of religions . . . whence, Hindu-Muslim friendship. It would be free from the injustice of one sex toward the other . . . whence, the emancipation of women. It would be free from the cruelties of perverted caste . . . whence, no Untouchability. It would be free from the despotism of wealth . . . whence, most of the Gandhian economic policy.

This idea of a Non-Violent Society helped Gandhi to clarify his thinking and carry it further. It helped him, for instance, in making up his mind about caste in general. While condemning the crazy tangle of sub-castes, and the taboos that went with it, he could see the merits of functionalism in the original four. A social division of labour was surely right, so long as it was a harmony, not a tyranny. Therefore he felt no need to challenge *karma* and *dharma,* as embodied in what he preferred to call the four divisions; but he restored some lustre to a horribly tarnished ideal.

A stress on the abuses of economic power gave unity to his own economics. Since large-scale capitalism meant oppression and class war, the non-violent axiom implied that there should be as little of it as possible. Where it had to exist, it should be de-fused, by a system bringing together management and labour; which was precisely what he had created at Ahmedabad. But the best course was to deliver men from wage-slavery altogether. For most Indians deliverance lay in cottage industry, manual work to supply their own needs, and so on. The spinning wheel was the key to unlock all such doors, the bond of brotherhood that united all Indians. When it returned to a village, everything else could return—including culture, Gandhi believed, 'the ancient rustic art and the rustic song'. Shaking off the bondage of drink and opium was part of the same liberation. Some day perhaps the liquor shops would be converted into restaurants and music-rooms.

Gandhi perceived wider implications. He moved toward the view that the State is evil, being coercive in its essence, an organ of privilege. Why should Indians in power be free from the vices of other rulers? Better than any existing State would be a co-operative federation of village republics. Even within these he demurred at western democracy, because it would mean that majorities could impose their will on minorities, and he had seen in the Transvaal how bitter the result could be. In a non-violent democracy, the majority would work with the minority to arrive at formulae for resolving disputes. The result would be, not 'the greatest good of the greatest number', but the good of all or Sarvodaya—the word he had used as the title for his version of Ruskin.

The mark of the Non-Violent Society would be unity in diversity; not fusion, but mutual respect. This was his proclaimed hope for India as a nation, and this was in keeping. The bottom-upward revolution would be, in effect, Satyagraha going on all the time. Satisfied that he had a policy which gave scope for his convictions, he began expounding it in *Young India* and *Navajivan*, and training another legion of shock-troops to implement it.

For his village audiences he hit on a visual aid. Holding up his left hand with fingers outspread, he would check them off with his right forefinger. 'This is equality for Untouchables; this is spinning; this is keeping off drink and drugs; this is Hindu-Muslim friendship; this is equality for women. And the wrist is non-violence.'

4

As early as June 1924 the outline of his intention was becoming clear. It made the Swarajists anxious. He seemed to be wandering off into a world of his own, and perhaps luring the No-Changers after him. His behaviour encouraged middle-class critics who argued that Gandism and civilized politics could not be reconciled at all. Among these was Sir Sankaran Nair, one of the thwarted mediators of 1921. As soon as his victim was safely in a cell he had published a carefully prepared diatribe entitled *Gandhi and Anarchy*. This—the most savage of a number of savage outpourings by moderates—accused the Mahatma squarely of hypocrisy. Non-co-operation, taken at face value, was nonsense. It was a trick to enlist support so that he could subvert civilization. He was 'an impulsive fanatic indifferent to facts,' and the nihilistic *Hind Swaraj* was his only sincere utterance. Sir Sankaran overreached himself. But Gandhi had disturbed even admirers by writing a preface to another book, *The Gospel of Swadeshi,* in which an

ashramite named Kalelkar preached a benighted parochialism as
God's will. The Mahatma's excuse (that the Gujarati original had
been mistranslated) did not really absolve him. Meanwhile the
launching of a Communist journal in Bombay, and the jailing of
four Communists, marked the dawn of a Left opposition as well as
a Right one.

Plainly he could not go very far without reviving a host of misgivings. Nor could he save Congress from a split by merely saying
he was neutral. The strains were too intense. That June he suggested
a token measure of solidarity which the All-India Congress Committee, to Das's irritation, adopted. All members holding office
should henceforth pay their dues by contributing two thousand
yards of self-spun yarn monthly.

While they were fumbling to fulfil this requirement, he was
pitched into a communal war. A Hindu author in Lahore published
an offensive pamphlet about Muhammad. It was called *Rangila
Rasul,* The Fun-Loving Prophet, and he was eventually murdered
for it. As it circulated, riots broke out in Delhi and spread to other
cities, till at Kohat near the Afghan border thirty-six Hindus were
massacred, a hundred and forty-five injured, and over three
thousand driven from the town. Congress asked Gandhi and
Shaukat Ali to investigate. Gandhi, however, was too deeply
appalled to content himself with investigation. In September, having
deputed Andrews to edit *Young India,* he started a three-week
fast at the Delhi home of Shaukat's brother, in penance for the sins
of the nation. Consciences were stirred. A conference of Hindus and
Muslims, with Christian bishops attending, assembled in the capital.
The fast went on for the full three weeks and ended in a scene of
holy amity on 8 October. Vinoba recited from the Upanishads. An
imam recited from the Koran. The missionary Andrews—large,
bearded, blue-eyed, a striking contrast—sang 'When I survey the
wondrous cross', which was supplanting 'Lead, kindly light' as
Gandhi's favourite Christian hymn. Das, Motilal Nehru and the Ali
brothers sat on the floor, and watched the exhausted Mahatma as
he took orange juice.

The ensuing lull was not peace, nor was it destined to last long.
The outrageous pamphlet continued to sell, the absurd provocations
continued to occur. Most communal strife arose from pressures on
rootless, inflammable mobs of town-dwellers; urban pressures which
Gandhi never fathomed. But, for the time being, applause was

general. Friends advised him that he could hold Congress together by accepting its presidency. He agreed to do so. At the December meeting in Belgaum he was elected in a cordial atmosphere.

Certain bargains were struck. He spoke unflinchingly of his faith in Satyagraha, reserved the right to name his successor, and virtually forced Congress to resolve that all its members, not only the office-holders, should pay their subscription in self-spun yarn. On the other hand he conceded the scrapping of non-co-operation, apart from the foreign cloth boycott. The politically minded could go their own way without restraint. That meant the Swarajists' way, into the councils. Annie Besant indeed reappeared with proposals of her own. She was now seventy-seven. The Mahatma had coaxed her back into Congress, and she had gamely taken spinning lessons from Devadas Gandhi. At Belgaum she produced a draft Home Rule Bill which she wanted to smuggle into the British Parliament as a private member's bill. This, however, inspired little confidence. It was the Swarajists (lately helped by police persecution) who emerged with Congress's support. They pursued their obstructive antics in the corridors of power.

Gandhi could not persuade himself that these political intellectuals were close to him, or that his interests were theirs. The emptiness of their professed Ahimsa could move him to tears. Even before going to Yeravda he had suspected that it was often an excuse for cowardice, the non-violence of the weak, not the brave. His presidential year was the only period of his Congress membership when he held office, yet it was also the only period when he showed any bitterness toward the class of men who still headed it. Sometimes he spoke of 'educated Indians' with a faint but uncharacteristic sneer. The estrangement had repercussions which never quite died away. He declined, in advance, an invitation to the Soviet Union, because he feared that Leninist ideologues would use him for violent purposes. When an American clergyman asked what caused him the most concern, he replied: 'The hardness of heart of the educated.' However, he checked his tongue. The most acid comment on the intelligentsia—that they leaped aboard his bandwagon when it was visibly rolling, and leaped off again when it slowed down—came from Jawaharlal Nehru. Jawaharlal preserved and published a significant letter from his own father. Motilal never turned against Gandhi, and he wore khadi and even hawked it in the street, to the merriment of the *Times of India.*

Yet in a phase of perplexity he wrote: 'I shall consult Gandhiji, but as you know, his hobbies do not interest me beyond a certain point.'

Most of the Mahatma's associates did prove themselves capable of gestures that cheered him. Rajaji spoke up for khadi more loudly than Motilal. Das, who was Mayor of Calcutta, made it the uniform of civic employees, and staged a public welcome for Gandhi while refraining from doing the same for British officials. But in June 1925 he died, to Gandhi's great sorrow. By that time it was clear that most Congress members were never going to pay their dues by spinning. On the disclosure that only eighteen thousand had qualified, the arrangement was made optional.

For several months during 1925 Gandhi was travelling, in indifferent health and without the Ali brothers to prop him. Khadi was his main theme. It had the immense advantage of yielding a measurable result. He toured Kathiawar, Central India, Bengal, Malabar, Travancore. When visiting the princely states, he pointed out that his constructive programme would apply there as well as in British territory. In fact he denied that his present measures were directly political at all. The boycott of foreign cloth meant precisely that: not a boycott of British cloth alone, nor yet a boycott of British goods generally. On 22 September, at Patna, he founded the All-India Spinners' Association as a branch of Congress. By the end of 1926 it had 42,952 spinners, 3,407 weavers, and 110 carders, working in 150 centres drawing people from 1,500 villages. The officers of the Association, besides himself, included Maganlal Gandhi, Rajendra Prasad, and Jawaharlal Nehru, the last as one of the secretaries.

As in 1921 he attracted huge crowds, and now, in cities, he had loudspeakers to help him. He raked in money like the most accomplished evangelist. When floral garlands were thrown over his neck, when addresses of welcome were presented in silver caskets, he auctioned them off or even sold them back to the donors. The difference from the year of Swaraj was one of emphasis. Khadi was so distinctively his own message that the chief effect of the tours was to restore and strengthen his personal cult. He was constantly slipping across the ill-drawn line which divides India's mortals from her gods. The *darshan*-seekers clambered all over him, yelling, pushing, covering his legs with scratches. A whole tribe, the Gonds, were already worshipping him. Once his train jolted to a sudden halt, and he learned with surprise that he had worked a miracle. A passenger had fallen off head-first without being hurt. Gandhi told him not to be silly: 'If I'd had anything to do with it, I wouldn't have let you fall.' At Dacca he had to calm down an effusively grateful old gentleman who swore that he had been cured of paralysis by repeating 'Gandhiji'. When a correspondent remarked that his name appeared as 'Mahatma Gandhi' in the list of officers of the Spinners' Association, he answered sadly that he was not responsible, and these were things which he simply had to put up with. His tour organizers tried to put him in first-class railway compartments, and when he stood firm, they would put him in a third-class compartment but keep all other passengers out.

The President of Congress was enjoying a triumph (if 'enjoying' is the right word). But the question persisted: how far was Congress with him? In the Hindu context, his steady growth as a religious folk-hero made his status as a nationalist more and more dubious. That issue needed to be faced.

When the ethical wisdom of a great culture has always despised the realm of history and human affairs—the realm where political events vulgarly happen—that culture will not readily find a place for ethics in politics. To Hindu thinkers political action is too base, too ephemeral for the truly wise, who should pursue their private *dharma* and their eternal release. The classic Hindu manuals of statecraft reduce government to a revolting 'science of punishment' in a context of jungle law. The dishonesty of public servants is taken for granted, not in the spirit of a western cynic who assumes a standard, but with the suggestion that no real standard exists. Legends tell of this or that virtuous rajah who made his subjects happy, but their welfare is a mystical consequence of his virtue, not an outcome of any specific qualities as a ruler.

Hence, when Gandhi had begun infusing his moral Absolute into politics, he had attempted something un-Hindu. His one major precedent was Asoka, another rare personality . . . and a convert to Buddhism at that. In 1921 he had succeeded for a time. But as soon as he confined himself to the role of a teacher, and let the Swarajists go their way, the two realms threatened to drift apart. The split which he felt as a personal alienation went deeper than personality. He could turn round and close it if anybody could, but the tendency of Hindu thinking was to pry it open. Politics were one thing, morals and religion another. To see that distinction working in practice, it was enough to glance at some of the nationalist newspapers.

As a public *guru* Gandhi had the problem of building a new continuity into Hindu minds. There was his own morally based social programme; there was also the amoral world of the politicians, concerned with Dyarchy and Dominion status, and also with 'progress', industry, and other matters outside his preferred range. Could he offer a logic or mystique which would fit both into a single pattern? In the pause that followed his khadi mission, it became plain that he could not. Without aid from some other mind he would never break through.

What Gandhi needed was a doctrine somewhat like Zionism. In Palestine Chaim Weizmann was already doing wonders with a policy which had been as loudly assailed as Gandhi's and by the same kind of people, educated liberals. Zionist institutions such as the kibbutz were not only remarkably Gandhian but inspired partly from the same source, Tolstoy. But the Zionists of Weizmann's school had all the Jewish awareness of history and the linkage of things. They related their programme to the Bible, the Dispersion, the Jewish plight in the modern world, and the Jewish sense of vocation—not by theological phrase-making but by informed reason and cultural insight. When they spoke of restoring Israel to its Land, they raised that almost infallible battle-cry, the reinstatement of long-lost glories; and they did so with a logical force which moved men of intelligence and ability, and even politicians.

To do likewise, Gandhi too would have had to draw on the past. He would have had to show how the ancient village-republics flourished, how the true India took shape in them, how they were ruined, how he proposed to restore them on a higher level, how a modern State could be raised on that foundation. If Zionism was too remote he could have found hints from an Asian in the teaching of Confucius, or for that matter Vivekananda. But he was too Hindu at heart—too much conditioned by a timeless universe where people use the same word for 'yesterday' and 'tomorrow', the same word for 'history' and 'myth'. He was not conscious of a coherent sequence in life, only of an Absolute and a disjointed series of moments. In thinking about the past he was sketchy and selective, in thinking about the future he avoided long-term planning. Occasionally he talked of a golden age of the Indian village, in the sixth century B.C., or in the mythical Krita Yuga. However, he talked vaguely and in a sermonising 'good old days' style. His Utopia appealed to villagers because it was spun (literally spun!) from familiar materials, and did not require them to leap into the unknown. But it hung in a void, not connected with anything else. Many who grasped it realized that it could be radical and exciting, a rebirth from fundamentals. An extremist who came to the Ashram to denounce Gandhi as a Tory went home saying he was the only true revolutionary. Not many, however, bothered to come. To them, to their brethren abroad, and even to sympathetic moderates of the Left like H. N. Brailsford, the Mahatma was atavistic. The Programme of the Communist International treated him as an enemy who had betrayed the mass struggle to an ideal of backwardness.

India in the middle 1920s had few Communists. Others, however, put awkward questions to Gandhi about his views on current issues, and how he saw his activities fitting in. He had a second brush with Tagore on the subject of spinning. The Poet argued that trying to liberate three hundred million people by making them all spinners was like urging them to drown the English by all spitting together; it was 'too simple for human beings'. Complaints came in against khadi as a material, in the conditions of modern living. It wouldn't stand up to the wear and tear of a factory. It was too heavy. It was hard to launder, and therefore unsuitable for children. Gandhi's answer was that with more skill there would be better khadi.

When he was in Delhi, Andrews introduced him to G. Ramachandran, who afterwards became a disciple and lived at the Ashram. Their conversations, published in *Young India*, brought up the recurrent topic of his attitude to machinery. Was he against it?

'How can I be,' said the Mahatma, 'when I know that even this body is a delicate piece of machinery?' What he opposed was slavery to machines, a machine-society. He approved of the sewing machine, 'one of the few useful things ever invented', and a product of Singer's love for his wife and his wish to lighten her labours.

'But,' said Ramachandran acutely, 'there would have to be factories for making sewing machines.'

Quite so, Gandhi replied, and they should be owned or controlled by the State. Was this the glimmering of a kind of Socialism? In the next breath he said that machinery, in the usual sense, was at best a necessary evil, and he would like to abolish it. Yet in practice he did move slowly toward acceptance of the machine age, though some of his disciples did not. The problem in his eyes was how to make machinery serve humanity. In 1926 he persuaded the Textile Labour Association to pass a resolution favouring nationalization of the industry. But he never declared for Socialism as the West pictured it. State action to change the economy struck him as a form of violence. He wanted to reach the same goal by consent. To the disgust of left-wingers, he consorted with industrialists like Ratan Tata as well as workers, preaching the interdependence of capital and labour, joint consultation, and sometimes paternalism. The rich were to regard their wealth as a trust.

These ideas, at least in the 1920s, were makeshifts. He had no reasoned policy, and shied away from industry because he saw it in terms of British industry, the ogre reflected in the horrible blank stare of the unemployed villager. To a financier he said: 'God forbid that India should ever take to industrialism after the manner of the West. The economic imperialism of a single tiny island kingdom is today keeping the world in chains. If an entire nation of three hundred million took to similar economic exploitation, it would strip the world bare like locusts.'

It was hard to pin him down. He could give an impression of sheer perversity. Somebody once told him that he always took the Muslim's side against the Hindu, the Untouchable's against both, and that he always sided with women. He laughed and did not resent it. To bridge the gap between himself and the politicians, he sometimes claimed that his programme was educational. It was training for mass action whenever a political crisis should require it—training of the people, and training for their leaders, who became fitter to lead through helping with the programme. Progress might not be apparent, but he believed, like Tolstoy, in sharp transitions. When India had enough real Satyagrahis they would 'transform the atmosphere in an immensely short time, even as one gentle shower transforms the plains of India into a beautiful green carpet in one single day'. But the argument, though sound as far as it went, was another makeshift. In Gandhi's hands it was weakened by his conviction that quality was more important than quantity anyhow. Victory would come through a comparatively small band of perfect warriors—even a single one, if he acted rightly at the right moment—rather than an army of second-raters. If so, the point of mass education was lost.

Continuity might, of course, have been created by way of religion. Gandhi's bent was in that direction. He seemed well qualified to invent a frankly religious nationalism. Surely he could evoke a unified vision of India and her destiny by unfolding the heritage of cult and myth and literature which he had studied in prison? Was he not the very person to carry on where the Hindu revivalists had left off—the mystic Ramakrishna, the intellectual Vivekananda, the activist Tilak?

Perhaps. But there was an obstacle.

XIII

A Saviour Saved

1

In November 1925 Gandhi resumed a project which he had twice
tackled and twice shelved without getting it under way. This was
the writing of his autobiography. It was a request performance,
which he undertook in some doubt. His strongest motive was that
it solved the problem of his expected weekly contribution to
Navajivan. He wrote in Gujarati, and the chapters appeared in the
paper as he produced them. Mahadev Desai, who was becoming
ever more indispensable as his chief secretary, translated them into
English for *Young India*. The first completed volume was not ready
till 1927, the second not till '29, with his prison book *Satyagraha in
South Africa* published between. However, the instalments were
widely read during the serialization.

Gandhi called this account of himself 'The Story of My Experiments with Truth'. Taken with its South African supplement, it
covers his life as far as the Nagpur Congress. The single major
omission among public events, for which there is no obvious reason,
is the sensational Benares speech of 1916. He draws heavily on his
memory and the result is sometimes confusing and inexact,
particularly on dates. But within its limits the book is impressive. The writer goes on and on with an utter, naïve honesty
which compels attention, and a wealth of illuminating detail. At
the end, a reader may well feel that he knows Gandhi thoroughly.

The trouble is that he does not. Gandhi as portrayed in his own
confessions is smaller, paler and less attractive than he was. Without prompting, we would never think of him as a Great Soul. His
quality can be seen fitfully shining through. But we have to look
for it, and only do so because of outside evidence that it must be
there. The cause is not humility, though his humility is genuine,
but a distortion of a subtler kind. The *Autobiography* is tinged by

252

a mood which Gandhi was prone to in the mid-1920s when alone with himself: a withdrawn, often anguished mood that narrowed him down.

In the introduction he says:

> My experiments in the political field are now known, not only in India, but to a certain extent to the 'civilized' world. For me, they have not much value. . . . But I should certainly like to narrate my experiments in the spiritual field which are known only to myself, and from which I have derived such power as I possess for working in the political field. . . .
>
> What I want to achieve—what I have been striving and pining to achieve these thirty years—is self-realization, to see God face to face, to attain Moksha [freedom from birth and death, salvation]. I live and move and have my being in pursuit of this goal. All that I do by way of speaking and writing, and all my ventures in the political field, are directed to this same end. But as I have all along believed that what is possible for one is possible for all, my experiments have not been conducted in the closet, but in the open.

It is dismaying to find him in the posture of a salvation-seeker, not unlike the Christians in his own story. Is all his devotion to the desolate and oppressed no more than a by-product of his spiritual exercises? Hardly anything in his earlier writings would lead us to think so.

. The passage must be read in the light of his comments on Chauri Chaura. He then said that he needed to undergo personal cleansing, so as to make himself a worthy leader. But the connection between that process and leadership became tenuous and esoteric. Purification meant working harder at *brahmacharya,* at self-control. The attempt drove him back into his private moral world. Somehow, he felt, his public world depended on this. Retrospectively he saw his long quest for a practical *rapport* with the Absolute as a more inward thing than it had actually been. He had 'really' been pursuing salvation all the time, whether he put it like that or not.

When he faced his moral self, as the telling of the story required, his spirits tended to wilt. All was far from well. He closed the introduction darkly.

> I must exclaim with Surdas:
> Where is there a wretch
> So wicked and loathsome as I?

> I have forsaken my Maker,
> So faithless have I been.

For it is an unbroken torture to me that I am still so far from
Him, who, as I fully know, governs every breath of my life, and
whose offspring I am. I know that it is the evil passions within
me that keep me so far from Him, and yet I cannot get away
from them.

On the last page, written three years later, his tone is much the
same if slightly more hopeful:

> Ever since my return to India I have had experiences of the
> dormant passions lying hidden within me. The knowledge of
> them has made me feel humiliated but not defeated . . . I must
> reduce myself to zero.

The passions that afflicted him were not solely carnal. He accused
himself of pride, for instance. But many passages in the *Autobiography*, and his choice of words in them, make it plain that sexual
unrest was mounting rather than declining. There is medical
testimony that he remained physically youthful to the last. Also, on
account of the nature of his programme, the presence and pressure
of women round him grew steadily more obtrusive. In May 1924
he told the readers of *Navajivan* about his 'bad dreams', and he
reverted to these a year later. His religion had always been morality.
But now, whenever public work was not forcing it into action, it
threatened to dwindle into an ingrowing, negative morality. During
these years he proved that he could be pious in an off-putting sense,
and show some of the cruder defects of the religious personality.

About the time when the *Autobiography* began to appear, some
Ashram schoolboys were caught in sodomy. Gandhi not only fasted
to atone, he publicized the affair in *Young India,* with a set of Rules
for Fasting. They are fairly sensible (conserve energy, don't think
about food, drink cold water a little at a time, sunbathe and use
enemas), yet as journalism it is all a shade peculiar. When a reader
bewailed the frequency of the kind of conduct that prompted the
fast, he came back with an almost unbalanced article on the 'sexual
microbe' in schools, the evil results of talking about intercourse as
natural, and—a sorry cliché—the effect of films.

He became capable, in flashes, of the holy vanity that shrugs off
blunders and shortcomings by dismissing the matters involved as
worldly trifles. The Indian author Frank Moraes was once showing

him round a college when they came to a room where students were playing ping-pong.

'Ah,' said the Mahatma, 'billiards.'

Moraes politely put him straight.

'Oh well, knocking balls back and forth, it's all the same.'*

The failing was harmless, at least when it was confined to everyday topics. But Gandhi's spirituality had a painful side. It could inject fresh poison into his own family. Even his all-passion-spent partnership with Kasturbai was marred by a lingering guilt which took pathetic forms. She was the only person he was afraid of. Once when Motilal Nehru and other notables dropped in at the Ashram, Bapu furtively prepared a meal for them himself, because Ba was resting and he dared not disturb her. When she found out she was annoyed anyway.

Such minor upsets were nothing to the catastrophe of their eldest son. All four had had a frustrating life. Bapu expected them to follow in his own path. He made them work for him and disapproved of their marrying. Admirers have praised him, quite justly, for enabling ordinary layfolk to practise ideals which only those in a religious calling could practise before; but to impose monastic rules on people who are not monks is scarcely the same thing, whoever they may be. In spite of resentments, three of the boys won through to a peaceful filial relationship. They aided the movement and endured suffering for it. They married—though Manilal had to wait till he was thirty-five. But Harilal was a harder case.

Father and son had quarrelled in 1911, Harilal complaining of paternal callousness toward himself and his brothers. Picking up a wife, he settled in India. Tension continued but with no fatal breach. Then his wife died in the influenza epidemic of 1918. Bapu objected to his taking another, and he rebelled. The revolt took the form of misbehaving in ways that would harm his father. Harilal got drunk in public, and kept company with dubious women. Also he exploited his parentage to raise cash for a shady business venture.

When a solicitor wrote on behalf of a swindled client, the Mahatma's handling of the scandal was curious, even allowing for the Indian lack of regard for privacy. Readers of *Young India* for 18 June 1925 were confronted with the lawyer's letter and his reply.

---

* At least two versions of this exchange are current. It would seem that Gandhi did not mix up the games, both of which he knew, but their names in the language he was using.

I do indeed happen to be the father of Harilal M. Gandhi. . . . His ideals and mine having been discovered over fifteen years ago to be different, he has been living separately from me. . . .

His commercial undertakings were totally independent of me. Could I have influenced him he would have been associated with me in several public activities and earning at the same time a decent livelihood. But he chose, as he had every right to do, a different and independent path. . . . He wants to become rich, and that too, easily. Possibly he has a grievance against me that when it was open to me to do so, I did not equip him and my other children for careers that would lead to wealth. . . .

There is much in Harilal's life that I dislike. He knows that. But I love him in spite of his faults. The bosom of a father will take him in as soon as he seeks entrance. . . .

Let the client's example be a warning against people being guided by big names in their transactions. Men may be good, not necessarily their children.

That last insufferable sentence is so grossly out of character as to make it clear that some warping influence is at work. Gandhi was fond enough of his eldest son to be hurt by him. On that point we possess what is lacking in almost all other cases, the first-hand written evidence of Kasturbai. But he was psychologically powerless to reduce the distance between them. His attitude was bedevilled by memories. 'I was a slave of my passions when Harilal was conceived,' he said. 'I led a carnal and luxurious life during his childhood.' Or perhaps Harilal was a punishment for sins in a previous existence?

2

The nature of Gandhi's preoccupations ruled him out as a successor to the great Hindu revivalists. He had a sound knowledge of his religion, and loved its literature. Yet when he discussed that literature he did so for only one purpose—to draw morals from it. Furthermore, they seldom added anything new to his stock-in-trade. He used the classics to support, or at most amplify, the moral views he already held and was determined to work with. If a text seemed to teach the wrong thing, so much the worse for the text. Then he would appeal to the 'spirit of Hinduism' as construed by himself. While the result might be wise and good, nothing but the extreme elasticity of Hindu belief saved him from being a heretic.

It is intriguing to see what he made of the epics, the *Ramayana* and *Mahabharata*. These are sacred books, and living sources of popular lore and myth, with a vast influence. Gandhi enjoyed listening to story-tellers reciting episodes from them, and he recommended them to westerners for the insight they gave into Hindu thought. But in his own hands their function was strictly and eccentrically didactic.

The *Ramayana*, which had enthralled him as a boy, remained in his eyes 'the greatest book in all devotional literature' . . . not a legend of love, adventure and battle, but a fable of perfect fidelity to vows. The *Mahabharata* made heavier demands on his skill as an interpreter. It is the nearest approach to the Bible in Hinduism. Its nucleus is a Sanskrit heroic poem about events during the formative era of the Aryan kingdoms. A dynastic dispute broadens into a war north of Delhi, with undertones of caste conflict and racial conflict. The virtuous party are the banished Pandava princes, who, in eighteen days' fighting on the plain of Kurukshetra, kill their usurping cousins and regain power. Their leader is the high-principled, rather weak Yudhishthir, who is sustained by the alliance between his brother Arjuna and the Lord Krishna. The basic epic was enlarged by generations of Brahmins, till its text was loaded with mythology and philosophy running to tens of thousands of verses, and including the *Gita* as an episode in the saga of Krishna and Arjuna. Hence, the *Mahabharata* as we now have it is a truly elephantine work. Still it contains fine poetry, dramatic stories, and as much of the history of ancient India as Hindus cared to remember.

Gandhi, however, brushed aside its claim to be in any sense a record of facts. He called it 'significant fiction', stating his view when writing on history in general: 'It is my pet theory that our Hindu ancestors solved the question for us by ignoring history as it is understood today and by building on slight events their philosophical structure. Such is the *Mahabharata*. I look to Gibbon and Motley as inferior editions of the *Mahabharata* . . . Truth transcends history.' Moralizing this poetic leviathan was none too easy for him. The *Mahabharata* upholds practices like suttee which he could not defend. Its heroes assert the idea of a just war, and the triumph of the righteous by force of arms. Moreover (as anyone will discover who reads the poem itself instead of digests), the righteous themselves are far from righteous. The Pandavas win by a succession of dirty tricks. Krishna—God Incarnate—turns the tide of war by a lie so vile that even the devout Yudhishthir is sickened. Yet he co-operates.

An apostle of Truth and Non-Violence could scarcely condone all this. Gandhi cut the knot by an inspired stroke. The *Mahabharata,* he declared, is 'a book written to establish the futility of war and violence'. Readers who plough impartially through the slaughter to the last lines of Book XI may well feel tempted to agree. But his judgement ranged him against the orthodox.

It was worse when he restudied the *Gita.* He had taken this up again in prison. A series of articles and lectures culminated in a Gujarati version with notes, which he published in 1929. Like Tilak, whose commentary he drew upon, he knew that anybody aspiring to expound Hinduism must prove that his teaching is in accord with the *Gita.* For himself the difficulty was that the *Gita* seemed to refute his cardinal tenet. Arjuna wants to abstain from violence, Krishna persuades him to be violent. The best Gandhi could manage here was to fall back on allegory. The battlefield is the human heart where good and evil contend. Selfless action must be undertaken to achieve moral victory. This implies the uprooting of passion, the Ahimsa of the mind. Therefore—etc. Again Gandhi found himself alone, apart from personal disciples. All the orthodox scholars dissented. They complained that he was biased by his fondness for Christianity.

He read European poets—Goethe, Tennyson, Wilde—in the same spirit as Asian poets. His response to poetry, and to art and beauty of most kinds, was still keen within the limits his outlook permitted. But it had grown more Tolstoyan, more tightly bound up with ethical implications and inwardness. He described Jesus as a supreme literary artist because he saw and expressed Truth. The beauty of a face in his estimation depended on character, not features; thus the homely Socrates would have been beautiful. The Taj Mahal made him think of all the forced labour that had gone into its building. His aesthetic sense only broke free in the presence of impersonal splendours. He gazed up at the stars, and contrasted the inadequacies of human art with the 'eternal symbols of beauty in Nature'.

Gandhi's convictions defined the outlines of a religion which can be summed up in a few sentences. God is Truth, or Truth is God. (He began by saying the former, like St Thomas Aquinas, but gradually shifted to the latter as less question-begging.) The way to God is Non-Violence. This is the secret of renunciation, and thence of right action, right speech, and right thought. Man goes on being reborn from time to time till he sheds self in the narrow meaning. Then he soars into the liberty of the Absolute, with the body's hindrances and the world's deceptions left behind. All the great religions are the same in their moral essence, and to that extent valid. Their creeds, myths and rituals are incidentals, always in some degree erroneous, and misleading if taken too seriously. There is no sufficient reason for anybody to leave one religion and join another. The highest common factor is what all should cling to.

In spite of his individuality Gandhi insisted he was a loyal Hindu, and, indeed, his prayers and hymns and vocabulary bore out the claim. Yet he also said he belonged to all religions. If all religions are equal, the remark makes sense. But he wavered on that point, especially when comparing Hinduism with Christianity. He addressed missionary gatherings, but could never quite reconcile himself to missionaries. More striking is his indifference to the larger life of Hinduism itself, the colourful company of the gods, the metaphysics of Vedanta. He could speak the language of priests and mystics without entering deeply into the world of either. Though he was open-minded about the supernatural, it had no place in his experience. He never saw visions. The inner voice which he trusted for guidance was a silent one.

Some would-be classifiers supposed him to be a Jain at heart. Bernard Shaw came to the same conclusion about himself. Gandhi was impressed by Jain teaching on the many-sidedness of reality— chiefly because he knew by this time that his own certainties were not everybody's. Jainism, however, has no God, no single Absolute, and on that subject he was firm. Satyagraha assumed such an Absolute. On this ground he ruled that a Jain could not be a complete Satyagrahi at all. More recently Professor Zaehner has tried to fit Gandhi into the Hindu scheme as the restorer of a humanist motif, traceable in the *Mahabharata* but almost forgotten. The key figure in this interpretation is Arjuna's elder brother Yudhishthir, who protests at the decrees of the gods and rises morally above them. Gandhi was, so to speak, Yudhishthir returned, a Hindu whose best was better than Hinduism.

At any rate he was no Ramakrishna. The contrast could scarcely have been sharper. The results of his study of the arch-seer were personal and surprising.

When an official biography was published, Gandhi was invited to write a preface. He did; but the apparitions and mystical adventures were alien to him, and all he could produce was a strangled paragraph.

> The story of Ramakrishna Paramahansa's life is a story of religion in practice. His life enables us to see God face to face. No one can read the story of his life without being convinced that God alone is real and that all else is an illusion. Ramakrishna was a living embodiment of godliness. His sayings are not those of a mere learned man but they are pages from the Book of Life. . . .

No author who cared much what he was saying could have let this go out over his name, with its flat phrases and jarring repetitions. Once when training a young journalist, Gandhi quoted just such a passage as an example of inattention. The book affected his thinking in a single respect only—by supplying hints toward a solution of the sexual problem.

Before his own *Autobiography* began coming out, he was already writing articles on this topic. As the serialization advanced it brought letters from readers wanting to argue or compare notes. He went on with the articles, reading Havelock Ellis and other experts to equip himself. Some were issued in book form as *Self-restraint versus Self-indulgence*. On top of his personal disquiet was a public dilemma: a conviction that birth control was necessary, coupled with a conviction that it must be achieved, somehow, through sublimation and not contraception.

Here as in most matters, Ramakrishna flew to extremes. The normal attitude of the Hindu holy man to a woman is to keep her at a distance, and think of her as a sister or mother. Gandhi approved without being fully able to imitate. But Ramakrishna's psychic gymnastics included working his way, with a lady tutor, through the sixty-four Tantra handbooks. These teach the student how to dwell among objects of desire instead of fleeing from them. He is to treat them as divine manifestations instead of sensual stimuli. Though bound by a vow of continence like Gandhi, Ramakrishna had a wife. Apparently he was not impotent. Yet they lived and slept together for over a year without intercourse—not mortifying lust (like certain early Christians noted by Gibbon) but floating above it, exalted by the divine in each other.

At least twice during his visions, Ramakrishna transcended male passions by becoming female. Behind this inversion was a theory explained by his biographer: 'If a man can so inoculate himself with the idea that he is not a man but a woman as to be to all intents and purposes a woman, that idea in turn may be made to give way to a higher one—that there is neither man nor woman.' To judge from a saying of Jesus recorded outside the Gospels, he too was familiar with this idea. Ramakrishna succeeded in self-identification with one of Krishna's girl playmates, and then with Radha, the god's mistress. In both cases he dressed for the part and it came with ease. Later he was able to make women feel that in some sense, quite unlike homosexuality, he was akin to them.

Gandhi was not the man to imitate such actions in detail. Yet he was more receptive in the mid-1920s than he would once have been. After ten years of India, his former trust in such antaphrodisiacs as a fruit diet had given place to the belief that *brahmacharya* was 'impossible to attain by mere human effort'. For a while his advice was mixed. In a letter to G. D. Birla, he described the 1920s as a sex-ridden age (what would he have said of the 1960s?), and recommended the Ramanama prayer as an aid to control. In an article on marriage he wrote rather desperately of cold baths and separate rooms.

But memories of Ramakrishna were now lodged in his mind, and even while all the fret was going on, a healing likeness was creeping into his life. True to his experimental temper, he sometimes ventured to join the still-handsome Kasturbai in the same bedroom. They would lie side by side in calm companionship. The subjective acrobatics of sex-change were not for him; yet a great deal of his social programme—the Ahimsa, spinning and so forth—had a feminine and maternal air. One woman at least, Mrs. Polak, did feel the affinity with him that others felt with Ramakrishna, and he was aware of such traits in himself as solicitude and intuitive discernment, even remarking that he was 'half a woman'. In his attempts to reduce self to zero he tended to equate 'self' with his aggressive, masculine qualities. Merely to damp them down would have meant becoming ineffectual. But with Ramakrishna in the background, the social programme could supply a spiritual haven. It was a realm where the dangerous male could merge into the safer female without loss of power. More than ever, the spinning wheel adjusted and soothed.*

Gandhi had not in fact reached the last twist of this particular knife. Peace, however, was becoming more conceivable. It was not in his nature to be lastingly morbid or turned inward. He bounced back. As Jawaharlal Nehru remarked, however forbidding he sounded in his writings, he was nearly always delightful face to face. When he wrote he was alone, able to pause and brood, but the presence of people set him in motion again. Human contact, debate, action, drew him out and rescued him. Even the slow lightening of the sexual worry was partly due to his plunging into public discussion about it and meeting other minds, living and dead.

The same contrast appeared in his religion. Summed up on paper, it looks jejune. As taught and practised by himself in society, it was radiant. From 1924 onward he was winning more and more disciples for religious rather than political reasons. Such was the millionaire Birla, now in his thirties. Birla was sceptical about non-violence, which he said might be mere inertia, and about Gandhian economics, which were out of tune with his own faith in industry. But the generosity of the Mahatma's version of Hinduism held his allegiance. Birla actually did regard his wealth as a trust, endowing schools, hospitals and temples, and providing funds to aid the emancipation of women and the education of Untouchables. He gave Gandhi money, and sought his advice on the spending of other sums. His many letters began 'Dear Bapu'.

Gandhi's salvation came through interaction with people. To say that he had developed a gift for love is, of course, to leave a query. It might have been the do-gooder's love for humanity, which can go with coldness and cruelty toward actual specimens. But it was not. His love for a variety of individuals—Vinoba, Das, Andrews, Mahadev Desai, Sarojini Naidu and many more—illuminated their lives and expanded his. Because of that gift, though at an age when most men are fixed in their habits, he was ready for the new comradeships which would have to take shape, if he was ever to lead India forward again.

* In view of sensitivity on the topic, it may be as well to state here that he explicitly recommended the study of Tantra. See Pyarelal, *Mahatma Gandhi—the Last Phase*, Vol. 1, page 589.

Those who knew Ramakrishna declare that after he finished his Tantric course he glowed, physically, literally. The same has been asserted of Gandhi by witnesses not at all prone to superstition.

3

There was now a Mahatma cult in the West also. It had originated during the Swaraj year with the Reverend John Haynes Holmes, an American minister, who hailed Gandhi in a sermon as the world's greatest man, and compared him to Christ. Dr Holmes's superlative was put on the title-page of the 1922 book of tributes, and his sermon was the first non-Indian item. Some were earlier— one by Gilbert Murray considerably so—but Holmes marked the transition from praise to more than praise. Andrews was among the writers, and might have been expected to go further in making the Mahatma known. However, despite their closeness and his own competence as a teacher, he found difficulty in condensing his master's thoughts. His main part in the revelation came later.

During Gandhi's imprisonment a vague curiosity spread without being satisfied. When French troops occupied the Ruhr, the German policy of passive resistance owed a debt to his example. Soon after his release he received a greeting from Marcus Garvey, the American Negro leader, in the name of 'the Negroes of the world'. 1924 was the year of the first British Labour Government. Bernard Shaw proposed that Gandhi's mentor Henry Salt should be given a peerage and made Secretary of State for India. MacDonald, hard pressed for talent, toyed with the notion but preferred another member of the same circle, Sydney Olivier. Salt himself contemplated writing a book on the erstwhile law student. He was deterred both by Shaw (on the ground that Gandhi was considered a saint, and *Saint Joan* had exhausted that theme) and by Olivier (on the ground that Gandhi was considered a crank, and the public would not be interested). He did note a suggestion of Olivier's that the Mahatma should be invited to England. This was to bear fruit. But the return of a Conservative Government headed by Baldwin ruled it out for the time being.

The major prophet was a genius in his own right, Romain Rolland, the French pacifist, novelist and musician. Rolland wanted to correct an impression in Europe that the Indian strategy was mere inert obstruction. He dreamed of an alliance between Satya-graha and Communism. His study *Mahatma Gandhi* appeared in 1924. Its sub-title, 'The Man who became One with the Universal Being', is a warning of its bias. It presents its hero as an eastern saint. The account of his youth is both idealized and Indianized; there is no hint that his London phase affected him. The political part is lucid but critical. Rolland thinks Gandhi has too rosy a view of human nature, and might do better to keep more aloof from politics, being too much of a saint, too pure. While averring that 'the Apostle of India is the Apostle of the world', he says the Apostle's message is peace through self-sacrifice. In fact a good deal of the revolutionary dream has oozed away in the telling.

But pacifism was in vogue, and Rolland opened a gate. Scattered westerners had been writing to Gandhi for years. Now a larger number wanted to join him. Tagore too became involved in a cloudy oriental enthusiasm. Before 1924 was out, Andrews noted a rush of letters asking about accommodation at Sabarmati and Shantiniketan. It reminded him of the ferment in the days of the Romantic poets. The prophecy spoken of by Shelley in the 'Ode to the West Wind' was, he exclaimed, trumpeting out of India.

His excitement was premature. Most of the inquiries were of little weight and led nowhere. One, however, stood by itself. It came from a Miss Madeleine Slade, aged thirty-two. The Slades were a well-off English family, whose residences had included Field Place, the Sussex home of Shelley. Her father was an admiral. At eighteen she had spent some months in Bombay, but among English society only. Solitary, privately educated, she was a music-lover and an excellent horsewoman, seeking a purpose and finding none.

Miss Slade's approach to Gandhi was roundabout. In her early thirties her single profound passion was Beethoven—coincidentally or not, one of the first Europeans to be influenced by Hindu thought. Wishing to discuss his work with Rolland, who was an authority, she took a course in French and went over to visit him. When the conversation drifted from music, Rolland happened to mention Gandhi as 'another Christ'. She read his book and saw her vocation, a path traced out for her in India when England was trackless.

But she did not rush to her Mahatma in a spiritual flurry. She sent him £20 and told him she would spend a year learning to spin, and to subsist on a vegetable diet. After that, would he accept her as a helper? He replied with guarded encouragement. By this time he undoubtedly knew, and shied away from, the sort of women who swoon at the feet of saints and sages. At the end of her year, he wrote, if she was prepared for hard work and the climate, he would welcome her.

She landed at Bombay on 6 November 1925. Devadas Gandhi met her. Next morning she reached Ahmedabad, where Mahadev Desai and Vallabhbhai Patel collected her from the train. Mahadev raised his eyebrows at the dismounting apparition—a graceful thoroughbred in khadi, which she had ordered from Delhi and given to her dressmaker to run up into a garment. They drove her to the Ashram and showed her into the building where Gandhi was. He rose from a mattress on the floor. In her own words: 'I was conscious of nothing but a sense of light. I fell on my knees. Hands gently raised me up, and a voice said, "You shall be my daughter".' This was his usual greeting to young women joining the community, but nobody had told her so. She looked him in the face. He seemed a little amused.

He was Bapu to her at once, and rechristened her Mira after a legendary woman mystic. When more fully accepted at the Ashram she became Mirabehn, Sister Mira. Her first job was to sweep out the lavatories. Mahadev gave her a spinning lesson with an Ashram wheel, and she started studying Hindustani. Gandhi did not disappoint her. She thought him an angel of graciousness, humility, and sunshiny humour. But she also had an observant eye for the people around him. His two secretaries, for instance. Mahadev—tall and good-looking, with a moustache and thinning hair—impressed her with his unfailing intelligence. The assistant Pyarelal was younger, thickset, and not so steady, being sometimes furiously active and sometimes absent-minded. However, it was clear to her that in choosing them Gandhi had applied a businessman's standards, and that he got a prodigious amount of work out of both by inspiring a loyalty which few businessmen could hope for.

About the other ashramites Mira was less happy. She quickly shed whatever illusions she had brought with her, and saw Sabarmati as it was, full of discord and mixed motives. In December Gandhi took her on his annual trip to Wardha before the meeting of Congress. As they travelled, the bedlam of Mahatma-worshippers at each station distressed her again. She glanced at his face during a demonstration, and saw a sternness that he never showed at the

Ashram. Plainly he recoiled from mindless emotionalism, especially when he was its object himself. Vinoba's Wardha community turned out to be far more sober and selective than Sabarmati, and it appealed to her more. After the glimpse on the railway she felt emboldened to tell Gandhi that she wished his own Ashram could be more like that. He replied that it was his policy to be unselective. But her earnestness was not lost on him. Gradually, she became a working partner.

To describe this partnership as the nearest thing to a love affair in his life would be libellously misleading. John Haynes Holmes, extending the biblical parallel, compared it to the relationship between Christ and his female disciples. Yet Gandhi avoided this. He never allowed Mira to treat him as a *guru*. In correspondence with her, when he touched on spiritual matters, he did so in a tone of discussion rather than instruction. A strange scene occurred when she wanted to wear a sari and he objected. The reason probably was that he mistrusted the garment as a token of romantic submission, in the manner of the swooners. Actually Indian dress can be an asset to a western woman anxious to make contact with Indians, and she carried her point. But Gandhi insisted that her sari should be of white khadi. Later on she changed to a compromise costume which saved her air of independence.

Though never abject, Mira clung to him—a scrawny, gap-toothed, nearly bald little man in his fifties—with a personal devotion that no other woman displayed. Whenever he went away she touched his feet in parting, and suffered torments during his absence, often becoming ill. She pursued him on his journeys with letters and flowers, and asked for bulletins on his weight. For years he fought back nobly, striving to divert the ardour from himself to his work, and not fully admitting her to his closest circle at the Ashram. But the fact remains that although he was ruthless enough to snub her, he never did. His response to Mira began early: she was among the first to notice, and evoke, his 'glow'. In all he wrote her 650 letters. Those which have been published give glimpses of a long story of alternate harmony and disturbance. They refer to uncharacteristic outbursts on his part, and to her 'haunting him in his sleep'.

Probably, on balance, the presence of Mira helped him along the road which Ramakrishna's exploits had pointed to. Her fervour forced the issue. Between upsets he achieved (because he had to, in self-defence) a state known to professionally-linked men and women, where something of sex persists, but is transformed by the Cause which they are serving together. She gave him honeymoons of activity.

Their immediate business after visiting Wardha was the Congress meeting at Cawnpore. As they drove through the streets in a horse-drawn tonga, another wild demonstration boiled up round them and the tonga was wrecked. Mindful of the Mahatma's special interests, the organizers invited him to inspect the latrines. He told Mira that he had lost his sense of smell—a slight tactical exaggeration—and made her come and help.

At the Congress session he handed over the presidency to Sarojini Naidu, the first Indian woman to hold that office. She was his own choice and she justified it, spending a large part of her term collecting for khadi. 'It takes a great deal of money,' she remarked, 'to keep Bapu living in poverty.' Bapu himself announced to Congress that he would withdraw from politics altogether for a year. Through 1926 he would stay in the Ashram, or at any rate go no farther than Ahmedabad. The silent year thus embarked upon included fifty-two Mondays which were literally silent. He then confined his communications to short written notes. This was a practice he had begun some years earlier to give himself a breathing-space. By 1926 he had discovered that silence had mystic virtues; he would recall the Trappists in South Africa, and say that on Mondays he could listen to the still small voice. But the basic motive was convenience. He was not unknown to alter the day to avert conversation with an unwanted caller.

During the year of withdrawal Gandhi was busy with journalism, Havelock Ellis and the rest, and sorting himself out. He campaigned against child marriage in articles that were reprinted, like most of what he wrote, throughout India. Chapter by chapter the *Autobiography* pounded on, through his student days and his South African adventures. Mahadev's English version was checked by Mira. She too remained within the Ashram, except for trips across the river into Ahmedabad. There she made friends with Anasuya-behn, Ambalal Sarabhai's labour-leading sister, who advised her on clothes. Her concern about the precise ethics of the sari, the half-sari and the full skirt was a counterpart to Bapu's sartorial strategy. In her own way, she was growing more like him than his male followers. She vowed *brahmacharya*. They jointly ran a new diet experiment, to see if the ashramites could survive on raw food alone. If this had worked, the saving would have been substantial. Bapu, however, had a fresh onset of dysentery, and Mira (as she informed the world in due course) became totally constipated. They restored the old menu. On another day Andrews came, and she put him through a Gandhian trial he had hitherto dodged—a spinning lesson. Unfortunately he was too fat to sit cross-legged on the floor, and his fingers lacked the touch. He looked at her in gentle bewilderment over the baffling *charkha,* and Bapu laughed heartily.

Bapu too had his interests across the river. He made a speech calling for more music in Ahmedabad. Culture, however, was unexpectedly overshadowed by euthanasia. The city was infested with stray dogs, diseased, scratching, and wretched. Ambalal Sarabhai rounded up sixty on his property and had them shot. Then a qualm of conscience attacked him, and he consulted Gandhi. The oracle was reassuring: 'What else could be done?' His words were reported and the Ahmedabad Humanitarian Society pounced on him. Was this Ahimsa? Was this Hinduism? He defended himself patiently. The dogs were a menace, causing hydrophobia cases by thousands. If nobody would look after them, it was the truest Ahimsa to put them out of their misery. Indians might learn dog care from the West. For three months he was deluged with angry letters, the ultra-non-violent Jains being especially abusive.

On a later occasion a calf fell sick at the Ashram. After a harrowing attempt to nurse it, Gandhi declared for mercy-killing. But among Hindus a calf was more explosive than dogs. Kasturbai led the opposition. He told her to tend the calf herself, and when she could neither feed it nor soothe its pain, she gave way. Her husband sent for Ambalal, who drove up with a doctor and an injection. When the animal was dead Gandhi wrote an article with the title 'The Fiery Ordeal', from a poem: 'The pathway of love is the ordeal of fire'. Again a swarm of critics assailed him. 'Some of them,' he commented, 'seem to have made the violence of their invective against me a measure of their solicitude for Ahimsa.' He was unrepentant. The incident had set people thinking. For himself, he was prepared to approve euthanasia even with human beings, if it was simply a question of easing the inevitable.

In the silent year the course of public events was mixed. Khadi was making fair progress, and a new national youth movement was taking shape. But the trend in Hindu-Muslim relations was ugly.

The Muslim League, swayed by Jinnah, was moving toward a revival of communal politics. Gandhi suspected the Government of favouring Muslims for divide-and-rule purposes. More riots— really a recrudescence of those of '24—broke out in Calcutta and other cities. Toward the close of the year Swami Shraddhanand, the hero of the Delhi *hartal,* was murdered while ill in bed by a Muslim who gained admittance as a religious inquirer.

To Gandhi this crime was not only a tragedy but a reproach; he had failed to solve the problem. In 1926 and the eighteen months after, most of his positive comfort came from abroad. More English enthusiasts made the pilgrimage. One was Muriel Lester, who stayed at the Ashram in October. She was a Christian pacifist and temperance advocate, a founder-member of the Kingsley Hall settlement in the East End of London. Sarojini Naidu had spoken there on the Punjab atrocities. Miss Lester noticed that the Mahatma had pictures of New Testament scenes on his wall. As she sat on the sand beside the river for prayers, he asked her to sing 'When I survey the wondrous cross'. On her return she published a pamphlet exposing the drug and liquor traffic in India, the Government's reliance on these for revenue, and its use of the money for a bloated arms budget.

Gandhi also saw a good deal of Horace Alexander, a prominent Quaker, and something of Fenner Brockway (now Lord Brockway). The latter went to Madras in 1927 to attend Congress as a fraternal delegate of the Independent Labour Party. A car accident disabled him. Every day during the session Gandhi looked in on him in hospital. For much of the time he was restless and in pain, but when the visitor pressed his hand, he settled down and the pain lessened. He registered the fact without explaining it, or feeling any particular need to.

Americans also were discovering the Mahatma. A missionary bishop, Fred Fisher, sailed to India to convert and went home converted, expounding his own version of the Gospel of Sabarmati. In this phase, when Gandhi was not active as a nationalist, many westerners could follow Rolland and look to him as a prophet with a world mission. Recoiling from war, capitalism and the jazz age, they saw what they desired to see, a pacifist and apostle of simple virtue. Politics receded. There was, indeed, a widespread impression that he was a spent force as a politician. Congressmen still came to him, but nothing resulted. When Lord Irwin—the future

Lord Halifax—succeeded Reading as Viceroy, there was not, as in 1921, an early audience. Gandhi for his part took no notice of the change.

The prophetic role was tempting, especially when it brought invitations to preach Truth and Non-Violence in the United States. But he temporized, saying he could not accept till he had a concrete success to show. Failing to coax him out of India, his foreign devotees went on seeking him there. Early in 1928 the Federation of International Fellowship met at the Ashram. On that and other occasions he did talk of an internationalism beyond nationalism, and affirm it as a goal. However, nationalism always came first. Each nation, he said, would have to find itself and be free to act for itself, before the nations could genuinely combine. India could lead. India's moral revolution could bring the brotherhood of Man. But this was how Gandhi put it, in an article published on 12 January 1928:

> My ambition is much higher than independence. Through the deliverance of India I seek to deliver the so-called weaker races of the earth from the crushing heels of western exploitation in which England is the greatest partner. If India converts, as it can convert, Englishmen, it can become the predominant partner in a world commonwealth of which England can have the privilege of becoming a partner if she chooses.

It was not exactly the language of vague fraternity. It was the first rumble of the Afro-Asian avalanche.

4

During this growth of his cult abroad, Gandhi's other activities remained in a minor key. At the 1926 session of Congress he opposed an 'independence' resolution as a pointless gesture of ill-will. Then he embarked on a fresh series of tours, talking about his social programme. He laid more stress at his meetings on the Un-touchability question, sitting among the outcastes himself where-ever they were segregated, and urging caste Hindus to join him. At a leper colony he insisted on shaking hands with the inmates. Local successes brightened the outlook. In one place the laundrymen vowed not to wash anything but khadi, in another an entire tribe swore off alcohol.

Three or four ashramites usually accompanied him. Mahadev was always among them, and sometimes Mira. She was making progress with Hindi and was an expert carder and spinner. Rajendra Prasad had sent her out with a khadi team in Bihar, where she looked in the face of poverty, and understood Gandhi as she had never learnt to do from Rolland. When she travelled with him, he deputed her to see to his own food and accommodation. The party made their longer journeys by train and then toured the villages by car, grinding slowly through crowds. Gandhi wore his assistants out with his passion for strict accountancy. All sorts of people gave money, including peasants who produced hoarded coppers out of knots in their clothes, and every gift had to be recorded. The job kept them up late between exhausting days. Gandhi had the ability to take his cat-naps while riding in the car. But the strain was too much even for him. He was addressing thirty meetings a week. At Kolhapur he endured seven in one day—Untouchables, women, children, non-Brahmins, Christians, khadi workers, students—and finally collapsed. Doctors thought he had had a slight stroke. After struggling on for another day or two without making any speeches, he agreed to rest.

The main trouble was his blood pressure. This now tended to rise under stress, especially when he was unsure of himself and groping for a decision. In 1927 he felt that he should be giving a lead toward Swaraj, but could not see how. He spent that April recuperating in Mysore. The doctors told him not to work, and advised recreation. He chuckled. Did they mean bridge perhaps, or backgammon? Games could not relax him, because, under his circumstances, they seemed a waste of time. The best recreation he could think of was to potter about with a tool kit, mending broken spinning wheels. He was in the closest approximation of his career to the mood of Hamlet. His membership of Congress became almost nominal. This year it carried the empty resolution on independence, at a debate he did not attend.

Recovery came by degrees. The patient was very thin and light, his weight fluctuating around a hundred pounds. However, he was active. For the first time since South Africa he rode a bicycle. In November 1927 he went to Ceylon, raising funds for khadi and talking to Buddhists. Two months later he blessed the marriage of his thirty-year-old son Ramdas, which was solemnized at the Ashram with full Hindu rites. About the same time there was some family heart-searching over the marriage of Devadas, a love match with Rajaji's daughter, whose caste was different. Gandhi softened the other parents' anxieties, but they agreed in insisting on a long probationary engagement.

Recovery as a leader came also. It was a gift from outside. Just when he might have yielded to his own demotion into a mere sage —a patron saint of conscientious objectors and prohibitionists— Britain herself conjured up a fresh army of rebels, and put it at his disposal.

Since becoming Viceroy, Lord Irwin had given few signs of his inclinations. He was a tall Tory patrician in his middle forties, the King's personal choice. Devoutly Anglo-Catholic, he was regarded by some as a very suitable ruler for a religious country. But he had once written that a man's duty as a citizen might override the commandments of his Church; and his political record was ambiguous. In Parliament he had argued that the British must 'fulfil the functions of a superior race' in order to govern 'black' nations . . . the 'blacks' in question being Egyptians. He was a friend and collaborator of George Lloyd, the Governor of Bombay who believed Satyagraha to be a dark conspiracy. On the other hand he had been the first Conservative MP to denounce the Black and Tans, and he was the first Viceroy to inspect the slums of Calcutta for himself.

In October 1927, at Mangalore, Gandhi received a message from this no-longer-new proconsul. He was to report in Delhi on 5 November. The meeting was attended by several other Indians, among them Vithalbhai Patel, who was now President of the Central Legislative Assembly, and gave Gandhi half his monthly salary. Irwin handed out a memo announcing that a parliamentary commission headed by Sir John Simon was coming to report on Dyarchy and the readiness of India for further constitutional progress. Gandhi read it, and looked up.

'Is this our only business?' he asked.

'Yes,' said Irwin.

The peremptoriness of the notice, and Gandhi's subsequent comment that a postcard would have done as well, inspired a legend that Irwin brought him twelve hundred miles simply to give him a piece of paper. Actually they had an informal chat afterwards. This went pleasantly enough. But Irwin took it for granted that the British Parliament would determine India's course, as a matter of right and duty. When it dawned on him that Gandhi did not, communication broke down. He stared at the Mahatma in bewilderment as if he had dropped from another planet.

Dyarchy in fact was not working well, from either side's point of view. Congress abstention had hobbled it at the outset. Most of the Indian ministers were puppets of the officials. The Swaraj Party, uncertain whether to sponsor positive measures or merely disrupt, had entangled itself in dubious bargains and lost ground at elections. Das was dead, Motilal Nehru disillusioned. In the words of Vallabhbhai Patel, a faithful No-Changer, those who set out to smash the Government had themselves been smashed. Business elements were cynical about a patriotic party which had failed to prevent a pro-British revaluation of the rupee, a pro-British Steel Protection Bill.

Alongside Congress new blocs were taking shape, such as the Mahasabha, a militant Hindu body formed as a retort to the Muslim League. Behind it were the forces of Tilakite tradition and the increasingly bigoted Arya Samaj, which prompted a remark of Gandhi's to Mira: 'You have to love humanity in spite of itself.' However sinister some of these trends might be, they were symptoms of a returning restlessness which could not be ignored.

The Simon Commission was set up by Lord Birkenhead, Baldwin's Secretary of State for India. He had opposed the Montagu-Chelmsford reforms, and maintained that India would not be fit for self-rule in any credible future. One of his motives for sending the Commission was that if he did not, a second Labour Government might soon take office, and send a commission which would come back with the wrong answer. He asked Irwin whether he thought it should co-opt Indian members. Birkenhead himself was of two minds: he fancied it might be a sound idea to have Indians on the Commission, so that their dissensions would furnish an argument for inaction. Irwin, however, had gathered round him a little circle of Indian advisers who counselled otherwise. They were all Liberals. He relied especially on Sir Tej Bahadur Sapru and M. R. Jayakar. These experts told him that it would be best if the Commission were composed solely of British MPs and peers. It would then be above Indian jealousies, and stand the best chance of enlisting Indian co-operation.

Simon, therefore, led a purely parliamentary group. The Labour Party joined in, sending Clement Attlee and another. But Irwin's experts had grossly misunderstood their own countrymen. Reaction was furious. The English politicians were going to come over, look at the natives, and go home to arrange their destiny for them. By a painful coincidence an insulting best-seller had just been published entitled *Mother India,* by Katherine Mayo. Gandhi, who had helped the author with her researches, led a chorus of indignant reviewers; he called the book a drain inspector's report. Delhi denied, in vain, that *Mother India* was officially inspired.

All the major political bodies—Congress, Muslim League, Mahasabha, even the Liberals—united to boycott Simon. He landed in Bombay on 3 February 1928 to be greeted with black flags, a *hartal,* and processions chanting 'Simon go back'. Indians who knew no other English learned that slogan. The same thing happened in every city. To Sir John and his companions, even the jackals seemed to be howling the three words. They were cut socially, and could get no Indians of consequence to talk to them or aid their inquiries. Gandhi scarcely mentioned them.

Many Swarajists drifted back to the idea of civil disobedience. His *Autobiography* and *Satyagraha in South Africa* set them talking. To his doubts of Indian courage and self-control they now had a partial answer. Three times in the past six years, local Satyagraha had been tried with success, not under his leadership but under his influence.

The first two cases had occurred while he was in prison. In August 1922 the Akali Sikhs had set out to evict the corrupt and British-protected guardians of the sanctuary of Guru-ka-Bagh, ten miles from Amritsar. A thousand settled near the sanctuary and four thousand at Amritsar, in the Golden Temple. Every day a hundred and twenty-five marchers in black turbans advanced on Guru-ka-Bagh, under oath to attempt an entry. British policemen with iron-tipped rods blocked the road and beat them. They were often carried back unconscious, but never hit the policemen. At last the Government handed over the shrine to an elected committee. Andrews watched the marchers, and they had Gandhi's encouragement so far as he could give it, but their movement was independent of him.

The second case was at Nagpur in June 1923, when the Government banned a procession with the unofficial national flag. Vinoba and Jamnalal Bajaj, the businessman who financed the Wardha Ashram, led two thousand demonstrators who paraded with the flag in relays for two months. Many of them, including Vinoba, were jailed, but finally a token procession was permitted.

The third case was at Vykom in Travancore just after Gandhi's release. A road which passed through a district full of Brahmins, and close to a temple, was closed to Untouchables. George Joseph, Gandhi's disciple from the southern Christian community, tried to escort an Untouchable along it. He was set upon and arrested. Dozens of volunteers promptly followed his example. The police threw a cordon across the highway, and the Satyagrahis stood in front of it in a posture of prayer. They continued to go there in four-hour relays, despite orthodox hooligans and floods that rose to their waists. Gandhi went to see for himself. He drew attention to Vykom in his papers, and sent Vinoba to direct operations instead of George Joseph, believing that a Hindu problem should be handled by Hindus. After sixteen months the Brahmins surrendered.

With the Simon Commission in their midst, nationalists looked to the inventor of the technique and wondered if he could see his way to act. A chance presented itself: marvellously enough, at Bardoli, where so many hopes had foundered. Its taxes were raised by 22 per cent. The peasants of that region are proverbially gentle (it is said that their dogs do not bark at strangers) but now they erupted. Gandhi spoke to Vallabhbhai Patel, who was Mayor of Ahmedabad in that year, and authorized him to lead the resistance. On 12 February 1928—the sixth anniversary of the halt—Bardoli, at last, stopped paying its taxes.

Vallabhbhai's precise mind and card-index memory made him a skilful organizer where organization was the prime need. The collectors' onslaught was ferocious. They drove families off their farms, grabbed the pots and pans in the kitchens, confiscated cattle and horses. 'At the rate the forfeitures are being served,' Gandhi wrote, 'practically the whole of the county of Bardoli should soon be in the Government's possession, and they can pay themselves a thousand times over for their precious assessments.' Everything hinged on Vallabhbhai's ability to keep eighty-eight thousand peasants in line, neither giving up nor resorting to violence. He managed it. Week after week, in the face of mass arrests, they stood firm. He vetoed every proposal for violence, such as planting spikes in the road to puncture the tyres of officials' cars, and violence did not occur. When the authorities tried to strip villages of all movable property, he told the peasants to dismantle their carts and hide the parts in different places.

Funds poured in from the rest of India. On an announcement that the land of Bardoli would be sold in its entirety to new occupants, Vithalbhai Patel broke his neutrality as President of the Legislative Assembly, and wrote to the Viceroy in support if his brother. On 12 June Indians observed 'Bardoli Day' with a *hartal*. Questions were asked in the House of Commons. On 2 August, anticipating Vallabhbhai Patel's arrest, Gandhi moved to Bardoli himself. Four days later the Government retreated. It restored the property and released the prisoners. An inquiry board upheld most of the peasants' claims, and the tax increase was cut to 5.7 per cent.

Gandhi had proved his point. The thing could be done. Vallabhbhai—henceforth known by the honorary title of Sardar, Leader—was fully persuaded, and he was a critical man whose certainties carried weight. Tagore praised Bardoli without his usual reservations: it was a story recalling the epic age.

While the battle was at its height, India's more ardent spirits had seen their opportunity. In the forefront was Subhas Chandra Bose. His slogan was 'Give me blood and I promise you freedom.' As head of a Congress volunteer corps he called himself the G.O.C., General Officer Commanding, with the result that his letters were apt to be delivered to an outraged Englishman with the same rank. His uniform was made in Calcutta by British tailors. That May he visited Gandhi at Sabarmati and urged him to lead national civil disobedience. The Mahatma, however, disliked his uniform and was cool to his suggestions. Finding the Swaraj Party immobile, Bose pressed Motilal Nehru to accept the presidency of Congress.

Bose, like Mussolini and Hitler, was not less formidable for being slightly absurd. He counted as a left-winger, and 1928 was a year of rapid labour organization and militant strikes. Conscious of danger in a quarter it had scarcely noticed before, the Government began arresting trade-unionists, Socialists and Communists. The atmosphere grew generally more harsh. Toward the end of the year, police armed with lathis (four-foot staves shod with metal) charged a peaceable anti-Simon rally in Lahore. Gandhi's colleague Lajpat Rai, now aged sixty-three, was struck over the heart by a muscular young Englishman and died soon afterwards. With Das and Lajpat Rai both gone, Gandhi was left for good or ill in a lonelier eminence, with few advisers of comparable stature. But he was no longer looking to his contemporaries. At another demonstration in Lucknow the police charged again. This time Jawaharlal Nehru was among the victims. On 3 December, during the annual stay at Wardha, Gandhi wrote him a momentous letter.

My love to you. It was all done bravely. You have braver things to do. May God spare you for many a long year to come and make you His chosen instrument for freeing India from the yoke.

In associating the younger Nehru with himself as a virtual crown prince, Gandhi showed a genius which saved his movement and his own future. Possibly he was helped toward the decision by the sudden death of Maganlal Gandhi, whom he had thought of as his heir. That blow was heavy, and the search for a substitute was natural. But instead of looking for a non-political heir, as Maganlal would have been, he reached out. He realized—an impressive fact in anyone nearing sixty—that to go further he would have to extend himself, through alliance with a younger leader; and his choice was correct.

Jawaharlal Nehru had now been under his spell for years. In 1923 he had spoken of the Mahatma as 'representing the soul of India'. In 1926 and '27 he had toured Europe, attending an Oppressed Nations' Conference and reporting on it to Gandhi. He returned to India in December 1927 and was struck by the revival of energy during his absence. He described himself as a Socialist and a believer in industrialization. But he saw Gandhi's radical implications better than most, and did not break with him. He was one of the first Hindus to achieve an historical perspective. Thanks to Marx and other westerners, he was able to combine his Socialism with Gandhi's programme in a synthesis that cohered well enough for joint action. This, plus his talent for being charming and tactful while taking a strong line, held together the younger and older nationalists.

To the objection that his heir was an atheist, Gandhi replied that Jawaharlal was nearer to God than many professed worshippers. To the objection that his master was not a Socialist, Jawaharlal replied that the Gandhian social regeneration at least pointed the way.

Their partnership did not instantly follow on Gandhi's letter. It matured in the stress of action, after a crisis which seemed to divide them. At Calcutta that December, Congress was to consider a draft constitution for a federal Dominion of India. Motilal Nehru— Pandit Motilal Nehru, as everybody called him—had drawn this up in consultation with members of all parties. Gandhi insisted that Motilal preside. Weary and disenchanted with politics, and downcast by Muslim hostility to his plan, the Pandit agreed only unwillingly. He insisted in his turn that the Mahatma should attend. 'You have made me sit in the presidential chair,' he wrote, 'and put upon my head a crown of thorns; but at least do not look at my difficulties from a distance.'

The debate was confused and unedifying. Jawaharlal and Bose argued that the draft was too moderate. They wanted full independence and an immediate bid for it. Congress might have been deadlocked, but Gandhi stepped in, proposing a compromise which was adopted with amendments. Britain should be given a year to accept the Nehru Constitution. Congress should spend that year organizing itself for combat, and then, if Britain had not responded, should launch 'a campaign of non-violent non-co-operation by advising the country to refuse taxation.'

Left-wingers complained at the year's grace. A large section of Congress opposed the compromise on this ground. Fifty thousand industrial workers swarmed round waving flags and demanding revolution. But on the main issue, the state of feeling was clear. Even Mrs Besant approved. The wheel had come round. The politicians, unable to rouse the people without Gandhi, were bringing him back with an ampler authority than ever.

XIV

Salt

1

Gandhi had been thinking of a tour of Europe. This was now out of the question. Instead (though still underweight even for him) he began another tour of India, preparing audiences for the clash. He went as far afield as Burma, which was then part of the Indian Empire. Meanwhile he was putting some final touches to his popular version of the *Gita,* which came out during 1929. Its readers could hardly fail to see a more concrete and timely allegory than he suggested himself. Krishna was summoning Arjuna to take up his weapons again.

When visiting Delhi in February about a new cloth boycott, Gandhi attended a tea party given by Vithalbhai Patel. The guests included Motilal Nehru, Jinnah, a couple of maharajahs, and the Viceroy. Patel had notions of ice-breaking. But Gandhi wrote in *Young India*:

> There cannot be much breaking of ice at a private, informal tea party . . . England will never make any advance so as to satisfy India's aspirations till she is forced to it. British rule is no philanthropic job, it is a terribly earnest business proposition. . . . The coating of benevolence that is periodically given to it merely prolongs the agony. Such occasional parties are therefore good only to the extent of showing that the bringing together of parties will be easy enough when both are ready for business.

Events bore him out. In March the Government launched its own preparations by arresting over thirty leading trade-unionists. Some were Communists, more were not. Eight belonged to the All-India Congress Committee. They were taken to Meerut where they could be tried without a jury. The charge was sedition, and the trial was drawn out for four years, to ensure their unavailability. Irwin

279

followed his March round-up with a Public Safety Ordinance, imposing it by decree when the Central Assembly, under the maddeningly resourceful presidency of Patel, refused to pass it. Fresh strikes broke out in protest. A Sikh terrorist, already guilty of an assassination condemned by Gandhi, retorted to the decree with a bomb outrage in the Assembly chamber. Simon was in the gallery and went home carrying that picture with him.

Gandhi's own reply to repression was a conference of the All-India Congress Committee, held in Bombay at Mani Bhavan. Congress was exhorted to build up its membership to at least three-quarters of a million in the next three months, to strengthen and spread its organization, and to support the constructive programme. In one respect there was a significant shift of emphasis. Much more was being said about the rights of women and their role in the struggle.

The British General Election in May restored Labour to office. MacDonald had lately voiced the hope for a Dominion of India within months rather than years. One of his first acts as Prime Minister was to summon Irwin home for consultations with himself and the Secretary of State, Wedgwood Benn. Needing Liberal support to survive, he felt bound to proceed on tripartite lines and work out a 'British' solution rather than a 'Labour' one. Though Congress was in a stronger position toward other political groups than Labour was, Gandhi pursued his own counterpart of the same policy. Reports were streaming in of police raids on homes and offices in search of subversive literature. The object, said Gandhi, was to 'overawe and humiliate'—the tested technique for the mastery of a hundred thousand people over three hundred million. The three hundred million must command respect, and unity was strength.

To avert a split between older and younger Congressmen, he declined invitations to be the next president, and manoeuvred Jawaharlal toward the chair. To avert a split between rich and poor, he urged Indian landlords and factory-owners to behave generously. To avert a far more terrible split between Hindus and Muslims, he sounded out the Ali brothers on the chances of inducing Jinnah to back Motilal's draft constitution. Their meeting, though cordial, was unfruitful, a negative success at most.

In October the Viceroy at last returned, having conferred with the Labour Cabinet and with Baldwin, Lloyd George, and many

more. Noting the alarm which was rising in India as the year ran
out, he issued a statement envisaging what he had turned down in
1927, an exploration of the issues with Indians taking part. His
statement affirmed the goal of Dominion status, although the Simon
Commission had not yet reported. This concession was balanced,
and in the eyes of many outweighed, by a proposal that the pro-
jected Round Table Conference should bring in the princely states.
Englishmen might welcome the romantic India of pomp and elephants and polo and cricket; they preferred silk to khadi. But to
bring in the princes meant bringing in such representatives of the
people as the dashing Maharajah of Alwar, a sadist, pervert and
suspected murderer who claimed descent from the Sun God; the
Maharajah of Jaipur, a youth who had been married at thirteen to
a woman of thirty; and the Nizam of Hyderabad, whose occasional
philanthropic acts (financed without trouble out of a fortune beyond computation) could scarcely outweigh his mean misgovern-
ment, his dirty and stingy habits, his eccentric cruelty to his own
children, or the harem and five hundred servants that went with
him when he travelled.

The Congress Working Committee met in Delhi to discuss Irwin's
announcement. Gandhi, Annie Besant, and both Nehrus were
present. They composed a counter-statement. This Delhi Manifesto
was politely grateful, but urged that the conference needed the right
atmosphere to work in. Political prisoners should be set free. At the
conference, Congress should have a special position. The programme should not be to debate Dominion status, but to draw up
a constitution taking that aim for granted.

Jawaharlal signed the Manifesto. He did so with deep misgivings
and no faith in MacDonald, but as Congress President-Elect he did
not want to break unity. Afterwards he regretted having signed it
at all, and joined S. C. Bose in criticizing the weakness of the older
leaders. Gandhi, however, persuaded him not to withdraw from the
presidency.

A meeting with Irwin was arranged for 23 December. The Viceroy appeared punctually in spite of another bomb. But the tone of
The Times had shown that his October offer did not have to mean
much, and the Opposition parties at Westminster had shown that
it did not have to mean anything. If he tried to implement it, they
would probably combine forces to throw MacDonald out. When
Gandhi pressed for a firm promise of Dominion status as the basis

of the Round Table Conference, it was not forthcoming. He subsequently told H. N. Brailsford that he realized power could not
be handed over at once, but it was vital that India and Britain
should meet as equals, and only a firm promise could establish that
point. The peace moves ended. Irwin was shocked at the Indians'
bad form in trying to pin an English gentleman down: 'They
really were impossible,' he wrote.

Congress assembled at Lahore in a temporary city of tents. His
waverings over, Jawaharlal presided. At forty he had climbed to an
astonishing height. He was President of the All-India Trade Union
Congress as well as Congress itself. He was a hero of the youth
movement and a chieftain of the Left. Now he spoke as a statesman-like rebel, warmly supported by Bose, who wanted to set up
a rival government on the spot. That was going too far. But Congress voted for complete independence, 'Purna Swaraj.' Its members
were advised to resign from the legislatures, and steer clear of the
Round Table Conference. As for the actual campaign, this was to
be conducted by the All-India Congress Committee in the Gandhist
style already foreshadowed. Gandhi himself was vested with full
powers to determine scope and timing. The President knew that
however much he might talk about Socialism and Youth, it was the
sixty-year-old Mahatma who knew India best and could mobilize
the masses.

At midnight on New Year's Eve, the delegates gathered round a
flagstaff on the banks of the Ravi. Upward against the sky rose the
tricolour of free India.

2

On 18 January 1930 Tagore came to Sabarmati. The movement
which he saw stirring on every side owed more to him than politicians acknowledged. He had been a pioneer of the boycott and the
renunciation of British honours; he had taught Indians to revere
Gandhi as a Mahatma; he had given prescient and constructive
warnings. Now he asked what was to come next.

'I am furiously thinking night and day,' Gandhi answered,
'and I do not see any light coming out of the surrounding darkness.'

His state of mind was not a mere reaction after the exaltation of

Congress. Two questions were oppressing him. First, there was his old problem of giving the issues that sharpness of definition which Satyagraha required. Second, there was his almost equally old problem of keeping the struggle within non-violent bounds.

He was as firm as ever in preferring no Swaraj at all to Swaraj attained the wrong way, and he was aware of ominous tensions. In a message to English friends he admitted that 'hatred and ill-will are undoubtedly in the air'. To him this danger was an argument in favour of civil disobedience rather than against it, because, if he did nothing, terrorists would take over the movement. But he knew by this time the dilemma of the leader who sincerely rejects terrorism yet whose programme is calculated to unleash it. His army had many combatants whom he might lecture and extract promises from *ad nauseam,* yet who would rush into plots, arson and murder as soon as opportunity served. The allaying of this anxiety was Congress's main motive in giving him its blank cheque. As a dictator he was not exposed to pressure from an unstable democracy. Nevertheless his freedom was not absolute. To dispel fears of another Chauri Chaura, he had to waive in advance the right of calling off any campaign if sporadic violence should occur. It would be for Congress to decide whether the situation was out of hand.

He gave reassuring interviews, he published Rules of Satyagraha, but he foresaw trouble. Nor could he hope to confine disobedience to a trained few. The world economic crisis was already bursting over India. A savage drop in the prices which peasants got for their produce was reflected in a decline in their consumption of staples —cloth, oil, sugar. Debts were mounting and farms breaking up. Within months, even if Gandhi did not proclaim non-payment of taxes, millions would cease to pay them from sheer lack of resources. Better an organized campaign than a jacquerie. However, the campaign had its own perils.

Gandhi tackled the first problem—defining the issues—at the end of January. Nothing could be settled till it became clear how much support Congress had. He named 26 January as Independence Day. Immediately before it, Irwin announced that the Round Table Conference would be advisory only. The national response on the 26th left no doubt. In every town and in many villages the flag was hoisted and a manifesto by Gandhi was read, calling for Purna Swaraj, and declaring it to be a crime against Man and God to submit any longer. While the Muslims as a community held aloof, and

their spokesmen talked of attending the Conference, a fair number
sympathized with Congress (in Bombay, thought Brailsford, about
one-third).

Four days later Gandhi published a programme giving the substance of independence as he conceived it. The items were meant to
cover the supreme evils of the British Raj. His choice was curious
but adroit. Purna Swaraj implied a ban on the liquor trade; revaluation of the rupee; halving of the land revenue, arms expendi-
ture, and the salaries of higher officials; abolition of the salt tax; a
protective tariff on foreign cloth, and controls over coastal traffic;
release of political prisoners; disbandment of the C.I.D.; and the
right to carry firearms for self-defence. With some of these reforms,
such as revaluation and the tariff, he was appealing to businessmen.
With others, such as the cut in land-tax, he was appealing to
peasants.

The list enabled the leaders to say, 'This is what we are fighting
for.' Still, it was ambiguous. Suppose the Viceroy himself offered
to carry out the reforms, should civil disobedience halt? Gandhi
said yes. His programme was a test of British willingness to relinquish power. Acceptance by Delhi would be tantamount to abdica-
tion—the change of heart which Truth-Force aimed at—and all else
would follow. Some dissented. He was fairly sure, in fact, that the
question was academic. Writing privately to Birla he said he did
not trust the British, and could not see himself conferring with them
on any currently credible basis. The British press had given his eleven
points a hostile reception. But his rules required that he should
make a genuine effort. He would ask the Viceroy to grant the reforms: failing which he would launch civil disobedience. Against
what precisely?

In the last week of February his inner voice was prompting him
toward a decision, and at the beginning of March his mind was
made up. The enemy line had a weak point where he could exert
maximum pressure with minimum risk of violence. He would summon Indians to throw off the burden of the salt tax by making salt
for themselves.

It was the weirdest and most brilliant political challenge of
modern times. The English laughed, their Indian flatterers echoed
them, the intellectuals of Congress were bewildered . . . and the
great motionless crust of India began trembling. Gandhi had
suggested defying the salt laws as far back as 1919, and his instinct

was sound. In a hot climate salt is almost a necessity for man and beast. The Hindu of past ages could pan his own, or pick it up out of natural deposits. His Mogul conquerors tried to tax it and thereby made such a tax hateful. It weighed heaviest on those least able to bear it. Under the British Raj the only legal salt was government salt from guarded depots. The price had a built-in levy—not large, but enough to cost a labourer with a family up to two weeks' wages a year. Yet eastward, westward and southward, at the end of all the sacred rivers, lay the open acres of God's salt water.

On 2 March Gandhi wrote to the Viceroy, beginning 'Dear Friend'. He reviewed the grievances covered by his eleven points, not omitting the highly apposite one about expensive officials.

> Take your own salary. . . . You are getting much over five thousand times India's average income. . . . I have too great a regard for you as a man to wish to hurt your feelings. . . . Probably the whole of your salary goes for charity. But a system that provides for such an arrangement deserves to be summarily scrapped.

He explained that he hoped to convert the British people through non-violence and suffering, and that if Irwin promised to grant his reforms it would 'open a way for a real conference between equals'. Otherwise, however, he would assemble a party at the Ashram on the 11th and set out to break the salt laws.

To show his freedom from race-hate he entrusted his message to an English Quaker, Reginald Reynolds, who arrived at the Residence wearing khadi and a sun-helmet. Irwin came in from a polo match, glanced at the letter, and handed it to his secretary, who dismissed it in four curt lines.

Meanwhile Gandhi had been training a picked band of ashramites. Little over a year before, the standards of the community had sunk so low that he considered changing the name, because 'Satyagraha Ashram' was no longer deserved. But now recovery was complete. Sabarmati stood at its zenith. As the days passed, reporters and photographers and onlookers gathered at the gate and in the adjacent fields, waiting, watching. Early on 12 March they heard the chanting of prayers. Then seventy-eight men and youths (all of whose names were printed in *Young India* for the benefit of the police) formed a column in the grounds. They included two Untouchables, two Muslims and a Christian. At their head the

Mahatma appeared, with an iron-tipped bamboo walking staff. He was perfectly frank about his intentions. The whole party would march to Dandi, on the coast 241 miles to the south, where sea-water evaporated on mud flats leaving a layer of salt; and they would pick some of it up. The rest of India should wait for that signal, or if he were arrested before getting there, should look to Jawaharlal—Pandit Jawaharlal as Gandhi now spoke of him—for guidance. 'We are marching', he said, 'in the name of God.' At half past six the column began to move through a cheering crowd, and soon it vanished into the distance. Some of the pilgrims were to come back to the Ashram as their home, but Bapu said he would not settle in it again till the tax was repealed.

On the Salt March he fully entered the world of newsreel and documentary. Henceforth we have many glimpses of him flickering in black and white, a brisk, mobile figure, with odd but illuminating moments of likeness to Charlie Chaplin. The marchers tramped along the dirt roads from village to village, through the green and brown plains of Gujarat, for more than three weeks. On the way Jawaharlal met them with other Congressmen. After a talk the Mahatma strode on again, staff in hand, a look of peace on his face. Decades later when other memories had dimmed, this was the picture that remained branded on Nehru's mind.

Villages were garlanded and flying the flag. Peasants knelt by the wayside. Gandhi would make a short speech about the subjects dear to his heart. He cited the *Gita*: Krishna stood for the right-eousness of the end, Arjuna for the purity of the means, and with the two together defeat was impossible. At sunrise and sunset he held prayer meetings in the open. Every day all his ashramites spun for an hour and wrote diaries. Some could not keep up with him on foot, and rode in bullock carts. A horse was kept in readiness for their leader, but he never mounted. Behind him the administration was silently crumbling as three hundred and ninety village head-men resigned their posts. Villagers joined the column as it surged through. When it neared Dandi the seventy-nine had swelled to thousands. Among them were numerous women—not only the poor, but wealthy ladies from Bombay, and orthodox Hindu aristocrats. India was at the same stage as South Africa in 1913, with the women and the masses committed.

The march approached its goal. Enemies in high places were no longer laughing. Instead they were sneering at it as propaganda. But they were unwise to belittle propaganda when they were duped by their own. Delhi debated whether to arrest the Mahatma and decided not to, because his arrest would cause disturbances, whereas the march was just a piece of charlatanism that held revolt in check without being dangerous.

Dandi takes its name from a lighthouse. It is in level country. Trees and scattered buildings lie well back from the coast. Land reclamation has altered the face of things, but all that matters is still there. A narrow track runs shoreward beside the mud flats and pools where formerly the waves swept in at high tide. Beyond a belt of scrub, with a lonely palm or two, are the beach and the line of foam. You cross over sand that is dry and soft on to sand that is firm. Right and left, north and south, the beach stretches away into infinity, a strip between sea and land: empty, without breakwaters or refuse, quiet and fearless. No monument disfigures that landscape anywhere. A plaque under a tree is all. The monuments are living ones—local people who were there, and still are, and cannot forget.

On 5 April the marchers poured along the road with the sunset in their eyes. They camped near the water. Night fell and passed, and all through it the ashramites were praying. Next day was the eleventh anniversary of the Delhi *hartal*. In the bright fresh minutes of the new morning, before its heat careered over the tree-tops, Gandhi waded into the ocean. From that huge and healing womb he presently turned back toward India, and paced over the sand to a spot where the salt lay thick. There he bent quickly over and scooped some of it up with his fingers. Sarojini Naidu, who was among the pilgrims standing nearest, cried 'Hail deliverer!' He straightened and held it out for all to see: the treasonable gift of God. So the evening and the morning were the first day.

3

It was like releasing a spring, Jawaharlal said. Within a week everybody seemed to be making salt, or reading Congress leaflets on how to make it, or hawking illicit packets of it. The product was poor stuff, but who cared? All round the coast, peasants and fishermen were digging into the natural deposits or setting out pans of brine to evaporate. In Ahmedabad Congress had its own depot, and sold the salt or gave it away to enormous crowds, besides auctioning the Mahatma's original handful for sixteen hundred rupees. In Delhi Vithalbhai Patel and other Assembly members resigned in protest against the law. One was Pandit Malaviya, who had not always supported Gandhi, but now bought some salt before an audience of fifteen thousand.

Blows began to fall. The police attacked the peasants with lathis and rounded up Congress Volunteers peddling salt in the streets. They arrested Ramdas and Devadas Gandhi, and several ashramites including Mahadev Desai. At Congress headquarters in Bombay they discovered rows of pans on the roof. During the raid sixty thousand people jammed the neighbouring streets, and hundreds were dragged off handcuffed or bound with ropes. Jawaharlal himself was arrested in Allahabad on the 14th and sentenced to six months, nominating his father to be Acting President of Congress. Disobedience spread through Maharashtra, Madras, Bihar, Bengal, the Punjab. Everywhere illegal salt factories were set up. The Mayor of Calcutta read seditious literature in public and was soon in jail, as were Rajagopalachari and both the Patel brothers. Processions of professors and students filed down to the sea and were imprisoned in batches. At Patna Rajendra Prasad accompanied a vast crowd toward one of the new salt depots. When the road was blocked they stayed where they were for forty hours. Prasad refused to disperse them. Mounted police galloped forward; the crowd lay flat, the horses shied and pulled up, demonstrators had to be hoisted bodily into trucks.

The Government ordered local officials to stamp out the illegal industry, and the officials resigned. It imposed a press censorship, and dozens of papers ceased publication rather than submit to it. Attempts were made to confiscate bags of salt. Satyagrahis never resisted arrest, but they did try to hang on to the bags, and were beaten, kicked, and squeezed in the genitals until they let go. Mass meetings and *hartals* in the cities greeted every major arrest. Normally these were peaceful, but at Karachi a riot broke out. Congress Volunteers rushed in to restore order and the police shot two of them dead. A month after the Dandi action at least sixty thousand Indians had gone to prison. Lord Irwin had succeeded in dispelling an impression at home that he was a weak Viceroy. According to a biographer, 'his religious convictions seemed to reinforce the very ruthlessness of his policy of suppression'.

Gandhi meanwhile had not moved very far. He had been holding conferences and issuing directives within a short distance of the beach. Besides the salt campaign, he called for an intensified cloth boycott and other measures on the same lines as in 1921. At a special gathering of women, he urged them to wear khadi and to go on picket duty outside the shops of liquor dealers and vendors of foreign cloth. As funds rolled in he ordered Congress workers to keep strict accounts. For some weeks his tone was restrained. But in the second half of April he noted signs that the movement was taking a more critical turn.

Sporadic tax strikes were reported. At Chittagong, non-Congress terrorists made a futile raid on the arsenal which resulted in six deaths. At Peshawar in the North-West Frontier Province, on the arrest of Ghaffar Khan, armoured cars were employed to scatter demonstrators. One vehicle was burnt without loss of life. Another, with the Deputy Police Commissioner aboard, drove full tilt into the crowd and opened up with machine-guns, killing seventy. On 25 April the police withdrew, leaving Ghaffar Khan's Khudai Khidmatgars or Red Shirts in control, the first Gandhist civic authority. When troops were brought up, two platoons of Garhwali Rifles—Hindus—refused to fire on the unarmed Muslim populace. The job had to be done by Gurkhas with aerial support. Seventeen of the mutineers were in due course court-martialled and given severe sentences. By Irwin's wish, this affair was hushed up and demands for an inquiry were rejected.

While the Peshawar issue hung in doubt Gandhi wrote to the Viceroy again, still beginning 'Dear Friend,' but protesting vigorously at the police violence. This, he warned, was likely to provoke counter-violence. To reaffirm Satyagraha he proposed, 'God willing', to lead his companions into a fiercer ordeal. They would march to the salt works at Dharasana and seek possession, asserting the right of the people to occupy a State-controlled property.

On the night of 4 May he was sleeping in a cot under a mango tree, at a village near Dandi. Several ashramites slept near him. Soon after midnight the District Magistrate of Surat drove up with two Indian officers and thirty heavily-armed constables. He woke Gandhi by shining a torch in his face, and arrested him under a regulation of 1827. After the morning ritual of prayer and tooth-cleaning (there were still a few teeth to clean) the prisoner left.

The 1827 regulation, passed in the Company era, enabled the Government to detain him without trial and with no fixed sentence. He was taken again to Yeravda, where some personal particulars were put down: height, five feet five; scar on right thigh, scar below left elbow, mole on lower right eyelid. They treated him gently and offered privileges which he refused. Imprisonment was again a welcome respite. He spent much of the time translating Hindu hymns, nicknaming his abode Yeravda Mandir —Temple.

The arrest set off a general *hartal*. The railway workshops and cotton mills of Bombay stood idle. At the industrial city of Sholapur, after a riot in which some policemen were killed, the textile workers raised the national flag and formed their own administration. Peace reigned until the authorities declared martial law and mowed down twenty-five people. At a subsequent clash in Barisal, where lathi charges had disabled hundreds of citizens, a furious mob locked the police in a school and set fire to it. This was Chauri Chaura over again—but with a difference. Congress Volunteers broke open the door and rescued the victims. Gandhi's lesson had been learnt. During these weeks there had, of course, been cases of stone-throwing and uglier hooliganism. But there had been no serious violence under Congress auspices, and amazingly little by rebels of any kind. The English had inflicted far more casualties in the name of law and order . . . yet not one Englishman had been killed.

On 17 May the *Manchester Guardian* published some remarks by the ever-perceptive Tagore.

> Those who live in England, far away from the East, have now got to realize that Europe has completely lost her former prestige in Asia. She is no longer regarded as the champion throughout the world of fair dealing and the exponent of high principle, but as the upholder of western race supremacy and the exploiter of those outside her own borders.
>
> For Europe this is, in actual fact, a great moral defeat that has happened. . . . Asia . . . can now afford to look down on Europe where before she looked up.

The communiqué justifying Gandhi's arrest claimed that his followers were out of hand and behaving violently. It was left to Dharasana to supply the only adequate comment. The promised raid on the salt works was undertaken on 21 May by 2,500 Satyagrahis under the leadership of Manilal Gandhi and Sarojini Naidu. Mrs Naidu addressed the weaponless army in their khadi and white caps: 'You will be beaten, but you must not resist. You must not even raise a hand to ward off blows.'

Dharasana is not far from Dandi. The salt-pans are in a vast, flat, brown expanse. Access is by a track that leads to a work area in the centre. From the work area, a causeway runs to the right and ends on slightly higher ground, with grass and cacti and trees, and a fair-sized house. When the Satyagrahis arrived in the early morning, they found the approaches cut across by a ditch. Farther on was a barbed wire fence protecting the work area, where the salt was stacked. Four hundred Indian policemen commanded by six British officers were waiting, some in front of the salt, many more on the higher ground to the right, where horses could be seen and the house had been commandeered as police HQ. An American journalist, Webb Miller, stood and watched.

In total silence the human wave rolled forward. It stopped near the ditch, about a hundred yards from the stockade. A picked group waded through the ditch and advanced toward the barbed wire. Officers shouted at them to go back. They went on. Someone gave an order. Policemen with steel-shod lathis, who had been edging in from the grassy slope on the right, charged over the level ground. The lathis fell on the marchers' heads. Not a single hand was raised. As the crack of each impact rang out clearly, the onlookers winced and gasped. One after another the marchers fell near the wire, stunned or tossing in agony with fractured skulls, their white khadi stained with red. When all were down, a second column advanced, heads high, silent, to the certain doom. Again the police littered the ground with bodies.

Changing tactics, parties of twenty-five entered the danger zone and sat down. Somewhere about this point the discipline of the police went to pieces in a frenzy. There was nothing to prevent them from picking the men up and carrying them off. Instead they kicked them in the abdomen and testicles, dragged them along and threw them into the ditch, and smashed their heads with lathis. These assaults drew irrepressible screams from them, but still no blows. The officers had far-sightedly provided stretchers. Hour after hour, as the day grew hotter, relays of bearers conveyed the victims to the trees. Here they were dumped down and placed under arrest,

as were Manilal and Mrs Naidu. The latter shook off an Englishman trying to haul her by the arm, and walked alone.

By eleven o'clock the temperature was 116 and no more volunteers were advancing. Miller crossed to the improvised hospital and
counted 320 injured prisoners. Many were unconscious or in torment from wounds. Two were already dead. For days, however,
these events were repeated.

Lord Irwin wrote to George V: 'Your Majesty can hardly fail
to have read with amusement the accounts of the several battles for
the Salt Depot.' Most of the casualties, he said, were shamming.
Such was the verdict of viceregal wisdom on a combat as decisive
as any in history. Truth-Force in practice had vindicated Gandhi's
faith. Here at last was the Non-Violence of the Brave in full
measure—'a perfect thing of its kind', in his own admiring words.
It was plain enough who had got out of hand, who had behaved
violently. If Irwin and the King were amused, others were not.
Miller's dispatch had been syndicated to over a thousand papers
throughout the world.

Raids on more of the depots followed. The most spectacular was
at Wadala on 1 June, with fifteen thousand taking part. The raiders
managed to carry off some salt. Already the Congress Working
Committee had authorized civil disobedience on a broader front.
The cloth boycott and liquor boycott were strengthened by mobil-
izing countless women as pickets. The forest laws were broken.
Business was withdrawn from British commercial firms. In various
districts, peasants who had the funds to pay their land-tax and rent
refused to do so. Congress's wealthier supporters discouraged such
action as a general policy. Some were landlords themselves.
But they stayed loyal to the movement, because of the rupee
exchange rate if nothing else, and ostracized the pro-British
minority.

The Raj was slowly running down. It could always be prevented
from actually stopping, but at what price? A correspondent of the
Observer reported growing defeatism. Repressive measures went on
and on with no end in sight. In their lathi charges, the police were
now apt to hit almost anybody of either sex, but were taught to be
discriminating in picking the vital parts of the body. They also
performed hundreds of official whippings. But in spite of these, and
the censorship and propaganda, there were few signs of a return
to co-operation. In June the All-India Congress Committee and

Working Committee were declared illegal. Motilal Nehru went to prison. From his own cell at Naini, Jawaharlal wrote to Gandhi:

> May I congratulate you on the new India you have created by your magic touch! What the future will bring I know not but the past has made life worth living and our prosaic existence has developed something of epic greatness in it. Sitting here in Naini Jail, I have pondered on the wonderful efficacy of non-violence as a weapon and have become a greater convert . . . than ever before.

About this time his enlarged vision began to express itself in the letters to his daughter Indira, the future Prime Minister, which were published as *Glimpses of World History*.

Meanwhile, as the number in jail rose from sixty thousand toward a hundred thousand, about one-eighth of them Muslims, the Viceroy had begun to think of a truce. Strictly he was doing his duty and could not be faulted. Yet his Christianity had, after all, something in it which forbade him to rest content with that. Also the state of world opinion was far from satisfactory. Cartoonists had portrayed an impish Mahatma putting salt on the lion's tail. When Lord Lothian said, 'What people in India want to know today is where they are,' David Low illustrated the remark by drawing a prison with the people of India crammed inside.

Irwin's term of office was nearing its close, but he was making a belated effort to understand Gandhi. He ought not to have found this difficult. He could have studied the *Autobiography* and the files of *Young India*. Or he could have talked with some of Gandhi's associates. Mira, for instance. He had been introduced to her when she was Madeleine Slade. Although she had let the side down, especially by publishing tactless articles on the police, she was English and at liberty. But he took neither course.* Instead he relied on experts (of the sort who had predicted that Indians would welcome the Simon Commission) and his own judgement (the judgement that had dismissed Dharasana as a joke). One of the fruits of his meditation was a scheme for trumping the Mahatma's potential ace by fasting himself—a project which he never put into effect, but discussed afterwards with an archbishop.

---

* Later, when he was Lord Halifax and Chamberlain's right-hand man in foreign affairs, he had to confer with Hitler; but he never bothered to read *Mein Kampf*. General Smuts did read *Hind Swaraj*, almost as soon as it came out.

In June the Simon Report appeared. While it remained silent on Dominion status, it wrote off Dyarchy as a fiction camouflaging autocracy, and advised the development of a federal India. Mac-Donald and Wedgwood Benn were anxious for Congress participation in the Round Table Conference. To the disquiet of bureaucrats and businessmen, Irwin took soundings. He did it through a journalist. The *Daily Herald* was then the Labour Party's organ. Its correspondent, George Slocombe, was allowed to interview Gandhi in prison. Gandhi held out for his eleven points, but offered to postpone some of them. In July Irwin's counsellors Sapru and Jayakar obtained his leave to confer with the Congress leaders. The Nehrus were courteously conveyed to Poona. There, with Gandhi, Mrs Naidu, and other members of the Working Committee, they met the two Liberals. The outcome was a letter dated 15 August stating that Congress wanted peace, but. . . .

> We have come to the conclusion that the time is not yet ripe for securing a settlement honourable for our country. Marvellous as has been the mass awakening during the past five months . . . we feel that the sufferings have been neither sustained enough nor large enough for the immediate attainment of the end.

The letter laid down conditions about the transfer of authority and the right to secede.

Gandhi's main thesis was the same as before. India had to be built up, morally and economically, to the point of confronting Britain as a power. The constructive effort, he wrote, was still the foundation of his campaign. 'Actual taking over of the Government machinery is but a shadow, an emblem. And it could easily be a burden if it came as a gift from without, the people having made no effort to deserve it.' He was sticking to his 1921 concept of the Counter-Establishment, in a context where it asserted itself by a more active defiance.

After the parley the thing was palpably beginning to happen. Bombay, for instance, had in effect two governments. The British administration retained the Europeans, the troops, the older Muslims. Most other citizens took little notice of it. Congressmen controlled trade and industry. Each onslaught by the authorities was answered with a *hartal* striking another blow at the Englishman's bank balance. Inspectors ran a permit system which kept out foreign textiles. Volunteers wearing khadi and Gandhi caps marched about the city banging on drums, chanting verses from the *Gita,* and leading the crowds in national songs. Outside the shops of merchants who had not joined the boycott, women in orange saris (a military colour) dissuaded customers from going in, and sometimes blocked the door if they tried. An endless procession went to jail, and always more women emerged from seclusion to take their places. Gandhi's portrait and the flags and emblems of Congress were everywhere. At mass meetings the people gathered and listened quietly to speeches which always included a brief sermon on non-violence. Here and in many cities, Jawaharlal's birthday on 14 November was observed as a national celebration. It resulted in a fresh flood of arrests.

In numerous villages of Gujarat, an area which was prosperous by Indian standards, the peasants were refusing land-tax. The Government would demand the tax three months before it was due, then seize the defaulters' farms, and sometimes, if they resisted, lock up the ringleaders in cages. At Borsad eighteen men unconvicted of any definite crime were shut in a cage thirty feet square for several days. Ultimately some of the villages stood deserted, except for a priest tending the temple or a peasant who had come back for a few hours to do some ploughing. Most of the inhabitants had fled from British India into the state of Baroda. Just across the boundary they could be seen camping in shelters made of palm leaves and matting, with their goods piled round, and their pictures of the gods and the Mahatma. 'We won't pay,' they said, 'until he tells us.'

4

From 12 November 1930 to 19 January 1931, the Round Table Conference met in London. Sapru, Jayakar and Jinnah were among the Indian members. It made some progress toward a constitution, fitting in the princely states, and MacDonald voiced a hope that Congress would attend the next session. This hint broke the deadlock. To the stupefaction of a Delhi officialdom under the delusion that it had won, or could win, the Viceroy released most of the Congress leaders. Gandhi came out of Yeravda on 26 January 1931, Independence Day.

The re-legalized Working Committee assembled at the Nehru

home in Allahabad, and agreed to negotiate, though without suspending the campaign. To their great grief Motilal died. He had been ill for some time, and told his son that nothing but a deep conviction would have induced him to go on fighting. The bereavement was more than personal. Gandhi had lost the last of his veteran advisers, and was compelled to feel his way on ground where he was not at home. However, he wrote to his 'Dear Friend' in Delhi suggesting a meeting.

Irwin had to tread carefully. Truth-Force had made him honestly want a settlement. He did not lack courage; he was leaving in a few weeks, and it would have been disastrous to go home in an atmosphere of defeat, under the fire of the Imperialists in his own party. But although he was willing to take risks, his study of Gandhi's character had not equipped him to communicate very freely. On 16 February he received the arch-rebel in a nervous mood, expecting all manner of oriental subtlety. The session took place in the splendid, inconvenient pink palace designed by Lutyens, which had happily been completed, at immense cost, just in time for the beginning of the end. In England, Winston Churchill uttered one of the most notorious and unlucky sentences in his career:

It is alarming and also nauseating to see Mr Gandhi, a seditious Middle Temple lawyer, now posing as a fakir of a type well known in the East, striding half-naked up the steps of the vice-regal palace, while he is still organizing and conducting a defiant campaign of civil disobedience, to parley on equal terms with the representative of the King-Emperor.

A series of bizarre confrontations ensued, while the seven hundred servants and A.D.C's hovered agape in the corridors. On the fourth of them the half-naked fakir was tended by his faithful Mira. He squatted on the floor, and when they took tea she knelt to serve him (with 'some filthy yellow stuff,' as an infuriated bureaucrat put it, 'which he started eating without so much as by your leave'). Mira's august compatriot was too well bred to comment. Once Gandhi evoked a polite laugh by fishing out a bag of salt as a reminder of the Boston Tea Party. The meetings, eight in all, went on for three weeks. Irwin's increasing respect was reinforced by religious sympathy. At one of their partings he said, 'Good night, Mr Gandhi, and my prayers go with you.' Sarojini Naidu spoke of their conference as a dialogue of two Mahatmas. On 5 March they signed what was known as the Delhi Treaty, or the Irwin-Gandhi Pact.

It looked like a compromise rather to Gandhi's disadvantage. He promised to discontinue civil disobedience—the word was carefully chosen—and failed to secure several concessions which he asked for. One was an inquiry into police conduct. The Government was bound to protect its servants, and Irwin brushed the issue aside as 'a matter of comparatively minor importance'. This was too much even for the loyal go-betweens Sapru and Jayakar, but Irwin, with a rare loss of temper, snapped 'Whose side are you on?' and they capitulated. In other respects he was less sensitive and more constructive. The Pact allowed people near the coast to make salt for their own use, and it allowed peaceful picketing. Confiscated property was to be handed back. Non-violent prisoners were to be set free, though not the Garhwali mutineers. A political clause endorsed the federal idea which was taking shape in London. This clause provided for 'safeguards in the interests of India' covering defence, minority rights, and other matters. If one emphasized the 'safeguards', the phrase implied that Britain could keep a substantial foothold. If one emphasized the 'interests of India', it left that question in doubt.

While Gandhi had not gained anything remotely like his eleven points, he had gained what he judged vital—negotiation instead of dictation. The Treaty embodied hitherto unheard-of formulae such as 'it is agreed'. He was not too worried about the safeguards, because he was not rigidly committed to complete independence. Dominion status might do, and some sort of British presence might go on, so long as the British were not present as masters, and India retained the right of secession. Meanwhile he had achieved a crucial change in relationships, giving time for his process of conversion to take effect. The Delhi officialdom, in its fashion, agreed. Ever afterwards it groaned over Irwin's move as the fatal blunder from which the Raj never recovered.

Nehru, however, was shocked by what he regarded as a surrender, and Gandhi had to have a long talk with him. The Congress meeting which had been impossible in December was held in March at Karachi, with Vallabhbhai Patel as president. Its mood at first was resentful. The Sikh bomb-thrower of April 1929 had just been hanged despite Gandhi's intercession, and renewed communal rioting was reported from Cawnpore. Some young left-wingers had the temerity to greet the Mahatma with black flags. Congress approved the pact after acrimonious debate, but reaffirmed the goal of Purna Swaraj, and interpreted the 'interests of India' clause so as to deprive Britain of all real power. It also adopted a charter of human rights proposed by Nehru, which reiterated Gandhi's points but added others of a Socialist kind. Gandhi, whose prestige steadily recovered throughout, was appointed as Congress delegate to the Round Table Conference in London, an arrangement for which MacDonald expressed a wish.

The Congress leaders hardly felt that they had won any victory. But the masses did. S. C. Bose, who distrusted the pact, travelled from Bombay to Delhi with Gandhi and saw ovations such as he had never witnessed before. The Mahatma had judged correctly. By all the rules of politics he had been checked. But in the people's eyes, the plain fact that the Englishman had been brought to negotiate instead of giving orders outweighed any number of details. The released prisoners came home to garlands and civic welcomes. The pickets strolled up and down and grinned at the police.

This elation did not last long. Irwin departed, and the new Viceroy was Lord Willingdon, the same who had been Governor of Bombay during the Kheda Satyagraha of 1918 and emerged with neither success nor credit. He made it clear that he had none of Irwin's respect for Gandhi and wanted as little as possible to do with him. By July the pact showed signs of crumbling because of British violations. Gandhi talked of staying away from the Conference, and even cancelled his passage. Affairs were patched up, unsatisfactorily and unhopefully, but—for the moment—patched up. The truce limped on and he consented to sail, chartering a special train to catch the last available boat.

He left a country for which he had accomplished nothing and everything. Purna Swaraj was nowhere in sight. What he had done was to liberate Indians' minds and teach them not to be afraid. No amount of pressure would push them down to where they had been before. They had picked up the salt and they would never drop it. With two classes of people, the effect of the struggle had been revolutionary. It would have been worth while, as Brailsford observed, if it had done nothing more than emancipate women. And as for the Satyagrahis who embraced non-violence as a faith and suffered for it, they were changed, changed utterly.

The impact on the opposition was less encouraging to Gandhi's beliefs. He had influenced Irwin, but not the permanent Indian Establishment. The servants of Delhi had not been softened by non-violent resistance, they had been brutalized. When Nehru looked in the faces of policemen rushing at him, he saw a hate previously unknown. Officers and district commissioners shared their attitude. Shelley had been right—

> Then they will return with shame
> To the place from which they came—

but the usual effect of the shame was not repentance, it was fury. The utmost that could be claimed was that some scattered Englishmen in India were now prepared to speak up for Gandhi and would not be frozen or frightened into silence.

At the highest levels, those who dealt with the Mahatma had formed an estimate of him which they passed on to their successors. It was a strange estimate, not because it was hostile, but because it was so wrongly hostile. Seemingly almost unaware of his real failings, they invented a bogeyman. He was commonly regarded as a crafty, enigmatic schemer; as a shifty Asiatic whom you never knew where you stood with; as a bogus Messiah who owed his power to willing exploitation of his own cult; as a sophist who obscured issues with mystical fog; as a hypocrite who preached peace while stirring up strife. When these views are placed alongside the mountainous evidence as to his real character, the problem is not to fit them in (which is impossible) but to account for them.

Some sort of objectivity can be reached on such questions as his alleged habit of confounding people by sudden changes. The fact is that when expounding his Absolute, and its social expressions in India, he was constant to the verge of boredom. Truth and Non-Violence, the spinning wheel, Hindu-Muslim unity . . . it is amazing that any man could bring himself to write and say so much for so many years, on the same themes, in the same style. Compared with the party leaders at Westminster he was so consistent as to be almost comic. Even his tactical zigzags were sometimes due, not to a zigzag in the mind, but to a moral rigidity so rock-like that the politicians never imagined he had it in him: over Chauri Chaura, for instance. His bargaining with the English was actually hampered by this. He could have oiled the wheels at any time if he had appreciated their fear that withdrawal would plunge India into chaos, and tried to calm it with concrete plans for the succession. But expediency as an honest motive was beyond him. He thought the choice for the English was the clear-cut thing it would have been for himself. Once they recognized a moral duty to go, they would go. As a result, he tended to treat their objections as excuses—a view which was partly right, but sometimes unfair and harmful. The kind of politician they supposed him to be would have been lavish with specious propositions to suit the moment. He never produced any.

On matters conceived to be secondary, Gandhi could indeed show a Hindu lack of coherence and sequence. He had flashes of insight, and made snap decisions which upset Nehru. 'My aim', he once wrote, 'is not to be consistent with my previous statements on a given question, but to be consistent with the truth as it may present itself to me at a given moment.' Also his pious tone and touches of vanity could be irritating. At times he was like Gladstone, who, it will be recalled, not only kept an ace up his sleeve but insisted that God had put it there. This fault appeared at its worst when Gandhi ascribed a change to a warning from his inner voice, instead of frankly confessing a mistake.

However, the substance of the British indictment is another thing. One cannot seriously believe that he had qualities of which there is no trace in dozens of volumes of articles, speeches and private letters, or in the reminiscences of people who knew him, including the critical and candid. One cannot believe that he was an astute, secretive Machiavelli, when a chorus of disgruntled colleagues headed by S. C. Bose assailed him for being the very opposite—for giving notice of all his moves, for refusing to conspire or plan in advance, for sidetracking and compromising and generally bungling. A foreign contemporary, the Director of the American Civil Liberties Union, expressed the same view of him to Nehru soon after the pact. Nor can one believe that he was devious, when even the changes he did go through were largely an outcome of openness: he thought aloud and in public, so that the trial-and-error which most leaders cover up was exposed to all.

As for his obscuring issues, and cheating the world with mystical phrases, it is salutary to read his words beside those of the British prime ministers of the period. He never discharged smokescreens of verbiage as MacDonald and Baldwin did. Nor was he so much as accused, by any responsible critic, of practising deception on their scale. One of his gravest shortcomings as a religious thinker was the way he over-simplified. On the other counts—for instance, that he posed as a Mahatma to awe a superstitious mob—no more need be said. The burden of proof was on those who made such charges, and they never even produced evidence.

Where did the Delhi demonology come from? Gandhi's biographer B. R. Nanda has remarked acutely that whatever he did, the English turned it against him. If he criticized them he was a demagogue, if he spoke amiably he was a hypocrite. When he launched a campaign he was fanatical, when he tried to modify it he was losing control, when he asked for an interview he was luring the Viceroy into a trap. He was mulish when firm, slippery when flexible. If he asserted himself he was a megalomaniac; if not, he was yielding to extremists.

This is a familiar frame of mind—that of the person who is out to smash, and who switches from argument to argument, attacking on an endless series of contradictory lines, the sole axiom being that he dare not concede a single point to the enemy. Englishmen could not admit that Gandhi succeeded essentially because he was in the right. Therefore he had to be a sort of malignant chameleon outsmarting plain, blunt John Bull. A ludicrous by-product was a partial adoption of the myth by Communists.*

But if Gandhi faced insuperable barriers among the English in India, his prospects among the English in England were brighter. He had friends there who did not fail him. MacDonald's mind had been warmed in advance by Olivier and Henry Salt—in fact, it was Salt who had planted the idea of inviting him in MacDonald's head. Admirers, especially among the clergy, were speaking out. People in general were not unkindly disposed. The stark outlines of the struggle had been softened for them by distance and censorship. Films of lathi charges were never shown, newspaper dispatches were kept in a minor key. Now the curtain seemed to be coming down with credit on both sides It had not been pleasant to persecute a saint, but Britain had kept her moral end up by supplying a saint of her own to do the persecuting. Lord Irwin had 'tamed' Gandhi. Having saved face, he had acted with generosity. The rebel was not

---

* See the paragraph by Palme Dutt quoted in the front of this book. Some of the 'expert' assessments betray an ignorance—and an unwillingness to look for truth—which would be incredible if it were not documented. I once talked with a former member of the administrative set who gave me what purported to be the real lowdown on the Mahatma, and then, when I happened to mention the Salt March, asked 'What was that?'

only responding but helping to maintain order. Ellen Wilkinson described him as Britain's best policeman.

Toward the end of August he arrived in Bombay on his way to London. The crowds cheered. His own feelings, fresh from a forbidding encounter with the new Viceroy, were apprehensive. But still, he was on his way.

XV

Conversion

1

Gandhi travelled with seven companions. He himself was the sole Congress delegate. Britain would have allowed more, but the Working Committee preferred to stay at their posts in case of trouble. If any agreement were reached in London they could be sent for. He took his two secretaries Mahadev and Pyarelal, and his son Devadas. G. D. Birla went to the Conference as an industrial spokesman. Mrs Naidu and Pandit Malaviya joined the party in their respective private capacities, and Mira in her own indefinable one. She was now a full member of Bapu's inner circle. He had abandoned all efforts to keep her at a distance when her mother's death left her grief-stricken and isolated. After an emotional meeting in June, he had tried hard to believe that she was devoted to what he stood for rather than himself, and written her a remarkable letter.

> You are on the brain. I look about me, and miss you. I open the *charkha* and miss you. So on and so forth. . . . All the time you were squandering your love on me personally, I felt guilty of misappropriation. And I exploded on the slightest pretext. Now that you are not with me, my anger turns itself upon me for having given you all those terrible scoldings. But I was on a bed of hot ashes all the while I was accepting your service. You will truly serve me by joyously serving the cause.

So here she was: Mirabehn, as her complete acceptance now made her for all.

At Mani Bhavan stacks of gifts were awaiting him. He ran a jaundiced eye over a whole bazaar of socks, shawls, bags, and much else. Mirabehn sorted them out and packed. On 29 August they sailed aboard S.S. *Rajputana*—second class, at Gandhi's insistence. He was annoyed to find how much luggage they still had, and

303

positively scathing about a folding camp bed ('I thought it was a bundle of hockey sticks'). When the ship put in at Aden he received a purse of 328 guineas from the Indian colony, and sent seven trunks back to India. Throughout the passage he kept to his normal routine of early rising, prayer, spinning, and open-air life. His party disembarked at Marseilles and went on by train, reaching London on 12 September.

The Conference was to be held at St James's Palace. Andrews and Polak, both in London, had been discussing the Mahatma's accommodation with his former guest Muriel Lester. She wanted him to stay at her Kingsley Hall settlement in Powis Road, Poplar. They agreed that he would like this, but thought the place too far out. While the prospect of five-mile journeys back and forth did not disturb him, he saw that some of his visitors might object. The final arrangement was that he should stay at the Hall himself among the English poor, but hire an office in Knightsbridge and station his secretaries there.

Kingsley Hall still exists, with a blue commemorative plaque. It is a square, flat-roofed brick building, in what was then a modern style. Today the Council flats tower above, but many of the old two-storey terraces are standing in the neighbourhood, and the 1931 aspect can be recaptured. When Gandhi arrived, it was soon clear that in terms of news value he surpassed everyone but the Prince of Wales. Pressmen surged into the Hall and filed astonishing stories, reporting, for instance, that a flock of goats was on the roof. Many Indians had been anxious over his costume—loincloth or *dhoti*, shawl, sandals, exactly as at home. This looked all the more grotesque because he now wore glasses. But it was not a mistake, it heightened his vividness. The fashionable plus-fours of that year prompted one of his few outright jokes: 'You people wear plus-fours, I wear minus-fours.' Among the journalists he was always in superb form. An interview that was caught for a few seconds on film looks like a comedy act with the reporter as straight man.

The day after his advent, the Columbia Broadcasting System elbowed its way into Kingsley Hall to enable him to speak to America. He sat unruffled eating his supper while technicians rushed to and fro with their apparatus. At 6.30 they were on the air. The harassed Miss Lester stammered an introduction with an eye on the door Gandhi was supposed to come through, and at the last moment he came through it. The radio microphone was strange to him. 'Do I talk into this thing?' he said, heard by millions of listeners. His broadcast, delivered without notes, appealed skilfully to American opinion. He spoke of India's past glories which could only be recovered through freedom, and stressed the unique nature of the struggle, its moral value, its significance for a world sick of bloodshed. His voice was distinct, but it went out with a background of tiny staccato noises caused by swings and seesaws in a playground close by. Afterwards he addressed a Kingsley Hall audience on prayer, and then drove off to meet the Prime Minister.

For several days the goodwill ran high. The weekly *Truth* indeed called him a humbug, the *Children's Newspaper* a simpleton. Churchill denounced him as an enemy of Britain, the Communists as a British catspaw. But such voices were less in evidence than those of another kind. Laurence Housman welcomed him at Friends' House. Cordial letters piled up, one of them from an Accrington textile worker, who assured him that Lancashire would be glad to see him despite the effects of the cloth boycott. He visited the House of Commons, talked to a gathering of Labour M.P.s in a committee room, and led them in prayer on the spot. He asked to see Henry Salt; the vegetarian presented himself, discoursed on ailments as ageing people will, but seemed rejuvenated. Meanwhile the journalists were discovering Mirabehn, who did the Mahatma's household chores. Men found her amusing, women less so.

At St James's Palace, however, the magic faded. Gandhi made an excellent first speech—again without a prepared text, in defiance of entreaties from Birla. Despite the pressures on him, he remained alert and punctual through most of the sessions. His daily drives gave him time to doze. But when actually conferring, alone in a foreign atmosphere, he was swamped.

British politics were working against him. MacDonald was still in office,. but as head of the National Government, expressive of a move to the right; and during the Conference a landslide election made it virtually Tory. The economic crisis was so acute that it was hard to arouse much concern for India. Moreover, Churchill and kindred spirits argued that loss of control over such a large portion of the Empire would be a deadly blow to hopes of recovery.

All the British emphasis lay on India's divisions. The Conference was a hubbub of noisy sectional interests, and stage-managed as such. The 112 participants included 23 from the princely states and 64 from British India, yet the peasant majority was unrepresented.

While the press recognized Gandhi as the chief nationalist spokesman, it stressed that he was only the leader of a party, and described this as a 'Hindu' party. The Government maintained that all minorities—Muslims, Sikhs, Untouchables, Christians, Parsees, Europeans—must be protected and satisfied before self-rule could be granted, and that any federal scheme must have a place for the princes. Gandhi believed that India's communal problems were due mainly to the divide-and-rule policy of the British regime. Swaraj could not wait till they were solved, it was the prerequisite of their solution. But the Conference was packed with carefully chosen minority figures, invited by Delhi and eager to oppose him. Even his old comrade Shaukat Ali was among them. He had no simple answer to their demands.

One issue on which he took a stand was the hardy principle of communal electorates. This provided that in assemblies based on a wide franchise, the Hindu population should elect one bloc of members, the Muslims another bloc, and so forth. It negated the Congress doctrine of non-sectarian national unity. Gandhi was willing to contemplate multi-member constituencies with reserved seats in a set proportion. Thus a mixed area might have two Hindu members and one Muslim. But a single electorate of all voters, Hindu and Muslim, should choose all three.

The question was taking a grimmer turn. A new plan envisaged that the fifty or sixty million Untouchables should have their own electorate distinct from the Hindus, a measure which would perpetuate their status. Here Gandhi was firm. 'If I was the only person to resist this thing,' he declared, 'I would resist it with my life.' But the Untouchables' spokesman at the Conference, Dr B. R. Ambedkar, favoured the plan. Ambedkar was a lawyer, a man of massive presence and stubborn intelligence. Educated at a Bombay missionary college and Columbia University, he had risen on a wave of Untouchable restlessness. The outcastes' political apathy had been jolted by the Christians who gave Ambedkar himself his start. Converts managed to rise in the social scale. The effect on their brethren was not mass conversion, but an ambition to go the same way by some other route. With that object, Ambedkar was trying to organize them into a party, virulently anti-Hindu. Gandhi urged that the only right answer was for caste Hindus to relent and absorb these people into their own community. However, when he clashed with Ambedkar—one of the few prominent Indians who loathed him—he created an unhappy impression of claiming to know what the Untouchables wanted better than their own leader. A similar refusal to admit that the Muslim League spoke for Muslims reinforced that impression. Jinnah said the League did speak for Muslims, and blocked him completely.

The outcome was a Minorities Pact. The Muslim spokesmen, Dr Ambedkar, and others, agreed to treat with Britain for separate electorates. Gandhi's counter-arguments were courageous, but tended to sound like mere debating points. He observed that in Europe, despite its class conflict, no question arose of separate electorates for the workers. Again, when MacDonald added up the minorities and said they amounted to 46 per cent of the population, he retorted that women were 50 per cent yet did not want a separate electorate. He was more right than wrong. Nevertheless the dispute damaged him. It seemed to give the lie to his pretensions to speak for India, or even for a majority. Onlookers failed to grasp that most of his Indian opponents—not all, but most—were men of straw.* The English could acknowledge that his ideals were high without feeling bound to respond to them, and then turn with relief to good fellows like the Aga Khan.

But Gandhi was far from downcast. Politics of the sort he heard at the Palace were not his major concern. The real conference, for him, was a grassroots dialogue with the people of England. Out-side official business he maintained a schedule which often cut his time for sleep to three hours. Kingsley Hall was much more than his lodging. He got up for prayers at four, and refused to adjust his watch for the end of Summer Time, after which he was dragging Mira and the rest out of bed at three. Some of the colossal resulting day was spent in spinning, or debating Hinduism with the resident social workers (he recommended, as ever, Max Müller). But more was taken up with expeditions and meetings. At 5.30 a.m. he strolled with Miss Lester through the grimy streets—Eagling Road, Three Mill Lane, Bow Bridge—and beside the canal. She took him into working-class homes, where the wives proudly showed him their rabbits and chickens, their pianos, and other treasures. He asked about the men's work, the rent, the drains, the dole.

* Whereas the earlier struggle had provoked anti-Gandhi books by Indians of unquestioned standing, the only such book to appear in the second struggle was a crazy tract by a nonentity, alleging that the cloth boycott was a Jewish plot and the Mahatma was an agent of the Elders of Zion.

The impression he usually made was good: 'just like one of us'. A labourer praised him as 'a fine chap, laughing and jolly', and admired him for getting up so early. He met countless children, with whom he made friends as easily as in India. They called him 'Uncle', and one urchin amused him by shouting 'Hey, Gandhi, where's your trousers?' His non-violence inspired some rousing arguments about what to do when another boy hit you. Finding that 2 October was his birthday, a group of children presented him with a basket containing two woolly dogs, three pink candles, a tin plate, a blue pencil, and some sweets.

His impact on the East-Enders was not something gradually built up. It was almost instantaneous. Very early in his stay he walked into a Saturday-night social at Kingsley Hall, an uproarious affair with a hundred guests. Miss Lester led him across the floor to meet a blind man, and complete silence fell while everyone watched. Women came forward lifting their babies for him to touch and hold. At another social he was urged to join in country-dancing, and did, to the dismay of a puritan.

He was well aware of the frightful level of unemployment, and the fact that his own cloth boycott was making it worse. Welsh miners came to Kingsley Hall to talk with him. He avoided lecturing proletarians on it directly, and perhaps it was as well that he did, because his private opinion was that they should refuse the dole as an insult and demand public works. But he tried to plant the Indian case in their minds. He spent a lively week-end in Lancashire, the area hardest hit by his policies. The mill-hands listened to him without hostility. An unemployed man remarked, 'If I were in India I'd say the same.' At the Greenfield Mill in Darwen, Gandhi posed for a photograph squeezed into a wildly incongruous group of hearty women, holding his arms and cheering.

By Government order, two bulky detectives from Scotland Yard protected him on his tours. He chatted with them, and kept on cordial terms through a round of meetings with public figures. Winston Churchill would not see him, but Randolph interviewed him. He visited Lord Irwin and Harold Laski. He renewed his acquaintance with Smuts, who happened to be in London, and who advised the Government to make its peace with him—advice which was suppressed in the papers. Lloyd George invited him to Churt and they talked for three hours; the eminent Celt, however, was impressed chiefly by the entry of an unknown black cat, who sat on

Gandhi's lap and then disappeared. Lady Astor was more reward-ing. She took the offensive, informing Gandhi sternly that the British had 'created something' in India. He replied by listing all that the Indians had created in the past fourteen years—the village revival, the improvements in temperance and drainage, the emanci-pation of women—and the last shot went home to her.

In London he had conversations with Evelyn Underhill, whose poems he had read in prison; with Krishnamurti, Annie Besant's young protégé who had resisted her efforts to make a Messiah of him; with Brailsford, whose reports on rebel India were helping to establish a truer picture; and with Bernard Shaw, who looked in at the Knightsbridge office. Shaw remembered the 1880s and knew that they were a pair, the two principal products of that remote ferment. With unaccustomed modesty he called himself 'Mahatma Minor' and Gandhi 'Mahatma Major'. They had a wide-ranging and hilarious chat which left Mahatma Major a little dazed. When asked for his own impression, Shaw answered: 'You might as well ask for someone's impression of the Himalayas.' Another who desired a meeting was Charlie Chaplin. Gandhi was not a filmgoer and could not place the name, but he liked what he heard. They met at the East End home of an Indian doctor and exchanged congenial views on the machine age. Chaplin's next film, *Modern Times,* bore a distinct Gandhian imprint.

An odder, almost surrealist occasion was a visit to Buckingham Palace. Amid a flurry of speculation as to what he would wear, Gandhi went to tea with George V and Queen Mary. He was dressed as usual. The King made solemn remarks about the wrong-ness of subverting 'my Empire', which Gandhi tactfully turned aside. When the ordeal was over, somebody asked him if he really thought he had had enough clothes on. 'It was quite all right,' he said; 'the King had enough on for both of us.'

His ventures farther afield included a trip to Canterbury, where Hewlett Johnson gave him a pleasant time. At Cambridge he wanted to be shown round Trinity because it was the college of Andrews and Nehru. At Oxford he stayed with Professor Lindsay, the Master of Balliol, and had a mixed reception from a party of dons. Among these were his early admirer Gilbert Murray, and Professor Edward Thompson, the future biographer of Tagore. They put him through an oral examination lasting three hours without shaking him. Gilbert Murray's enthusiasm had waned;

Thompson subsequently observed that he now understood why the Athenians made Socrates drink the hemlock. Lindsay, on the other hand, was not averse to using the word 'saint'.

He addressed the boys at Eton, but greatly preferred the Montessori Training College, where he at last discovered a system of education which he could digest himself. Maria Montessori addressed him as 'Noble Master', and he had to cope with a good many persons of the kind who employ such phrases. Through Kingsley Hall there tramped a procession of Swedish missionaries, German Anthroposophists, veterans of Tolstoy Farm, prohibition zealots. Americans and French and Swiss turned up at all hours.

Also he was a star speaker at meetings, dozens of them. Socialists and Quakers, Indians and M.P.s, students' unions and Women's Institutes and the London School of Economics—all pressed in with invitations which he accepted. The American Journalists' Association staged a meatless banquet at the Savoy. He was guest of honour at a luncheon with Fenner Brockway in the chair. He appeared, of course, at the London Vegetarian Society, with Henry Salt on the platform beside him, and startled some of the vegetarians by drinking cider. When he spoke on British-Indian relations, his message was always the same. He wanted an honourable partnership, with India in the Commonwealth, but by choice and not compulsion. His public utterances, however, were less effective than his personal contacts. His level and restrained style, so potent in India among spellbound adorers, struck audiences in England as merely tame; and by his reluctance to be amusing in a set speech, he threw away one of his assets.

Yet where his subject demanded a wholly grave treatment, the best of him did come through. The Columbia Gramophone Company asked him to make a recording, and he read an article on God which he had written for *Young India*. The record can still be heard at Mani Bhavan. Here and there it achieves a rhythm and power that place Gandhi among the major prophets.

> In the midst of death, life persists. In the midst of untruth, truth persists. In the midst of darkness, light persists. Hence I gather that God is Life, Truth, Light. He is Love. He is the Supreme Good. But he is no God who merely satisfies the intellect, if he ever does. God to be God must rule the heart and transform it.

2

He stayed in England twelve weeks. His performance at St James's Palace was summed up by Andrews as a magnificent failure. Others said it was simply a failure. In the end he neither gained anything nor yielded anything. With the new Secretary of State for India, Sir Samuel Hoare, he was on terms of mutual respect. But Sir Samuel pushed ahead with his own constitution-making. This provided for a Federal Council based on a jigsaw of electorates and special interests. It would be free to govern India, so long as it had no control over the armed forces or foreign policy or four-fifths of the budget, and accepted a heavy over-representation of Muslims and princes, plus a viceregal veto.

The deadlock clouded Gandhi's success with the public, but did not blot it out. Henceforth there would always be an abundance of English people who knew he was not an impossible fanatic. Few took his side, but a much larger number would object to any attempt to crush him. His well-wishers complained that the press had fastened on incidentals—the loincloth, goat's milk and so on. But in the age of the Image and the Hidden Persuaders it is no longer so certain that the bias harmed him. Cartoons were good-humoured.

On 5 December he left England for the last time. The party travelled via Paris to Switzerland to visit Romain Rolland, who had never actually met his Mahatma. Rolland lived at Villeneuve on Lake Léman. The announcement of Gandhi's advent exposed him to a barrage of letters. They came from milkmen offering to supply 'the King of India', from a Swiss band volunteering to play under his window, from Italians seeking supernatural tips for the next lottery. Hotels were crammed and journalists encamped round the house.

On a wet Sunday evening Gandhi arrived with Mirabehn, Devadas and the secretaries, and the Scotland Yard detectives, who were still with him by his own request. Rolland afterwards described that moment:

> The little man, bespectacled and toothless, was wrapped in his white burnous, but his legs, thin as heron's stilts, were bare. His shaven head, with its few coarse hairs, was uncovered and wet with rain. He came to me with a dry laugh, his mouth open like a good dog panting, and flung an arm around me.

The next day was a silent Monday and Rolland held forth while his guest scribbled notes. On Tuesday they conversed. On the following two days Gandhi addressed audiences in Lausanne and Geneva, standing up well to prolonged heckling. He also expounded Truth-Force to the pacifist Pierre Ceresole, suggesting that it might be the 'moral equivalent for war' desired by William James. On Friday and Saturday the colloquy with Rolland continued.

They discussed the state of Europe, and art, and non-violence, and crime, and labour, and God—an eternal principle, Gandhi said, not a person in the anthropomorphic sense. Rolland found his outlook, in some respects, a trifle bleak: he agreed that the search for truth should bring joy, but had to be prompted into doing so. On the Saturday evening they turned to music. The Mahatma revealed an expert knowledge of Indian religious chants, which he had been unobtrusively collecting for years. But as for Beethoven, although Mira had come to Rolland and thence to Sabarmati because of him, Gandhi had never bothered to make his acquaintance. Would his biographer supply the defect? Rolland played a piano transcription of the Andante from the Fifth Symphony. He followed with Gluck's 'Elysian Fields' as an encore. Apparently these pieces reflected his own concept of Gandhi. One notes the limitations of the pacifist. If Beethoven's symphonies contain any echo of this particular Great Soul and his career, it is surely in the first movement of the Ninth.

From Villeneuve Gandhi went on to Rome. Prudently declining an invitation to be the guest of the Italian Government, he stayed with a friend of Rolland's. But Mussolini, scenting possibilities in the demise of the British Empire, summoned him to an audience. It took up, and wasted, a quarter of an hour. Gandhi disliked the dictator's melodramatic gaze and array of weapons. Mussolini asked his opinion of the Fascist state, and he replied, 'You are building a house of cards.' More amusing if not more appropriate events were a Rome-Naples rugger match and a parade of Fascist youth who fired a salute. Tolstoy's daughter was in the city, and he sought her out. During the call a basket of figs from the Queen of Italy was delivered to him by a princess. The Pope would not see him, probably for political reasons. But he made the round of the Vatican, savouring the library and pausing before a life-size crucifix in the Sistine Chapel. The figure fascinated him. He studied it from various angles for several minutes. 'That was a very wonderful crucifix,' he remarked as they walked on. 'One can't help being moved to tears.'

It was a premonition, perhaps. They embarked aboard S.S. *Pilsna* at Brindisi on 14 December, saying good-bye to the detectives, but not to a Swiss couple who wanted to see India and whom, on impulse, Gandhi invited to come with him. Trouble began during the voyage. The *Giornale d'Italia* published a faked interview, putting unpleasant threats in his mouth about using boycotts to worsen the British depression. This was quoted in *The Times* and destroyed much of the goodwill he had toiled to create. Mirabehn—who was handling most of his press relations—cabled a denial from Aden, but, as usual, the truth did not overtake the falsehood. Two years later the story was still drearily turning up in his correspondence with Hoare.

Their ship docked at Bombay on the morning of the 28th. Gandhi drove to Mani Bhavan like a victor, past decorated buildings and roaring crowds held back with difficulty by Congress Volunteers. It was another of his silent Mondays, but he had to make an exception. The tone of his press conference was buoyant. Then he joined the Working Committee in private, and heard what had been happening while he was at sea. It was now plain that Congress had been living for months in a fool's paradise. While the Round Table lulled suspicion, Lord Willingdon had been planning a counter-stroke. He entirely lacked Irwin's nuances. Gandhi, for him, was simply the opportunist and fraud of official myth, using Congress as a tool. Sir Samuel Hoare warned that this was a mistake which would recoil. But the National Government, after smashing Labour in the autumn election, authorized him to smash Congress.

During December Delhi had begun employing emergency powers in three areas—the North-West Frontier Province, the United Provinces, and Bengal. In the first of these Ghaffar Khan, the most resolutely non-violent of all Gandhists, was charged with insurrection. In the second, Congress backing of four local rent strikes was answered by confiscations of property, arrests without warrant, and imprisonments without trial. In the third, minor terrorist outbreaks were made the pretext for similar measures. Bengal had a new Governor, Sir John Anderson, with experience of Black and Tan work in Ireland.

The Irwin-Gandhi Pact was dead. Willingdon accused Congress of aspiring to become an alternative government. It did; but so does any opposition party. To infer the propriety of annihilation was to assert undisguised autocracy. Where Irwin had balked, Willingdon went forward. On the day of Gandhi's return, Ghaffar Khan and Nehru were already in prison, and the Government was considering his own exile to the Andaman Islands. That evening he spoke at Azad Maidan to a crowd of two hundred thousand, reaching all of them through loudspeakers. He referred to the arrests and ordinances with a rare touch of bitter humour: 'I take it these are all Christmas gifts from Lord Willingdon, our Christian Viceroy.' Yet he made a bid to resuscitate the pact. Willingdon's secretary offered him an interview, provided nothing was said about the ordinances. He tried again, passing on some resolutions of the Working Committee, which showed that it might be hard to prevent a resumption of civil disobedience. Though he undertook to see that no resumption occurred so long as they were talking, the Viceroy treated his warning as a threat, and broke off all correpondence.

On 2 January 1932 Gandhi composed a public statement. The Government, he declared, had banged the door in his face. A fiery ordeal lay ahead. But India's quarrel was with measures, not men. Non-violence must be observed in thought, word and deed. Through a journalist he appealed to his 'numerous American friends' to exert their influence. It was his first hint at a factor which was to assume steadily greater importance. Moderates and businessmen besieged Mani Bhavan with ideas for mediation. Most of them had to be dealt with by Vallabhbhai Patel. The Mahatma himself spent 3 January working on messages to various groups, and writing letters, including one to Tagore, whom he urged to give his best to the 'sacrificial fire'. He assured an English clergyman that he harboured no illwill toward Englishmen, and found a moment to send engraved watches to his Scotland Yard detectives as keepsakes.

In the small hours of 4 January, two police cars pulled up in front of Mani Bhavan. Officers climbed to the terrace, where Gandhi was asleep in a tent. Devadas ran ahead to wake him. He smiled without speaking; it was Monday again. Mirabehn packed his jail kit—sandals, a mattress, a portable spinning wheel, extra clothing and food. Detained as before under the 1827 regulation, he went off to Yeravda with Patel as his fellow-prisoner. Mahadev Desai and Vinoba Bhave were arrested about the same time. Vinoba was kept apart, but after several weeks Mahadev was allowed to join the Mahatma.

To begin with, this term was like its predecessors. Gandhi finished a commentary on the Ashram vows which he had started in 1930, entitled *From Yeravda Mandir*. He read Upton Sinclair's *The Wet Parade* and Kingsley's *Westward Ho!* He also read many papers, though he was no longer an editor or contributor, because *Young India* and *Navajivan* were suppressed. But then a subtle difference crept in. Far off, not very effectively yet, but visibly, Truth-Force was sowing the disquiet it was intended to sow. People in Britain who had found the Mahatma entertaining and thought-provoking could not feel easy at his going home into a trap. A sort of anthology which Andrews had finally compiled was becoming known. Pamphlets were calling for his release. One was written by Polak and published by the Quakers. Another, by Carl Heath, hailed him as the prophet of a new type of society, compared Willingdon most unfavourably with Irwin, and proposed a campaign by Christians to deliver the Hindu who was the best Christian of all. Ellen Wilkinson went to India with a delegation, and reported indignantly in the *Manchester Guardian*.

For a while these rumblings of conscience carried no weight. On 4 January, as Gandhi vanished into Yeravda, the Viceroy had struck at his followers with terrific force. Months of meticulous preparation bore fruit overnight. At home, Hoare told the Commons that there would be no second drawn battle. A vocal group of Conservatives, headed by Churchill, praised the new measures as the firmest since the Mutiny. In a single day all the leaders of Congress were rounded up. Congress itself was outlawed with all its subsidiary bodies. The Government assumed powers to sequester its property, bank balances, and schools. Its press was banned. The postal services were denied to its officers. These blows, which were accompanied with loud protestations of civic virtue in the face of a menace, appeared to be mortal. Although Congress just survived, it had to resort to secrecy, thus belying its Gandhist principles.

Civil disobedience broke out on a large scale, but in a changed spirit. This time Delhi held the initiative. The Satyagrahis were merely resisting. Most of them abstained from violence; the labour militants who might have done otherwise were still undergoing their long-drawn trial at Meerut. The cloth boycott, the tax strikes, the defiance of forest laws and salt laws, were desperately renewed. In January and February, authorities armed with a 'Civil Disobedience Manual' convicted 32,600 people of political offences. They treated entire districts as hostile, and forced the population to carry identity cards and submit to curfews. The victims of the lathi charges included Nehru's old mother, whom a policeman beat over the head and left unconscious by the road. A month later she visited her son in prison. She was bandaged and radiant.

After February activity slowly waned. Arrests fell off. In the prisons, whipping and hard labour and calculated brutality to women induced about one in ten to recant. Resisters who could stand everything else were sometimes unnerved by prison lavatories —rows of holes so close together that each user touched the next, who might be a criminal or pervert. Outside, censorship and the internment of journalists left Satyagrahis in the dark. A new Government tactic split their ranks. This was the wholesale seizure of property, not simply their own, but that of their relatives and parents. Guilt by association was now part of Indian law. Several ashrams founded in imitation of Gandhi's were dissolved. Sabarmati itself was spared, but Kasturbai had her first taste of jail.

Mirabehn remained free for a time and issued news releases. However, when her exposure of certain police practices led to questions in Parliament, she received a three months' sentence. She wrote to Bapu asking his advice about reading. He recommended the Hindu epics. The *Ramayana* had lately been enjoying a vogue, because it could be construed as patriotic allegory. Rama stood for Gandhi, the demon Ravana was the British Raj, and so on. But comforting fables were no substitute for success. Ravana was winning.

And then he made a false move. In March, the British Government had announced that it was drawing up its new scheme for communal electorates. Gandhi warned Hoare that he would hold out against an Untouchable electorate to the limit—if necessary, by fasting to death. Sir Samuel told him that nothing was settled and his views would be considered. On 17 August, however, Mac-Donald published a Communal Award defining separate electorates for Hindus, Muslims, Sikhs, Europeans . . . and Untouchables. Gandhi wrote: 'I have to resist your decision with my life.' On 20 September he would begin starving himself. The Prime Minister answered that the Award took his protest into account. It did not separate the Untouchables completely. Each of them would have two votes, one in his special group, the other with the Hindus. The Government had debated whether it would be enough to reserve some seats on the legislatures for what it called the Depressed Classes. But its judgement was that without a distinct electorate, such members would be dependent on the votes of caste Hindus, and therefore hamstrung.

Gandhi wrote back that the question was one of religious principle. He objected to the whole communal scheme, but the Untouchable part was the breaking-point, a classic Satyagraha issue. Segregation undid all the work of Hindu reformers and could not be compensated by extra votes. The outcaste status would be written into the constitution. Therefore, his fast must proceed. He was presently to find support in surprising quarters—from Lionel Curtis, for instance, his opponent in South Africa, who described the communal policy as the worst British blunder. But at the time he seemed once again to have committed hara-kiri. MacDonald was puzzled and offended, Ambedkar and many more condemned the fast as a stunt to recapture the limelight. Andrews noted with distress how it was resented in England as blackmail. Nehru suffered another of his qualms about the Mahatma's conduct. As he put it in his autobiography, 'I felt angry with him at his religious and sentimental approach to a political question.' Surely, moreover, Gandhi was diverting energy and attention from the main battle? If he died, India would be left desolate to no purpose. But after a day or two Nehru came out of his depression. The Mahatma had proved before that he had a knack of doing the right thing at the psychological moment. His lieutenant waited.

The Mahatma meanwhile was busy explaining that his fast was not meant to coerce the British, but to sting Hindu consciences and inspire action. MacDonald had implied that Britain would accept an alternative solution if Hindus and Untouchables could agree on it. Even before the 20th, signs that Gandhi had judged correctly began to appear. An Untouchable leader, M. C. Rajah, broke away from Ambedkar and supported him, as did Muslim spokesmen. The moderate Sapru urged Delhi to release him. Rajendra Prasad called upon Hindus to let Untouchables into their temples and schools. Pandit Malaviya convened a conference. Rajagopalachari summoned all India to pray and fast on the 20th.

The fatal day dawned. Gandhi wrote to Tagore saying he would 'enter the fiery gates' at noon, and asking for the Poet's blessing or criticism as he saw fit. It was a blessing which he received. Tagore's mind was already made up. Before the staff and students at

Shantiniketan, he rose in a black robe and spoke of the sin of division for which Mahatmaji might soon sacrifice his life. If Mahatmaji died because Hindus acquiesced in the Award, with its institutionalized affront to humanity, they would all share the guilt of murder.

Tagore was asking, in effect, for a miracle. Yet it was happening as he talked. In Allahabad the keepers of twelve temples had opened them to the outcastes. The Kalighat Temple in Calcutta and the Ram Mandir in Benares followed almost at once. Day by day the papers carried reports of hundreds more precincts, in the princely states as well as British India, which the excluded were entering. In Bombay a women's organization arranged ballots in front of seven temples, and the vote for admission was 24,797 to 445. Caste Hindus ate in the streets of Delhi with Untouchable scavengers and sweepers. Resolutions against discrimination were rushed to Yeravda and piled five feet high in the yard. Nehru, confirmed in his faith once more, could only marvel. 'What a magician, I thought, was this little man sitting in Yeravda Prison, and how well he knew how to pull the strings that move people's hearts.'

Gandhi reclined on a white iron cot in the shade of a mango tree, with Mahadev Desai sitting near, and Mrs Naidu in attendance. He read and wrote and sipped water, with a dash of salt or soda bicarbonate. His wife was transferred from Sabarmati Jail to be with him. 'Again the same story!' she murmured as she approached.

He weakened before their eyes, under a psychological as well as a physical strain. A group of Hindus parleyed frantically with Ambedkar. Birla was one of them. They met first at his Bombay house, afterwards moving to Poona to be near the prison. Together with Rajendra Prasad, Sapru and others, he groped for a formula. In the end it was Sapru who hit on it. The upshot, after much consultation with the sinking Mahatma, was a new pact to replace the Communal Award. The Depressed Classes were to have 147 reserved seats in the provincial legislatures (MacDonald had proposed 71, Ambedkar wanted 197). Hindus and Depressed Classes would vote together. But all Untouchable candidates would be chosen in primary elections by Untouchables only. This plan would prevent caste Hindus from keeping the more active ones out of politics. The bargaining was tough and complex. Sometimes Gandhi seemed to be offering more than Ambedkar asked. As usual, he would yield surprisingly on details, so long as he saved the principle.

On 25 September the Poona Pact was ratified at a joint conference. Its text was wired to London, where Andrews and Polak were to submit it to the appropriate ministers. The day was Sunday and the ministers were out of town; MacDonald was at a funeral in Sussex. He came back to No. 10 and conferred with Hoare till midnight. Gandhi was dying. At last, during the morning of the 26th (afternoon in India), simultaneous announcements in London and Delhi approved the pact. Tagore came to Yeravda and sang a hymn as Kasturbai raised a glass of orange juice to her husband's lips.

For the first time Gandhi had imposed his will on a British Government. When the entire fabric of nationalism was crumbling, he had halted the Imperial trend toward fragmentation and demoralization. He might or might not have achieved the same political end without fasting. At least the fast gave urgency; MacDonald recoiled from the prospect of his dying in a British jail, the Indian negotiators recoiled from the prospect of his dying anywhere. But the question is pointless. It was not the pact as such that mattered, it was the lightning-bolt of truth. He had revived spirits. Untouchability was not dead, but it would never be the same. An India going to pieces under pressure had pulled itself together and again had a moral advantage over its masters. The Viceroy had failed, as, indeed, anyone so stubbornly and wilfully wrong about an opponent deserved to fail.

This crisis was an event of a kind already noted in Gandhi's writings, a sudden twist at the moment when all is lost. According to his theory, such twists are inherent in Satyagraha because of the contact with God, who takes charge when the human pattern dissolves in exhaustion. The reversal in 1932 was a proof so dazzling that he took it as a revelation. For the time being, his war on Untouchability should take precedence over other pursuits. This was the inward revolution which India needed.

Henceforth he called the Untouchables 'Harijans', Children of God—a term which has passed into India's vocabulary, though it has not always been popular with the Children themselves. Still in Yeravda, he founded an eight-page weekly, *Harijan*, which became his new mouthpiece, and a Harijan Sevak Sangh or Order for the Service of Harijans. Here Birla came into his own. On Untouchability the millionaire was whole-heartedly with the Mahatma. Another follower who rose to distinction on this issue was

Chhaganlal Joshi, a Bombay sociologist who had walked beside Gandhi on the Salt March. In February 1933 the weekly and the organization made their début. The first number of *Harijan* contained articles by Gandhi and Mahadev, a poem by Tagore, even a note (though a surly note) from Ambedkar. The Sevak Sangh was launched with Birla as President and a governing body of caste Hindus. However, it drew in Harijans later.

This new programme settled the fate of the Ashram. During the wave of punitive expropriations Gandhi had thought of disbanding it, not caring to keep a home when so many were losing theirs. Then, in April 1933, scandalous rumours reached him about a visit by a too-charming American lady. He wrote to Mirabehn lamenting the rarity of complete *brahmacharis*, and affirming his matured doctrine on sex:

> How to use the organs of generation? By transmitting the most creative energy that we possess from creating counterparts of our flesh into creating constructive work for the whole of life, i.e. for the soul. We have to rein in the animal passion and change it into celestial passion. . . .
>
> The burden of the Divine Song is not 'fly from the battle' but 'face it without attachment'. Therefore you and I and every one of us have to stand unmoved in the midst of all kinds of men and women.

At Sabarmati not all had stood unmoved. However, he could now wind up the experiment without admitting defeat. The ashramites could hand over to the Harijans.

Slowly, a bargain was taking shape. The Government would let him go if he would concentrate on the Children of God. His progress toward freedom was halting. There were further fasts (not 'unto death'), including a long one in May for self-purification, and various releases and re-arrests, none too creditable. But he was convinced of the divine presence. He ascribed the May fast to a mystical command unique in his life. At the end of July, temporarily at liberty, he dissolved the Ashram as a community and handed over its buildings and land to the Harijan Sevak Sangh. Thereafter it functioned mainly as a trade school. A march with the departing inmates led to a further imprisonment, but on 23 August his faith was justified. He was out of custody—officially, on medical grounds.

His new base was Vinoba's ashram at Wardha. For ten months,

beginning on 7 November, he went on tour again, working exclusively for the Harijans. He raised about sixty thousand pounds, and organized informal dinners and concerts bringing Harijans and caste Hindus together. Once more the problem of dirt engrossed him. He trained the despised scavengers to become skilled sanitary engineers, and induced Brahmins to clean latrines. He persuaded villagers to let Harijans use the common well and wash at the bathing place. Ultimately, he hoped, the Harijans would be absorbed into the castes according to their vocations.

Enmity sprang up on all sides. The Harijans themselves were distrustful, and sometimes pelted well-meaning Hindus with stones. The orthodox poured kerosene into the wells, beat Harijans who aspired above their station, charged them with sorcery, whispered that Gandhi kept mistresses, and tossed bombs at him. Angry *sadhus* abetted them. But the change in attitudes did gradually progress. Vinoba and many Congressmen helped the work. Caste Hindus adopted Harijan children, universities created Harijan bursaries, municipalities provided washing facilities, and more and more temples were thrown open. A clause in the Poona Pact urging the removal of Untouchable disabilities by law was slow to take effect, but reforms trickled through—sooner in the best of the princely states than in British India.

Gandhi's belief in the special concern of God sustained him against hostility. But it also aroused more hostility. The sour Ambedkar accused him of insincerity. Some Congress activists, out of prison, resented what they thought a betrayal of nationalism, and its sanctification with religion. In January 1934 the Mahatma tried his supporters very far when an earthquake in Bihar took thousands of lives and he spoke of it as a divine judgement on Untouchability. Even Nehru, even Tagore, protested at this. The supreme gesture which had saved so much seemed to have left him subtly altered, off-centre. For the first time since 1928, Indians asked whether he was effectually a national leader at all.

That question was not being answered in India but in England.

3

The direct collision of forces was over. By May 1933 mass civil disobedience had almost petered out. At that point Gandhi, having consulted such Congressmen as he could reach, suspended it in the vain hope of getting Willingdon to receive him. Then he stopped it. After July the only acts of disobedience were token protests by individuals. About these he was unhappy, because he felt that his own release bound him in honour not to sanction provocation. On 7 April 1934, after a discussion with some ashramites, he called a final halt. The Government let most of its prisoners go, and allowed Congress to re-form in June with a view to contesting elections. The ban on several affiliated bodies, such as Ghaffar Khan's Red Shirts, was not yet relaxed.

Nehru, downcast, felt that he had drifted apart from Gandhi. In August they exchanged letters. Nehru spoke of a sense of spiritual defeat. Congress had become cowardly and lost its ideals. Demagogues and reactionaries were the inheritors. Congress Socialism was largely verbal legerdemain: 'A person who declares himself to be an engine-driver and then adds that his engine is of wood and is drawn by bullocks is misusing the word engine-driver.' Gandhi replied that while he understood Nehru's grief, he did not see any rift between them. 'I am the same as you knew me in 1917 and after.' It was a time for reconstruction.

He was hinting at his own next move, another partial withdrawal. Congress's resort to underground methods had disturbed him, and he heard tales of corruption. When Nehru's complaint arrived he had just written to Mirabehn that he was thinking of resigning his membership. In October 1934 Congress at last reassembled in Bombay, and he did resign. He displayed the utmost tact, saying he realized that many members, especially left-wingers, had ideas of their own, and that non-violence for most was a policy rather than a creed. Personal loyalty to himself should not inhibit a thorough sorting-out. Meanwhile he backed Nehru as Congress's 'rightful helmsman'. Congress, in return, backed his constructive programme.

This retirement was more nominal than real. He bequeathed Congress a tightened-up constitution which affected all its subsequent functioning. The leaders, in general, did not cease to consult him, nor did they venture on major steps against his advice. The Working Committee often met at Wardha. But he now had a rival of the first magnitude. Subhas Chandra Bose was in virtual revolt. The previous year, with Vithalbhai Patel, he had issued a manifesto asserting that Gandhi had failed and that fresh leadership was required. In 1934 he expanded this thesis into a book, *The Indian Struggle*. Still a valuable account of the movement, it shows how the sequel of the Round Table Conference forced an unresolved problem into the open.

What exactly was Satyagraha for? What kind of victory did it aim at? In twenty-eight years Gandhi had never fully explained. To Bose, the goal was obvious. Congress was fighting for political independence, a transfer of power. Gandhi's techniques were obviously potent, but their success was to be gauged by progress toward the goal as defined. If progress flagged, Congress should turn to other methods, not excluding violence. The ambitious Bose veered away from democracy because he did not trust the people to vote as he wished. Later he proved his willingness to try almost anything to get the British out and himself in. But his own defects did not cancel his criticism of Gandhi's.

Besides decrying the Mahatma's lack of guile and diplomacy, Bose argued that his method was stultified by the philosophy underlying it. Rather than estrange anybody whatever, Gandhi had combined Indians of all sorts into a spurious brotherhood too broad to be strong. On the one hand he was deferential to the rich. On the other he conceded enough to the militants to keep them in line, but never enough to swing Congress leftwards. Though a great reformer, he was no revolutionary. Furthermore he insisted on playing two discrepant roles, as nationalist leader and as world teacher. In London, the second role had lured him into a useless and dangerous fraternization with the enemy. Bose preferred the Irish rebels who, when dealing with Lloyd George, kept strictly to themselves.

Granted his premiss, he had a case. Communists indeed had anticipated his argument and carried it further. A party pamphlet of 1931 accused Gandhi of 'posing as a saint' in order to control the national movement and frustrate it, in the interests of the British and Indian plutocrats and princes. Indian Communists eventually dropped the charge, but not before a query had been started in many minds.

Gandhi never replied to Bose directly. However, he made his answer apparent. It was not a defence in detail but a rejection of the premiss. He was sincere about Swaraj in the political sense . . . but not for its own sake. Satyagraha was not a mere tactic to secure the transfer of power. In its full unfolding it was a revolution in its own right. True Swaraj was a state of mind rather than a political deal. Gandhi stood for a permanent revolution, a limitless regeneration of human nature through Truth and Non-Violence.

Again and again he declared, 'Ahimsa comes before Swaraj'. The surface meaning was that he would not countenance violence to achieve independence. But his maxim had deeper implications. Social work remained dearer to him than political work. The Non-Violent Society, the self-reliant Indian commonwealth, mattered more than autonomy as such. It could not indeed be fully realized without a transfer of power, and its building tended in that direction. But the mere transfer, without social renewal, would be barren. As the revolution of Truth-Force was going on all the time— through the constructive programme, if in no more spectacular way —Gandhi was content to focus his energies on the moment and not plan in advance. 'One step enough for me,' he said, quoting Newman's hymn as before. Sooner or later the British would be converted. He would not look so far ahead, or make guesses as to what lay farther on still.

An American disciple, Richard B. Gregg, grasped his point of view perfectly and urged it on Nehru. Nehru was too politically minded to concur. However, his future leadership was founded on his skill in reconciling both positions, Bose's and Gandhi's. As a Socialist he dissented from many of the Mahatma's ideas. But he still approved the main drift of Satyagraha, so long as it was regarded as foundation-laying. Gandhi's 'one step' could be made fairly acceptable to him, so long as he was free to look ahead to the next, and plan for that himself.

His verdict on non-co-operation and civil disobedience over the past fourteen years was therefore more favourable that Bose's. He stated it in a letter to Lord Lothian.

Of course these movements exercised tremendous pressure on the British Government and shook the government machinery. But the real importance, to my mind, lay in the effect they had on our own people, and especially the village masses. Poverty and a long period of autocratic rule . . . had thoroughly demoralized and degraded them. . . .

Non-co-operation dragged them out of the mire and gave them self-respect and self-reliance . . . they acted courageously and did not submit so easily to unjust oppression; their outlook widened and they began to think a little in terms of India as a whole; they discussed political and economic questions (crudely no doubt) in their bazaars and meeting places. . . . It was a remarkable transformation and the Congress, under Gandhi's leadership, must have the credit for it. It was something far more important than constitutions and the structure of government. It was the foundation on which a stable structure or constitution could be built up.

All this of course involves a cataclysmic upheaval of Indian life. Usually in other countries this has involved a vast amount of hatred and violence. And yet in India, thanks to Mahatma Gandhi, there was, relatively speaking, exceedingly little of this. We developed many of the virtues of war without its terrible evils.

In the middle 1930s Indians could think of this process as still going on—subject to one condition. Were there any signs that a 'stable structure', a 'constitution', were getting closer? Had Gandhi's lengthy innings even begun to vindicate him by converting the rulers?

Bose said it had not. The first hint that it had came from Mira-behn. In June 1934 she set off for England and America on a speaking tour. In her native land she had news value which she exploited ably. Lloyd George received her; he was somewhat shaken by the return of the mysterious black cat. Among the Americans, she met Eleanor Roosevelt and told reporters that Gandhi, for her, was Christ. She got home in November and hastened to the Messiah at Wardha. He was cheerful but subdued. The sullen aftermath of the struggle oppressed him, he said, like an indigestion. But Mirabehn assured him that she had noticed a shift in English thinking, especially at working-class level. Sympathy for him was no longer confined to Quakers, Socialists and eccentrics.

She was not indulging her fancy. An open-minded interest actually had grown up. It was reflected in the publication of the first Life by an uninvolved English observer, Glorney Bolton's *The Tragedy of Gandhi*. In some respects this was critical, but it was full of praise for his non-violence, his championship of the outcastes, his success in creating Indian self-respect. Bolton predicted that the English would put up a statue of him as they had done for Washington. Meanwhile politicians were no longer afraid to say, like Viscount Samuel, that he had 'taught the Indian to straighten his back, to raise his eyes, to face circumstances with steady gaze'. Churchill's reiterated maxim 'Gandhi and all he stands for must be crushed,' and his insistence that Indian self-rule would worsen British unemployment, sounded increasingly shrill and jarring.

Nehru might lament (as he was still lamenting a year later) that hardly anyone in England understood how India's heart had been wounded by what he called the indecency and vulgarity of the great repression. He was too gloomy. The pause for reflection, the unease of conscience at the repeated jailing of manifestly good men and women, the pressure from Americans who had been told more of the truth—all these factors were bringing a slow change. Reports from missionaries on Congress's social work in the villages, and the contrast with government neglect, were seeping into the public consciousness. The doctrine of the white man's burden was ceasing to inspire or convince. As for the English in India, nobody could expect them to alter. But Gandhi had worn them down. Kipling, in his story *Thrown Away*, observed that it was fatal for them to take anything seriously except the noonday sun. Now they had been forced for years together into a seriousness that left them drained. Though they would never welcome an unwinding dictated from Whitehall, most of them were too tired to fight against it.

Baldwin resumed the premiership in 1935 and sensed the national mood. He came nearer to splitting his party over India than over anything else, but he judged rightly that Churchill no longer had a following zealous enough to make the split actual. In August a new Government of India Act became law, going well beyond what had been envisaged at the Round Table. It was meant to set up a federation combining the princely states with the eleven provinces of British India, Burma being separated. Dyarchy would go on at the centre, but not in the provinces, where the elected legislatures would enjoy greater powers. This Act left several questions unanswered—for instance, how far the provincial governors would be able to thwart the Indian ministries. Mistrust among the princes prevented the Act from ever being fully effective. Nothing, however, could wipe out the fact that the electorate was vastly increased. Henceforth India would have more than thirty million voters.

G. D. Birla spent several weeks of that year conferring with politicians in London, including Churchill. When he returned in September he went to Wardha as Mirabehn had done. Much would depend, he thought, on the spirit in which the constitution was worked. But he had noticed heartening symptoms. Even Churchill had talked to him quite constructively, and said Gandhi had risen in his esteem because of the Harijan campaign.

Ironically, few Indians grasped what had happened. Nehru and Jinnah both condemned the Act. So, at first, did Gandhi himself. They saw it as no more than a sugar coating for continued British ascendancy. Yet whatever lingering hopes it embodied, it did in practice concede just enough. The enlarged electorate and the new provincial system gave Congress the leverage it required to heave India over the top. A real transfer of power might be delayed for ten or twenty or thirty years. But it would come, if Congress remained resolute that it should. Britain no longer had the will to hold out for ever. To that crucial extent Satyagraha had done what it was meant to do. It had converted the opponent.

XVI

Twilight and Sunburst

1

Unmoved by the change he did not believe in, Gandhi was turning away from politics. If the rest of his life had followed the course he wished for, he would have spent it in relative quiet, building up rural India behind Nehru. It looked, briefly, as if he might manage the rural part of this programme. The quiet was always more elusive.

The same Congress session which accepted his resignation also gave its blessing to a new society under his guidance, the All-India Village Industries Association. It was launched in Wardha. That district suited him, partly, perhaps, for the symbolic reason that it was the geographical centre of the peninsula. The association had the backing of wealthy friends, and Tagore sat on the advisory board. Sheth Jamnalal Bajaj, the financial sponsor of Wardha Ashram, gave Gandhi a house at nearby Maganwadi, where he lived during 1935, making it the headquarters of the association.

As always he attracted disciples, whether he wanted them or not. About twenty joined him. They were a curious group. One walked in his sleep, and another, who suffered from St Vitus's dance, would hurl himself out of bed and grab the sleep-walker, causing yells that woke the whole house. At this juncture Mirabehn intervened. Exploring the country east of Wardha, she discovered a village called Segaon where Jamnalal owned a farm and orchard. It had no shops and no post office. Only a dirt road linked it with the outside world. The climate was extreme, malaria was rampant. But Segaon was untouched by civilization, and many of its six hundred inhabitants were Harijans. This, she decided, was the place for Bapu, the raw material for a model village.

Unfortunately Bapu was ill. She hurried from Segaon to see him.

328

His attendants shut her out, saying she would put up his blood pressure. After hovering devastated for several days she was admitted on rationed time with Jamnalal present. Bapu liked the Segaon scheme, but everyone else opposed it, and blamed Mirabehn for using undue influence. In February 1936 he wrote to her that he was prepared to go to Segaon so long as she was not there herself. Finally he won over Jamnalal and carried out a reconnaissance. On 16 June, in a mud-spattering downpour, the move took place. At first he lived in a hut with two Harijans, and allowed Mirabehn, who had settled in a neighbouring village, to visit him only once a week. But when she went down with typhoid, he nursed her himself.

This disturbance was part of a phase of personal tension. Gandhi was sixty-six. Yet the tremors of the flesh could return. Ramakrishna's lessons, indeed, had not been forgotten, and never would be. Sometimes the Mahatma surrounded himself with women helpers. He affectionately patted their cheeks or rested his hands on their shoulders, confirming his own tranquillity. They were fond of him, vied for his favour, served him loyally, and usually remained unmarried like Sonja Schlesin, the prototype of them all. But as for himself, the cure was imperfect. While in Bombay during 1936 he again felt sexual desire in a dream. It shook him. For six weeks he observed a special vow of silence. Then he discussed the dream with his female clerical staff, noticeably not putting his hands on their shoulders, and confessed to the world in an article in *Harijan*. 'I ultimately conquered the feeling, but I was face to face with the blackest moment of my life and if I had succumbed to it, it would have meant my absolute undoing.'

His home at Segaon became virtually another ashram, which governed the life of the small community. He presided with Kasturbai—Bapu and Ba as at Sabarmati. The volume of his mail, averaging a hundred letters a day, created a problem; not only because of the lack of postal services at Segaon, but because items went astray to another place of the same name. Gandhi's colony was eventually renamed Sevagram, Service Village. Jamnalal built a better road, and had a telephone installed, but civilization's impact was slight.

Gandhi was working on the Non-Violent Society. In his year at Maganwadi and the three subsequent years at Segaon, this was his main concern. He was increasingly convinced that Ahimsa should be all-pervasive, a universal love. Purely as a mode of political action, it was apt (as he had long since grasped) to be merely an expedient or a cover for cowardice. Even the brave tended to think in terms of dramatic clashes, with no foundation in social virtue or service. Now, as he recruited fresh volunteers for village work, he insisted on his version of evangelical poverty.

Hind Swaraj still enshrined his social ideal. He saw no reason to change it, and said so. Once or twice he described the village of his imagination. The fullest attempt is a product of later days, but reflects what he was thinking at Segaon.

> It is a complete republic. . . . Every village's first concern will be to grow its own food crops and cotton for its cloth. It should have a reserve for its cattle, recreation and playground for adults and children. Then if there is more land available, it will grow *useful* money crops, thus excluding . . . tobacco, opium and the like. The village will maintain a village theatre, school and public hall. It will have its own water works ensuring clean supply. . . . Education will be compulsory up to a final basic course. As far as possible, every activity will be conducted on a co-operative basis.

Rural electrification, with publicly owned power-houses, was part of his developed vision. The dream was still an essentially moral one, a protest of the Simple Lifer against the city's corruption. Gandhi thought his village republic would be far more law-abiding than present society, and would cure its rare delinquents instead of punishing them, a practice he had grown to detest.

As he began trying again to lift actual villagers toward the modest yet remote goal, his outlook became more fluid, radical, and adventurous. Thus, while pushing on with Harijan work, he also showed a warmth contrasting with earlier caution toward conduct that ignored social distinctions entirely: marriage, for instance, between couples of different caste or religion. His attack on under-nourishment and under-employment broke fresh ground. The slump and the fragmentation of peasant holdings had undone much previous progress. But now, through his village laboratories, Gandhi strove most resourcefully to renew the advance. (Delhi regarded his programme as a cunning plot to form an underground movement, and wasted its agents' time in futile efforts to unearth evidence.)

He started a campaign for unpolished hand-pounded rice, to replace the denatured mill product. He experimented with soya beans, peanuts and palm sugar. He launched a bee-keeping project. He published recipes for salads made from wild plants, discussed the merits of milk and bananas, instructed his readers on manure. Home spinning and weaving remained his chief remedies for seasonal unemployment. Few Congressmen endorsed khadi as a permanent policy; by itself, it meant permanent poverty. But they supported it as a short-term cure, because it was simple and the tools were cheap. Khadi therefore progressed. It progressed indeed very slowly—from five thousand fully equipped villages in 1934 to fifteen thousand in 1940, out of seven hundred thousand. However, the Village Industries Association was busy diversifying as the Spinners' Association could not. Gandhi sponsored paper-making, mat-weaving, oil-pressing, and home manufacture of new foodstuffs.

His spirit was strictly practical. In advocating what looked to some like a backward step, he was not glamourizing backwardness. 'I have no partiality', he wrote, 'for return to the primitive methods . . . for the sake of them. I suggest the return, because there is no other way of giving employment to the millions of villagers who are living in idleness.' Some of the industries were by-products of Harijan work, and the deliverance of millions not from idleness but from foulness. When he found that the outcastes who skinned carcases were not paid, and ate the carrion as their reward, he demanded that the job should be put on a cash basis, and then started tanning classes where the skinners were taught to do it better and to make use of the flesh and bones.

Also, he at last resumed the school project which he had reluctantly left to die in Champaran. Gandhian 'Basic Education' was one of his last inventions. The idea was his own, with touches of Montessori. But in October 1937 he entrusted the planning of the curriculum to a committee under Dr Zakir Husain, a learned and not uncritical Muslim. Children went to his primary schools from seven to fourteen. The teachers used the vernaculars, plus compulsory Hindustani as a common language. Handicrafts were the foundation—spinning, carpentry, horticulture, animal care, and so on. Vinoba, who had experimented in this field, acted as a consultant. The crafts took up three hours and twenty minutes a day. Music, drawing, arithmetic, citizenship, history, science and languages took up the residual two hours, different subjects being

treated on different days. The allocation of time varied somewhat
and is in any case misleading, because the academic subjects were
also taught through the crafts, on a learning-by-doing theory. When
a farm animal died, the older pupils might learn how to dispose of
the carcase and learn some physiology in the process. When an
eclipse was due, they would make simple instruments to observe it,
and learn about eclipses. One of the familiar trials of the teacher
was turned to account in characteristic style. The Mahatma devised
a moveable latrine, so that children who left the room could manure
the fields. He reckoned fifty to an acre.

Schools in India were financed out of the provincial budgets,
and a third of the provincial revenues came from taxes on drink.
Gandhi's ideas about prohibition—for which, in spite of America,
he had a rather painful enthusiasm—made him unwilling to plan
educational expansion if it depended on the liquor trade. Hardly
any of the parents could afford fees. Instead, he proposed that the
schools should pay their own way by marketing the products of
the handicrafts. His advisers calculated that such a scheme might
provide minimal salaries for the staff, but could never meet the cost
of equipment and maintenance. It was clear, moreover, that most
of the products would not be saleable unless the pupils spent
enough time on them to become skilled. Then the school would
degenerate into a workshop or market-garden. Gandhi had to settle
for only partial self-support.

But he stood by his ashram principle that all should do physical
labour, though by choice, not compulsion. The purely intellectual
or professional worker was always in some degree a parasite. One
could spin if nothing else. This doctrine implied that the ideal
society would be levelled by the kind of work people did, free from
extreme class differences in a common frugality. It gave a leftish
tinge to his utterances. He welcomed the rise of a Socialist bloc in
Congress headed by Jayaprakash Narayan. Sometimes, in these
later years, he professed to be a Socialist himself—to the distress
of Nehru, whose own Socialism stressed heavy industry, with the
rural programme as a balancer only. Sometimes Gandhi even professed to be a Communist. He had first met Indian Communists in
1931. Mrs Naidu had a son in the party. In effect he told its
members that they were not true Communists, and he was.

If the words 'Socialism' and 'Communism' were employed as
they were originally, his claim had substance; and he shared Lenin's

view of the State, in its existing forms, as an instrument of exploitation. But while the Socialism he aired in *Harijan* did provide for publicly owned factories, it shied away from expropriation of capitalists and enforced land reform. Gandhi knew quite well that India's plutocrats held the poor by the throat and wrung fortunes out of them. Yet he never got beyond his old maxim that they should learn to be trustees and behave responsibly. Labour could and should combine—he still worked staunchly for his Textile Labour Association—but chiefly with a view to co-partnership. Militancy should go no further than strikes or other non-violent action against otherwise incurable wrongs. The goal was not a People's Republic but a de-centralized federation of little units.

There was the deeper question of religion. Gandhi was a humanist if anyone ever was, yet not in the irreligious sense of most humanists of the Left. As the years passed he stressed the divine Absolute more and more, asserting that disbelievers in a Supreme Being could not be perfect Satyagrahis. 'Disbelievers' meant Buddhists and Jains as well as Marxists. He once took issue with a Buddhist on prayer. Though agreeing on the uselessness of crude petitions to a heavenly father, Gandhi argued that prayer was valid, as an aspiration to closer union with the great Reality. He buttressed his Socialism with a proverb about the land belonging to God, which he construed as conferring title on the people.

Nevertheless he remained untempted by religious organizations. Moral Re-Armament sometimes seemed to be talking his language, but he said it was a cult for the 'haves' with no message for the 'have-nots', and would not touch it. Christian missionaries, notably John R. Mott, made the pilgrimage to his home without budging him.

They were far from being his only visitors, or the only people anxious to get his ear. Politicians came and went, most of them friendly. Gandhi in fact was an oracle. But he showed no sign of ossifying into a Grand Old Man. The ever-vivacious Mrs Naidu nicknamed him Mickey Mouse. A more solemn lady was Margaret Sanger, who arrived while he was still at Maganwadi to argue about birth control. Gandhi stood where he had for a long time. Birth control was necessary, but artificial aids led to self-indulgence and were therefore demoralizing and enfeebling. Intercourse should occur solely for the sake of offspring, and his preventives against excess of offspring, apart from restraint, were in essence the Irish preventives: late marriage, many celibates. He condoned the 'safe period' because it was a form of restraint, but contraception not at all, or only in exceptional cases. Mrs Sanger made no impression. As before, he had reached a religious position—in this instance, roughly, the extreme Catholic position—by a non-religious route. He did not appeal to divine law but to practical, if unconvincing, psychology.

Other foreign visitors included Yone Noguchi, the Japanese author, and Lord Lothian. Also he was in closer touch with American Negroes. Delegations arrived in 1936 and after. They had a special interest for him because of the parallel with South Africa. 'A civilization', he once declared, 'is to be judged by its treatment of minorities.' With some foresight he suggested that Negro campaigners for civil rights might be the future standard-bearers of non-violence.

Some of the visitors came to stay. Such was the Polish engineer Maurice Frydman, who appeared at Segaon that August. The settlement also recruited a Sanskrit scholar who was a leper; a Japanese monk who worked like a demon; and a professor who had previously lived in a jungle naked, though at Segaon he dressed. On the fringes was Mirabehn, studying animal husbandry. At one point, weighed down with aimlessness and despond, she went to a Himalayan summer resort for a rest cure. The simultaneous presence of Subhas Chandra Bose prevented the cure from being entirely restful.

Gandhi seldom rested. He slept in the open, and took massages and daily walks, but never fully relaxed. The sultry climate so far from the sea was not good for him. In February 1936 the quarrels which preceded the Segaon move had their share in causing a mild nervous breakdown. In 1938 he suffered another, apparently because Kasturbai had gone into a temple which was still closed to Harijans. A long-drawn, largely successful, but gruelling battle for the release of some alleged terrorists took its toll. Like everyone else at Segaon he contracted malaria. Only a holiday at Juhu Beach averted a serious decline.

The tension of 1936 had been aggravated by family trouble. Harilal Gandhi was publicly deriding his father, threatening to turn Muslim or Christian, and getting drunk and disorderly. When one of his misdeeds was reported in the papers, Kasturbai (who had been saddled with the upbringing of his four neglected children) dictated a letter to him—a pathetic appeal to a disintegrating creature in his late forties.

My dear son Harilal, I have read that recently in Madras policemen found you misbehaving in a state of drunkenness at midnight in an open street and took you into custody. Next day you were produced before a bench of magistrates and they fined you one rupee. They must have been very good people to treat you so leniently. . . .

I do not know what to say to you. . . . Think of the misery you are causing your aged parents in the evening of their lives. Your father says nothing to anyone but I know how the shocks you are giving him are breaking his heart. . . .

I am told that in your recent wanderings you have been criticising and ridiculing your great father. This does not behove such an intelligent boy as you. . . . He has nothing but love in his heart for you. . . .

For sheer shame, I am unable to move about among my friends and strangers. Your father always pardons you, but God will not tolerate your conduct. . . .

Every morning I rise with a shudder to think what fresh news of disgrace the newspapers will bring. I sometimes wonder where you are, where you sleep, what you eat. . . . I often feel like meeting you. But I do not know where to find you.

That May, Harilal went over publicly to Islam. Gandhi wrote an article in *Harijan* casting doubt on his sincerity. It is a genuinely saddened and saddening article, yet, like his previous outpouring on the same·subject, it leaves an unpleasant taste. The wound never healed.

Awareness of personal shortcoming was perhaps a motive behind one of his most important speeches. During his first Indian jail term, a study group had been formed called the Gandhi Seva Sangh, to explore the wider social implications of his ideas. In 1936 this was reconstituted under K. G. Mashruwala, a softly efficient veteran of the salt adventure, who later succeeded Gandhi as editor of *Harijan*. Addressing the members on 28 March, the Mahatma warned them against the inherent danger in using his name. He was simply a preacher of Truth and Non-Violence, in that order. They should rid themselves of the habit of searching in his writings for textual authority. 'There is no such thing as Gandhism, and I do not want to leave any sect after me.'

2

While the Mahatma was entrenching himself at Segaon, Congress was grappling with the Government of India Act. Most of the leaders had denounced it a shade too vehemently. As the provincial elections neared, it was plain that their results were not going to be totally meaningless. Should Congress contest them? Gandhi spoke up in favour and decided the issue. 'India,' he said, 'is still a prison, but the superintendent allows the prisoners to elect the officials who run the jail.' Congress could use the machinery set up by the Act, even to thwart what he suspected to be its intention. Thirty million voters were thirty million voters. It would be absurd for the only real national movement to turn its back on them.

Nehru, who had been to Europe, returned in March 1936. Congress met at Lucknow soon afterwards. He was far from happy about it, complaining that it was divided, out of touch with the masses, and down to 457,000 members. But with Gandhi's support —now more determined than ever, because there was no other way of holding together the Left and Right—he was again installed in the presidency. That title would obviously carry more weight in India if Congress took office in any of the provinces. In his presidential address Nehru said he was willing to contest the elections for propaganda purposes, but not to co-operate with the Raj by accepting office. Congress, however, remained non-committal on the second point.

Sardar Vallabhbhai Patel and Rajendra Prasad (who led what the Left now stigmatized as the Old Guard) opened the marathon election campaign on 7 July. This was still under way in December when Congress held its next full session. As a gesture toward Gandhi it met for the first time in a village, Faizpur. Delighted at the choice, he organized a display of village industries, and directed the putting up of ingenious temporary buildings made of bamboo. Nehru continued as President.

Membership had risen to 636,000. It was a hint at the election results, which were out in February 1937. The Round Table myth that Congress was merely one faction among many went up in smoke. Congress led the polls in nine of the eleven provinces. In Bombay, Madras, United Provinces, Bihar, Central Provinces and Orissa, the party achieved a clear majority. An agreement with a minor group later gave it a majority in the North-West Frontier Province also. As for the Muslim League, its performance bore out Gandhi's contentions. It was an Imperial scarecrow. Put to the test in the communal electorates, it polled less than 5 per cent of Muslim votes. Nor did the Harijans evince much zeal for Ambedkar's men. Only 13 of these got through to the reserved seats, compared with 78 Congress Harijans.

Candidates with Gandhi's backing had fared especially well. Secure in his prestige, he urged Congressmen to shoulder the burden of office. When Nehru and Bose demurred, he persuaded them to approve if the British governors would promise not to interfere with administration. Weeks of paralysis ensued while the position was clarified. Gandhi served as an intermediary with the new Viceroy, Lord Linlithgow. (Delhi construed his conduct as a trick to enhance his own importance.) In June he at last extracted the required undertaking, and enabled the Government of India Act to work. Six Congress ministries took office. A seventh province followed quickly, and two more subsequently.

Congress in the legislatures was the political arm of Congress outside. All elected members signed a pledge of obedience to the party's higher command. With a common policy thus ensured, Gandhi began offering advice to the incoming ministers. They should regard their salary of five hundred rupees a month as a maximum, and try to live on less. They should travel third class. They should move promptly to ban the liquor trade, support Basic Education, relieve indebted peasants, and convert the prisons into workshops for rehabilitation. He did not carry all his followers; Rajagopalachari, now heading the Government of Madras, showed symptoms of restiveness.

Nehru was uneasily aware of certain appearances.

What of the masses? . . . They must be puzzled to see some of their old comrades who were in prison with them but yesterday, sitting in the seats of the mighty in those imposing structures which have been the citadels of British Imperialism. Red-liveried chaprasis hover about them and the enervating perfume of power surrounds them. What has happened to these comrades of ours? they must wonder. . . .

We have not left them and we are their comrades as of old. Though some of us may sit on chairs of state, the same khadi covers our bodies, the same thoughts fill our minds.

Under the spur of scrutiny from below, and from above too, the Congress ministries gave government a brisker tempo. Englishmen in the Civil Service had difficulty adjusting. But they did not see the altered relation as a fundamental threat to themselves, and their behaviour, on the whole, was correct. Official hindrance came more in the form of subtle discouragement. It held back support for Gandhi's educational schemes, because these were not oriented toward preparing young Indians for the service of the British Raj. Prohibition made little headway. More was achieved with reforms affecting the Harijans. In 1938 Bombay and Madras removed their disabilities, so far as legislation could. But Congress proved itself not so much by any particular acts as by showing it could govern at all.

Much depended on Nehru and Bose. By fitting the movement which Gandhi had created into a political mould, Nehru was preventing any reversion to the Hindu divorce of moral wisdom from practical statesmanship. So far, so good. However, his own failings contained the seeds of trouble. The Pandit was the same age as Gandhi had been in Champaran, but he had not revealed the same judgement of character, or the same flair for making full use of others' capacities. There was no clear sign of a Nehru team taking shape to succeed to the Old Guard. As for Bose, he was pulling apart toward a mirage of armed revolt led by himself. He opposed what he described as the Gandhi Wing in Congress—meaning the block of votes which Patel could usually deliver through the party machine—and resented Nehru's reluctance to organize the rest as a counterpoise.

To the Mahatma, 1938 brought anti-climax and worse. Congress membership had shot up to three million, but mainly because office meant jobs, and place-seekers could join the party without running the risks formerly entailed. Quality was declining, corruption and ostentation were seeping in. Gandhi spoke out in *Harijan,* and exerted his influence to unseat one of the prime ministers. The governments' use of force against strikers and communal rioters made him despondent. In February, at Haripura, Congress hoisted Bose into its presidency. He rode in a chariot drawn by fifty-one bullocks. The bamboo buildings were more showy without being more efficient. All the time, as the delegates cheered and voted, a long-lowering cloud was growing darker.

The Muslim League's electoral failure had occurred when its

leader was only recently back from a long stay in England. Nehru, indeed, thought Jinnah was finished. The Congress ministries brought in Muslims if they were willing to sign the Congress pledge. Jinnah retaliated by setting out to turn his League into a popular party. Seizing on every rumour of anti-Muslim discrimination, he conjured up an image of Congress in office as a Hindu dictatorship working through the British Raj. Against this the League was the sole defence, the sole instrument for getting the benefit of the much-touted separate electorates.

Austere and arrogant, upper-crust, well dressed in European style, Jinnah did not suggest a demagogue. Yet possibly he was helped by being so wildly unlike Gandhi. His débâcle in 1920, when he felt that his inferiors had ousted him, rankled perpetually. Most of the grievances he exploited were feeble, and some were imaginary. At one point he was offered an impartial inquiry and turned it down. But while Bose was taking over the reins of Congress, Jinnah was gaining ground. On 28 April Gandhi conferred with him, and failed. Jinnah would only come to terms on a basis of sectarian politics, with Gandhi and Congress leading the Hindus, and leaving the Muslims to himself and the League. Even then Congress would have to make grotesque token concessions like promising not to sing 'Bande Mataram'. Gandhi sent his intractable visitor away, and sank into his first real crisis of confidence. The demands Jinnah had put were only a beginning. A new word, a new slogan was being uttered, so monstrous to him that his mind reeled from it in helpless dismay: *Pakistan*.

The idea that Indian Muslims should be a distinct nation was broached in 1933 by an undergraduate at Cambridge. His plan was that north-western India should secede and combine with neighbouring areas to form an Islamic empire. Hence the name—'P' for Punjab, 'A' for Afghania (i.e. the North-West Frontier Province), 'K' for Kashmir, 'I' for Iran, 'S' for Sindh, 'T' for Tukharistan, 'A' for Afghanistan, and 'N' from the end of Baluchistan. This acrostic, in Persian or Urdu, would mean 'land of the pure'. In 1938 Jinnah was well on the way toward adopting the scheme. He pointed to the Sudeten German agitation, which Hitler harnessed to disrupt Czechoslovakia, and said the Muslims should learn from it. British policy, as prone as ever to play up communal tension, cautiously encouraged him. The Mahasabha and other organs of Hindu chauvinism grew stronger as a retort.

To Gandhi the conception of nations based on religion was absurd and repugnant. If, as he maintained, Indian nationality had room for all religions, then Muslim nationalism was a treacherous irrelevance. It was not as if the Islamic conquerors had remained a separate race like the English. Most Indian Muslims in the twentieth century were of mixed blood and convert ancestry. Even if Jinnah's claim were conceded, it was wholly illogical as it stood. Why stop at the Muslims? Why not a Sikh nation, a Parsee nation, a Christian nation? Indians of different religions mingled everywhere; the character of a given area was a matter of percentages. At a loss, the Mahatma consoled himself by touring the North-West Frontier and meeting the faithful Ghaffar Khan and his men, Muslims all. He tried to form inter-communal peace brigades. Maulana Azad and other eminent Muslims remained loyal to Congress. But on 17 June 1939 Gandhi wrote to the author of a book on this problem: 'The disease has gone too deep for books to help. Some big action is necessary. What, I do not know as yet.' It was the first shadow of the end.

He was witnessing one of the bitterest phenomena of a bitter decade, the lie becoming truth. Year after year, he and other enlightened Indians had rebutted British allegations of communal hate and Muslim separateness. Yet now the hate and the separateness were real. The same was happening elsewhere in the long debates over Communism and pacifism. People of goodwill had argued tirelessly, and with justice, that the propagandist picture of the Soviet Union was false; but now Stalin was making it true. They had argued that the causes for which nations were stirred up to fight had always been bogus; but now Hitler confronted them with a crisis which was different, and vindicated the Blimps who talked of preparedness.

Those who held out usually suffered a loss of contact with reality. Even Gandhi was not exempt. He had never been either a Communist or a pacifist in the western sense. However, his faith in non-violence had to endure the test of Fascist aggression, and in that context it rang hollow. His sympathy for the victims was profound. He condemned the futility of the League of Nations, called for world government, and sent messages to such resisters as Negrin, the Prime Minister of Republican Spain. But his advice to the Spanish, and to the Abyssinians, Chinese and Czechs, was to practise non-co-operation and 'perish unarmed in the attempt'.

Truth-Force would convert even dictators, if only there were enough martyrs.

Like Lord Irwin, who was now Lord Halifax and Foreign Secretary, Gandhi could not comprehend a Hitler at all. Surely nobody could be quite incapable of a moral response? Surely it was a matter of degree? His Jewish friend Kallenbach came over on a visit, and remarked that he could not bring himself to pray for the Fuehrer. Gandhi could. His prescription for the Jews was not Zionism (toward which he was vacillatingly cool, despite appeals from the philosopher Martin Buber) but Satyagraha as in South Africa. While the Nazi press assailed him for his pronouncements, the Jews did not find them helpful. After the war and the horrors of the 'final solution', he said: 'The Jews should have offered themselves to the butcher's knife. They should have thrown themselves into the sea from cliffs. . . . It would have aroused the world and the people of Germany.' In fact he failed to answer the question which no pacifist ever has answered: Even if you are a saint yourself, what right have you to ask the same of everyone else?

His disorientation was showing itself in other ways. A renewed growth of Indian industry and the Left shook his hold on Congress. Early in 1939 Bose was re-elected against the Mahatma's candidate, an unprecedented defeat. The Working Committee, including Nehru (who was getting sick of Bose), forced him to stand down. But the damage was done. He formed his own Forward Bloc within Congress.

Meanwhile Gandhi was embroiling himself in another contest, which he came very close to botching completely. Soon after the Congress ministries took office, popular leaders in several princely states had begun a struggle for constitutional rule. Nehru gave them moral support. Mysore, Travancore, Jaipur and Hyderabad all passed through internal crises. The upheaval came to a head in Rajkot, Gandhi's boyhood home. Here Vallabhbhai Patel led civil disobedience aimed at extorting a political amnesty and reforms. The sovereign—or Thakore, to give him his correct title—promised to appoint a commission with reformers in the majority. Then, having secured the backing of an alliance of other princes, he broke his word. Civil disobedience was resumed. Kasturbai joined it and went to jail. Her husband, unwilling to think the worst of a dynasty the Gandhis had served, got it into his head that the Thakore had been prompted by a British political agent. The truth was that the Thakore needed no coaching in duplicity beyond what he was receiving from Durba Virawala, his own minister.

Gandhi took up residence. After a quixotic effort to 'free' the Thakore, he grasped the facts a little more accurately. On 3 March 1939 he terrified his doctors by beginning a fast, and sent a wire asking the Viceroy to intervene. The Chief Justice of India arbitrated in favour of Gandhi and Patel. The Thakore made concessions, and then raised further issues. Tortuous bargaining ensued. Finally Gandhi's conscience smote him. He had done wrongly to coerce his antagonist by bringing in Delhi. He said he was sorry, and relinquished the concessions, which were scarcely his to relinquish. In response to his pleas the prisoners were released. But the sole response otherwise was a little constitutional window-dressing, which left the citizens no better off.

Govind Dass Consul, the author of a short Life of Gandhi, records a conversation at this time between two politicians. One said: 'I am losing faith in the old rogue and his roguery. I ask you, is every step backward really a step forward?' The other took up the impudent word. 'Oh, you can depend on him all right! Roguery is the principle he works by. Can't you see, it takes a rogue to know a rogue? That's how he dominates his own herd, and the white rogues of the bureaucracy too.' The dialogue was untypical, but a few years before, it would have been unthinkable.

During this Rajkot tragi-comedy, Lord Halifax had been suffering his own disillusionments. German troops occupied Prague and the Chamberlain policy of appeasement collapsed. In July, Gandhi wrote to Hitler begging him to spare mankind.

3

On 1 September Germany invaded Poland. Two days later Britain declared war, and Lord Linlithgow followed suit on behalf of India. He did so in virtue of his viceregal powers, pitching more than three hundred million people into the conflict without consulting a single one of them. Many Indian patriots—Birla, for instance—had at last come to believe that they were on the road to Dominion status. But the Viceroy seemed to confirm the sourest cynicisms of Congress. As soon as an issue arose which really mattered, the puppet-show ended and autocracy returned.

S. C. Bose wanted to embrace Britain's difficulty as India's opportunity. His Forward Bloc muttered about a rising. Gandhi, Nehru, and most Congressmen disowned him. Seen from their angle, Britain and Germany were both imperialist powers. But no sane person could doubt where the war guilt lay, or which of the two was preferable. Linlithgow, realizing his blunder, did his best to atone by inviting Gandhi to Simla. There the Mahatma made his sympathies clear. At the notion of Westminster Abbey or the Houses of Parliament being destroyed by bombs, he almost wept. Britain had his moral support. No more than that. He remained wedded to non-violence, although, he said, 'In the secret of my heart I am in perpetual quarrel with God that he should allow such things to go on.'

This was his personal position throughout the first half of the war, and he was firm in it while others were contradicting themselves. But as a public figure, he was drawn into conflicting statements of day-to-day policy by the oscillations of Congress. Since most members of the Working Committee did not believe in non-violence as a moral axiom, they were prepared to fight against Hitler on terms. The Viceroy's declaration of war had killed any chances that their terms would be easy. On 14 September they adopted a resolution drafted by Nehru, asking for a constituent assembly and a sharing of power. If these were granted they would assist the war effort. Gandhi recognized that his views could not be imposed on his colleagues. His own advice was to go frankly one way or the other: either stand aloof, or help unconditionally. But he loyally backed the resolution, and, at a second conference with the Viceroy, pressed him to accept it.

All he got was a nebulous promise of changes after the war. To this the Working Committee replied with a reversion to the tactics of 1920. During October and November the Congress ministries resigned, leaving the governors in charge. India at war stood deadlocked. The princely states were of course committed, and supplying their expected quota of good soldiers, but the provinces wavered. Gandhi, Nehru, Prasad and Jinnah all had talks with the Viceroy and each other, without finding a formula. The implacable Jinnah reviled Azad, rejoiced at the ministries' demise, and urged his supporters to celebrate that event as a deliverance. Linlithgow co-operated, treating the Muslim League as if it spoke for all the Muslims of India.

In March 1940 the League met at Lahore and voted for a separate state as its goal—not perhaps the huge Pakistan of the original concept, but something like it. The Pakistan preached by Jinnah was indeed so vaguely defined that it soon became a Muslim Land of Cockaigne, a repository for every dream, a salve for every disappointment. It would spell power for the politician, office for the office-seeker, profit for the businessman, relief from taxes for the peasant, higher wages for the worker, religious purity for the mullah. The mystique of the two nations was enthroned, and Mohamed Ali Jinnah was the Anti-Mahatma. It had taken him nineteen years.

Meanwhile, life at Sevagram (as Segaon was now called) had become lustreless. Bapu, adrift, was prone to changes of mood. He did not lose his own mental balance, but he unsettled the other residents. At a bad moment Mahadev Desai told Birla that the place was like a madhouse. Birla suspected that the situation was worse than it looked. Having squeezed out Gandhi's usefulness, Congress was going its own way and might well be close to dropping him.

Bapu and Ba took comfort from a visit to Tagore at Shantiniketan. The Poet said: 'We accept you as our own, as one belonging to all humanity.' The Mahatma said: 'Even though I call this visit a pilgrimage . . . I am no stranger here. I feel as if I had come to my home.' Noting how their controversies had passed into limbo, he rejoiced at his late and glorious discovery that there was no real divergence. Tagore appointed him as a kind of executor to settle the school's finances after his death—a trust which he discharged, in spite of immense preoccupations. They shared a bereavement in April when Charles Andrews died. He had been a devoted friend to both, and never grudged what that friendship cost him in English respect.

People asked the inevitable question: What should we do if India were invaded? Gandhi's answer appeared in *Harijan* on 13 April.

> If the worst happens, there are two ways open to non-violence. To yield possession but non-co-operate with the aggressor. Thus supposing that a modern edition of Nero descended upon India, the representatives of the State will let him in but tell him that he will get no assistance from the people. They will prefer death to submission. The second way will be non-violent resistance by

a people who have been trained in the non-violent way. They would offer themselves unarmed as fodder for the aggressor's cannon. . . . The unexpected spectacle of endless rows upon rows of men and women simply dying rather than surrender to the will of an aggressor must ultimately melt him and his soldiery.

But in private Gandhi was more and more doubtful whether the masses would ever be adequately 'trained in the non-violent way'.

Two months later the question ceased to be academic. German victory in France raised the possibility of a British collapse in Asia. Gandhi had no criticism for Pétain's surrender or Roosevelt's non-belligerence. He wanted an Anglo-German parley, and, on one of his less felicitous impulses, offered to go to Germany. Linlithgow politely turned him down. Bose talked to him for the last time, suggesting a revolution. This was the current policy of the far Left, under Communist influence. But Gandhi's South African ruling still stood: a Satyagrahi never takes advantage of an opponent's difficulties. 'We do not seek our independence out of Britain's ruin,' he wrote. A query perhaps hovered over what he counted as ruin, since he was counselling Britain to stop fighting and render Hitler's victories hollow by non-violent resistance.

Vocal India was not with Bose. The Congress moderates, led by Rajagopalachari, were now ready to come to Britain's aid without making extreme conditions. The Liberals were ready to do likewise with no conditions. The religious pressure-groups professed the same readiness with a special motive—that of getting weapons and training, to be employed later against adherents of the other religion —but the immediate effect was no different. On 21 June the Congress Working Committee rejected both revolution and non-violence (its first explicit break with Gandhi) and resolved on a fresh appeal to the Viceroy. Despite the snub Gandhi went to see Linlithgow on its behalf, and returned with an offer to broaden Indian participation in the Government. He was not impressed, but Rajagopalachari and Patel favoured further discussion. Gandhi saw how his old comrades were thinking and made no attempt to dictate. Only Ghaffar Khan took his side, and Rajaji's resolution went through. To the anguish of leftists such as Jayaprakash Narayan, the Committee informed Linlithgow that if he would accept the principle of independence, and form a suitable government as a step towards it, Congress would throw its full weight behind the war effort.

Linlithgow's reply on 8 August was chilling. Apart from an enlargement of the Executive Council, his proposals were too hazy to provide any basis for consent. He spoke of safeguards for minorities, in the tone which Congress associated with evasion and gerrymandering. At the crisis of the German war, with Churchill at Downing Street, British policy was to tighten up. Even before sending his reply the Viceroy had prepared emergency orders curtailing freedom of speech and other liberties. In secret memoranda he made it clear that the regulations could and should be directed against nationalism.

With the orders in force, the All-India Congress Committee gathered in Bombay on 16 September. Somewhat ignominiously the Congressmen asked Gandhi, whose leadership they had so lately rejected, to give them a lead. Guided partly by intuition, partly by a shrewd appreciation of Delhi's motives, he resolved on civil disobedience against the new measures only. Individual resisters, beginning with members of his own circle, would affirm freedom of speech in defiance of the law. Having given the Viceroy advance notice, he called upon Vinoba to make the opening move, propelling him into the limelight for the first time and introducing him with a manifesto in praise of his virtues. On 17 October Vinoba made an anti-war speech near Wardha and went to prison. Nehru was to go next, but the Government hauled him in before he could speak. Patel and others followed in a quickening tempo. By the end of 1940 nearly four hundred members of the legislatures were in jail. During this and the ensuing year, more than twenty thousand protesters were convicted, among them several ex-ministers. Vinoba got himself imprisoned three times by speaking again as soon as he was let out.

The campaign, however, was dull compared with its predecessors. Censorship of news cut the volunteers off from each other. Gandhi temporarily suspended *Harijan* and advised Satyagrahis to become 'walking newspapers', carrying information from place to place. Also he tried patiently to draw the volunteers into constructive work. But the fire never blazed, and disputes arose over aims and methods. Bose's Forward Bloc clamoured for blood. Their chief, despairing of a national movement which he wrote off as static and hidebound, vanished altogether. Then his Congress colleagues were alarmed to hear him introduced on the Berlin radio. They hoped the broadcasts might be a trick, but decided gloomily and correctly that the voice was his.

After the German attack on Russia in June 1941, fresh dissension was inspired by the Communists' claim that the war was now quite different and should be supported. This view had weight with Nehru and the trade unions. By December it was widespread. On the 4th of that month, though civil disobedience had not been called off, Linlithgow judged rightly that it had spent itself, and released the imprisoned members of the Working Committee. Gandhi, foreseeing war without limit, and perhaps fearing the effect of Bose's allegations on German strategy, composed an open letter to Hitler. Starting with his habitual 'Dear Friend,' he warned the Fuehrer that Indian nationalists had no use for Nazism and would never become its fifth columnists. Granted, they opposed British rule, but they did not seek to overthrow it by force, and certainly not with German aid. Mankind yearned for peace, he added; the Indians had desisted from even a non-violent struggle; could not Hitler respond? The letter remained unpublished, and probably never reached its addressee.

As before, the course of events lifted the Mahatma out of his doldrums. Pearl Harbor brought Japan and America fully into the war. The recent Churchill-Roosevelt Atlantic Charter had not been meant to apply to India, but on becoming a belligerent ally Roosevelt ventured to broach the topic. Churchill's reaction was so explosive that the President said no more. However, he exerted some pressure indirectly, and sent Colonel Louis Johnson to India as a personal envoy. When Singapore fell and the Japanese advanced across Burma, the prospect of an invasion of India became real, and the cry for an acceptable government correspondingly urgent. Many Indians felt sympathy for the Japanese, few wanted Japan to win. The people would fight, Nehru declared, but as free citizens, not as slaves. This was the tenor of a Congress resolution passed at Bardoli. Gandhi recognized again that he was in a minority, and again withdrew rather than split the ranks by holding out for non-violence or trying to keep civil disobedience going. Nehru, he said, was his political successor and could take over. He had never looked more unlike the dictator he was accused of being. Yet within a few months the dictatorship of Congress was in his hands.

On 22 February 1942, Roosevelt stated that the Atlantic Charter did, in his view, apply to all nations. Marshal Chiang Kai Shek, who then controlled most of independent China, visited India and urged Britain to make a genuine offer. The pressures were too heavy even for Churchill. In March an offer was made. Its bearer was Sir Stafford Cripps, a good choice on several grounds—as a Socialist contemporary with Nehru, as a friend and well-wisher of the Congress leaders, and also as a vegetarian of austere moral rectitude. He had learnt his diet from Dr Edmond Székely, a social and medical theorist after Gandhi's own heart. If he had talked to Gandhi about Székely he might at least have created a helpful atmosphere. Unfortunately he stuck to politics. The Mahatma met him in Delhi, listened to the offer, and advised him to go home. The Working Committee debated it till 9 April and reached the same conclusion. So did the Muslim League, the Mahasabha, the Ambedkar organization, and the Liberals.

The offer was an advance on its precursors. It embodied a clear pledge of Dominion status after the war, with nothing to prevent India from opting out of the Commonwealth. This, however, was hedged with clauses about the right of regional non-accession, which would (at least on paper) have allowed Jinnah and the princes to shatter the sub-continent into 564 separate countries. Nor were the proposals for an interim war government any more cogent. On 12 April Cripps returned empty-handed, under the mistaken impression that Gandhi had sabotaged his efforts.

India was now gripped by foreboding. To the horror of the inhabitants of the prospective war zone, Delhi was preparing a scorched-earth policy, not in the Russian spirit of voluntary sacrifice, but as a tactic to be imposed on a confused and apathetic people too poor to endure it. Japanese bombs fell on the coast, rumours swept inland, and at Sevagram, like an uncompromising sun piercing the clouds, Truth burst on its worshipper once more. As he pondered the Cripps mission and its failure, on a silent Monday, Gandhi suddenly knew that this was the climax. This was the beginning of the ultimate crisis with nothing beyond it. Again iniquity had come to a head in an evil to be resisted at all costs. But the evil was no longer a Rowlatt Act, a provincial reign of terror, an infidel treaty, a bad tax, or a denial of elementary freedom. It was the British presence itself—at least in the diseased form it had assumed under stress.

Disenchantment with Cripps had destroyed the last remnant of Gandhi's loyalty. The Sahib was not even a protector. Singapore had gone down at a push, its native population sullenly indifferent. The British Raj in India was fast sinking into the same degradation, with the same results likely if the Japanese marched in. It was not so much a government as a garrison, a bankrupt and panicky garrison, threatening action almost as savage as war itself against a people it had lost. Indeed it had already started that action, wrecking the economy of the border zone by a blind destruction of river craft. Only a supreme shock could restore the English to moral sanity; only such a shock could brace the Indians themselves to resist a new conqueror, as their Malayan and Burmese brethren had not. Gandhi challenged the Englishman with the simplest and most tremendous of all his slogans: Quit India.

He did not coin it himself. His own phrase was 'orderly withdrawal'. The other, however, was soon the accepted version. The forces which he unleashed on that April day were to go on working for five years, till the slogan was fulfilled. One of the last and cruellest of India's misfortunes under the Crown was that after giving the impulse, Gandhi was deprived of all power to guide.

His agent in publishing his summons was Mirabehn—perhaps because she was English. Apart from himself, she was the first of many whom the renewed touch of the Absolute revived and exalted. Over the past two or three years she had gone through a season of depression. Once Bapu astonished her by suggesting she should marry a Punjabi acquaintance, but nothing came of this. She had found no peace at Sevagram, where she spent her time spinning prodigiously, dreaming of a hermitage, and looking after some pet toads. From this decline into a pattern of spinsterhood Bapu rescued her with a draft Quit India resolution for Congress. If it appealed to her, she was to take it to the Working Committee at Allahabad. She alone; Mahadev was not going. Mahadev, as a matter of fact, would not have been the ideal companion. His judgement of her in 1942 was that she was full of spirit, but not equally full of knowledge. Bapu, however, knew what he wanted. He was anxious particularly that he should not seem to be applying pressure, either by going himself or by sending a secretary who would have the air of a proxy.

Nehru met Mirabehn at Allahabad, not concealing his surprise at her being the dispatch-bearer. The Working Committee read the resolution and discussed it heatedly for hours, referring back to her to find what it meant. Rajaji moved into opposition and resigned, but most of the rest approved strongly. Purpose was returning. They adopted the draft with certain amendments.

What did 'Quit India' mean? At first Gandhi interpreted it in the plainest sense. 'Leave India to God,' he wrote in May. 'If that is too much, then leave her to anarchy.' In more sober terms, what he proposed was that India should be left in a neutral status like Ireland's. Then the Japanese might well turn away, rather than add three or four hundred millions to their enemies. If they did invade, Indians should practise non-co-operation or take to the hills, but never submit or collaborate. It was pointed out, however, that such a sweeping proposition would lose foreign sympathy, especially Chinese and American. By June Gandhi was suggesting that India might strike a bargain with the Western allies allowing their forces —including British forces—to use her territory for the duration. But 'quit' meant 'quit'. The Raj must be dismantled, at once and for ever. Any further British presence was a matter for India's consent. As for the method of persuasion, it could only be full-scale Satyagraha all over again. That would be rebellion; it would look like exploiting Britain's difficulties; it would probably lead to acts of violence . . . but these things could not be helped.

On 4 June the American journalist Louis Fischer arrived at Sevagram. He had already discussed Gandhi with Linlithgow, who said: 'The old man is the biggest thing in India.' The Viceroy foresaw the end, which he assumed would come after the war. 'We are preparing for our departure.' Now Fischer interviewed the 'old man' daily for a week, and talked with associates in between. His long report, which was published in book form with a preface by Carl Heath, helped to refurbish Gandhi's prestige beyond the reach of censorship, and to keep his claims before English-speaking readers through the latter part of the war.

Fischer's portrait of the Mahatma at seventy-two was careful and interesting, in one respect unconsciously—at their first meeting, he seemed tall. Later the account was expanded in a biography.

> His body did not look old. He did not give one a feeling that he was old. His head showed his age. . . . His upper lip, covered with a black-and-white stubble moustache, was so narrow that it almost met the fat, down-pointed nose. . . .
>
> He wore his dentures only for eating and took them out and washed them in public; he wore gold-rimmed bifocals; he shaved his face every day with a straight razor. . . .
>
> His facial features, with the exception of his quiet, confident eyes, were ugly and in repose his face would have been ugly, but it was rarely in repose. . . . He spoke with a low, sing-song, undistinguished voice . . . and he gestured eloquently, but not always, with the fingers of one hand. His hands were beautiful.

Kasturbai sat with him at meals, toothless, not speaking, but often looking at him. Obviously he wanted her near. When he went out he walked briskly in stupefying heat, but with his forearms on the shoulders of boys or girls from the community, who competed for the honour of being his walking-sticks. At meals, thirty people sat cross-legged, a prayer was chanted ending 'shanti shanti shanti' ('peace'), and then Fischer was expected to eat with his fingers like everybody else. A good deal of their conversation went on under these conditions. Even in Gandhi's room, where the sole decoration was a picture of Christ, they were seldom alone.

The Mahatma talked about diet, and reincarnation, and Upton Sinclair, and Eleanor Roosevelt, and Dr Kellogg of the cornflakes. He reminisced a little, but was far more concerned with the present than the past. His remarks on the communal problem, the constructive programme, and the plan for civil disobedience, contained nothing new, but much that Fischer realized would be new to his public, and dispel misunderstandings. Gandhi refused to be drawn into speculation about what would follow independence. He asked Fischer to take a message to Linlithgow; perhaps a clash could still be averted. Also he entrusted him with a letter for Roosevelt. 'America and Britain', he said, 'are very great nations, but their greatness will count as dust before the bar of dumb humanity, whether African or Asiatic. They and they alone have the power to undo the wrong.'

Caught by the spell of his personality, Fischer wondered what the secret was. The word 'passion' took shape in his mind. A subdued, purring passion. He put it to Mahadev, who agreed. 'This passion', the secretary explained, 'is the sublimation of all the passions that flesh is heir to—sex and anger and personal ambition. . . . Gandhi is under his own complete control. That generates tremendous energy and passion.' In Hindu terms, *brahmacharya* was perfected. Actually (as appeared later) Gandhi himself did not think so.

Mirabehn, who had been probing bureaucrats on the implications of the scorched-earth policy, returned to Sevagram in July and found Bapu at the top of his form again, inspired and glowing. He asked her to go to Delhi and explain his intentions further. She must make it clear that he regarded even his rebellion as a friendly gesture. Mirabehn dutifully made her way to the capital and stayed at Birla House, a building belonging to the millionaire, who had placed it at their disposal. She failed to penetrate to the Viceroy but conveyed the message to his secretary.

The Working Committee met on 14 July. By this time Nehru had completely convinced himself that Gandhi was right. True partnership, brought about by shock treatment and a total British reversal, was the sole route to Indian effectiveness. He was disturbed by signs that Bose's pro-Axis propaganda was making inroads, and by rumours that that elusive person would return under Japan's aegis, with an army recruited from Indian prisoners of war. Certainly things would not stand still. The committee called for a transfer of power, and reinstated Gandhi in his 1930 rank of generalissimo for whatever struggle might ensue. On 8 August the All-India Congress Committee voted likewise in Bombay, with the addition, sponsored by Nehru and Azad, that a free India would fight aggression with arms as well as non-co-operation. Such protests as there were came from the Communists, whose unreserved backing of the war effort made them the Raj's only organized allies. No date was fixed for civil disobedience. Gandhi proposed to make a last overture to the Government before giving the signal. Meanwhile he exhorted Congress members to think of themselves as free and act in that spirit.

Delhi struck first. Before dawn on the 9th he was arrested, together with most of the Congress officers (148 in Bombay alone), and Vinoba, Mahadev and Mirabehn. The last two accompanied him to his place of internment, the Aga Khan's palace at Poona. Kasturbai could have stayed out. But she elected to deputize for her husband at a meeting he was to have addressed, and in that way she managed to join him.

XVII

Anti-climax

1

Their quarters were a row of rooms, side by side in a long building. Sarojini Naidu was interned with them. Gandhi had talked of fasting, but he decided to wait, and sent a message to Vinoba at Wardha jail, asking that intrepid disciple to drop plans for a fast accompanying his. After four hectic months the strain on the Mahatma might have been dangerous. Worry over this probably hastened a tragedy, the collapse of Mahadev. Within a few days of arrival at the palace-prison he had a heart attack. All attempts to revive him failed, and he died. Though only fifty, he had said he did not wish to outlive Gandhi. Kasturbai lamented: 'Bapu has lost his right hand, and his left hand! Both his hands has Bapu lost!' Demonstrative emotion was checked, as always, in Bapu's presence; but Ba was not far wrong. Few employers can have been blessed with such a secretary for so many years. Mahadev's records, which reflect a care far beyond the call of duty, make him the nearest approximation to a Boswell in India. His death in harness was a species of martyrdom.

He was cremated, and they raised a mound over the spot where his ashes lay. On it Mirabehn moulded the sacred word OM, with a cross and a crescent. Every morning Bapu silently put flowers on the mound, outlining the cross with tiny blossoms.

The Government had no wish to be harsh with him. Pyarelal, the other secretary, was transferred to the palace. Pyarelal's sister Dr Sushila Nayyar (afterwards the Indian Minister of Health) was already there as a medical attendant on Kasturbai. When a few weeks had elapsed, newspapers were allowed. So were private visits, though not contacts with politicians. Reports that trickled in were heavily censored, but terrible enough. The mass arrests, when Congress was still hoping for a settlement, had thrown the country into confusion and anger. A 'Quit India' revolt was actually flaring up, which the

imprisoned leaders were powerless to control. It was violent—a foretaste of many bitter fruits of the last attempt to suppress the
Mahatma.

This revolt took the form of a guerrilla war, waged chiefly by
fugitive left-wingers. The rebels cut telegraph wires, attacked railway stations, derailed trains, burned down post offices and assaulted
the Raj's representatives. At one stage communication between Bengal and the rest of India was almost disrupted. Local governments
sprang up at Midnapur and Satara and over large parts of Bihar.
Troops as well as police had to be employed to quell the uprising.
By mid-September about fifty had been killed on the side of authority, and over six hundred on the other. The fight raged on into 1943.
Then, with thirty-six thousand in jail again, it gradually flickered
out. But its end brought no feeling of reconciliation. As the revolt
receded, famine advanced. A million and a half people died through
what Indians blamed as government negligence, a view not devoid
of factual support.

Meanwhile the Japanese, threatened in the rear by the resurgent
Americans, had let their opportunity pass. Their intelligence service was poor, and they were afraid to risk their army in such a terri-
fying country. Linlithgow, responding a little to the Congress case,
had reformed his Executive Council so as to give Indian members
a large majority. They were advisory only and did not speak for the
major parties. However, in the last part of 1942 a steady recovery
was going forward. Altogether two million Indian volunteers joined
the armed forces—an impressive number, until one states it as a percentage of the population. When the Japanese turned west again
they were driven back. But the British success remained incomplete.
During the campaign Subhas Chandra Bose appeared in the border-
lands with a government of sorts, and an Indian National Army
twenty thousand strong. His legend had power if his government
did not, and it survived his own accidental death, which many
Indians refused to believe in.

During the revolt and the changes at Delhi, Gandhi was corresponding with Linlithgow. He protested at British propaganda, disclaimed responsibility for the violence, and asked that Congress's
leadership be absolved of guilt. The Viceroy stood firm despite a
bad press in America and China, and statements in defence of his
prisoner by General Smuts and Bernard Shaw. Like Lord Willingdon he fancied he had drawn Congress's sting. He had more justi-

fication, not because Congress was really beaten, but because the terrorism had undermined its moral position. The rank and file had taken part, and so had a few of the larger fry who escaped the net. Nevertheless Gandhi could fairly argue that the leaders deserved to be cleared—especially of the charge that they were fifth columnists.

On 10 February 1943, having given the usual warning, he began a three-week fast, taking no nourishment but a minimal amount of fruit juice. The Viceroy's Council debated what to do. Should they let the fast run its course, with a grave risk of his dying in British detention; or should they let him out on some sort of parole? Linlithgow decided to take the risk. He told Gandhi he was breaking his own rules. Fasting was supposed to prod the consciences of friends, not to coerce opponents. For once, somebody at Delhi had taken the trouble to read the Mahatma's writings. His reply describing the fast as 'an appeal to the Highest Tribunal' was less than satisfactory; it suggested that he was prodding the conscience of the Almighty. He would have done better to say he was trying to influence his fellow countrymen on the Council. Three of them did resign in support. The Viceroy rejected all appeals, and sent doctors to keep Gandhi alive. The fast ended punctually without mishap. Its main result was an attempt by Sir Tej Bahadur Sapru, the mediator of 1931, to soften Delhi's attitude. Linlithgow remained adamant. When his term of office (prolonged owing to the war) expired in October, Gandhi wrote once more, reproaching him for the grief he had caused by countenancing untruth. The departing Viceroy's answer was as dusty as ever.

Life in the Poona internment suite had been, and continued to be, a dragging nightmare of inaction. Bapu and his five companions were reduced to the unprecedented need of killing time. He read books, but without the eager appetite of the 1920s. Again poetry and drama helped: he extended his knowledge of Shakespeare, Shaw and Browning. His main interest for a while was Communism. Although put off by the style of *Das Kapital*, he ploughed through it and went on to further works by Marx, Engels, Lenin and Stalin. Pyarelal gathered that the course had confirmed him in his own brand of Communism, which was closer to Marx's forerunners than to Marx, and had not won him over to the idea of class war.

At other times he reverted to one of the first serious pursuits of his life, and gave Kasturbai lessons. They smiled together over her struggles with Gujarati script, her failure to memorize the rivers of the Punjab, and her statement under oral examination that Lahore was the capital of Calcutta. Once Ba asked Bapu why he had brought such miseries on the people by defying the Government. Wasn't there room in India for English as well as Indians? Yes, he replied quietly, they were welcome if they stayed as brothers and not as rulers.

He desired a religious symbol to keep before him on days of silence. Mirabehn wrote OM on cardboard with 'Hey Rama', O God, underneath. Sarojini Naidu applied her rich imagination to the observance of Hindu festivals as these came round. The party celebrated the birthday of Krishna, and warmed to Mrs Naidu's spirit and fortitude. In default of festivals and reading matter they played games—badminton and ping-pong, and *carrom,* a kind of shuffleboard. Bapu's half-hearted attempt at badminton was hopeless and he gave up. Ba enjoyed *carrom.* She practised by herself and became adept.

But the wonderful old lady was flagging at last. She grew depressed, and suffered from heart palpitations and bronchitis. In December 1943 her illness became serious. She asked for Dr Dinshah Mehta, a nature-cure therapist who had treated her husband, and also for a practitioner of Aryuvedic or traditional Indian medicine. Bapu requested permission for them to come. The Government was slow to grant it. By February 1944 hope was waning. Sons and grandchildren were allowed to visit the palace. Devadas sent for penicillin, then hardly known in India, but Bapu preferred to leave her in peace rather than torture her with injections.

One of her last wishes was to see Harilal. On 21 February he lurched into the sickroom, drunk. She wept and beat her forehead, and they hustled him out. The crisis came next day. Bapu was sitting with Ba's head resting in his lap. Her breathing altered. Gently he asked: 'What is it?' The answer was sweet and clear, with a tone of wonder, as if at a sudden strange rapture: 'I don't know what it is.' That was the end. She went before him into the presence of Truth.

He said not a word, but signed for the body to be laid out. Women washed it and decked it with flowers. Incense was burnt, verses of the *Gita* were read. He sat in contemplation, not speaking aloud, but once murmuring a little. On the 23rd they cremated her on the same site as Mahadev, with a small crowd looking on.

By her own request she was wrapped in a sari made of yarn spun by her husband. Devadas lit the pyre. Afterwards they found her bangles intact among the ashes, a token of salvation.

Gandhi returned and sat on his cot. 'I cannot imagine life without Ba,' he said. 'Her passing has left a vacuum which never will be filled.' The new Viceroy, Lord Wavell, sent his condolences. Gandhi wrote back: 'Though for her sake I have welcomed her death as bringing freedom from living agony, I feel the loss more than I had thought I should. . . . We were a couple outside the ordinary. . . . She became truly my *better* half.' A memorial fund was launched, to be devoted to the welfare of village women and children.

Six weeks later Gandhi himself had an attack of malaria, with a temperature of 105. He held out against quinine for a couple of days and then took it. The fever passed, but hookworm and amoebic dysentery followed. Under the pressure of public anxiety, the Government yielded to his doctors' advice and set him free. On 6 May, with his companions, he emerged from his last imprisonment. All told he had spent 249 days in African jails and 2089 in Indian ones. Amid sighs of relief and good wishes from every side, he went to stay at Juhu with his old host Shantikumar Morarji. Other guests were Mrs Naidu and Mrs Pandit, Nehru's sister. Learning that he had never seen a feature film with a soundtrack, the Morarjis arranged a private showing of *Mission to Moscow*, a wartime production based on a book by an American diplomat. Gandhi did not enjoy it. The spectacle of such serious business being conducted in a milieu of cocktail parties and provocatively dressed women jarred on him. They tried an Indian film with happier results. However, his self-treatment during convalescence did not include much entertainment. It consisted mostly of long periods of silence. He would plant a chair on the Juhu sands near the water-line and sit in it looking like Canute. After a month he felt fit enough to resume work at Sevagram.

2

His first concern was to publish his long-forbidden rejoinder to the British version of what had happened in 1942. Then he approached the new Viceroy, reviving proposals for conditional co-operation with the war effort. The reply was a blank negative. Wavell, a capable soldier and a cultured man, had gained much goodwill by prompt action to relieve the famine. But he never succumbed to the Mahatma's spell, and was disposed to accept the bureaucrats' reading of his character.

In their correspondence Gandhi assured the Viceroy that his last essay in national Satyagraha was a closed chapter. The reasons for this retreat were not merely strategic. Events had proved that the non-violence which he supposed the masses to have learnt from him was in most cases superficial, and an outcome of weakness rather than strength. It worked when he was favourably placed to make it work. In 1930 he had got the movement off on the right lines himself, and retained a high degree of control even from prison. But in 1942 the rising had been independent of him, and no real Satyagraha had occurred. A minority had been violent, a majority had done nothing. Gokhale's warning long ago—that he made demands beyond people's capacity—sank in at last.

What then were the prospects for the future? Should he take a hint from the ex-Tilakite Aurobindo, now a sage in Pondicherry, who was offering a Hindu version of Nietzsche? Aurobindo said humanity was simply inadequate; to solve its problems it must evolve into superhumanity. Gandhi could not go so far. But he did revert toward the view he had expressed in the 1920s when writing on *brahmacharya*. Ordinary sensual man was 'animal-like' and below true manhood. The converse was that by drastic action, human beings could (so to speak) be rewound and put right. They could realize their full potentialities and thus measure up to the imperatives of Truth.

The Mahatma pursued this thought along two related lines. He made a fresh scrutiny of the nature-cure theories which he had absorbed as a student from the pamphlets of Allinson, and applied on and off throughout his life. Dinshah Mehta, the doctor he had summoned for Kasturbai, ran a clinic in Poona. Here Gandhi observed techniques by which the body could allegedly perfect itself without drugs, and become a firm support for the controlled mind. After a sketchy trial in a village, nature-cure was added to khadi and the rest of his social causes. It included hygiene, sunbaths, hip-baths, massage, milk, and fruit juice, plus recitation of the Ramanama prayer, his favourite meditation on the name and nature of God.

Together with this, he adopted Shaw's belief that to attain fruition mankind must live longer. However, he was still unwilling to admit that mankind would need to be radically altered. The ability was there, if only it could be drawn out. According to a text in the Upanishads the true span of life is 125 years. If we never reach it, that is solely because of our own faults. Gandhi took heart from this passage and said he would make 125 his target. So should everybody. It was a matter of will and self-realization. If people could only learn to strangle that fretful, craving, contemptible little sham ego! If they could only learn to work out their salvation in detachment, enriching the world as their gifts dictated! What might they not accomplish? When Louis Fischer came to see him again, he said: 'I want freedom for full expression of my personality. I must be free to build a staircase to Sirius if I want to.'

But at least one highly formidable ego was delaying that project. As Congressmen drifted back into the legislatures, tactical questions arose over bargains with Muslim politicians. Gandhi tackled Jinnah. During the repression of Congress the Muslim League had flourished exceedingly with British blessings. Rajagopalachari, estranged from the Congress leadership by the Quit India resolution, had sought a basis for joint action with it. Gandhi had received him cordially in prison and called him 'the keeper of my conscience'. Now, at liberty, it was time to test his formula. This envisaged a series of plebiscites conceding the possibility of a small Pakistan. In July 1944 Gandhi sent off a letter beginning 'Dear brother Jinnah,' a salutation which he later changed to 'Quaid-i-Azam', Great Leader, as the other liked to be addressed. Replying, Jinnah always began 'Dear Mr Gandhi'. When they met during September, he insisted that the Mahatma should come to him at his Bombay house.

Their talks foundered, partly on the psychological clash, partly on Jinnah's demands for Congress-League equality, and for the partition of India before the British Raj was withdrawn. He also rejected Rajaji's plebiscites, putting forward a counter-scheme of his own. In each province with a Muslim majority, however narrow, qualified Muslims alone should vote. A majority of these, however narrow, should then be enough to take the province into Pakistan. Arithmetic showed that on this basis, less than two million enfranchised Punjabis could decide the fate of the twenty-eight million inhabitants of the province.

About this time Sapru and other Liberals set up a committee to draft an Indian constitution. Gandhi worked with it. Jinnah refused, saying he did not want one constitution but two, one for the Hindu 'nation' and one for the Muslim 'nation'. The irony was that whereas the religious Gandhi was fighting for a secular state, his arch-rival, a Muslim so lax as to border on agnosticism, was riding to power under the banner of theocracy.

The mingled hope and gloom of the war's last year had their repercussions on Gandhi. He voiced his sympathy for Warsaw and the people of Poland, but observed that there were war criminals at top levels in all the major countries. The outside world was far from forgetting him. Hints at a recommendation for the Nobel Peace Prize had never gone any further, and did not now. But in April 1945, when UNO was founded at San Francisco, journalists asked him for comments as a matter of course. Mostly he generalized about the need for world government, a non-vindictive peace, and racial equality. But he again spoke of India as a leader in that direction. 'India's nationalism spells internationalism.' 'Freedom of India will demonstrate to all the exploited races of the earth that their freedom is near.' San Francisco prompted a letter from Sonja Schlesin. She had not forgotten him either.

Wavell was in London. A weighty *Times* correspondence had shown that despite Churchill's reluctance to preside over the liquidation of the Empire, the demand for a British move was overwhelming. The diehards of the Army and Civil Service in Delhi, and those of big business in Bombay and Calcutta, might say otherwise. But they were insufficiently aware of the background— a background of changing minds (the continuance of Gandhi's conversion process) and economic and military erosion. On 14 June Wavell returned. He released all the Congress leaders, and summoned them to a conference at Simla on the 25th, together with Jinnah and other politicians. Gandhi was not a delegate, but he went to Simla and took part in the discussion between sessions.

As an opening step, the Viceroy proposed to turn his Council into an interim government, with ministers from the major parties. He would retain his veto only under strict limitations. Congress approved. Then Jinnah queried a clause about Hindu-Muslim parity. Congress took it to mean simply a fair representation for both religions, which would permit its own current president,

Maulana Azad, to be a minister. Jinnah insisted on adding a political sense. The only true representatives of Islam were members of his League. Therefore, he claimed all Muslim nominations for himself. Wavell could not persuade him and would not proceed without him. The conference broke up. Curzon's monster, political Islam, had grown too big for his successor to cope with.

This turned out to be the last bid for an Indian settlement under Churchill. The third Labour Government took office toward the close of July, headed by Attlee, whose service on the Simon Commission had given him a special interest in India. Memories of prison and lathi charges during the last Labour premiership made Indians tepid in their welcome. The realization that the end was truly in sight began with an event which was a legacy of S. C. Bose, and a posthumous triumph. After Japan's defeat the soldiers of his National Army fell into British hands. Wholesale charges of desertion or treason could not be pressed. However, some of their officers had allegedly committed war crimes. GHQ put three of these on trial in Delhi—a Hindu, a Muslim and a Sikh. It thus united the communities in furious protest. Nehru and other notables defended the accused. Gandhi himself spoke on their behalf, and fraternized with National Army soldiers who were not on trial. The proceedings took on the air of a test of strength, and it was GHQ, in consultation with Whitehall, that yielded. Sentences were passed but not carried out, and no more of the presumed criminals were tried. Indians sensed that the will to hold firm had gone. So did the British officers of the armed forces. Their no-surrender spirit gave way to resignation. In February 1946 the Indian Navy responded with a mutiny. Disaffection was also noted among the police, and riots over shortages raged almost unchecked in several cities.

Elections for the provincial and national assemblies placed Congressmen in most of the non-Muslim seats. Thanks to Ghaffar Khan, they won most of the Muslim seats as well in the North-West Frontier Province. But elsewhere the League captured the Muslim seats, and claimed a mandate for Pakistan. Jinnah was coming into his kingdom.

On 24 March a British Cabinet Mission with all-party support arrived in Delhi. It consisted of Sir Stafford Cripps, now President of the Board of Trade; Lord Pethick-Lawrence, Secretary of State for India, and an old acquaintance of the Mahatma; and A. V. Alexander, the First Lord of the Admiralty. Gandhi, more acute than some of his colleagues, expressed an immediate if cautious trust. This time the mission was not a hoax. This time, surely, they meant it. He came to Delhi at Pethick-Lawrence's request and lived there for the next few months.

His role in the discussions was unofficial but crucial. While never delivering prepared speeches or formal statements, he explained the issues as he saw them himself (he did not profess to speak for Congress) with tact and lucidity. On 16 May a proposal emerged for a federal constitution in three tiers—a Union of India at the top, provinces and states at the bottom, and in between, voluntary groupings of regions which would allow Muslim cohesion without secession. A constituent assembly was to be formed, with a structure safeguarding minority rights. India would be free to remain in the Commonwealth or not.

The princes and the League accepted the scheme, though Jinnah interpreted it in a manner which gave no hope of stable working. Gandhi welcomed it with reservations, which grew more pronounced but never caused him to change his mind, and he eventually carried Congress with him. Most of the opposition came from the Left. But while Congress agreed to join in the Constituent Assembly, it would not join in an interim government, unless it could instal a Muslim minister of its own choosing. To renounce that claim would be to capitulate to Jinnah's mythology and become merely the Hindu organization. Wavell wanted to form a combined Congress-League ministry. Gandhi told him that he could not ride two horses at once. The difficulty grew clear when Jinnah again refused to tolerate Muslim ministers who were not Leaguers, and declined to sit at the same table with the 'traitor' Azad. The Cabinet Mission went home at the end of June with the long-term scheme approved but no government in being.

Wavell broke the deadlock, after a fashion, by ruling that neither party could veto the nominees of the other. Jinnah retorted on 27 July by withdrawing his acceptance of the federal scheme, and announcing a boycott of the Constituent Assembly. The League's next step would be direct action to achieve Pakistan. 'We have forged a pistol,' he said, 'and we are in a position to use it.' Someone ventured to ask if the direct action would be non-violent. He refused to 'discuss ethics'. On 12 August the Viceroy invited Nehru to form an interim government, while keeping the door open for the League. Jinnah, however, declared that the interim government would embody 'the caste Hindu Fascist Congress' seeking to rule over the Muslims and other minorities with the aid of British bayonets. He would give his answer on 16 August, which he had fixed as Direct Action Day. The day dawned, and Muslim gangs in Calcutta began a prolonged massacre of Hindus which took more than five thousand lives.

The perpetrators of what came to be known as the Great Killing were well prepared, well armed, and not noticeably checked by the police. However, Hindu reprisals inflicted heavy losses. Nehru took office as Prime Minister on 2 September. The new Congress President, Gandhi's Champaran helper Professor Kripalani, spoke with pride of breaking into the citadel of power. Muslims hoisted black flags and rioting spread through India. Under intense pressure from the Viceroy, Jinnah consented to join the Government. But his five ministers included an Untouchable from Ambedkar's anti-Gandhi group, whose presence made nonsense of his religious platform, and could only be construed as a species of sabotage. Furthermore Liaquat Ali Khan, the Leaguer who became Finance Minister, told a press conference that he did not regard the Government as a coalition. The League admitted no joint responsibility. Nor would it take part in the Constituent Assembly.

Gandhi was still in Delhi, living on the fringe of the sweepers' colony. Here a cluster of huts, built under his direction by homeless Harijans, became the nucleus of a sort of town. His own home was a single cell in a row with a small temple in the middle. It faced a patch of grass where he held prayer meetings. The Harijans came to him with their problems, and he played with their children, telling them to learn to read and keep clean. From the city beyond, the visitors had been streaming in for months—the British and Indian politicians, the correspondents, the tourists with cameras. His prayer meetings gave him a daily forum. They were ecumenical gatherings, with readings from the scriptures of all the major religions. He gave talks (published as articles) about the gods and the moral virtues and leprosy and prison reform and growing more food: an endless series of topics, on all of which he had things to say that were worth hearing.

When Nehru became Prime Minister, Gandhi told his audience it was a red-letter day for India. Behind his satisfaction, however, there was a gnawing anxiety that rapidly worsened. A year earlier he had sounded Nehru out with a long letter. In this he reasserted the main principles of *Hind Swaraj,* stressed Truth and Non-Violence as mankind's sole hope, and argued that India's proper social unit was the transfigured village of his dreams. Nehru had replied disquietingly. Why did the village have to be the embodiment of the ideal? After all, India would need heavy industry anyhow, to maintain independence and raise the standard of living. As for *Hind Swaraj,* it struck him as 'completely unreal' and he had not looked at it for years.

Now that this unamenable heir was Prime Minister, Gandhi stood by him and never allowed his rare public criticisms to sound resentful or hostile. Privately he became a prey to doubts. Nehru had never concealed his aim of advancing beyond the Gandhi programme, yet he had seemed sincere in his endorsement of that programme as far as it went. But had he been so? Had any of the Congress leaders been so, except perhaps for a faithful few like Sardar Patel? As 1946 neared its close Gandhi fell into moods of sick mistrust, when he feared that the past quarter-century had been a delusion, that the politicians had exploited him for his influence and were casting him aside.

What was left of the constructive programme, or the doctrine of Ahimsa? He was trying to reinvigorate Basic Education, Harijan work, and all the rest, under a joint planning board. Mirabehn was doing well with a cattle-breeding project. An agricultural team was studying how to grow more food. But he could not shake off a suspicion that the spirit had altered. The Spinners' Association seemed obsessed with output statistics and the narrower economic aspects. As for Ahimsa . . . within a few yards of his own Delhi lodging he had to endure the sight and sound of drilling, as the young zealots of the RSS (Rashtriya Sevak Sangh), a Hindu storm-troop body, openly prepared to slaughter the Muslims. They were taught to regard him as their chief enemy. The counter-massacre in Calcutta had been largely their doing.

That October the communal fury began to look like a prologue to civil war, vindicating the diehards' most vicious forecasts. Appalling reports came in from eastern Bengal. There had been more mass killings in Chittagong and Noakhali. Muslims set fire to Hindus' houses, defiled their temples, forced them to profess Islam and break Hindu commandments, and raped their women. Refugees poured into Bihar telling their stories to the press. 25 October was proclaimed Noakhali Day, and Hindus paraded chant-

ing 'Blood for blood'. The resultant riots in Bihar during the following week piled up a verified total of 4,580 corpses.

These events drove Gandhi toward despair. First Bengal, now
Bihar, the cradle of Satyagraha in India! He was especially
revolted by the assaults on women, which lacked even the excuses
Jinnah provided. Behind the immediate nightmare were even
grimmer implications. With such savagery rising to the surface, most
of the armoury of non-violence was useless. Should the Constituent
Assembly fail to arrange the transfer of power, he could not launch
civil disobedience. It would mean a gigantic Chauri Chaura throughout the peninsula. India's fate, therefore, depended on the professional politicians; and early in November it became apparent what
they were capable of. Nehru toured Bengal and Bihar with three of
his ministers, and threatened to restore order by aerial bombing,
the Englishman's method in the Punjab and on the North-West
Frontier. As Gandhi privately remarked, his protégé was learning
to act like the Sahibs even before they had gone.

During the ministerial tour he was in Calcutta. Demonstrators
with placards had recently burst into his Delhi prayer ground
demanding that he take action over Bengal, and he felt bound to
try. In Calcutta he drove with the provincial premier, a Muslim,
through streets that were almost empty and piled two feet deep
with refuse which nobody had ventured out to collect. Rows of
houses and shops were gutted by fire. He experienced 'a sinking
feeling at the mass madness that can turn man into less than a
brute'.

From Calcutta he wrote to Nehru.

> A deep bond unites me with Bihar. How can I forget that?
> If even half of what one hears is true, it shows that Bihar has
> forgotten humanity. . . . My inner voice tells me, 'You may not
> live to be a witness to this senseless slaughter. . . . Does it not
> mean that your day is over?' The logic of the argument is driving
> me irresistibly toward a fast.

Fasting seemed to be the only form of Satyagraha that was still
possible. But he decided against it. His place was in Noakhali,
where the Muslim terrorists had reduced much of the Hindu population to a panic-stricken rabble. He would go there to restore Hindu
courage, if he could, and make peace between the communities.
Muriel Lester, who was in India again, had already gone. She

warned him of the signs that more sinister forces were at work than mere hooliganism. Somebody had supplied the Muslims with lathis; with petrol (which was rationed) for arson; and with stirrup-pumps.

He left Calcutta on 6 November. Noakhali is a densely inhabited region forty miles square, in the delta where the Ganges and Brahmaputra converge. Access is tortuous even for rural India, because of the watercourses. Large boats and small boats, bullock carts and bicycles all have their uses, and the traveller may have to change from one to another and resign himself to very slow progress. When Gandhi came, about four-fifths of the population was Muslim. Some of the villages lay in ruins. He embraced the challenge with sombre satisfaction. 'My present mission', he wrote, 'is the most difficult and complicated one of my life. . . . "Do or Die" has to be put to the test here.'

Some Bengali politicians went with him. So did Pyarelal and Sushila Nayyar, several relatives and in-laws who were helping him, and a skeleton staff. He dispersed them relentlessly into separate villages to work alone, without protection or medical aid. As for himself, he set up headquarters at Srirampur with three companions—Manu Gandhi, the granddaughter of a cousin; Parasuram, a stenographer; and Professor Nirmal Kumar Bose, a scientist from Calcutta University, who had got leave of absence to join him as secretary and interpreter. Bose's links with the Mahatma went back more than a decade. He was the author of one of the most carefully reasoned analyses of Gandhian theory.

Gandhi remained in Noakhali for four months. He tramped from village to village as a pilgrim, often barefoot, depending largely on local hospitality. Again and again he risked injury visiting places that could only be reached by swaying bamboo bridges, ten or fifteen feet above ground, spanning patches of marsh. To achieve confidence he practised walking on poles at floor level. In all he stayed at forty-nine villages. At each he held prayer meetings which were in effect open forums, and did his best to leave an inter-communal peace council functioning. The Muslims' attitudes varied from place to place. His simple talks on the unity of God and the virtues of true Islam attracted many of the poor. So did his perfect impartiality, and his readiness to listen to grievances and relieve the sick. But fanatics strewed his path with brambles and broken glass; while the wealthier, more politically-minded hung menacing placards on the trees, and advised the peasantry to keep away from his meetings, if they knew what was healthy for them.

This Noakhali pilgrimage was a grapple with the Absolute. The atrocities on both sides since Direct Action Day had put the break-down of non-violence in a more lurid light. As British power declined, spectres which Gandhi had assumed to be dead were again on the prowl. An ancient Hindu concept of holy warfare or *dharma yuddha*, invoked in the past when Hindus fought Muslims, was inspiring their descendants. Gandhi now wondered if non-violence under his leadership had actually concealed worse evils than the weakness he already acknowledged. In many cases, he began to suspect, it had been cowardly hypocrisy. Indians had abstained from violence merely because they were frightened of the police and troops. With that fear receding, their true character was reasserting itself. After twenty-six years of lip-service to Ahimsa they were as violent as any other people.

Yet in the deepest trough of despond, Gandhi blamed himself. As always he believed that if he had failed to teach Ahimsa, it was because he had failed to make himself a good enough teacher. His wanderings through Bengal were a penance, a practical examina-tion of conscience. The hope of living to be 125 faded from his mind; he had not the heart or the composure. A poem of Tagore's haunted him, 'Walk alone'—a strange and sad irony for someone who, in the body, never did walk alone. Once again he was striving to perfect *brahmacharya*, to reduce self to zero, to divest himself of everything but God's presence. In January 1947 he wrote to Mirabehn that if he could entirely empty his being, God would possess him. Then he would become a fit instrument at last.

3

His tone was grave. Yet the final spurt of his *brahmacharya* showed that he could still startle the faithful. Over the years his experiments in self-control had taken a novel shape, which suddenly became patent in their sight. The last surprise of Gandhi's career was no solemn attainment of the Holy Grail. It was a characteristic blend of the deeply serious and the semi-comic.

In 1936, the year of tension and the bad dream, it had looked as if his audacities among women might cease. But after reflection he took the dream as a challenge. Certainly he could not dispense with women. He was inclined to see them as the future leaders of Satyagraha. The proper course was not to take flight but to press on and call the devil's bluff.

This meant pursuing the Tantric course that Ramakrishna had given the hint for. At Segaon, Gandhi went on trying to soft-pedal his more masculine qualities and cultivate his odd feminine streak —the almost motherly traits that went with the spinning wheel. But also, piecemeal and quietly, he resumed the scheme of conduct which he had favoured at Tolstoy Farm, with its mixed bathing and sleeping. A western parallel is perhaps to be found in the more responsible forms of the Naturist cult. Gandhi's innovations account for the phrasing of his sole letter to Winston Churchill. Hearing (not quite accurately) that Churchill had called him a naked fakir, he commented that he was indeed trying to be a fakir and also naked, and that the latter was more difficult. He meant it literally. Besides keeping his own clothes to a minimum, he inveighed against the muffling-up and false modesty imposed on Indian women. Tranquil uninhibitedness became his goal, to be achieved through habit, and spiritual exercises such as the Ramanama prayer.

During the argument which at length flared up, he described his ideal *brahmachari* as a man who by 'constant attendance upon God' is 'capable of lying naked with naked women, however beautiful they may be, without being in any manner whatsoever sexually excited'. As the notion took hold of him at Segaon, it affected both himself and the other inmates. Ashramites of opposite sexes nursed each other in illness without restraint; he set the example himself with Mirabehn. Sometimes he received visitors in the bathroom, and had his massage administered by young women.

The next step was that one or other of the young women would sleep in his room. He did not contrive this to test himself, a practice which he condemned as foolhardy. But if the evening found them together, more or less in the line of duty, they might stay together. In the haphazard Indian atmosphere, and the extreme non-privacy of the ashram, the situation was less peculiar than it would be to a western taste. Also he kept the door open. Normally, all was peace. If he did feel disturbed, he noted it as a sign that his self-control was imperfect, and recited the Ramanama. As for the girls, they would not, of course, have thought of him sexually in any case. But if no ideas at all were put in their heads, they were presumably making progress in their own self-control.

For a long time these experiments were not widely known. The English found out when a policeman happened to call at night. However, they judged it unwise to release his scandalized report. In 1939 accusations were made—not for the first time—by orthodox Hindus wishing to discredit Gandhi because of his Harijan work. He replied with a light-hearted though not very explicit personal statement, in the course of which he said that if he wanted women as charged he would not be afraid to take them, publicly and polygamously.

It was the pilgrimage in Noakhali that brought a crisis. The Mahatma's assistant Professor Bose came to him with a sophisticated insight such as he had not often been exposed to. Bose knew and was unhappy. Some of Gandhi's female disciples, he thought, showed neurotic symptoms and a misplaced possessiveness. Gandhi himself went through fussy, prying phases. The mysteries of the senses seemed to interest him a shade disagreeably. He asked people how they felt when others touched them—to Hindus, a shocking question.

His experiments had begun moving toward a climax with the advent of Manu, his cousin's granddaughter. Kasturbai was nursed by the girl, and entrusted her to Bapu's care. He wrote her a letter saying: 'I have been father to many but to you I am a mother.' Though nineteen years old, she averred that she had never felt any sexual impulse. Not unnaturally a query arose in his mind as to whether this assertion was true, and what it implied if it was. But a young woman with the right kind of innocence might be a promising *brahmachari* herself. He tried to sift Manu. Within a year or so of Kasturbai's death, uneasiness was spreading even to friends like Birla who were not in his closest circle.

When she wanted to go to Noakhali, where he was almost without other companions except Professor Bose himself, he weighed the issues carefully. This would be the ultimate trial. But it would come in the course of duty, not through his own devising. If he could perfect his own *brahmacharya,* and if Manu possessed the cool and crystalline balance he dared to hope for, all would be well. Public opinion had no terrors for him. She could join him at Srirampur, he said, so long as she was completely frank and co-operative. But if he detected any ambiguity in her, she would have to leave. Manu replied that to her he really was more like a mother than a male guardian. In Noakhali she attended to his travelling kit, and aided the mission in such ways as she could; he looked after her with the deepest solicitude; and they slept in the same bed.

Professor Bose had it out with him, querying this whole course of sexual exercises on two grounds. First, whereas everything else in Gandhi's life had been open, this was semi-secret. Hushing it up as if it were shameful made it actually shameful. Secondly, what about the girls? Did they understand and concur, or was he simply using them for his own self-discipline? To the first point, Gandhi answered that he saw no reason to tell everybody. Later he admitted that although no active hushing-up was intended, he ought perhaps to have said more. But he would publish the whole story when he was ready. As for the second point (which Bose was not alone in raising), he insisted that they did understand, and benefited. Spiritual progress at another's expense was a contradiction in terms.

While Gandhi and Manu were at Haimchar, in February 1947, the major scandal broke. Anguished outcries went up from his disciples. Some deserted him. When he aired the topic at prayer meetings, and sent the transcript of his remarks to *Harijan*, two members of the staff resigned rather than print it. He wrote to Kripalani asking him to take soundings among the Congress leaders. Kripalani found time, in the death-throes of the British Raj, to compose a long and somewhat embarrassed answer. Gandhi was unrepentant. He told inquirers that he held 'radical views of *brahmacharya*', and urged them to study the Tantra cult. Several objectors were won over. Ghaffar Khan, who had come to labour among fellow-Muslims in riot zones, watched the couple with his cloudless heroic eyes and was persuaded and touched. The ancient wonder-worker had invented a new human relationship. The intimacy which ought to have been repellent was not.

Manu assured Bapu that she was wholly with him. However, she suggested that they should keep a little more distance, and they did. The storm was generally forgotten in the turmoil of India's greater storm. But in May she added a footnote to their relationship by coming down with appendicitis. After an ineffectual essay in nature-cure he allowed an operation, and asked the surgeon for permission to be present. With gauze over his face the Mahatma sat on a chair throughout, perfectly silent, contemplating the ordeal of Manu's body. In the last few months of his life they were together again. He felt no regrets. His spiritual mistress had taken him over the final hurdle. 'Sixty years of striving', he said, 'have at last enabled me to realize the ideal of truth and purity which I have ever set before myself.'

4

On 20 February 1947 Britain agreed to do what Gandhi had demanded—quit India. The Government announced that power would be transferred by June 1948 at latest, to whatever authority the Indians succeeded in setting up. In the House of Commons the Opposition censured this action, but in the Lords, by a statesman-like speech, Halifax averted a hostile vote. He remained Satya-graha's most distinguished convert. To carry out the transfer, Lord Mountbatten was to become Viceroy. The manœuvre was masterly. There is some reason to think that Attlee, consciously or otherwise, took up a hint dropped by Birla. At any rate he not only forced the Indians' hand without angering them, he also associated his policy with a non-party figure of royal prestige, unquestioned patriotism, and outstanding ability, a man whom the Right could not decently attack.

Lord and Lady Mountbatten landed on 22 March. The new Viceroy made it clear at once that he was the last. Nehru welcomed his coming. Jinnah greeted him with the comment that partition was the only solution, and underlined it with further direct action. Gandhi meanwhile was in Bihar. He had left Bengal on 2 March and was struggling to prove, in what had once been Gandhist country, that Hindus and Muslims could co-exist. In villages wrecked by riots he exhorted Hindus to restore property looted from Muslims, and repair the houses they had smashed. Ghaffar Khan helped, his soldierlike faith unbroken.

There were flashes of hope. The Viceroy, setting to work with tact and energy, invited Gandhi to confer with him. The Mahatma took a train to Delhi and got on exceedingly well with both Mount-battens. All mistrust of Britain was over. From 31 March to 12 April six meetings took place. While in the capital he addressed an Asian Relations Conference, attended by delegates from most countries of the continent, including five Soviet republics. He still felt able to speak of Asia as the world's teacher. Zoroaster, Buddha, Moses,

Jesus, Muhammad, were all Asians. Asia's vocation was neither to ape the West nor to take vengeance: it was to carry wisdom to the nations that had invented the atomic bomb, and were recoiling into despair at their own creation. On 15 April, at Mountbatten's request, Jinnah actually joined him in a declaration denouncing violence and calling upon the communities to cease from incitement. And the Finance Minister, a Muslim Leaguer, gladdened his heart by announcing—seventeen years after Dandi—the repeal of the salt tax.

But the trend toward partition was inexorable. The eruptions in Bengal and Bihar, and now in the Punjab also, had killed united India. The League had exploited them, and Congress had acquiesced in regional splits within the Constituent Assembly. To Gandhi all splits meant the vivisection of India. He resisted them as long as he could. He even suggested to Mountbatten that power should be handed over to Jinnah, who could turn the entire sub-continent into Pakistan if only he would keep it intact. Hindus shared Gandhi's horror at the blasphemy of dividing the body of Mother India. But too few shared his steadfastness. The Congress leaders felt increasingly bound to settle for a political deal (getting rid of the headache by cutting off the head, as some put it) and turned from Gandhi as unrealistic. The orthodox supremacists of the Mahasabha and RSS wanted an all-India Hindu Raj, and turned against Gandhi as a pro-Muslim and traitor. As he returned to the Bihar treadmill, he was beginning to receive insulting and threatening letters. By June most of his mail was hostile.

Mountbatten had become convinced that 1948 was too far off, and that a unitary constitution could not be forced through. Quickening the tempo, he secured approval from Congress, League and Sikh representatives and the British Government, and published his own plan on 3 June. It provided that the Muslims in the legislatures of decisively Muslim provinces could opt for secession. Mixed provinces could be partitioned. The inevitable result would be a mainly Hindu India, and a Pakistan in two widely separated pieces. The princely states could choose their own course. Technically the plan envisaged, not one independent country or two, but 564. However, the states would certainly adhere to India or Pakistan. The Muslim League scented a possibility that princely allies might form Pakistani enclaves right across India, and ratified the scheme. Many of its members were publicly shouting slogans about their imminent conquest of the Hindus. Congress accepted joylessly. Anxious eyes turned toward the Mahatma. Would he advise against the plan? Would he sabotage it by fasting? No. Mountbatten gently persuaded him, and on 4 June, wearily and reluctantly, he gave way. He could not prevent the birth of this fragmented India. He merely wondered if there was any place for him in it.

The Indian Independence Act, passed by Parliament without a division, provided for the two Dominions to come into being on 15 August. Apparently that day marked the triumph of Gandhi's efforts. A national rising on an unprecedented scale had ended foreign rule in what was, after all, an amazingly short time. India (and Britain) had been spared the horrible 'war of liberation' which would certainly have broken out sooner or later if he had not taken the lead. The final settlement had come by consent. He was well aware of that last fact, and his praise for Britain was unstinted. But on the day of independence he was in Calcutta staying with a Muslim. The smoke of burning houses hung in the air, the pavements were slippery with blood, shed in fresh riots which he was toiling to calm. The renewal and regeneration he dreamed of had not happened—only a transfer of power, in the midst of spiritual tragedy.

On 15 August he did nothing unusual. The Hindus and Muslims whom he had brought together celebrated together. He did not celebrate. The BBC begged him for a message, but he gave no message. In his own eyes he had failed. For whatever time might be left, he wished simply to retire to his village and start again.

To a correspondent who was still friendly, Dadabhai Naoroji's granddaughter Kurshed, he recalled the Upanishadic prayer: 'O Lord, lead us from darkness into light.' To Tagore's secretary Amiya Chakravarty, grieving at the death of a cousin, he wrote:

> Dear Amiya, I am sorry for your loss which in reality is no loss. 'Death is but a sleep and a forgetting.' This is such a sweet sleep that the body has not to wake again and the dead load of memory is thrown overboard. So far as I know, happily there is no meeting in the beyond as we have it today. When the isolated drops melt, they share the majesty of the ocean to which they belong. In isolation they die but to meet the ocean again. I do not know whether I have been clear enough to give you any comfort. Love, Bapu.

XVIII

Climax

1

He had built better than he knew. The non-violence of so many years could not be cancelled by the violence of one. Over most of the country the flags changed painlessly. The solid achievements of the dead Raj passed to its heirs without fatal damage. Fears over the princely states were generally dispelled. Five hundred and fifty acceded quickly to the Indian Union, three to Pakistan, without breaking up the map. During British rule the rajahs had stood for a semblance of nationality. Now that this ghostly function was gone, nearly all of them bowed to facts and resigned their powers. Another sign of hope was the conduct of the Indian Army. Throughout the turmoil, despite a rapid hand-over to Indian officers, it had held firm against communal propaganda. After its division between the Dominions, Hindu and Muslim units behaved correctly toward each other. Ill-treatment of civilians occurred, but no major military clash.

Furthermore, partition in practice turned out not to be a rigid segregation of the communities. Pakistan was smaller and less formidable than the League had intended. The Indian Union preserved more than vestiges of Gandhi's ideal. It was a secular state enfolding every religion, not a mere Hindustan. Within its frontiers it contained all the chief Hindu holy places; but it also contained about forty million Muslims. An inter-communal society could still be realized.

The special impress of Gandhi's personality was neither effaced nor ignored. This showed vividly in the contrast between Bengal and the Punjab, where, just after independence, fresh riots began. It had been proposed that Lord Mountbatten should bridge the gap between the Dominions by staying as Governor-General of both. Jinnah had taken the Pakistani governor-generalship himself, and

374

tension continued. But while the Punjab blazed, Bengal, under the spell of the Mahatma's presence, subsided. On 18 August the Hindus of Calcutta flocked to a Muslim festival chanting the old unity slogans. Mountbatten wrote to Gandhi: 'In the Punjab we have 55,000 soldiers and large scale rioting is on our hands. In Bengal our forces consist of one man, and there is no rioting.'

As the Congress Raj took shape it was apparent that nearly all the leaders were, to a greater or less extent, Gandhi's people. Nehru and Sardar Patel, Rajaji and Rajendra Prasad, even some of the Socialists and Communists—they had entered public life as his aides, they had won their spurs in his campaigns. Because of him, the new India had more women in high places than any other Commonwealth country. Mrs Naidu was Governor of the United Provinces, Mrs Pandit was leading the India delegation to the UN.

On the last night of August a gang of Hindu youths smashed the windows of the Calcutta house where Gandhi was sleeping, and burst in. He got up and faced them unflinchingly, his palms joined in greeting. One tossed a brick, another brandished a lathi. Police arrived and cleared the house, and then had to use tear gas to disperse a crowd of Muslims who had gathered outside, accusing the Hindus of a knifing. But despite appearances civic tension had slackened. When Gandhi resorted to his personal weapon and fasted, delegations converged on him with promises of good behaviour. Five hundred policemen, including their English officers, fasted a day in sympathy. Gang leaders wept at the Mahatma's bedside. On 4 September a number of citizens' representatives signed a pledge, and Gandhi drank lime juice. Calcutta was quiet. It remained so. *The Times* echoed Mountbatten: he had done what an army could not have done.

From Bengal, and from Bihar too, the demons were departing. But their departure seemed to be only a migration. Westward of Delhi fifteen million people were on the move, as minorities in each Dominion fled to the other. The triumphant Muslims of Pakistan were closing in on the local Hindus and Sikhs. In one village, children were torn to pieces. In another, seventy-three women drowned themselves in the same well as a Muslim mob advanced on them. A column of Hindus and Sikhs fifty miles long rolled toward Delhi out of the divided Punjab. The refugees went on foot or in such carts as the Muslims had not stolen, carrying, or abandoning, the sick and aged. Smallpox ravaged the column and vultures hovered overhead. Inside India the fanatics of the RSS launched reprisals of equal vileness, which sent Muslims scurrying toward Pakistan. Deaths were said to be rising into the hundreds of thousands.

Gandhi left for Delhi on 7 September. He found the city in the grip of communal rioting, provoked by stories heard from the first wave of refugees. Hindus had attacked mosques and turned some of them into temples, installing images of the gods, which to Muslims were idols and an unspeakable pollution. Inside and outside the capital displaced persons of all religions were encamped. Gandhi's own quarters in the Harijan colony were packed with the waifs of partition, Hindu and Sikh. He went to Birla House.

There he lived in a ground-floor room 25 feet by 16 (for him, very spacious) and slept outside on the terrace. Adjacent was a bathroom where he took baths in the European style, relaxing in hot water, and sometimes following up with a cold shower. His health improved if anything, and he did not seem to have aged since the 1930s; his weight, at 113 pounds, was more than it had been in his frailest phase, and his pulse was a steady 68. With him at Birla House were Pyarelal, Manu, and Abha Gandhi, the young wife of another of his cousinly relatives.

Promptly he plunged into relief work among the sufferers of all three communities. Messages came in from the squalid camps of the eastern Punjab pleading for him to visit them. But many of the Hindus were bitter against him as pro-Muslim, and they inflamed the RSS further. No danger deterred him. He drove out to a Muslim school at Okla, where Zakir Husain, who had built up Basic Education, was under siege with the staff and students. Muslim houses throughout the neighbourhood were ablaze, Muslims seeking to escape by swimming across the Jumna River were seized by Hindus or Sikhs and held under. Gandhi could not save the village, but he averted an assault on the school. Day after day he toured the refugee camps without escort. He even spoke to an RSS rally. Meanwhile he went on calmly with his regular prayer meetings, which anyone could attend without screening. He held them in the garden of Birla House, leaving his room by a French window and walking unguarded through a long pergola. Daily he risked a demonstration by reading from the Koran as well as other scriptures, politely requesting any objectors to keep quiet.

As usual he discoursed on a wide range of topics. The message of love, forgiveness and self-control took priority. But this had to be applied : to Kashmir, for instance. The Maharajah, himself a Hindu, ruled over a mainly Muslim population. He had not yet joined either Dominion. Soon after Gandhi's arrival in the capital, tribesmen from Pakistan infiltrated Kashmir. Pakistani troops followed them. The ruler applied for Indian protection. On 29 October India announced the accession of Kashmir, and sent in its own troops. Skirmishing broke out with the Pakistanis, who raised the cry of holy war. Gandhi hesitated and then bestowed his approval on the Indian action. In a situation where nobody would practise Ahimsa as he understood it, violence, as always, was preferable to cowardice. Nehru had submitted India's case to UN, and this Gandhi regretted, because it entangled the problem in irrelevant power politics. The parties ought to solve it themselves, perhaps with the aid of a British mediator (he suggested Philip Noel-Baker). A plebiscite might be held. On the whole he would be glad to see Kashmir a part of India. Its presence, with a Muslim majority, would mean a step away from religious politics toward his all-embracing secular state. Kashmir might some day prove that Pakistan was unnecessary.

His voice was heard with respect, but the trend of politics and public opinion still seemed to be against him. The angry letters piled up, the attendances at his meetings dwindled. In November Kripalani resigned as President of Congress on the ground that Nehru and Patel, the Prime Minister and Deputy Prime Minister, were no longer taking him into their confidence. Gandhi went to the meeting of the Working Committee that debated his successor. It was a silent day, but he handed Nehru a written nomination— Narendra Dev, a Socialist who had lived at Sevagram. Nehru supported him, but others opposed, and no vote was taken. After the morning session, Nehru and Patel took Rajendra Prasad aside and urged him to be a candidate. They did so without consulting Gandhi. Prasad went to Birla House and informed him. The Mahatma disliked the offer and persuaded him not to stand. Subsequently, however, Prasad changed his mind and was elected. Since Champaran he had never once gone against his chief. Now he did.

This defection was a challenge to Gandhi's faith that as his *brahmacharya* progressed, his influence would increase. At the zenith of detachment which he felt himself to have attained, he ought to have been the potent agent of God. Bengal and Bihar had confirmed his faith; Delhi had not. The axioms of his life pointed to some ultimate victory, yet its shape was slow to emerge. He cast about. Much of December was taken up in consultations with his constructive workers, whom he was beginning to see as the nucleus of a new kind of movement, to mobilize the masses and purify politics at the grassroots. Also he considered going to Pakistan, perhaps even settling there. The condition of the smaller Dominion was fluid. Jinnah, his object gained, had no purpose left and was fast losing authority. Ghaffar Khan and his supporters were fighting to preserve a Gandhian enclave by way of Pathan autonomy.

At the turn of the year the sense of an imminent yet undefined climax was spreading to the Mahatma's friends. John Haynes Holmes, the American minister who had once compared him to Christ, wrote after a visit: 'You were never so great as in these dark hours.' Suddenly the solution began to unfold. Its opening phase was a repetition of what he had done in Calcutta. Delhi's riots had simmered down in response to his presence, but without security or genuine relaxation. The Muslims were being killed by inches, as he put it. Mobs of refugees were evicting them from their houses amid applause, and although the police intervened, they had to use force.

On 13 January 1948 Gandhi embarked on his last and greatest fast, without warning Nehru, Patel, or his own doctors. He would stop, he said, when the capital proved its change of heart and made amends to the victimized minority. But the fast was addressed to the consciences of all, in both countries. He summoned them to pause and reflect. If Hindus, Muslims and Sikhs recovered their sanity; if even one of the three communities did so; if Pakistan became truly *pak*, pure . . . then he would go his way in light and peace.

The fast affected him quickly. His weight dropped. Water caused nausea, and his kidneys partially failed. From the third day he spent much of the time lying on a cot in a porch at Birla House, with his knees drawn up and a white khadi cloth covering everything except his face—a foetal posture straining toward a rebirth. Hour by hour Indians and foreigners filed past, with prayers, tears, and gestures of salutation. The world outside waited for news. Even at this extremity he was still, in his fashion, a politician. During a bath he dictated a letter to Pyarelal. The Indian Government was hanging on to five hundred and fifty million rupees, Pakistan's share of the assets of undivided India. He asked that the money be handed over.

It was. On the 17th, in spite of a virtual cessation of urine, his weight was stabilized at 107 pounds and he impressed visitors as serene. The payment was a good augury for peace.

Rajendra Prasad was interviewing members of dozens of organizations, trying to adjust disputes and formulate a joint pledge that would satisfy the Mahatma. On the 18th he led a deputation a hundred strong to Birla House. Nehru and Azad had already arrived, together with the High Commissioner for Pakistan, and representatives of the police, the Hindus, the Muslims, the Sikhs, the Christians, the Jews, and even the Mahasabha and RSS. Prasad showed a pledge guaranteeing the Delhi Muslims against further harm. They would enjoy complete freedom to travel, assemble, and hold their annual fair. Mosques would be returned.

Gandhi replied that an armistice in Delhi was not enough unless it was clearly understood to be the first step toward peace everywhere, a reunion of hearts. He wept for a moment and resumed in such a faint voice that Dr Sushila Nayyar, who was in attendance, had to repeat his words to the gathering. What did the Mahasabha intend? Would the zealots of both parties give their promise that they were not merely seeking a truce to prepare a fresh onslaught on the infidel? Would the Muslims let him go to Pakistan?

After many pleas and a tense pause, he consented to break his fast. Prayers were recited and hymns sung. As he sipped orange juice he remarked that if the pledge was honoured, it would restore his wish to live to 125. Though he was very weak, his effervescence returned in a matter of hours. To Nehru, who had been deeply shaken and started a sympathy fast of his own, he sent a note later in the day punning on the meaning of *jawahar*: 'May you long remain the jewel of India.' The Pakistani Foreign Minister told the UN Security Council that as a result of the fast, a 'new and tremendous wave of feeling and desire for friendship between the two Dominions' was sweeping the sub-continent. A rift had opened in the clouds. If they dispersed, Gandhi would have accomplished his miracle.

2

Almost at once the logic of the fast began working out toward its term. An officer of the Mahasabha showed his disapproval of a reprieve for the Muslims by repudiating the peace pledge. Gandhi, carried in a chair to his prayer meeting on the 19th, murmured regrets. He still assured everybody that he thought himself a failure. But he was not cast down. He was beyond ever being cast down again. To Mirabehn he scribbled a card: 'All anxiety is over.' He was planning his mission to Pakistan, and drawing up a political testament. This took the form of a draft resolution for the All-India Congress Committee, declaring that Congress had outlived its usefulness as a party, and should be turned into a democratic social-service body based on the villages. His own aim, after the final pacification, was to go back to Sevagram and immerse himself in the constructive programme.

He worked rapidly and cheerfully, knowing quite well what to be prepared for. On the 20th he was again carried to his meeting. At question time a man stood up and urged him to proclaim himself an incarnation of God. Gandhi smiled. 'Sit down and be quiet,' he said. While the meeting was in progress a near-by explosion frightened the audience. Uncertain what had happened, but determined to prevent any panic, he told them not to worry and went on speaking. But in fact someone had tossed a home-made grenade at him over the garden wall. An old woman grabbed the assassin and the police took him in charge. Gandhi asked them to treat him kindly. He was a bitter young Hindu from the Punjab, Madan Lal, who had sheltered in a Delhi mosque and then been expelled when the mosque was given back to its owners. Madan Lal was a member of a gang, most of them from Maharashtra, Tilak's country. They regarded Gandhi as a traitor to Hinduism. The success of his fast, and above all the disgorging of the five hundred and fifty million rupees, had driven them to desperation. Among them was an aristocratic Brahmin thirty-five years old, Nathuram Vinayak Godse, editor of a Mahasabha weekly in Poona.

Madan Lal did not betray his fellow-conspirators. But Gandhi never supposed that he was alone. 'If I am to die by the bullet of a madman,' he said to visiting friends, 'I must do so smiling. Should such a thing happen you are not to shed one tear.' On the 26th, still kept as Independence Day in memory of 1930, he talked as coolly as ever. Independence was disillusioning, but he hoped that the worst was over and the liberation of the masses was dawning. He warned against corruption, unnecessary strikes, economic mismanagement.

The next day brought him an American caller, Vincent Sheean.

Most Americans wanted to discuss politics with him. Sheean was more interested in his personality and beliefs. Arriving heavy with forebodings of doom, he sat before the Mahatma and listened, while Manu, Abha and others looked on. Afterwards he recalled the talk as strangely disjointed, yet wholly luminous. Gandhi seemed to speak in a celestial shorthand. He touched on the *Gita* and his own allegorical reading of it, which so few Hindus accepted. He dwelt lovingly on memories of his mother and nurse, who had taught him the value of taking vows, and on the fufilments he had found in constructive work. 'Avoid power,' he said; 'it corrupts.' Sheean asked him which side he took in the Hindu philosophic debate on the reality of the world of experience. 'I don't think it an illusion,' Gandhi replied. 'You could call it the world of "appearances" perhaps. It is real, but its reality comes from God.' He had been re-reading the Upanishads. The first verse of the *Isa Upanishad*, he suggested, was the sum of human wisdom:

The whole world is the garment of God.
Renounce it then, and receive it back as the gift of God.

(A loose paraphrase, but a fair one.) Sheean was his last disciple. Their dialogue went on in snatches from day to day but was never finished.

Friday, 30 January, was an important date. Gandhi was concerned for the Government. Some of the constituent parts of Congress looked like splitting off. Nehru and Patel, temperamentally dissonant, were drifting apart. Nehru remained left of centre; Patel was conservative, and suspected of being more anti-Muslim than he cared to admit. Gandhi wrote Nehru a note urging that the two of them should stick together for India's sake. Also he arranged for Patel to come to Birla House before evening prayers and discuss their differences.

He spent the morning answering letters. 'Tomorrow', he explained, 'I may not be here.' Early in the afternoon he received another journalist, Margaret Bourke-White, who wanted to interview him for *Life* magazine. She queried him about the atomic bomb. He had already written of the moral danger in even making it. Now she asked: If an aircraft actually drops one on a city, what should believers in Ahimsa do? Well, he said, if the bomb is actually falling, Ahimsa is the only thing it cannot destroy. The soldiers of non-violence should not dive for the shelter. They should stand firm in their thousands, looking up, watching without fear, praying for the pilot. Their sacrifice would not be in vain.

This was his last message to the world. At four, Patel came for their conference. Half an hour later Abha brought Gandhi a meal: goat's milk, vegetables, oranges, and a kind of sauce made with ginger and melted butter. He was due in the garden for his prayer meeting at five. Almost on the hour, they were still chatting. Abha picked up his watch, which he had set aside, and silently showed it to him. 'I must tear myself away,' Gandhi exclaimed. A little vexed at being unpunctual, he took his leave and started along the pergola. Abha was on his left, Manu on his right. He rested his forearms on their shoulders, taking some of the load off his legs. They joked about some carrot juice Abha had given him for breakfast, and his unusual inattention to time that day. 'Bapu,' said Abha, 'your watch must be feeling quite neglected.' 'You two are my timekeepers,' he answered. 'But you don't look at the timekeepers either,' said Manu.

It was nearly ten past five. They came out on open grass and climbed the steps to the garden prayer ground. Several hundred people were waiting. Most of them stood up. Those directly in front of Gandhi parted each way to make a lane, some bowing to his feet as he went by. He took his arms off the girls' shoulders and raised them in greeting.

Suddenly a man in a khaki jacket pushed through from the right. It was the conspirator Godse. Manu thought he was a pilgrim prostrating himself in the Mahatma's path, and as they were late, she put out a hand to check him. He thrust her away so hard that she stumbled. Two feet from Gandhi he actually did make a brief bow. Then he raised a pistol and fired three shots. The first bullet entered Gandhi's abdomen and came out through his back. It caught him in mid-stride. His foot touched the ground but he stayed upright. The second passed between his ribs and also came out at the back. A bloodstain appeared on his white shawl. His hands sank. The third bullet struck his chest above the right nipple and lodged in the lung. His face turned grey. His left forearm returned for a moment to Abha's shoulder. In these last instants, bystanders heard him gasping the divine name Rama. Then he crumpled and fell backwards, his glasses dropping off, his sandals coming away from his feet.

The gardener recovered soonest. He seized Godse and held him till others dragged him off into custody. Gandhi was carried indoors. Patel, who had not yet left the grounds, rushed back and felt his pulse. Pyarelal telephoned for a doctor. He came in ten minutes but could do nothing. All was over, quickly and mercifully.

3

'Life', Gandhi had once remarked, 'is perpetual triumph over the grave.'

Mountbatten, Nehru, Azad, Devadas Gandhi, and many more joined Patel at Birla House. The corpse lay with its head resting on Abha's lap, and calm on its face. The Prime Minister knelt and sobbed. Even to Devadas, who had memories which none of the mourners shared, his father's body seemed to glow. The Governor-General took command and saw that the vital things were done. He did not forget to draw Nehru and Patel aside and remind them of the Mahatma's last wishes.

Nehru broadcast the news, speaking impromptu in a choked voice.

> The light has gone out of our lives and there is darkness everywhere and I do not quite know what to tell you and how to say it. Our beloved leader, Bapu as we call him, the father of our nation, is no more. Perhaps I am wrong to say that. Nevertheless, we will not see him again as we have seen him these many years. . . .
>
> The light has gone out, I said, and yet I was wrong. For the light that shone in this country was no ordinary light. The light that has illumined this country for these many years will illumine this country for many more years, and a thousand years later that light will still be seen in this country, and the world will see it and it will give solace to innumerable hearts. . . .
>
> There is so much more to do. There was so much more for him to do.

Politicians, journalists, countless Indians of all sorts, added their homage. Thousands wept in public. Jinnah's comments were more restrained, but the Pakistani newspapers spoke up generously. 'All Muslims are bowed in grief', said a leading article, 'at the ghastly ending to so great a life.' Pakistanis realized that Gandhi had died for his defence of their own people. The Hindu saint was a martyr for the Muslims. His murder, which was a direct consequence of his fast, completed its effect. The persecutions and threats of war faded into limbo, the two countries began learning to co-exist. He had accomplished his miracle.

At Birla House they washed the body, and dropped a garland of homespun yarn over the head. Devadas allowed a brief lying-in-state with a rose-strewn blanket up to the waist, but the chest bare. In repose, his thin legs hidden, Gandhi had an astonishingly fine physique. Ramdas arrived by air at 11 a.m. on the 31st, and even Harilal was present, though he kept in the background. The body was dressed in khadi and placed in an open coffin on a converted army vehicle, which two hundred uniformed servicemen drew through the streets, the motor silent. Every diplomatic mission sent a wreath. Very slowly the cortège moved through the crowds. Six thousand soldiers, sailors, airmen and policemen, and citizens beyond counting, marched in front and behind. The Governor-General's bodyguard of lancers rode in the procession. Hymns of all religions went up from the onlookers, mingling with the old victory shout of 'Mahatma-Gandhi-ki-jai!'

Toward half-past four the funeral carriage was nearing the Jumna River. At Raj Ghat a pyre had been heaped up. Three Dakotas of the Indian Air Force flew overhead, dipping in salute and showering rose petals. Bearers laid the body on top of the sandalwood logs, its head to the north. Ramdas lit the pyre amid a vast wail from the crowd. Devadas tended it and sprinkled incense. Wrapped in thick smoke, it blazed for fourteen hours while priests recited the *Gita*. When all was still and cold, the ashes of the Mahatma were gathered up and placed in an urn. Godse's third bullet was found among them. Grains of ash were given to a number of friends. However, most of the remains were immersed in the Ganges at Allahabad, at the same place as Kasturbai's had been. The principal figures in the ceremony were Nehru, Patel, Azad, Mrs Naidu, Ramdas, Pyarelal, Sushila, Manu, and Abha. As the boat bearing the urn slid out on to the water, thousands of people waded and swam around it. The urn was inverted, the guns of the fort fired a salute, the ashes rode seaward and the funeral hymn was chanted:

Holy soul, may sun, air and fire be auspicious unto thee. Thy dear ones on this earth do not lament at thy departure, for they know that thou art gone to the radiant regions of the blessed. May the waters of all rivers and oceans be helpful unto thee, and serve thee ever in thy good deeds for the welfare of all beings; may all space and its four quarters be open unto thee for thy good deeds.

Throughout these days the world's condolences and praises had flowed in. Delhi counted more than three thousand unsolicited messages from abroad. The Pope, George VI, the British Prime Minister, the Presidents of France and China and the United States, the Archbishop of Canterbury, the Dalai Lama, Albert Einstein and Léon Blum and General MacArthur—a long parade of eminences paid tribute to the peacemaker, the 'spokesman of the conscience of all mankind', the 'most remarkable man of the century'. The United Nations flag dipped to half-mast; the Security Council paused while its members, including the hard-faced Russians, honoured the departing Great Soul.

So the flood of valediction poured on, mixing the sincere and the perfunctory, the touching and the commonplace. But one at least of the multitude spoke with a poet's tongue. It was Sarojini Naidu, and the words that matched the hour were hers.

May the soul of my master, my leader, my father, rest *not* in peace! Not in peace—my father—do not rest! Keep us to our pledge! Give us strength to fulfil our promises—your heirs, your descendants, guardians of your dreams, fulfillers of India's destiny.

Epilogue

Twenty years afterwards what remains, what continues?

In India the Mahatma is still a presence as few of the dead are in any country. It need not mean much that streets and buildings bear his name, that politicians invoke him, that leader-writers use his sayings to buttress their arguments. What is far more arresting is the way people of all sorts are so ready to talk about him and discuss what he means to them. I have seen a Gujarati school-inspector demonstrate exactly where Gandhi stood, how he acted, during the remote days of the salt campaign; I have heard an engineer's wife at Juhu say, 'He used to walk on the beach near here,' in the tone one might have heard by the Sea of Galilee about A.D. 50.

However, this mass memory draws distinctions. Publicists may point out that cottage industry schemes still go on under State patronage, and that Gandhi's birthday is marked by spinning ceremonies in which Government ministers take part. But if you talk about him to ordinary folk they seldom think of such things. His detailed programme has faded. For them he lives as India's *guru*, a Moses, a moulder of the national moral character. 'He taught Indians to be patriotic and self-reliant,' they say. 'He taught the importance of everyday concerns as well as high politics. He taught brotherhood and no class distinction. He taught that Indians must stand on their own feet and supply their own needs. That they must hate nobody, not even the British, and be brave and straightforward, and grasp that their only enemy was fear.'

He has half-outsoared mortality. Over a bench in an Ahmedabad textile mill I have seen a row of pin-ups portraying the worker's favourite gods, and Gandhi—no other human being. Stalls in bazaars offer cheap pictures of him with his three bullet wounds which are as purely iconographic as the Sacred Heart. In a Bihar village I heard a minstrel entertaining the peasants with a song which, my guide explained, was 'a national song about Gandhi and how he told the Englishman to go'. The song went on and on. Presently the guide spoke again: 'Now it is a story of Krishna.' Gandhi had blended into Krishna with no audible break.

386

His social impact has been unequal. The improvement in the status of women is among his most striking legacies. Very little remains of the drive for economic equality and the rural commonwealth. The former Untouchables are better off, but they have a long way to go. A Gandhi Memorial Trust, formed soon after his death, sponsors a medley of welfare projects, and has plans for his centenary year. What those who remember him tend to miss in his would-be heirs is his genius for improvisation, for making the best use of modest resources. The most effective of the disciples is Vinoba, whose land-reform movement—a co-operative system called Gramdan, village-giving—has taken the constructive programme some distance further. Gramdan has the support of no less a person than Jayaprakash Narayan, who sees it as the authentic Indian Socialism. Whatever its future, the most interesting fact about it is that it is not a slavish Imitation of the Mahatma, but an attempt to carry on where he left off.

The survival of the ideal of Ahimsa is a disputed question. Nehru's non-alignment in foreign policy was said to reflect it. But many Indians have debased the Gandhi techniques with senseless obstruction and hunger strikes for unworthy ends. The brief Kashmir war of 1965 was regarded in England (partly owing to biased press accounts) as the final betrayal. However, in India at the time, I noticed two things—one small but significant, the other crucial. When Delhi held the Dussehra festival, which includes the burning of demon effigies, a proposal was aired that the biggest effigy should be made to look like the President of Pakistan. The Government vetoed this. Hate was out. The other point concerned India's Muslims. When the fighting began, westerners forecast a communal explosion. The Muslims would become a Pakistani fifth column. But they did not. They remained good citizens under stress, and some served well at the front. Gandhi had at last been proved right, and Jinnah wrong. The secular state does work, the theory of implacable feud is dead. Only a year or so after Kashmir, the Muslim Basic-Educationist Zakir Husain became President. India still embodies the vision, however blurred, of a union of peoples.

A simple Gandhi revival is hardly likely. But India's internal crisis may well bring a revival of the Gandhian spirit of self-reliance, and a reawakening of some of the ideas in a new setting. The need, perhaps, is for a national leader standing in relation to the Mahatma somewhat as Kennedy to Roosevelt. Much the same could be said of his legacy to the world outside India. Afro-Asian nationalism was set off by him but has not walked in his footsteps, and followers like Martin Luther King and Danilo Dolci have gone only so far. As he foresaw himself, it would be misguided trying to piece together a Gandhi sect or party, however relevant some of today's problems may make him appear. But it is easy to imagine some rising leader being influenced by his life and thought. Truth-Force and the Non-Violent Society may come back in a new guise. It is a measure of his stature that they do not seem like dead issues.

What was the secret of his spell? Cliché descriptions like 'Hindu saint', 'father of his country', are empty and misleading. If we must label him, the best clue was supplied by Bertrand Russell, who once suggested that the key public figures of the twentieth century would be manipulative idealists—people who have the same gifts as the great leaders of the past, but use them to reshape society rather than to gain power or wealth as such. Russell's prototype was Lenin, but Gandhi fits equally well.

Leadership is a quality which has lately been much discussed, especially in the business context. Researchers like Vance Packard, the author of *The Pyramid Climbers,* have compiled lists of traits which outstanding chief executives tend to possess. Gandhi had them all—sustained energy, deftness and timely ruthlessness in handling people, the capacity to think to the purpose and somewhat intuitively, zest and fluency with ideas, an ability to bounce back constructively when thwarted or criticized, a love of running things, and a never-despairing passion for the Cause which infects others. Yet we cannot rest content with putting Gandhi in the same class as a corporation president. Mahadev Desai was right. The inner-most secret was not merely passion, but passion with a divine focus. Where the executive's passion is for his organization, Gandhi's was for the Absolute . . . or God or Truth or whichever word we prefer.

To call him a saint, in the sense of a very good person, is beside the mark. His faults could be depressing, and even his goodness was off-beat. But he had the rarer and truer sainthood which ritual canonization purports to recognize. He was raised, by communion with whatever it is that religions call God, on to a level where human nature is changed and ordinary understanding falls short. To those nearest him he transmitted a touch of the Absolute, a *something* of staggering directness. No everyday calculation of self-interest, respectability, or conventional virtue could compete with it.

Even if described thus, he sounds more like a saint of the traditional kind than he was. His uniqueness appears in the title of his autobiography. It was the story of his experiments with Truth. He discovered how to combine mysticism with humanism. To him, God was 'there', and relevant every instant. But God was not a dispenser of laws or dogmas. He was a goal to strive toward, a flashing beacon, an object of quest, largely unknown and everlastingly sought for. Everything Gandhi did was done by way of reasoned experiment, starting from what he could see and touch. Even his religious observances like the Trappist silence on Mondays had vulgarly practical beginnings.

He was willing in principle to do anything the agnostic humanist would do, in the same liberty of mind, with only this difference: that if objective search led him toward a religious position he would accept that result and stick to it, instead of reversing engines and trying to explain it away. Nor was he rationalizing religious conclusions which he was set on reaching anyhow (a charge made against philosophers like St Thomas Aquinas). When life convinced him that Hindu teachings were false, as with the crueller caste laws, he was prepared to incur loss and hostility by saying so. His rule was, in St Paul's words, to try all things and hold fast to that which was good. God did not command him to spin. But spinning could lead to God. The theory of non-violence with all its branches was rooted in his vision of humanity's quest, its need to shake off entangling greeds and hatreds, so as to move through love nearer to the divine Truth. That process had no limit. He became, therefore, a supreme and quintessential revolutionary, an apostle of endless transfiguration, for whom the most towering achievement was no more than a step and very likely a disappointing step.

To most religious believers, God exists and enjoins us to think and do certain things. To agnostics, he probably does not exist and is in any case an irrelevance. To Gandhi, he existed, but as the goal of a quest to be carried on in perfect freedom. Man should not live by the alleged presence or absence of the Absolute, as a given law of life like breathing, but by its possibility.*

---

* I have taken a hint here from a strange and little-known essay by B. K. Mallik. This professes to be based on a revelation from the Mahatma after his death, and is so far above the usual standard of 'spirit messages' as to be puzzling. But I have not, of course, adopted any ideas from it which are not to be found in his earthly works.

The implications of Gandhi's teachings, if applied to present politics, are beyond present scope. At any time and for any hopeful world-betterer, they imply this at least—an intense awareness of personal responsibility, a readiness to do things oneself and shoulder the burden, instead of relying on committees and governments. They imply, further, a readiness to go fearlessly down to fundamentals in search of one's vocation, and to do extraordinary things which may be quite foreign to normal methods and approved channels. The flash of Truth, when it flashes at all, gives the landscape new contours. The Absolute cuts across the trends. It may dictate something very like a rebirth of human nature, a clean break, a fresh start.

Lastly there are three sets of people for whom the Mahatma has, I submit, a distinctive and enduring value.

The past decade has witnessed a number of 'protest' movements, anti-nuclear and otherwise, which have owed Gandhi a debt and employed such phrases as 'civil disobedience'. They have risen, and they have declined. If we ask how they went astray, the main answer is obvious. They lapsed into negative rancour, never *for* anything, perpetually snarling at the public villains of the moment, and stultifying themselves through errors of judgement because they got the villains wrong. There is no point in raking over controversies which, though more recent than Gandhi, are infinitely more out of date than he is. But there is some point in noting that he foreshadowed the failure and diagnosed it in advance, simply by teaching that it is no use being merely 'anti', and that without the non-violence of the mind, Truth is lost.

Secondly, if Gandhi reconciles mysticism and humanism, does he leave the religious personality any special role in the struggles of mankind? He does so, surely, with his theory of suffering, his doctrine that martyrdom is part of the method. Humanism of the agnostic sort finds it hard to fit suffering in. It conceives progress as progress in welfare. That is a sound enough objective, but it induces a temptation to decry fortitude and approve of conduct which past generations would have thought ignoble. Pain is just something to get rid of. No reason exists why anybody should forgo a higher standard of living. By contrast, the religious believer can fit suffering in. He can give a value to pain and deprivation willingly borne. This may be illusion or masochism or whatever the humanist cares to explain it away as—but it is a fact, and Gandhi gives it a practical function. Indeed it may well be asked whether religion has any serious future if it fails to exhibit the Satyagrahi spirit, and if the faithful persist in acting like respectable cowards sheltering behind fairy-tales, with their faith reduced to an insurance policy.

Finally, the Mahatma has a special meaning for another nation besides his own. Because of him Britain learned as important a lesson as any country has ever learnt. It was not a lesson given entirely from outside, but one that Britain evolved out of her own better conscience, which unwittingly made Gandhi its agent. Henry Salt, Annie Besant, John Ruskin, G. K. Chesterton, never knew what they were doing. Yet they formed his mind and they returned him to India as a genius whom India could not have reared unaided. In all his campaigns he took for granted an essential British decency which they had helped him to trust. After 1930 the better conscience spoke up again, and louder. In response to Gandhi Britain resigned a world mission which had outlived whatever rightness it had, and turned back to a humbler and saner quest for self-realization. The quest has yet to reach its term, but the movement is no longer the wrong way. It is unthinkable that the realm of Elizabeth II would commit another Amritsar massacre, or present the perpetrator of such a crime with twenty thousand pounds. Gandhi did that for us. He was the only result of Britain's Indian conquests that was quite certainly for her good.

Bibliography

ALLINSON, T. R. *Hygienic Medicine*. 1886

ANDLEY, C. B. L. *Gandhi the Saviour?* 1933

ANDREWS, C. F. *Mahatma Gandhi at Work*. 1931

'ARGUS'. *Gandhism cum Non-co-operation Exposed*. 1921

ARNOLD, Edwin. (1) *The Light of Asia*. 1879; (2) *The Song Celestial* (i.e. *Bhagavad Gita*). 1885

BESANT, Annie. (1) Ed., *Gandhian Non-co-operation: or Shall India Commit Suicide?* 1920; (2) *Why I became a Theosophist*. 1889

Bhagavad Gita. See ARNOLD, (2); DESAI, (2)

BIRKENHEAD, The Earl of. *Halifax*. 1965

BIRLA, G. D. *In the Shadow of the Mahatma*. 1953

BLAVATSKY, H. P. *The Key to Theosophy*. 1889

BOLTON, Glorney. *The Tragedy of Gandhi*. 1934

BONDURANT, Joan V. *Conquest of Violence: The Gandhian Philosophy of Conflict*. 1965

BOSE, Nirmal Kumar. (1) *My days with Gandhi*. 1953; (2) *Studies in Gandhism*. 1940

BUTLER, Joseph. *The Analogy of Religion*. 1884 edition

BYLES, Marie B. *The Lotus and the Spinning Wheel*. 1963

Cambridge History of India, vol. vi. 1958

CARLYLE, Thomas. *On Heroes, Hero-Worship and the Heroic in History*. 1901 edition

CARPENTER, Edward. *Civilisation: its Cause and Cure*. 1889

CHAUDHURI, Nirad C. *The Continent of Circe*. 1965

CONSUL, Govind Dass. *Mahatma Gandhi, the Great Rogue of India?* 1939

DE RIENCOURT, Amaury. *The Soul of India*. 1961

DESAI, Mahadev. (1) *Diary*. 1953; (2) *The Gita according to Gandhi*. 1946; (3) *The Nation's Voice*. 1932. This contains Gandhi's Round Table Conference speeches in 1932, followed by Mahadev's narrative of the visit to England; (4) *A Righteous Struggle*. 1951

NOTE: Mahadev wrote accounts of other passages in Gandhi's career, but as these are largely incorporated in the biographies, especially Tendulkar (2), they are not noted separately.

DHAWAN, Gopinath. *The Political Philosophy of Mahatma Gandhi*. 1962

DOKE, Joseph J. *M. K. Gandhi: an Indian Patriot in South Africa*. 1909

DUTT, R. Palme, *The Problem of India*. 1943

Encyclopædia Britannica, art. 'Porbandar'

FISCHER, Louis. (1) *The Essential Gandhi.* 1963; (2) *The Life of Mahatma Gandhi.* 1951; (3) *A Week with Gandhi.* 1943

GANDHI, M. K. (1) *An Autobiography: the Story of My Experiments with Truth.* 1949; (2) *Bhagavad Gita* commentary. See DESAI, (2); (3) *Collected Works.* In progress. 1958 on; (4) *The Earliest Writings of Mohandas Karamchand Gandhi.* Facsimiles of his 1891 articles in *The Vegetarian,* and interview. 1948; (5) *Freedom's Battle.* 1921; (6) *Harijan.* 1933 on; (7) *Hind Swaraj.* English version with preface in context of the non-co-operation campaign. 1921; (8) *Hindu Dharma.* 1950; (9) *Letters to a Disciple* (i.e. Mirabehn). 1951; (10) *Mahatma Gandhi, his Life, Writings and Speeches.* 1918; (11) *The Nation's Voice.* 1932. See also DESAI, (3); (12) *Satyagraha.* Selected writings on this theme. 1951; (13) *Satyagraha in South Africa.* 1928; (14) *Self-restraint versus Self-indulgence.* 1927; (15) *Swaraj in One Year.* 1921; (16) *Towards Non-Violent Socialism.* 1951; (17) *Young India.* 3 vols. Collected contributions. 1922 on. The historical introductions by Rajendra Prasad are important.

GREGG, Richard B. *The Power of Non-Violence.* 1938

GRIFFITHS, Sir Percival. *The British Impact on India.* 1952

HANCOCK, W. K. *Smuts: the Sanguine Years.* 1962

Harischandra. English adaptation by G. C. V. Shrinivasacharyah. 1897

HEATH, Carl. *Gandhi.* 1932

HOLMES, John Haynes. *My Gandhi.* 1953

HOYLAND, John S. *Indian Crisis.* 1943

JHAVERI, Vithalbhai. *Gandhiji and Mani Bhavan.* 1959

KAYE, Sir John, and MALLESON, Col. G. B. *History of the Indian Mutiny.* 6 vols. 1888-9

KINGSFORD, Anna. *The Perfect Way in Diet.* 1881

KINGSFORD, Anna, and MAITLAND, Edward. *The Perfect Way: or, the Finding of Christ.* 1890

KOESTLER, Arthur. *The Lotus and the Robot.* 1960

LESTER, Muriel. *Entertaining Gandhi.* 1932

Life of Sri Ramakrishna. Authorized biography, anonymous. 1924

Mahabharata. Ed. and trans. by M. N. Dutt. 3 vols. 1895 on

MAITLAND, Edward. *The Story of Anna Kingsford and Edward Maitland.* 1905

MALLIK, B. K. *Gandhi—a Prophecy.* 1948

Manu. In *Sacred Books of the East,* No. 25. 1886

MARSHALL, Anne. *Hunting the Guru in India.* 1963

MAYNE, John D. *Treatise on Hindu Law and Usage.* 1878

MIRABEHN (Madeleine Slade). *The Spirit's Pilgrimage.* 1960

MORAES, Frank. *The Story of India.* 1942

MORTON, Eleanor. *Women behind Mahatma Gandhi.* 1954

MÜLLER, Max. *India—what can it teach us?* 1892

NAIR, Sir Sankaran. *Gandhi and Anarchy.* 1922

NANDA, B. R. *Mahatma Gandhi.* 1958

NEHRU, Jawaharlal. (1) *Autobiography.* 1936; (2) *A Bunch of Old Letters.* 1960

NORMAN, Dorothy. *Nehru: the first sixty years.* 2 vols. 1965

PANIKKAR, K. M. (1) *Common Sense About India.* 1960; (2) *The Foundations of New India.* 1963.

PARKER, Joseph. *The People's Bible.* 1886.

POLAK, H. S. L., BRAILSFORD, H. N., and PETHICK-LAWRENCE, Lord. *Mahatma Gandhi.* 1949

POWER, Paul F. *Gandhi on World Affairs.* 1961

PRABHU, R. K., and KELEKAR, Ravindra. *Truth Called Them Differently.* 1961

PRASAD, Rajendra. *Satyagraha in Champaran.* See also GANDHI (17)

PRICE, M. Philips. *A History of Turkey.* 1956

PYARELAL. (1) *Mahatma Gandhi—the Early Phase.* 1965; (2) *Mahatma Gandhi —the Last Phase.* 2 vols. 1956, 1958

RAI, Lala Lajpat, and others. *Mahatma Gandhi: the World's Greatest Man.* 1922

RAM, Suresh. *Vinoba and his Mission.* 1962

RAMACHANDRAN, G. *A Sheaf of Gandhi Anecdotes.* 1945

RAMAKRISHNA CENTENARY COMMITTEE. *The Cultural Heritage of India.* 3 vols. 1936. Contains articles on the Brahmo Samaj, the Arya Samaj, Ramakrishna and Vivekananda.

Ramayana. See TULSI DAS

ROLLAND, Romain. *Mahatma Gandhi.* 1924

ROSENTHAL, Eric. *Encyclopædia of Southern Africa.* 1961

RUSKIN, John. *Unto This Last.* 1901 edition

SALT, Henry S. (1) *Company I have Kept.* 1930; (2) *A Plea for Vegetarianism.* 1886

SEN, N. B. *Wit and Wisdom of Mahatma Gandhi.* 1960

SHEEAN, Vincent. *Lead, Kindly Light.* 1950

SHUKLA, Chandrashanker. *Incidents of Gandhiji's Life.* 1949

SLADE, Madeleine. See MIRABEHN

SPATE, O. H. K. *India and Pakistan.* 1957

STAMP, L. Dudley. *Asia.* 1957

STEPHENS, Ian. *Pakistan.* 1963

TENDULKAR, D. G. (1) Ed., *Gandhiji.* 1944. A volume containing essays and recollections by many writers; (2) *Mahatma.* 8 vols. 1951 on

THOMPSON, Edward. *Rabindranath Tagore.* 1948

TOLSTOY, Leo. *The Kingdom of God is Within You.* World's Classics Edition, with other Peace Essays. 1936

TULSI DAS. *The Ramayana.* Trans. by F. S. Growse. 1914

WILLIAMS, Francis. *A Pattern of Rulers.* 1965

WILLIAMS, Howard. *The Ethics of Diet.* 1883

WILLIAMS, Joshua. *Principles of the Law of Real Property.* 1887

WINSTEN, Stephen. *Salt and his Circle.* 1951

ZAEHNER, R. C. *Hinduism.* 1962

ZINKIN, Taya. *Gandhi.* 1965

Index

Abdulla Sheth, 49, 50, 58, 67, 70, 160
Absolute, the, *see* God
Afghans, 18, 192, 203, 216
Afro-Asian nationalism, vii, 52, 270, 388
Aga Khan, 135, 237, 307, 352
Ahimsa, *see* Non-Violence
Ahmedabad: G. in, 14, 148, 167-71 (mill strike), 186, 193, 195, 232 (trial), 268; Vallabhbhai Patel in, 146, 170, 275; Mira in, 265, 267; Congress activities, 226, 287; mentioned, 213, 386
Alam, Mir, 111-12, 115
Alexander, A. V., 361
Alexander, Horace, 269
Ali brothers, Shaukat and Mohamed, Muslim nationalists: official restraints upon, 173, 217, 224, 227; association with G. in Khilafat campaign, 201, 203; in Swaraj campaign, 214, 219, 220, 221; in Hindu-Muslim pacification, 244; later attitude to Congress, 237, 280, 306
Allahabad, 69, 155, 288, 296, 318, 349, 384
All-India Spinners' Association, 246, 331, 364
All-India Village Industries Association, 328, 331
Allinson, Dr T. R., 31, 38, 92, 358
Alwar, Maharajah of, 281
Ambedkar, Dr B. R., Untouchable politician, 306-7, 317-8, 320, 337, 348, 363
Ampthill, Lord, 118, 139
Amritsar, 193-5, 198-9, 274, 391
Anasuya, Anasuyabehn, sister of Ambalal Sarabhai, 167, 169-70, 173, 186, 267
Anderson, Sir John, 313
Andrews, Rev. Charles Freer, missionary and teacher: association with G.'s activities, 142, 164, 172, 225, 244, 304, 319; comments and observations of, 149, 173, 196, 222, 264, 274, 311, 317; G.'s attachment to, 262, 309, 344; as author, 263, 315; as spinner, 268; death, 344; mentioned, 249
Aquinas, St Thomas, 259, 389
'Argus', 222
Arjuna, 39-40, 104, 133, 139, 144, 257, 279, 286
Arnold, Sir Edwin, 35, 36, 39-41
Arya Samaj, 25, 27, 129, 135, 190, 273
Ashram, Satyagraha: at Kochrab, 148-51; at Sabarmati, 167, 170, 176-83, 239-40; activities of G. at, 148-51, 176, 186, 193, 216, 227, 232, 239, 255; residents, visitors and functions, 155, 177, 240, 249, 264-6, 269, 270, 271, 276, 282; in Salt March, 285-6; survives in 1932, 316; turned into Harijan centre, 320
Asiatic Department, in Transvaal, and policies, 78-9, 96, 108, 115, 122, 125; Asiatic Law Amendment Ordinance (the 'Black Act'), 96-7, 105-7, 113-14, 122
Asoka, 18, 23, 247
Astor, Lady, 309
Atlantic Charter, 347
Atomic bomb, vii, 372, 381
Attlee, Clement, 273, 361, 371, 385
Aurobindo, extremist and philosopher, 19, 134, 135, 136, 358
Autobiography, G.'s, 235, 252-4, 260, 267, 274, 293
Azad, Maulana Abul Kalam, Muslim politician: work for Hindu-Muslim unity, 136; in Khilafat campaign, 201, 203; in Swaraj

campaign, 214, 226; in Congress leadership, 201, 237, 340, 352; Jinnah's hostility to, 343, 361, 362; at Birla House, 379, 383; at scattering of G.'s ashes, 384

Bacon, Francis, 46
Bajaj, Jamnalal, 274, 328-9
Baker, A. W., 52, 54, 62-3
Balasundaram, 61, 70, 187
Baldwin, Stanley, 263, 273, 280, 300, 326
'Bande Mataram', song and slogan, 135, 218, 339
Banerji, Kalicharan, 76
Banerji, Surendranath, 135
Banker, Shankarlal, 185, 186, 197, 232, 234
Bapu, 'Father', affectionate title for G., 91, 124, 239, 262, 265, 329
Bardoli, 225, 228-9, 275-6
Barisal, 290
Baroda, 295
Basic Education, 331-2, 364, 376
Becharji Swami, 13, 15
Beethoven, 264, 312
Benares, 76, 152-5, 199, 252, 318
Bengal: as intellectual centre, 24, 129; partition, 134-6; anti-British disturbances, 135, 212, 288, 313, 354; G. tours, 246; riots and pacification by G., 364-7, 372-3, 375; mentioned, 238
Bentinck, Lord William, 21
Bernhardt, Sarah, 132
Besant, Annie: as exponent of Theosophy, 35, 41, 129, 147; in Benares, 76, 152-4; and G., 41, 76, 115, 147, 152-4, 174, 207, 222, 245; and Indian politics, 147, 156, 166-7, 173, 185, 198, 203, 226, 245, 278, 281; mentioned, 34, 36, 234, 309, 391
Bettiah, 159, 163
Bhagavad Gita: its literary character and themes, 39-40, 104, 144, 149, 257; G.'s study and exposition of, 39-40, 88, 92, 110, 216, 232, 258, 279, 286, 320, 381; application to Indian nationalism, 133, 139, 279; public recitation of, 295, 356, 384; mentioned, 35
Bhatt, Shamal, 13
Bhave, Vinoba, disciple: joins G., 155; G.'s regard for, 178, 262, 346; at Wardha, 217, 239, 266, 320; in various campaigns and activities, 244, 274-5, 321, 331, 346, 353; imprisonments, 314, 346, 352; mentioned, viii, 387
Bible, 42, 54, 63, 110, 257
Bihar: G.'s Champaran campaign, 157-66; civil disobedience in, 288; earthquake, 321; riots and pacification by G., 365, 371, 372, 375; mentioned, 271, 336, 386
Birkenhead, Lord, 273
Birla family, 128; G. D. Birla, philanthropist, 136, 155, 261, 262, 284, 303, 305, 318, 319, 326-7, 342, 344, 369, 371; Birla House, Delhi, 351, 376, 378-9, 381-4
Birth control, 36, 37-8, 92-3, 260, 333-4
Blavatsky, Madame, 35, 41-2, 44, 64, 92
Blum, Léon, 385
Boehme, Jakob, 235
Boers, 51, 56-7, 73-4, 77, 79
Bolton, Glorney, 325
Bombay: G.'s arrivals and departures on voyages, 16, 46, 47, 142, 302, 313; Congress, foundation and activities in, 26, 152,

397